Professors Speak Out:
The Truth About Campus Investigations

Nicholas H. Wolfinger,
Editor

Professors Speak Out:
The Truth About Campus Investigations

Nicholas H. Wolfinger,
Editor

Academica Press
Washington~London

Library of Congress Cataloging-in-Publication Data
Names: Wolfinger, Nicholas H. (editor)
Title: Professors speak out : the truth about campus investigations |
Wolfinger, Nicholas H.
Description: Washington : Academica Press, 2025. | Includes references.
Identifiers: LCCN 2025930017 | ISBN 9781680535563 (hardcover) |
9781680535570 (paperback) | 9781680535587 (e-book)

Contents

These are cases involving allegations of sexual misconduct of various kinds, most of which involve course content or off-color language.

These are cases involving allegations of racism or racial insensitivity.

Religion and Politics **325**

These cases involve allegations of religious insensitivity, including allegations of anti-Semitism or anti-Christian bias, or investigations fueled by political pressure.

**Postscript: How to Safeguard Your Academic Career
by Stephen Porter** **387**

Acknowledgments

John F. Kennedy is generally credited with saying that victory has a thousand fathers but defeat is an orphan. Most non-fiction books, my own included, have lengthy lists of acknowledgements but little mention of setbacks.

This book stands JFK's wisdom on its head. All the stories herein had their origins in defeat, instances when colleges and universities abused their power to investigate and sanction the contributors. The book had its own Bay of Pigs when the first publisher pulled out. Academica Press president Paul du Quenoy deserves great thanks for taking a chance on this book after so many publishers turned it down. Bob Frodeman started out as my co-editor before he, too, turned the book down. I thank him for his initial efforts, not to mention the fine chapter he contributed. Finally, my old friend Andy Roth lent his incomparable editorial eye to the introduction. Andy has edited more books than anyone I know, and once again he's worked magic.

The biggest thanks go out to the 21 academics who took the time to write about their experiences. For some of you, it wasn't easy to reopen old wounds, especially when your careers had been destroyed in the process. Thank you for taking the time to tell your stories. I appreciate your efforts, and I'm sure many readers will too.

So this is an easy choice: this book is dedicated to you, the contributors, and all the other academics who have had their lives upended by unjust investigations.

Introduction

Our colleges find themselves caught in (take your pick) the cross hairs of the right, the tentacles of the left, the vise grip of bureaucracy, the cultural contradictions of capitalism. Or all of the above.
A.O. Scott

The professors are the enemy.
JD Vance

What's a good career choice for people who are both brilliant and prickly? Higher education was once the obvious answer. Academia has long been known as a refuge for oddballs, scholars with dazzling intellects but who struggled to wear matching socks, let alone play well with others. Research universities hired the people who did the best scholarship. Whether they could get along with their colleagues didn't matter so much. Many of us have had the experience of a college instructor who was awkward or even downright rude, but a fantastic teacher—or a terrible teacher, but a first-rate scholar.

This understanding of the professoriate, if once true, isn't true any longer. Professors are now routinely disciplined for all manner of infractions related to their speech, in and out of the classroom, and for their behavior on and off campus. What changed? In a word, everything. The campus bureaucracy changed, the student body changed, the bureaucracy's relationship to students changed, the composition of the professoriate changed, the media ecosystem changed, and government oversight of higher education changed. The result has been an epidemic of academic investigations.

Professors are now investigated for every conceivable reason. To be sure, some investigations involve allegations of genuine misbehavior that is no longer swept under the rug. More often, faculty members are investigated to settle scores, or as a product of hyper-sensitivity to conduct that once would have passed unnoticed. And with increasing frequency, faculty members serve as proxies in the ideological conflicts that roil contemporary America.

Fragile Customers

Many disciplinary proceedings against faculty are initiated by students, perhaps responding to a brusque instructor or course material that rubs them the wrong way. In earlier years, a student might have groused to their friends, or perhaps confronted a professor directly. Now these complaints are more likely to be directed to a faculty member's department chair or a campus bureaucrat. In an era of cancel culture, professors are almost uniquely susceptible.[1] What other workplace consists of an individual employee regularly addressing tens or hundreds of people?

Students have always taken issue with their professors, but there's been a sea change in how they register their grievances. Today's students are less inclined to view challenging course content as grounds for legitimate disagreement, instead taking moral offense and sometimes even seeing a controversial lecture as *dangerous*.[2] A University of Sussex faculty member was assailed for the "harm" her work caused to trans and nonbinary students.[3] Northwestern University students denounced an essay by a professor as "terrifying" in its "chilling effect" on students' ability to report faculty misconduct.[4] And at Old Dominion University, student demonstrations against sociologist and pedophilia researcher Allyn Walker touched off a firestorm that culminated in administrative leave and, ultimately, Dr. Walker's resignation.[5]

Put yourself in the position of these students. If you believed that your professors were causing grievous harm to vulnerable groups, wouldn't drastic forms of retaliation against these malefactors be justified? Students seem to think so, and increasingly lodge complaints against their instructors. Sometimes they're encouraged to do so by other faculty members, especially younger ones, who may agree about the putative harm their colleagues are causing.[6] And while it's hard to measure the frequency of student complaints against faculty, the available data are discouraging. According to the Foundation for Individual Rights and Expression, the number of professors investigated for their speech jumped from four in 2000 to 145 in 2022.[7] Undergraduate students were responsible for initiating more than half of these investigations. And these, it should be stressed, are only the tip of the iceberg. Faculty investigations almost invariably take place behind closed doors. Word gets out only when a professor is well known, files suit against their employer (or former employer), or chooses themselves to raise a fuss.

Why did students become so much more likely to complain about their professors? One plausible explanation is the "coddling" theory proposed by Jonathan Haidt and Greg Lukianoff:

> [T]he new problems on campus have their origins in three terrible ideas that have become increasingly woven into American childhood and education: What doesn't kill you makes you weaker; always trust your feelings; and life is a battle between good people and evil people.[8]

In previous generations, Haidt and Lukianoff note, aggrieved college students protested against their universities: for free speech, for divestment from apartheid-era South Africa, against American wars in Vietnam and Iraq. Until the recent spate of pro-Palestinian protests, modern students have sought the protection of their universities through trigger warnings and safe spaces. Sometimes students have even protested to demand the intercession of their colleges. Implicit in all these requests is the notion that exposure to noxious ideas is injurious (consider the earlier examples, where students denounced faculty using words like "harm," "terrifying," and "predator.") The causes of this new fragility, suggest Haidt and Lukianoff, stem from generational shifts in parenting, education, and social media (shriller voices have blamed everything from moral collapse to "late capitalism.") These trends have been highlighted by the social justice movements of the last few years, especially #MeToo and #BlackLivesMatter.

At the root of all this lies a shift in metaphor that expresses a fundamental change in culture: the idea that students are customers. And, of course, the customer is always right. This inverts the traditional understanding of the role of the professor vis-à-vis students, which was long conceived in terms of mentor and pupil. Of course, there were problems with these metaphors too: the blind acceptance of the mentor's views, and sometimes the stifling of heterodox thinkers. But they were tokens of a cultural milieu that assumed that elders had wisdom to impart to new generations.

The upshot of this cultural change has been a student body far more likely to complain about their professors. And unlike in years gone by, university administrators have been receptive to student complaints.[9] As college costs soared and campus bureaucracies mushroomed, universities increasingly competed to recruit students.[10] Ten years ago *Forbes* wrote of a "college amenities arms race" as universities raced to install climbing walls, lazy rivers, and other fun stuff to attract undergraduates.[11]

It's not a huge speculative leap of faith to suspect that these new funding imperatives might change how universities responded to student complaints, especially in an era when the faculty is increasingly composed of easily-fired contingent instructors.[12] Student complaints, no matter how frivolous, have to be taken seriously. Universities need not always discipline the offending faculty member, but must at least give the appearance that complaints are being carefully considered.

As this book will show, it's often the investigation itself that's the punishment. I endured a Zoom hearing that lasted over three hours, but I got off easy.[13] The University of Central Florida subjected psychologist Charles Negy to nine hours of hearings as part of an inquest launched after a tweet, before firing him from his tenured professorship (he was reinstated after filing suit).[14] Teresa Buchanan, a contributor to this volume, was fired from a tenured position after a hearing that lasted eleven and a half hours, *all in a single day*. And Harvard's Tyler VanderWeele describes months of spending six hours a day dealing with the fallout of a student mob.[15]

Twisting Title IX

Even if the student body and its relationship to higher education hadn't changed, investigations against the faculty would have increased thanks to a sea change in how colleges think about sexual misconduct, and how they go about adjudicating allegations of rape and sexual harassment. This sea change arrived in the form of federal guidance issued in 2011 that greatly expanded the implications of Title IX.[16]

Some background is necessary. Title IX is the common name for the 1972 civil rights legislation now known as the Patsy T. Mink Equal Opportunity in Education Act. Most people think of Title IX in relation to women's participation in college sports, but it mandates gender equity in all aspects of higher education. Its main text is just 37 words:

> No person in the United States shall, on the basis of sex, be excluded from participation in, be denied the benefits of, or be subjected to discrimination under any education program or activity receiving Federal financial assistance.

This was a laudable development in America's long arc towards justice. My 2013 book *Do Babies Matter? Gender and Family in the Ivory Tower* explored the barriers women face in becoming tenured professors, and made recommendations that have been implemented by numerous universities.[17]

As chronicled by political scientist R. Shep Melnick, a long, winding road connected Title IX to sexual misconduct on campus. Federal courts wrestled for years with the relationship between sexual misconduct and Title IX before the Clinton Department of Education issued the first guidelines in 1997. The guidelines operated under the theory that there were a few bad apples on campus, subject to sanction for misconduct that was "sufficiently severe, persistent, or pervasive to limit a student's ability to participate in or benefit from an education program or activity, or to create a hostile or abusive educational environment."[18]

All that was thrown overboard by the federal guidance issued in 2011.[19] In response to concern from scholars and activists about campus sexual assault, the Department of Education's Office of Civil Rights issued new instructions to all American institutions of higher learning.[20] Behind the 2011 Dear Colleague Letter to colleges and universities was a theory about the cause of sexual misconduct on campus. The Clinton-era notion of a few bad apples was discarded. Instead, the problem was deemed endemic. Here it's worthwhile to quote Melnick at length:

> First and most important, [the Department of Education's] OCR and the White House repeatedly insisted that campuses around the country were experiencing an "epidemic" of sexual assault so extensive that it could be adequately addressed only through a

"sea change" in our attitudes about sex. According to a report issued by the White House Council on Women and Girls, "Sexual assault is pervasive because our culture still allows it to persist." Consequently, "violence prevention can't just focus on the perpetrators and the survivors. It has to involve everyone." Moreover, prevention programs must be "sustained (not brief, one-shot educational programs), comprehensive, and address the root individual, relational, and societal causes of sexual assault."[21]

Never mind that campus sexual assault had fallen by 50 percent between 1997 and 2011, per federal statistics. What's more, female college students are less likely to be sexually assaulted than young women who aren't in college.[22]

The 2011 Dear Colleague Letter changed everything. The definition of sexual misconduct went from "severe, persistent, or pervasive" to "unwelcome conduct." Colleges and universities were directed to employ a minimal burden of proof when adjudicating allegations of misconduct, the "preponderance of evidence" standard, sometimes referred to as "50 percent and a feather." (Previously college investigations of sexual misconduct had relied on the more rigorous "clear and convincing evidence" standard used in some civil proceedings.) Colleges were required to allow *accusers* to appeal verdicts of innocence, thereby creating the sort of double jeopardy that's alien to criminal law. Cross-examination in proceedings, even through an intermediary, was strongly discouraged.

Despite all this, the 2011 DCL was vague in how colleges should move forward on the new mandate. The Letter itself was only nineteen pages long. But far less vague were the compliance mechanisms: the threat of inclusion on a federal blacklist and, theoretically, the loss of federal funding (although this has never happened). This meant that colleges faced pricey compliance reviews if they showed insufficient vigor in investigating misconduct.

The 2011 Dear Colleague Letter therefore created incentives for colleges to investigate every allegation of sexual misconduct, no matter how frivolous. Federal legislation originally intended to promote gender equity in higher education became a framework for punishing things like a faculty member's poorly conceived test question about bikini waxing.[23]

A married couple teaching at Arizona State University was targeted by a colleague competing for a professorship at a better school.[24] Remorseful lovers also learned to push the Title IX button, as did university administrators who sought to silence outspoken faculty members.[25]

It's for these reasons that there are many vocal critics of how campuses conduct Title IX investigations, including 28 faculty members at Harvard Law School, former ACLU head Nadine Strossen, former Virginia governor Douglas Wilder, United States senators Lamar Alexander (R-TN) and Sheldon Whitehouse (D-RI), and even the late Ruth Bader Ginsburg.[26]

We should applaud the fact that universities now crack down on bad behavior that used to be routinely tolerated. Sexual misconduct is still too common on college campuses, and universities still often fail in rooting it out. The unsuccessful Title IX investigation of former Michigan State University doctor Larry Nasser, now serving life in prison, makes this point painfully clear.[27] At the same time, the 2011 federal guidance has given rise to large campus bureaucracies, part and parcel of a broader growth in college administrations in recent decades. Although national statistics are hard to come by, the *New York Times* reported that higher education administrators increased by 60 percent between 1993 and 2009, ten times the growth rate of tenure-line faculty positions.[28] Harvard now employs over 50 Title IX coordinators responsible for policing and adjudicating sexual misconduct on campus.[29] With staffing like this, it's inevitable that faculty members will come under administrative scrutiny, whether or not they deserve it. That is just how bureaucracies work.

We know more about campus investigations for sexual misconduct than we do about other kinds of faculty investigations. They've been the focus of no less than four books. A well-researched depiction of a Title IX sex investigation even appeared in a novel, Scott Johnston's *Campusland*.

Based on the cases that have been publicized, Title IX sex investigations have many unique qualities. The participants are enjoined to secrecy, but it's sometimes an open secret given how wide-ranging the investigations tend to be (in the course of my first inquest, the investigator interviewed every single one of my departmental colleagues).[30] The investigation bureaucracy varies widely. Some schools rely on the single investigator model, in which a sole functionary serves as investigator, prosecutor, judge, and jury.[31] Others rely on an adversarial system more reminiscent of civil proceedings. The credentials of the investigators vary just as much. Some are outside attorneys, others are veteran campus apparatchiks. Still others are part of a burgeoning national community of professional Title IX bureaucrats.[32] Finally, campus investigations are responsive to the broader ideological climate of the campus. Laura Kipnis's investigation at Northwestern was presaged by students protesting her and denouncing her work (she experienced a Title IX investigation on the basis of an article she wrote).[33] Florian Jaeger's budget-busting external investigation resulted from agitation by his colleagues, upset that he'd been exonerated by a previous internal investigation.[34]

Thanks to the work of Kipnis and others, we have a fairly good sense of how universities conduct misconduct investigations, and it's sharply at odds with legal proceedings. Generally you are not informed of the allegations against you. Instead, you're invited in for an interview, sometimes after months of quiet investigation, and given ample opportunity to incriminate yourself. Sometimes you aren't allowed to bring a lawyer with you, but may be allowed a "support person." Meanwhile, campus adjudicators are typically trained to believe that anyone accused of sexual misconduct must be guilty. At Middlebury College, for instance, the investigators are trained to "start by believing" the accuser, while asking themselves whether the accused is "who he said he is."[35] Inconsistencies in an accuser's story are typically explained away as the lingering consequences of trauma.[36] It was for reasons like this that Oberlin College reported guilty determinations in 100 percent of the sexual misconduct cases it adjudicated during the 2015-2016 academic year.[37]

The politics of Title IX continue to be topsy-turvy. The Trump Department of Education withdrew the 2011 Dear Colleague Letter and issued more balanced guidelines, a move that drew praise from liberal observers.[38] The Biden Department of Education, in turn, released revised guidelines in April of 2024 that chart a middle course between the Obama and Trump guidelines.[39] Some protections for accused students and faculty were left in place, but the new guidelines eliminate the requirement for all parties to participate in live hearings.

But does it matter? The 2011 guidelines are gone, but the college bureaucracies established in their wake remain—and it's not as though college tribunals were paragons of due process in the first place.[40] After all, the rules instituted by Secretary DeVos, Trump's DoE secretary, were not met with the wholesale termination of college bureaucrats. Harvard still has its 50 Title IX coordinators. At a minimum, it would require repeated legal challenges for colleges to reform how they go about adjudicating sexual misconduct cases.

Academic Hit Lists

Universities are politically progressive places.[41] It has always been thus, but the leftward trend has accelerated in recent decades. Professors have long been in conservative crosshairs, but social media has transformed the landscape in a way that makes faculty members much more vulnerable.[42] An army of digital soldiers now stands ready to target faculty members, and universities have often capitulated to public pressure and investigated faculty members who attract conservative animus.

Conservative outrage towards lefty academics has long been mobilized via professor watchlists (At least three contributors to this volume have been named on these lists). Lists of faculty "radicals" date back to the 1930s, but went mainstream after activist David Horwitz published *The Professors: The 101 Most Dangerous Academics in America* in 2006.[43] In 2016, influential conservative activist Charlie Kirk, head of Turning Point USA, launched professorwatchlist.org, a glossy website dedicated to "unmasking radical professors." Users can search by name, by college, and submit tips. Its entries, patently tendentious, are amply sourced and include pull-quotes intended to provoke outrage ("This country was founded on genocide and slavery. That is not some rhetorical device. It is historical truth," says Russell Rickford, a Cornell University historian.)[44]

Although the Watchlist is a good source for identifying faculty guaranteed to provoke conservative ire, other sites have been more influential in ginning up controversy about faculty members. Particularly important are campusreform.org and thecollegefix.com. The modus operandi of these sites is best captured by the journalist Kevin Drum's neologism, *nut-picking*.[45] Historian David Boshko describes in colorful terms how campusreform.org and thecollegefix.com conduct business:

> They find something really dumb a fringe wackjob college professor said and share it all around and have a bunch of people freak out about how evil liberals are how they are about to bring in a reign of darkness upon the land and blah blah blah.[46]

These conservative websites are effective at mobilizing public opinion, especially when their stories are picked up by general interest conservative media like Fox News. Once a faculty member is mentioned, universities are flooded with complaints.[47] Some colleges aggressively shield their faculty members from public outrage, but others succumb and investigate, or even terminate, targeted faculty members. Faculty are especially vulnerable to these onslaughts when they teach at smaller schools in conservative states, or at religious colleges.

Unlike the other sorts of cases discussed here, investigations resulting from public pressure are easy to learn about. Two examples will suffice.

Lora Burnett taught history at Collin College in Texas until 2020, when she was fired over tweets that criticized her school's COVID response and implored Vice President Mike Pence to "shut his little demon mouth up."[48] She ultimately sued and received a golden parachute.

Fresno State English professor Randa Jarrer waited less than an hour after the 2018 death of former First Lady Barbara Bush before tweeting "Barbara Bush was a generous and smart and amazing racist who, along with her husband, raised a war criminal." After a barrage of criticism, Fresno State President Joseph Castro sought to mollify protestors by intoning "this was beyond free speech" and promised a "long investigation" of Professor Jarrer. Castro apparently lacked faith in his school's ability to conduct a long investigation, as the case against Jarrer was dropped less than a week later.[49]

Perhaps the different outcomes in the Burnett and Jarrer cases can be explained by politics: Burnett taught in Texas, Jarrer in California. It may also have mattered that Burnett taught at a community college, while Jarrer is a productive scholar at a four-year school. Both cases ultimately produced outcomes supporting the faculty: Jarrer kept her job, while Burnett got a payout. Nonetheless, the fact remains that in both cases the colleges bowed to publish pressure and launched investigations in response to constitutionally protected speech.

Plenty of conservative faculty are targeted for their politics; one example is the aforementioned Charles Negy, from the University of Central Florida. The tweet that landed him in hot water was about "Black privilege." But the impetus for Negy's investigation originated from within his university, as investigations from the political left almost invariably do. There are no established left-leaning counterparts to conservative sites like the one maintained by Turning Point USA, no notable liberal watchlists of "fascist" professors.[50] Of course this doesn't mean that faculty are immune from left-leaning Twitter mobs. My third investigation resulted from my being dragged on Twitter.[51] But there aren't prominent progressive blogs trying to do the work of landing faculty in hot water.

The examples shown here demonstrate that the modern media ecosystem is effective in ginning up outrage against faculty members. Given the political polarization in America and conservative denunciations of colleges as indoctrination factories—consider the recent fuss about "critical race theory"—these attacks may well escalate in the years to come. Universities, especially in red states, won't always shield their faculty members. Even when they do, investigations will be the norm.

The Hothouse

A final explanation for the uptick in faculty investigations requires a short detour into recent American politics. As we'll see, ideological trends coupled with the unique features of the academic workplace led to a spate of investigations over the past few years.

The Democrats, the center-left party in a two-party system, has long been more of a coalition party than its conservative counterpart, counting in its ranks non-white voters, educated professionals, and less well-off working class whites. Starting around 2011, about half the white progressives in America acquired far more left-leaning attitudes about topics related to race, gender, and immigration. In many instances, these white progressives came to have more left-wing attitudes about race than did their non-white coalition partners.[52] Hitherto fringe ideas like reparations and decriminalizing the United States-Mexico border entered the discourse. So too did new solipsistic and totalizing understandings of racism, from best-selling authors Ta-Nehisi Coates, Ibram X. Kendi, and Robin DiAngelo. These changes were mirrored by the adoption of a new vocabulary of race relations ("whiteness," "structural racism," and so on) in prestige media like the *New York Times* and the *Washington Post*.[53]

And then Donald Trump was elected president. The progressive angst was instantly visible in the estimated four million people who participated in the national Women's March immediately following Trump's inauguration.[54] This public display was met with both soul-searching and inquiry, but soon gave way in the popular imagination to the trope of reporters (or social scientists) talking to white working class voters in Iowa diners.[55] Meanwhile, left-leaning organizations roiled and churned in their powerlessness over the new political order, a dynamic that was turbocharged in 2020 by COVID lockdowns and the murder of George Floyd. Many lefty nonprofits, NGOs, and faculty committees ground to a halt, consumed by recriminations and the tests of ideological purity that Barrack Obama famously denounced as circular firing squads.[56]

This was the state of affairs depicted by Ryan Grim in a widely publicized analysis written for the *Intercept* in 2022.[57] Right-wing takedowns of liberals are easily ignored by progressives, but Grim was a liberal writer at a liberal publication. His article told of organizations paralyzed by internal allegations of racism, sexism, and myriad other –isms, with countless hours spent in struggle sessions, anti-racism trainings, and nonstop identitarian backbiting. If there was any good news for progressives, it was Grim's sense that the dysfunction had peaked and was starting to abate. This assessment is supported by sociologist Musa al-Gharbi, who presented extensive quantitative data to suggest that the Great Awokening was winding down.[58] And a recent data analysis conducted by the *Economist* came to the same conclusion.[59]

How did these dynamics play out in colleges and universities, replete with bereft progressives, subsequent to the election of Donald Trump in 2016? Seething at their impotence when it came to national politics, progressives could act closer to home. Professors may have felt alienated from their countrymen, but they could fight perceived manifestations of Trumpism in their own universities. "That is a big part of the reason why, from 2016 to 2020, some of the most intense energy on the left was devoted to getting rid of anybody who supposedly threatened to pollute the moral purity of their community," writes the political scientist Yascha Mounk.[60] The *annus horribilis* of 2020—COVID lockdowns, the murder of George Floyd and the ensuing riots and protests, Trump's attempted coup—produced long Zoom meetings devoted to race and race relations, with the attendant allegations and investigations. It's no surprise that the lion's share of chapters in this book, mostly solicited in 2022, involve allegations of racism. Finally, the election of Joe Biden and unified Democratic government produced its own set of stressors, as progressives quickly started asking why change wasn't happening fast enough.

The broader social and political environment was conducive to an atmosphere where allegations of racism, sexism, homophobia, and other forms of prejudice would be aggressively pursued, but why should higher education have spawned so many investigations in the past few years? In *The Canceling of the American Mind: How Cancel Culture Undermines Trust, Destroys Institutions, and Threatens Us All*, Greg Lukianoff and Rikki Schlott lay the blame entirely on Herbert Marcuse, a Nazi refugee philosopher who penned celebrated defenses of illiberalism in the 1960s.[61] Marcuse became a prominent theorist of the New Left (for instance, striking French workers graffitied "Marx, Mao, Marcuse!" in 1968), and a bugaboo to generations of conservative writers.[62]

It seems implausible that a single long-dead scholar is entirely responsible for the surge of faculty investigations, or cancel culture more broadly.[63] He's hardly the only prophet of illiberalism on either the left or the right, and it's hard to identify any modern political discourse that pays him heed (or even knows who he is). His work appeared 60 years ago, in an era of considerable ideological tumult, but long before the modern wave of faculty investigations. Why did it only become relevant now?

A more plausible explanation should acknowledge the political composition of the modern academy, as well as its unique features as a workplace. Academic departments, the primary employment unit in higher education, offer an unusually stable workplace. Tenure guarantees lifetime employment, and it is difficult to change universities as a tenured faculty member. As a result, the same people are often working together for decades, which allows minor disputes to fester and the narcissism of small differences to assume outsized importance. Perhaps this is the logic behind Sayre's Law: the conflicts in academia are so great because the stakes are so low.[64]

Of course the dynamic fueling Sayre's law have persisted since scholars were first organized into academic faculties, but the context has changed. The Great Awokening brought identitarian concerns about race (and to a lesser extent gender and sexual orientation) to the fore for a number of progressives—and as we have noted, by the 2010s progressives comprised the vast majority of academics. These new racial attitudes were duly abetted by high profile books by Ibram X. Kendi and his peers. Professors soon experienced the national shock presented by the rise and fall of Trump and Trumpism.[65]

And this didn't happen in an institutional vacuum. At the same time, students were suddenly filing a lot more complaints about their teachers. University administrators were newly empowered, and, thanks especially to the 2011 reappraisal of Title IX, had new resources for conducting investigations. In such an environment, it's hardly surprising that some faculty disputes were now continued by other means. If you really want to sideline a colleague in a departmental power struggle, what better way to do that than to accuse her of racism? A Title IX complaint can also be a good option if she had once implored you to "go fuck yourself"—since the f-word frequently has a sexual meaning, its utterance can be treated as sexual misconduct. At the very least, your unfortunate colleague will be saddled with a solid month's worth of meetings. If you get lucky, your adversary just might be fired outright. Lukianoff and Schlott report that more tenured faculty members have been fired in the United States over the past ten years than during the Red Scare of the 1950s.[66] And while the Great Awokening may be losing steam, it that doesn't mean working conditions for professors are improving. The October 7 terrorist attack on Israel and the ensuing war in Gaza have touched off a new round of recrimination, chilled speech, and investigations.[67]

Finally, it's not a surprise that the surge in faculty investigations comes at a time when the professoriate is increasingly comprised of contingent faculty: almost two-thirds of faculty positions are now non-tenure track.[68] Universities are to blame here in two separate ways. First, they've sought to save money by replacing career employees with a fungible workforce of gig workers. Second, they've perpetuated what's been called *elite overproduction*: universities have churned out far too many Ph.D.s than can be absorbed by the workforce, most notably by university faculties themselves.[69]

The result is a lot of frustrated doctorate recipients, people who spent up to a decade in graduate school and can't find the tenure-track jobs they were promised. Many hang around academia in contingent faculty positions. These academic sharecroppers—in the memorable words of long-term adjunct professor Wendell Fountain—are poorly paid and lack job security compared to tenure-track faculty.[70] Consequently it's easier to replace them in response to a student complaint—or, really, for any other reason. And as sociologist Neil Gross has pointed out, their low pay and lousy working conditions may well make contingent faculty more likely to misbehave.[71] Gross describes several adjunct professors fired from their jobs over louche tweets. Another sociologist, Musa al-Gharbi, recently offered a more comprehensive version of this theory: the educated elite, in search of scarce academic jobs, are perpetually engaged in symbolic conflicts. Under this theory, academics compete to demonstrate the strongest devotion to social justice ideals, and punish those who fail to live up to manifestly impossible standards. This dynamic is most evident when graduate students or junior faculty members join or direct online mobs targeting their senior colleagues. This behavior is apparent in several of the stories presented in this book.

About this book

The following twenty chapters consist of faculty members recounting their experience of being investigated by the universities where they teach. As we've seen, these investigations have become a routine feature of modern higher education. Some of these investigations concern alleged sexual misconduct. These cases range from professors swept up by rapidly changing norms to bad faith accusations used to settle personal conflicts. Many other chapters involve a professor voicing an unpopular opinion (or at least unpopular within the precincts of contemporary academia), most often about race and ethnicity. These cases go to the heart of academic freedom and the right of faculty to engage with ideas in the classroom and the public square, and they've mushroomed in an era of political polarization and social media mobs.

This book reveals an academy under siege, with the attacks coming from across the political spectrum. In conservative states, lawmakers are targeting professors with content restrictions, exemplified by the recent spate of laws purporting to ban "critical race theory." Professors have long been a favorite target for conservative activists, and these attacks have exploded in the social media era. On the left, criticism often comes from within the academy itself, as professors find themselves denounced by idealistic students or (often younger) colleagues.

Universities have responded by developing Byzantine bureaucracies for investigating and punishing academic misconduct, often though muddled and opaque disciplinary proceedings. Investigations can last for years, with a professor's reputation besmirched whether or not he or she is formally exonerated. Long accustomed to the norms of free speech and open inquiry, academics now fear being punished for the slightest transgression, punishment that may entail dismissal from a tenured position. This is the environment that led *Vox* to pseudonymously publish an article titled "I'm a Liberal Professor, and my Liberal Students Terrify Me" in 2015.[72] Yet the author got his title wrong. His essay should have been titled, "I'm a Liberal/Conservative Professor, and *All* My Students Terrify Me."

Professors deserve the opportunity to tell their side of the story. All university stakeholders and society at large should be interested in what they have to say. University disciplinary procedures have high stakes—a tenured professorship and millions of dollars of grant money may hang in the balance—but all too frequently make a mockery of the due process that's the hallmark of a liberal society. Academics will want to learn how to safeguard their careers. Campus bureaucrats want fairer processes that better balance competing interests at their institutions. And everyone should be interested in ameliorating the now-routine injustice in a central institution of American society.

There are numerous critiques of the contemporary university as intolerant and censorious. This book is different in two ways. First, it offers professors the opportunity to speak for themselves. Second, to the extent possible there is no ideological agenda. I'm not a conservative who seeks to undermine American higher education, nor am I a progressive who views universities as engines of social justice. This book is devoted to chronicling miscarriages of justice against faculty members no matter where they land on the political spectrum.

Broadly speaking, all of the faculty stories in this book involve identity: sex, race and ethnicity, or religion. Coming on the heels of the Great Awokening and the 2020 racial reckoning, it's not a surprise that a plurality of chapters speak to allegations of racism, broadly construed. The next largest bloc involves allegations of sexual misconduct, a natural outgrowth of the radically revised guidelines on campus sexual misconduct issued by the U.S. Department of Education in 2011. Finally the book contains several chapters about religion, including allegations of anti-Semitism and anti-Christian bias.

This range of topics reflects what I believe to be one of the book's great strengths: its diversity. To be sure, the book is diverse on traditional metrics like the race and sex of the authorship. But the book is also diverse in ways that are often ignored by the academy. Its chapters depict conservative scholars being attacked for their politics, and left-leaning authors being attacked for theirs. Some of the left-leaning authors were assailed by conservatives; others were assailed by scholars and activists farther to their left. The occupational credentials of the contributors are just as diverse. One holds the rank of distinguished professor at a research university; another was a part-timer teaching a single college class in her area of expertise. The book's authors also span the range of academic fields, from chemistry to philosophy. Outside of the academy, the authorship includes an Air Force colonel, an Antifa activist, and a successful professional artist.

Perhaps most important are the consequences of the investigations described herein. One contributor was visited by the FBI. Another was denounced by both his governor and his senator. At least three authors came to fear for their physical safety. More than one of us was denounced on national news. Some of us were mobbed on social media and received thousands of threats. In many cases our deans and administrators were flooded with demands that we be punished. In others, (in)justice was meted out privately.

The career implications of our investigations run the gamut. Some of us escaped with the proverbial warning to straighten out and fly right, usually with the suggestion that the punishment would be worse next time. For these scholars, the consequences of investigation were limited to the time and energy these inquests inevitably entail—and the chilling of individual expression that comes from being under institutional scrutiny. And the other end of the spectrum, some of us were fired from our jobs or forced into early retirement. Vibrant careers were ruined, with millions of taxpayer's dollars squandered in research grants lost and exorbitant outlays to outside investigators. Many of us have also paid tens or hundreds of thousands of dollars to lawyers.

I should note that several colleges and universities successfully prevented faculty members from telling their stories here. Of the many scholars I solicited for this book, three expressed an interest in contributing but said they were muzzled by non-disclosure agreements. Two of the three had left their universities, so violating their NDAs presumably meant the loss of retirement benefits, or perhaps legal action. A fourth scholar penned a chapter for this volume, then withdrew it on the advice of her attorneys. All four teach or taught at top-ten schools, while one can reasonably described as one of the most eminent scholars in his or her field alive today.

The goal of this book is to draw attention to the proliferation of unjust faculty investigations. In theory, I could have screened contributors to ensure only the most outrageous investigations of the most sympathetic professors. Yet cherry-picking a roster of contributors wouldn't seem intellectually honest. Professors aren't categorically lovable and beneficent like Albert Einstein, or whimsical oddballs like the Nobel Laureate physicist Richard Feynman. Many are stubborn, dogmatic, or cantankerous. Some delight in provocation.

So it is with the 22 contributors to this volume. Some will seem entirely sympathetic, others less so. Some were investigated for what will strike most readers as bullshit allegations. Others were doggedly defending unpopular opinions. Indeed, some of the things the contributors did and said don't sit well with me. Some of them take political positions that are far from mine.

And that's the point: academic freedom is similar to freedom of speech in one key respect. It's easy to defend higher education, academic freedom, and open inquiry when we like the results of that inquiry. True academic freedom also demands accepting the results we don't like.

All of the consequences described here and elsewhere in the book have one thing in common: they undermine academic freedom and freedom of expression. No matter how small a price some of us paid, going forward we'll be more careful about what we say and what we study—provided we're still able to teach and do research after the investigations finally end.[73] This is a sanction that's inimical to the basic mission of higher education in a free society.

Endnotes

[1] I use the term "cancel culture" with ambivalence, as I find it both vague and ideologically laden. It's used here because it's the term the broader public uses. German, Komi T. and Greg Lukianoff. "Don't Stop Using the Term 'Cancel Culture.'" *The Daily Beast*, March 25, 2022. Available at https://www.thedailybeast.com/dont-stop-using-the-term-cancel-culture (accessed April 23, 2023).

[2] Lukianoff, Greg and Jonathan Haidt. *The Coddling of the American Mind: How Good Intentions and Bad Ideas Are Setting up a Generation for Failure.* Penguin, 2018. For a historical view of paternalism at American colleges and universities, Godanson, Rita. "The Coddling of the American Undergraduate." *The Hedgehog Review*, Spring 2024. Available at https://hedgehogreview.com/issues/missing-character/articles/the-coddling-of-the-american-undergraduate (accessed March 20, 2024).

[3] Adams, Richard. "Sussex Professor Resigns after Transgender Rights Row." *The Guardian*, October 28, 2021. Available at https://www.theguardian.com/world/2021/oct/28/sussex-professor-kathleen-stock-resigns-after-transgender-rights-row (accessed March 24, 2023).

[4] Kipnis, Laura. "My Title IX Inquisition." *The Chronicle of Higher Education*, May 29, 2015. Available at https://laurakipnis.com/wp-content/uploads/

2010/08/My-Title-IX-Inquisition-The-Chronicle-Review-.pdf   (accessed April 24, 2023).

[5] Svrluga, Susan. "ODU Professor Placed on Leave amid Uproar over Research into 'Minor-Attracted Persons.'" *Washington Post*, November 17, 2021; Stelloh, Tim. "Virginia Professor to Step Down after Backlash to Research on 'Minor-Attracted' People." *NBC News*, November 24, 2021. Available at https://www.nbcnews.com/news/us-news/virginia-professor-step-backlash-research-minor-attracted-people-rcna6709 (accessed November 4, 2024).

[6] The obvious evidence on this point are the proclamations of the faculty "mentors" themselves, often appearing in Twitter pile-ons of targeted professors. I myself was denounced in this way by a colleague. Many would-be faculty saviors are quite forthright in targeting their colleagues. Consider this statement of principles from a guest editorial in *Inside Higher Ed*: "Even more so than the bedrock notion of free speech, academic freedom can become a powerful weapon to be used against vulnerable populations." Scott, Inara. "You're a Professor, Not an Oracle." April 18, 2022. Available at https://www.insidehighered.com/views/2022/04/19/academic-freedoms-protections-are-not-unlimited-opinion (accessed April 1, 2024).

[7] Until recently FIRE was known as the Foundation for Individual Rights in Education. "Scholars Under Fire: Attempts to Sanction Scholars from 2000 to 2022." n.d. Available at https://www.thefire.org/research-learn/scholars-under-fire-attempts-sanction-scholars-2000-2022 (accessed April 24, 2023).

[8] https://www.thecoddling.com/ (accessed 4/28/2023). Haidt and Lukianoff develop their theory in Lukianoff, Greg and Jonathan Haidt. "The Coddling of the American Mind." *The Atlantic*, September 2015. Available at https://www.theatlantic.com/magazine/archive/2015/09/the-coddling-of-the-american-mind/399356/ (accessed April 28, 2023); Lukianoff and Haidt 2019.

[9] Guilbault, Melodi. "Students as Customers in Higher Education: The (Controversial) Debate Needs to End." *Journal of Retailing and Consumer Services* 40 (2018): 295-298.

[10] On expanding campus bureaucracies, Campos, Paul F. "The Real Reason College Tuition Costs So Much." *The New York Times*, April 4, 2015; on the growth of student recruitment, Han, Crystal, Ozan Jaquette, and Karina Salazar. "Recruiting the Out-of-State University: Off-Campus Recruiting by Public Research Universities." Report prepared for the Joyce Foundation, 2019.   Available   at   https://www.dropbox.com/s/f1j45l5eylmy0ub/joyce_report_rotated.pdf?dl=0 (accessed May 13, 2023).

[11] Newlon, Cara. "The College Amenities Arms Race." *Forbes*, July 31, 2014. Available   at   https://www.forbes.com/sites/caranewlon/2014/07/31/the-college-amenities-arms-race/?sh=6e5e78a54883 (accessed April 24, 2023); Woodhouse, Kellie. "Lazy Rivers and Student Debt." *Inside Higher Ed*, June 14, 2015. Available at https://www.insidehighered.com/news/2015/06/15/are-lazy-rivers-and-climbing-walls-driving-cost-college (accessed April 24, 2023).

[12] On the growth of contingent faculty, AAUP, The Annual Report on the Economic Status of the Profession, 2021–22, June 2022. Available at https://www.aaup.org/file/AAUP_ARES_2021%E2%80%932022.pdf (accessed November 4, 2023).

[13] Wolfinger, Nicholas H. "The New Dirty War Against Faculty." *Arc Digital*, November 1, 2021. Available at https://www.arcdigital.media/p/the-new-dirty-war-against-faculty (accessed 5/8/2023).

[14] Nine hours: Harris, Samantha. "The Floridian Inquisition." *Quillette*, August 13, 2020. Available at https://quillette.com/2020/08/13/the-floridian-inquisition/ (accessed April 27, 2923); fired and reinstated: Levenson, Michael. "University Must Reinstate Professor Who Tweeted About 'Black Privilege.'" *The New York Time*s, May 19, 2022.

[15] VanderWeele, Tyler J. "Moral Controversies and Academic Public Health: Notes on Navigating and Surviving Academic Freedom Challenges." *Global Epidemiology* 6 (2023): 100119. Available at https://www.sciencedirect.com/science/article/pii/S2590113323000226 (accessed January 6, 2024).

[16] This account draws heavily on the two monographs that explore how Title IX came to be associated with sexual misconduct on campus. Johnson, K.C. and Stuart Taylor, Jr. *The Campus Rape Frenzy: The Attack on Due Process at America's Universities*. Encounter Books, 2018; Melnick, R. Shep. *The Transformation of Title IX: Regulating Gender Equality in Education*. Brookings Institution Press, 2018. Also useful is the long essay that provided the title of this section, Shibley, Robert L. *Twisting Title IX*. Encounter Books, 2016. There have also been three book-length Title IX investigation memoirs: Kipnis, Laura. *Unwanted Advances: Sexual Paranoia Comes to Campus*. Verso Books, 2018; Klein, Alex. *Aftermath: When It Felt Like Life Was Over*. Republic Book Publishers, 2020; Viren, Sarah. *To Name the Bigger Lie: A Memoir in Two Stories*. Scribner, 2023.

[17] Mason, Mary Ann, Nicholas H. Wolfinger, and Marc Goulden. *Do Babies Matter? Gender and Family in the Ivory Tower*. Rutgers University Press, 2013.

[18] Office of Civil Rights, Department of Education. "Sexual Harassment Guidance 1997." Available at https://www2.ed.gov/about/offices/list/ocr/docs/sexhar01.html#:~:text=Sexual%20Harassment%20Guidance%201997&text=Under%20Title%20IX%20of%20the,receiving%20Federal%20financial%20assistance2. (accessed April 27, 2023)); "bad apples:" Melnick, R. Shep. "The Strange Evolution of Title IX." *National Affairs*, Summer 2018. Available at https://www.nationalaffairs.com/publications/detail/the-strange-evolution-of-title-ix (accessed April 27, 2023).

[19] Johnson and Taylor 2018; Melnick, *The Transformation of Title IX* , 2018.

[20] U.S. Department of Education, Office of the Assistant Secretary. "Dear Colleague Letter." April 4, 2011. Available at https://www2.ed.gov/print/about/offices/list/ocr/letters/colleague-201104.html (accessed April 25, 2023).

[21] Menick, *National Affairs*, 2018.

[22] Sinozich, Sofi and Lyn Langton. "Rape and Sexual Assault Victimization Among College-Age Females, 1995–2013." U.S. Department of Justice, December 2014. Available at https://bjs.ojp.gov/content/pub/pdf/rsavcaf9513.pdf (accessed April 27, 2023).

[23] Foundation for Individual Rights in Education. "Ouch! Brazilian Wax Test Question Nets Howard University Professor a 504-day Title IX Investigation, Sanctions." July 6, 2017. Available at https://www.thefire.org/news/ouch-brazilian-wax-test-question-nets-howard-university-professor-504-day-title-ix (accessed April 26, 2023).

[24] Viren, Sarah. "The Accusations Were Lies. But Could We Prove It?" *The New York Times Magazine*, March 18, 2020.

[25] Remorseful lovers: Soave, Robby. "Chicago Expelled a Male Student 4 Days Before Graduation Because His Ex Made a Dubious Sexual Violence Claim." *Reason*, November 12, 2018. Available at https://reason.com/2018/11/12/chicago-sexual-students-expelled-title/ (accessed November 4, 2024). A contributor to this volume previously recounted how his university forced him out of a tenured professorship, in part for asking forbidden questions. Frodeman, Robert. "Ordeal by Title IX." *Quillette*, August 13, 2020. Available at https://quillette.com/2020/08/13/ordeal-by-title-ix/ (accessed April 29, 2023.).

[26] Clarida, Matthew Q. "Law School Profs Condemn New Sexual Harassment Policy." *The Harvard Crimson*, October 15, 2014. Available at https://www.thecrimson.com/article/2014/10/15/law-profs-criticize-new-policy/?ref=quillette.com (accessed April 26, 2023); Wilder, L. Douglas. "Due Process Means Fairness for All." Wilder Visions, June 4, 2020. Available at https://wildervisions.com/2020/06/04/due-process-ensures-the-truth-will-out/ (accessed April 26, 2023); Strossen, Nadine. "Why Safety Culture & Distorted Title IX Are Bad for Men, Women & Free Speech - Nadine Strossen." Available at https://www.youtube.com/watch?v=2pIXER_ExFs (accessed April 26, 2023); Kruth, Susan. "Senators Ask Key Questions at Hearing on Campus Sexual Assault," June 30, 2014. Available at https://www.thefire.org/news/senators-ask-key-questions-hearing-campus-sexual-assault (accessed April 26, 2023); Rosen, Jeffrey. "Ruth Bader Ginsburg Opens Up About #MeToo, Voting Rights, and Millennials." *The Atlantic*, February 15, 2018. Available at https://www.theatlantic.com/politics/archive/2018/02/ruth-bader-ginsburg-opens-up-about-metoo-voting-rights-and-millenials/553409/ (accessed April 26, 2023).

[27] A Title IX investigation of Nasser failed to find any evidence of misconduct, revealing the folly of university bureaucrats conducting felony investigations. Kitchener, Caroline. "The Nassar Investigation That Never Made Headlines." *The Atlantic*, January 29, 2018. Available at https://www.theatlantic.com/education/archive/2018/01/the-nassar-investigation-that-never-made-headlines/551717/ (accessed April 29, 2023).

[28] Campos 2015; Yascha Mounk recently reported that the ranks of academic administrators grew 139 percent from 1976 to 2011, or almost twice as fast

as the growth in the number of faculty members. Mounk, Yascha. *The Identity Trap: A Story of Ideas and Power in Our Time*. Penguin Press, 2023, 100.

[29] Harvard University, Office of the Provost, Office for Gender Equity. Available at https://provost.harvard.edu/people/roledepartment/title-ix (accessed April 23, 2023).

[30] Wolfinger, Nicholas H. "How I Survived the Title IX Star Chamber." *Quillette*, August 24, 2017. Available at https://quillette.com/2017/08/24/survived-title-ix-star-chamber/ (accessed May 8, 2023). The Title IX investigator also sought interviews with graduate students, although none complied with his request.

[31] "Proposed Title IX Regulations: A Single Investigator Is Not Enough." FIRE, July 25, 2019. Available at https://www.thefire.org/news/proposed-title-ix-regulations-single-investigator-not-enough (accessed April 26, 2023).

[32] Title IX investigators have their own national organization, ATIXA. Available at https://www.atixa.org/ (accessed May 8, 2023).

[33] Kipnis, Laura. "My Title IX Inquisition." *Chronicle of Higher Education*, May 29, 2015. Available at https://laurakipnis.com/wp-content/uploads/2010/08/My-Title-IX-Inquisition-The-Chronicle-Review-.pdf (accessed April 28, 2023); see also Kipnis 2018; Gerson, Jeannie Suk. "Laura Kipnis's Endless Trial by Title IX." *The New Yorker*, September 20, 2017. Available at https://www.newyorker.com/news/news-desk/laura-kipniss-endless-trial-by-title-ix (accessed May 29. 2024).

[34] The investigation was conducted by Mary Jo White, formerly President Barrack Obama's head of the Securities and Exchange Commission, and cost University of Rochester $4.5 million. Perhaps coincidentally, Rochester's president resigned the day White delivered her report exonerating Jaeger. That same day, some of Jaeger's colleagues held a press conference to dispute White's findings and vow further inquiry. Jaeger, a German immigrant, remains on the faculty at Rochester, while some of his colleagues have moved on to new jobs at better universities. Herzog, Katie. "How an Academic Grudge Turned into a #MeToo Panic." *Reason*, March 14, 2022. Available at https://reason.co3m/2022/03/14/how-an-academic-grudge-turned-into-a-metoo-panic/ (accessed April 28, 2023). An anonymous collective largely supportive of Jaeger has created an extensive archive on his travails, https://thejaegercase.com/ (accessed January 31, 2024).

[35] Taylor, Stuart. "Why Campus Rape Tribunals Hand Down So Many 'Guilty' Verdicts." *Washington Examiner*, November 9, 2017.

[36] "Fallacies of Victim-Centered Methods." SAVEServices.org, n.d. Available at https://www.saveservices.org/sexual-assault/investigations/ (accessed April 26, 2023).

[37] "Cultivating Campus Climate: How Oberlin Meets the Challenges and Opportunities." Office of Equity, Diversity, and Inclusion, Campus Climate Report, Oberlin College, Spring 2016. Available at https://www.oberlin.edu/

sites/default/files/content/office/equity-diversity-inclusion/documents/
oberlin_campus_climate_spring_2016.pdf (accessed April 26, 2023).

[38] Bazelon, Lara. "I'm a Democrat and a Feminist. And I Support Betsy DeVos's
Title IX Reforms." *The New York Times*, December 4, 2018; Ullman, Buddy
"Title IX Reforms Will Restore Due Process for Victims and the Accused."
Newsweek, June 12, 2020. Available at https://www.newsweek.com/title-ix-
reforms-will-restore-due-process-victims-accused-opinion-1510288
(accessed April 28, 2023); Wolfinger, Nicholas H. "A Plea for the New
Department of Education Guidelines on Campus Sexual Misconduct."
Institute for Family Studies blog, August 31, 2020. Available at
https://ifstudies.org/blog/a-plea-for-the-new-department-of-education-
guidelines-on-campus-sexual-misconduct (accessed April 28, 2023).

[39] Montague, Zach and Erica L. Green. "Biden Administration Releases Revised
Title IX Rules." *The New York Times*, April 19, 2024.

[40] Historian Alan Kors and defense attorney Harvey Silverglate wrote about unjust
campus proceedings in 1999, over a decade before the 2011 Dear Colleague
Letter kicked the star chambers into overdrive. Kors, Alan Charles, and
Harvey Silverglate. *The Shadow University: The Betrayal of Liberty on
America's Campuses*. Simon and Schuster, 1999.

[41] The best data I'm familiar with are more than fifteen years old, but nonetheless
reveal a heavily leftward tilt among the professoriate. Neil Gross and Solon
Simmons. "The Social and Political Views of American Professors." Paper
presented at a Harvard University Symposium on *Professors and Their
Politics*, 2007, 41. Available at https://citeseerx.ist.psu.edu/document?
repid=rep1&type=pdf&doi=bb515236a3a001d4f90f606088888651f253641
4 (accessed April 27, 2023); see also Neil Gross. *Why Are Professors Liberal
and Why do Conservatives Care?* Harvard University Press, 2013. For more
recent data, Kaufmann, Eric. "Academic Freedom in Crisis: Punishment,
Political Discrimination, and Self-Censorship." Center for the Study of
Partisanship and Ideology, Report No. 2. March 1, 2021. Available at
https://cspicenter.org/wp-content/uploads/2021/03/AcademicFreedom.pdf
(accessed April 27, 2023). It's worth pointing out that academia isn't unique
in this regard: all the professions have become more left-leaning over the past
40 years as society has polarized along educational lines. https://twitter.
com/adam_bonica/status/1174536380329803776 (accessed 4/27/2023), data
obtained from https://data.stanford.edu/dime (accessed April 27, 2023).

[42] The classic evidence on this point is William F. Buckley's broad indictment of
his alma mater, *God and Man at Yale* (Regnery, 1951), but the animus is
much older. Stanford University forced out economist Edward Alsworth Ross
in 1900 for his support of populist Democrat William Jennings Bryan and of
left-wing political positions more generally. Eule, Brian. "Watch Your
Words, Professor." *Stanford Magazine*, January/February 2015. Available at
https://stanfordmag.org/contents/watch-your-words-professor   (accessed
April 28, 2023). Ross's firing and several similar incidents led to the
formation of the American Association of University Professors in 1915.

[43] On the 1930s watchlist, Tiede, Joerg. "The 'Professor Watchlist' of the 1930s." *Academe* blog, American Association of University Professors, November 24, 2016. Available at https://academeblog.org/2016/11/24/the-professor-watchlist-of-the-1930s/ (accessed April 28, 2023). The author of the watchlist, activist Elizabeth Dilling, also fingered Albert Einstein, Eleanor Roosevelt, New York Mayor Fiorello LaGuardia, Mahatma Gandhi, British Prime Minister Ramsay McDonald, and the ACLU as communist agents. The watchlist is available in its entirety at http://moses.law.umn.edu/darrow/documents/The_Red_Network_1934.pdf (accessed May 26, 2023). Dilling went on to be acquitted of sedition during World War II, and published numerous other scurrilous works. Interested readers are directed to *The Octopus*, her exposé about the purported Jewish threat to America. https://ia800900.us.archive.org/18/items/DillingElizabethTheOctopus_2019 03/Dilling%20Elizabeth%20-%20The%20Octopus.pdf (accessed May 26, 2023).

[44] Turning Point USA Professor Watchlist, n.d. "Russell Rickford." Available at https://www.professorwatchlist.org/professor/russellrickford (accessed April 28, 2023).

[45] Drum, Kevin. "Nutpicking." *Washington Monthly*, August 11, 2006. Available at https://washingtonmonthly.com/2006/08/11/nutpicking/ (accessed April 28, 2023).

[46] Boshko, David. Blog comment. Available at https://acoup.blog/2020/07/03/collections-the-practical-case-on-why-we-need-the-humanities/comment-page-1/ (accessed April 28, 2023).

[47] Complaints to college administrators are typically accompanied by death threats to the offending faculty member. Women receive rape threats, while non-Whites get racial slurs. Hans-Joerg Tiede, Samantha McCarthy, Isaac Kamola, and Alyson K. Spurgas. "Data Snapshot: Whom Does Campus Reform Target and What Are the Effects?" Blog, American Association of University Professors, Spring 2021. Available at https://www.aaup.org/article/data-snapshot-whom-does-campus-reform-target-and-what-are-effects (accessed June 6, 2024).

[48] Simone Carter. "Collin College to Pay $70,000 to History Professor Let Go amid Free Speech Debacle." *Dallas Observer*, January 26, 2022. Available at https://www.dallasobserver.com/news/history-professor-fired-for-tweets-lora-burnett-to-receive-70000-from-collin-college-13285526 (accessed April 29, 2023).

[49] Anna North. "The Controversy over a Professor's Tweet Calling Barbara Bush a Racist, Explained." *Vox*, April 25, 2018. Available at https://www.vox.com/2018/4/20/17257076/barbara-bush-death-randa-jarrar-fresno-state-professor-tweets-free-speech-college (accessed April 29, 2023); "Fresno State University: Professor Randa Jarrar's Tweets following Death of Barbara Bush Lead to Investigation." FIRE, n.d. Available at https://www.thefire.org/cases/fresno-state-university-professor-randa-jarrars-tweets-following-death-barbara-bush-lead (accessed April 29, 2023).

[50] A newly prominent form of watch list targets allegedly anti-Semitic or anti-Israel faculty members. Perhaps the most prominent of these sites is the Canary Mission, launched in 2014 (www.canarymission.org, accessed January 28, 2024). Had I solicited contributors after the October 7, 2023 terrorist attack against Israel, it's likely that much of this book would be devoted to allegations of anti-Semitism or Islamophobia.

[51] Wolfinger 2021.

[52] Yglesias, Matthew. "The Great Awokening." *Vox*, April 1, 2019. Available at https://www.vox.com/2019/3/22/18259865/great-awokening-white-liberals-race-polling-trump-2020 (accessed February 1, 2024); see also Chait, Jonathan. "Not a Very P.C. Thing to Say." *New York*, January 27, 2015, available at https://nymag.com/intelligencer/2015/01/not-a-very-pc-thing-to-say.html (accessed May 30, 2024). For recent academic treatments of the Awokening, see Engelhardt, Andrew M. "Trumped by Race: Explanations for Race's Influence on Whites' Votes in 2016." *Quarterly Journal of Political Science* 14, no. 3 (2019): 313-328; Yancey, George. 2023. "Identity Politics, Political Ideology, and Well-being: Is Identity Politics Good for Our Well-being?" *Sociological Forum* 38:1245-1265. Available at https://onlinelibrary.wiley.com/doi/pdf/10.1111/socf.12966 (accessed February 2, 2024). Finally, it should be noted that White progressives aren't alone: attitudes on race and immigration have trended leftward in recent years for nonwhite Democrats as well, according to recent data from political scientist John Sides. Available at https://threadreaderapp.com/thread/1844770314426662977.html (accessed October 11, 2024).

[53] On the media, Goldberg, Zach. "How the Media Led the Great Racial Awokening." *Tablet*, August 4, 2020. Available at https://www.tabletmag.com/sections/news/articles/media-great-racial-awakening (accessed February 1, 2024). This phenomenon is not limited to the United States. Rozado, David. 2023. "The Great Awokening as a Global Phenomenon." arXiv preprint. Available at https://arxiv.org/ftp/arxiv/papers/2304/2304.01596.pdf (accessed February 2, 2024).

[54] Waddell, Kaveh. "The Exhausting Work of Tallying America's Largest Protest." *The Atlantic*, January 23, 2017. Available at https://www.theatlantic.com/technology/archive/2017/01/womens-march-protest-count/514166/ (accessed February 1, 2024).

[55] For a rumination on the origins of the Trump-voters-in-diners trope, Mack, Doug. "Why Are Journalists Always Visiting Diners in Trump Country?" thecounter.org, October 22, 2020. Available at https://thecounter.org/trump-rust-belt-diner-presidential-race-election-2020/ (accessed January 9, 2024). Of course there was also serious social science about the 2016 election. One of the best studies is Sides, John, Michael Tesler, and Lynn Vavreck. *Identity Crisis: The 2016 Presidential Campaign and the Battle for the Meaning of America*. Princeton University Press, 2019.

[56] Pengelly, Margin. "Barack Obama Warns Progressives to Avoid 'Circular Firing Squad.'" *The Guardian*, April 6, 2019. Available at https://www.the

guardian.com/us-news/2019/apr/06/barack-obama-progressives-circular-firing-squad-democrats#:~:text=%E2%80%9COne%20of%20the%20things%20I,squad'%2C%20where%20you%20start%20shooting (accessed January 28, 2024).

[57] Grim, Ryan. "Elephant in the Room." *The Intercept*, June 13, 2022. Available at https://theintercept.com/2022/06/13/progressive-organizing-infighting-callout-culture/ (accessed January 28, 2024).

[58] al-Gharbi, Musa. "The 'Great Awokening' Is Winding Down." *Compact*, February 8, 2023. Available at https://musaalgharbi.com/2023/02/08/great-awokening-ending/ (accessed January 29, 2024); see also al-Gharbi, Musa. "The Great Awokening of Higher Ed Has Ended—But Is It Too Late?" The Liberal Patriot blog, June 21, 2023. Available at https://www.liberalpatriot.com/p/the-great-awokening-of-higher-ed (accessed January 29, 2024). A recent review offered preliminary evidence that scientific censorship peaked in 2020 and is on the decline. Clark, Cory J., Lee Jussim, Komi Frey, Sean T. Stevens, Musa al-Gharbi, Karl Aquino, J. Michael Bailey et al. "Prosocial Motives underlie Scientific Censorship by Scientists: A Perspective and Research agenda." *Proceedings of the National Academy of Sciences* 120, no. 48 (2023): e2301642120. Available at https://www.pnas.org/doi/pdf/10.1073/pnas.2301642120 (accessed September 1, 2024). One of the authors, Lee Jussim, is a contributor to the current book. Finally, corporate America, a powerful trailing indicator, appears to be running away from public manifestations of lefty cultural politics. Writing for *Business Insider*, Emily Stewart calls it the "great un-wokening." Stewart, Emily. "Woke No More." *Business Insider*, May 9, 2024. Available at https://www.businessinsider.com/woke-capitalism-reversal-google-unilever-bud-light-esg-dei-2024-5 (accessed May 19, 2024).

[59] *The Economist*. "America Is Becoming Less 'Woke.'" September 19, 2024.

[60] Mounk 2023, 116.

[61] Lukianoff, Greg and Rikki Schlott. *The Canceling of the American Mind: Cancel Culture Undermines Trust and Threatens Us All—But There Is a Solution*. Simon and Schuster, 2023, 37.

[62] On "Marx, Mao, Marcuse!" see Breen, Benjamin. *Tripping on Utopia: Margaret Mead, the Cold War, and the Troubled Birth of Psychedelic Science*. Grand Central Publishing, 2024, 265. A more sophisticated version of this theory was proposed 25 years ago, long before the Great Awakening and the surge in faculty investigations, by Alan Charles Kors and Harvey Silverglate. Kors and Silverglate, who founded theFIRE.org that same year, traced the throughline from Marcuse to critical legal theory. In hindsight this looks like a plausible etiology of what was to come in the 2010s, but it can't account for all the changes on campus chronicled here. Perhaps illiberal academic theories can provide a compelling post-hoc explanation for a relentlessly investigated faculty, but Marcuse and his intellectual progeny can hardly constitute a sufficient condition in light of the other changes to higher education described here. Kors and Silverglate 1999. Finally, it's worth

noting that another scholar has attributed wokeness to right-wing scholars, the Third Reich-friendly Carl Schmitt and Martin Heidegger. Neiman, Susan. *Left is not Woke*. John Wiley & Sons, 2023.

[63] Musa al-Gharbi's opus on wokeness concluded the same thing: "Wokeness is clearly not a result of people being indoctrinated into social justice activism through a deep reading of primary texts. . . ." al-Gharbi, Musa. *We Have Never Been Woke: The Cultural Contradictions of a New Elite*. Princeton University Press, 2024, 53.

[64] Per the Wikipedia page on Sayre's Law, political scientist Wallace Stanley Sayre's eternal wisdom has variously been attributed to many eminent scholars, including Daniel Patrick Moynihan, Richard Neustadt, and Woodrow Wilson. Available at https://en.wikipedia.org/wiki/Sayre%27s_law (accessed January 30, 2024).

[65] Donald Trump won the 2024 presidential election as this book was going to press.

[66] Lukianoff and Schlott 2023, 27; Lukianoff, Greg. "The new Red Scare taking over America's college campuses." *Washington Examiner*, September 23, 2023. Available at https://www.washingtonexaminer.com/opinion/beltway-confidential/2743162/the-new-red-scare-taking-over-americas-college-campuses/ (accessed June 15, 2024). Investigations that didn't end in termination surged even more in the past decade—and as has been shown here, this is just the tip of the iceberg.

[67] Lennard, Natasha. "University Professors Are Losing Their Jobs over 'New McCarthyism' on Gaza." The *Intercept*, May 16, 2024. Available at https://theintercept.com/2024/05/16/university-college-professors-israel-palestine-firing/ (accessed May 22, 2024); see also Afzal-Kahn, Fawzia. "The New McCarthyism on US Campuses." *Counterpunch*, December 11, 2023. Available at https://www.counterpunch.org/2023/12/11/the-new-mccarthyism-on-us-campuses/ (accessed May 30, 2024). Fawzia contributed a chapter to this book.

[68] AAUP 2022.

[69] Turchin, Peter. "Political Instability May Be a Contributor in the Coming Decade." *Nature* 463, no. 7281 (2010): 608. Turchin has developed his theory of elite overproduction in numerous other works. For an application to higher education, Smith, Noah. "The Case of the Angry History Postdoc." Blog, May 28, 2024. Available at https://www.noahpinion.blog/p/the-case-of-the-angry-history-postdoc (accessed June 3, 2024).

[70] Fountain, Wendell. *Academic Sharecroppers: Exploitation of Adjunct Faculty and the Higher Education System*. Authorhouse, 2005.

[71] Gross, Neil. "Professors Behaving Badly." *The New York Times*, September 30, 2017.

[72] Schlosser, Edward (pseudonym). "I'm a Liberal Professor, and My Liberal Students Terrify Me." *Vox*, June 3, 2015. Available at https://www.vox.com/2015/6/3/8706323/college-professor-afraid (accessed April 23, 2023).

[73] Perhaps the flurry of academic investigations is already succeeding in chilling academic freedom. A national sample of faculty members collected in September and October of 2024 indicates that 91 percent of faculty members think that academic freedom is under threat in America, while 55 percent say that academic freedom is under threat at their own universities. Even if we take the lower number as more indicative, it still points to a pervasive problem. Quinn, Ryan. "Many Faculty Say Academic Freedom Is Deteriorating. They're Self-Censoring." *Inside Higher Ed*, November 13, 2024. Available at https://www.insidehighered.com/news/faculty-issues/academic-freedom/2024/11/13/many-faculty-say-academic-freedom-deteriorating?utm_source=Inside+Higher+Ed&utm_campaign=74375c35ae-DNU_2021_COPY_02&utm_medium=email&utm_term=0_1fcbc04421-74375c35ae-236599654&mc_cid=74375c35ae (accessed November 18, 2024).

Sex

The 'Skittish' University[1]

Patricia A. Adler and Peter Adler

"Curiouser and curiouser!" cried Alice, in Lewis Carroll's 1865 *Alice in Wonderland* classic. This observation is apt today. Colleges and universities around the world are undergoing a period of turbulence and turmoil, battered from both the Right and the Left, from within and without. How they are transformed and weather this storm remains is an open question. We write today to discuss, from the inside, one particular incident that occurred to the lead author, Patti Adler, at the University of Colorado in the fall of 2013 through spring of 2014, that has been cited by the American Association of University Professors as one of the most egregious violations ever of Title IX and academic freedom and made a matter of public record.[2] Drawing from this case and events since then, we discuss and analyze developments that threaten North American institutions of higher education. Though a coauthored piece, for convenience we use the "I" form in presenting this story.

As some readers will know, I have joined the ranks of an elite group: the tiny number of tenured faculty members terminated or "asked to leave" their jobs. A 2005 *Wall Street Journal* article estimated that only 50 to 75 tenured professors out of 280,000 are fired each year.[3] My exit from academia resulted from a controversial decision made by my University in December of 2013 that rebounded globally, concerning a pedagogical device I had used in my class for over 25 years that, in the climate at that time, was deemed too great a risk to the University.

Peter and I moved to Boulder, Colorado in 1987 when I started working at the University of Colorado. I began teaching "Deviance in U.S. Society" that first semester and it quickly grew into the most popular class on campus, specifically mentioned in several college guide books. It enrolled 500 people every semester, so that over 27 years, I've taught this class to around 25,000 students. In one lecture I used a role play exercise ("the skit") to outline the eight features of a deviant subculture and to illustrate one of them: a system of status stratification. I used the example of prostitution (now preferably called "sex work") to portray six strata of prostitutes: sexual slavery; crack-addicted prostitutes; male and female streetwalkers and their pimps; sex workers in bars; brothels; and escort services. One of the didactic purposes of the skit was to open students' eyes to the wider array of life options, lifestyles, motivations, living conditions, working conditions, careers, violence, and degradation that exist among the different strata of prostitutes. Twelve participants joined me in performing the skit each time, role playing their parts from scenarios that I continually updated for my questions and narratives, drawing on academic research, investigative journalism, first-person accounts, and documentaries. Over the 27 years that I've featured this role—play exercise in my class, twice annually, there have been over 500 people portraying various roles. In all of this time, there has never been a complaint.

To personalize my mass class, I used both TAs (grad students) and Assistant TAs (ATAs). The latter were outstanding undergraduate students who I recruited from the previous semester to help me write and, with the TAs, grade non-standardized exams. They also enabled me to personalize the class beyond what the TAs could offer since they were stretched so thin with so many students. The ATAs were offered the first right of refusal to play roles in the skit, and after that I opened it up to volunteers from among former ATAs, friends, publishers' reps, and others. These were prized roles, and some former ATAs even drove or flew back to Boulder to participate in the skit. It was the highlight of the semester, and there was never a paucity of volunteers.

In the fall of 2013 the skit ran on November 5. The next day I heard that one of my second-year TAs, Vanessa Roberts, had been badmouthing me after the skit in her discussion section. On November 7, after our weekly TA meeting, I asked Vanessa if she could stay afterwards to talk for a few minutes. She had two concerns: (1) that evolving cellphone technology and social media might cause participants to worry about being embarrassed by students posting pictures of them; and (2) that participants might feel uncomfortable portraying their roles but not want to tell me for fear of retribution. We brainstormed about how to ameliorate this and I thought we had a productive meeting, coming up with new recruitment strategies and precautions.

But five days later, on November 12, Vanessa sent me an email confessing that she had brought her concerns about the ATAs to the department chair earlier in the semester. She explained her motivation for this by saying that she was just trying to protect the ATAs from feeling uncomfortable. But as I later learned, this account was spurious because she had surreptitiously begun trying to usurp my role from the beginning of the semester, undermining me and empowering herself. She held a meeting with my incoming staff while I was away at an international conference and told them that I was scary and standoffish, encouraging them to come to her with complaints about me behind my back.

Apparently, after hearing of Vanessa's concerns, chair Joanne Belknap immediately referred the case to the Office of Discrimination and Harassment (ODH). In so doing, she violated formal and informal department policies by failing to discuss it first either with me or with the Executive Committee. This raises the question of why chair Belknap took this case, a "concern" and not an actual "complaint" right away to ODH. Several possible explanations can be conjectured.

First, as an ardent feminist, she had never liked the skit and saw this as her chance to do something about it. Perhaps that's because she has a degree in Criminal Justice and teaches courses on Violence Against Women, while I'm a Sociologist who teaches Deviance. Criminal Justice is an applied, ameliorative, and value-laden discipline, while I come from an ethnographic, inductive, value-neutral tradition. She told me that I should have infused the material with more of a victimization perspective.

Second, it's hard to talk about a critique from the Left, but some Feminists view sex workers as victims of their traffickers, pimps, johns, the criminal justice system, and a patriarchal system more generally and want to save them. In contrast, there are people who view sex workers as women who have rights, free will, and agency and want to support their rights. My skit challenged the orthodoxy of both sides philosophically.

Third, some people believe that political correctness, a vital concept, has over-reach. We all probably agree that words have power and should be wielded sensitively, but does that leave no room for role-play or for different pedagogical devices?

Fourth, a new and inexperienced chair that semester, Belknap was apparently sending every concern she received to ODH in a knee-jerk manner. In her first three months on the job she referred a total of three cases to ODH. This contrasts with the 10-year tenure of the previous three chairs, during which no cases were referred. With the report filed, ODH opened their investigation. For one month, no one came forward. Vanessa did not qualify as a complainant herself because she had never been a skit participant. With no complainant, ODH did not have a case.

Their investigation stalled, the investigators then decided to investigate the *content of the skit*. On November 5, uninvited and unannounced, the two ODH investigators violated their policies and procedures and attended the skit. This represents a *key turning point*, because they expanded their focus from the power imbalance issue (professor-staff) to one of classroom content, a *violation of my academic freedom*.

After the skit, they tried more actively to drum up complainants from actual skit participants. Vanessa called each of my current ATAs, and the graduate (Janet Jacobs) and undergraduate (Hillary Potter) chairs, all ardent feminists, tried to solicit complaints from current and former (going back several years) TAs and ATAs. It was a witch hunt!

In the meanwhile, I didn't know what to do. Should I contact ODH preemptively? Should I wait for them to finish their investigation and contact me? I wanted the opportunity to present the didactic value of the skit and to see what they thought. I figured I could always stop using ATAs or just drop the skit if they informed me that it was a problem. So I waited. I didn't worry too much about it, after all, what could they do to me? I headed off to Thanksgiving break thinking that maybe the whole thing would just die.

Wrong! On December 5, the week after Thanksgiving and the second to last week of classes, the ODH investigators decided to take action. Without ever communicating with me, they called an emergency meeting with the dean and associate dean of arts and sciences, the chief University counsel, the head of ODH, and the chair of sociology. I was not invited to this meeting, and at this point I had still never been officially notified that there was an investigation. They presented a case to the administrators that they thought the skit was a "risk" to the University. The lawyer was concerned. This alarmed the deans. They brainstormed about what they could do to avert this dire threat. On the advice of the lawyer, dean Steven Leigh made his dynamic decision: I had to be removed from teaching Deviance immediately.

But apparently this was not enough. What else could they do to deal with this problem? How could they make it disappear? What if they could "*convince*" me to *retire immediately*? If this could happen, the lawyer and dean asked ODH, what would happen to the investigation? They do not investigate retired faculty, ODH said, and the investigation would go away. A plan was hatched.

That afternoon chair Belknap called me into an emergency meeting. As she delivered the verdict she told me that she had "*good news*" and "*bad news.*" The good news was that they were offering me an Early Retirement Buyout (known around campus as the "cash for clunkers deal," a term apparently referring to their using it to encourage the retirement of "deadwood" faculty). This deal, for which I had previously applied and been denied (because, they told me, of my outstanding value to the University), consisted of two years' salary spread out over five years. The bad news was that I had to take it *immediately*. I would have one week to finish up my classes, empty my office, and get out. If I declined to take it there would be severe hazards. First, I would be removed from teaching Deviance, my signature course. But second, even if I no longer taught it, if even one person ever came forward at any time in the future to complain about having felt uncomfortable (not only a skit participant, but also any of the 25,000 plus students who had ever taken the class), I could be found guilty of violating the University's sexual harassment policy and fired for cause. Third, if fired for cause, I would lose my retirement benefits, which included supplemental health insurance for my family for life.

The next day (December 6) the contract appeared in my box. I was amazed! Normally the wheels of bureaucracy grind exceedingly slow, but in less than 24 hours this paperwork was issued and signed by the chair, the dean, and the associate vice chancellor for faculty affairs.

What to do? On the advice of the faculty ombudsperson, I scheduled two meetings for Tuesday of the last week of school, December 10. In the morning, a colleague who sat on the ODH Board and I met with the ODH investigators. They first confirmed for us that this whole ruckus was completely confined to the skit. Despite their efforts, they had found no complainant and so they technically had no investigation and no case. But they pointed out three risk factors. First, the student portraying the slave role talked about how she had been trafficked from Latvia to America and used a fake accent. This might have offended students from that nation (protected class: national origin). Second, the student playing the role of a straight male streetwalker used the street vernacular "faggot" to refer to his customers (protected class: sexual orientation). Third, the student playing a pimp bragged about how he used a combination of love and fear to manipulate his women, and mentioned beating a woman who held out on him (protected class: gender). They confirmed one other thing: that there had never been a complaint made against me in my 28 years of teaching this course. I offered to drop the skit, but they said it was out of their hands.

Next, another colleague and I met with the dean and associate dean. They made the following points. First, I was in violation of the University's IRB because I had used students in a skit without institutional approval. Really, we thought? IRB for a classroom exercise? My colleague, who served on the IRB, pointed out that IRB approval is only required for research, which this classroom role play wasn't. My dean, an anthropologist by training, assured us three times that he knew better and that we were wrong. Second, the dean also said that in this *"post—Penn State environment,"* if he knew about a *"problem"* and didn't "do anything about it," then the University could be at too much risk. Was I being analogized to Jerry Sandusky, the repeat child molester who had coached at Penn State? I argued that he was doing something about it: he was talking to me and I agreed to drop the skit. But it didn't matter. It was too late! Third, if I did not sign the early retirement agreement and retire immediately, there would be the dire consequences that the dean and lawyer mentioned. I asked the dean for a one-year extension so that I didn't feel like I was being ignominiously and unceremoniously kicked out of my job on one week's notice, but he said absolutely not. And, moreover, he said that if I tried to delay my retirement for one year and a retroactive complaint came forth, even after I had signed, it would "damage the deal" and I would lose the buyout. The pressure to make a decision was intense. Fourth, if I signed the agreement I would have to relinquish my tenure, my right to due process, and my right to file a grievance through the Tenure and Privilege Committee of the University of Colorado system. That sounded kind of scary. I didn't think that a full professor could be pressured to leave so quickly without being notified at some point that there had been a problem and given the opportunity to fix it. When I asked about where my *due process* had been in this decision so far, the associate dean said, "What do you mean? You're getting it now!"

Shell-shocked, I went back to my department and told my colleagues in the hall what had happened. I said goodbye. I cried. They were stunned. And scared. The situation resonated with them personally, having a chilling effect. Could ODH walk into any classroom unannounced and uninvited and, in the absence of a complaint, go to the administration and get a tenured faculty member pressured to resign? Every single person to whom I spoke brought up some topic they discussed or lecture they gave that could potentially cause offense: racial privilege, immigration, sexism, theory, environmental politics, inequality, and more.

On the last Thursday of the semester, December 12, I went to class. I said goodbye to my students, tearfully thanked them for being such an amazing group, and told them that this would be the last class I would teach, ever. Most of the 500 people stood up three times to give me standing ovations, and then 200 of them came down to the front to hug me, to cry with me, and to tell me how much they had loved the class. By the time I got back to my office the shit storm had begun. Students were rampaging all over campus and calling their parents.

Then they went to the media. They began with the social media where they started a Change.Org petition that received over 3,500 signatures and comments as well as a Help Save Patti Adler's Job Facebook page that got over 500 postings and members. The mainstream media followed next. The first article came out in the local Boulder paper on December 13, the next day. *Inside Higher Education* published an article three days later

(December 16). *The Chronicle of Higher Education,* carried the story on December 17. I was deluged with hundreds of emails a day, phone calls, and media inquiries. The story was carried on CNN, MSNBC, AP, Reuters, The Huffington Post, and others. CU became the butt of a joke on the Jay Leno show.

Back at CU, protests erupted. Even though classes had ended, students held a rally. Faculty members on my campus freaked out. My department held an emergency meeting on the 17th. The Boulder Faculty Assembly held an emergency meeting on the 18th.

Support poured in from all over the country and the world, and numerous letters and emails were written to the chair, dean, provost, chancellor, and board of regents. Public letters and statements denouncing the University and supporting me were made by the state and national branches of the AAUP, the American Sociological Association, the Midwest Sociological Society, the Society for the Study of Symbolic Interaction and its European branch (the EU SSSI), the Society for the Study of Social Problems, the Foundation for Individual Rights in Education, the National Coalition Against Censorship, the American Civil Liberties Union, and a lot of other organizations. I was still freaking out, but I was buoyed by this amazing support.

The University then tried to respond to the waves of negative publicity released. Each response seemed more bungled than the last. They first had to address queries about the dean's IRB allegation. Mark Miller, a University spokesman, responded to inquiries from the press by reiterating dean Leigh's statement that this classroom exercise violated the University's human subject's policy. But by the next day they backed off that explanation when members of the board and others pointed out that IRBs focus on research, not classroom activities. A week later spokesman Mark Miller, who had recently been hired, "left the job to spend more time with his family."

Next, questions were raised about the *post-Penn State allegation*: How were volunteer students acting out roles in a classroom exercise equivalent to the forcible violation of underage boys by a retired coach in a locker room? The answer, I think, is that what the dean had in mind with regard to the Penn State affair was not the sexual abuse of young boys, but, instead, what happened to the university officials who covered up that abuse: the ex-athletic director, the former vice president, and the former president, all faced very serious criminal charges. So what motivated the lawyer and the dean, I suggest, was the fear that if they failed to act very quickly and extremely vigorously to deal with any occurrence at the University of Colorado that some, however unreasonably, might think was problematic, they might very well wind up facing serious charges themselves. This allegation was never retracted.

On December 16, provost Russell Moore sent out an email blast to all University of Colorado faculty, staff, and students. In it he suggested that I had violated the University's "sexual harassment" policy and possibly created a "hostile environment." He then said that CU had heard from "a number of concerned students" who said there would be retribution if they did not participate in the skit. He closed by saying that anyone found in violation of these policies was subject to "discipline up to and including termination." The AAUP demanded that he withdraw these allegations, but he declined.

Then, several days into the controversy and shortly after a closed-door meeting with faculty representatives, the university suddenly raised a new issue, which it now said was the main concern: the "photo consent allegation" claiming that students were being photographed or filmed without their consent during the skit. "With any course involving something unusual, like photographing students, we ask for consent forms to be signed," dean Leigh said. By this time it was clear that they were clutching at straws.

In response to attacks from the AAUP and other organizations about violations of academic freedom, the dean then lied, claiming that there had been ongoing concerns over the Deviance course for years, and that they had not been dealt with in an effective manner. To save face, given all of the negative publicity, the University had to reverse course about their insistence that I be removed from teaching the Deviance course. They deflected the decision by calling for a review of the course by the faculty in sociology. An ad hoc committee of senior full professors was assembled, despite the fact that the University was closed for the holidays, to review the course. The AAUP rejected this suggestion, arguing that this course, taught successfully for over 25 years, had no business being subjected to this extraordinary level of review.

Over winter break things continued to churn, with accusations and allegations flying and being aired in the media. I had to hire a lawyer (at $400 per hour). The stress my husband and I were under was intense, and high blood pressure and palpitations drew him to the emergency room at one point. The sociology committee approved the course without change, except to suggest that I should consider using consent forms for skit participants. Because of all the support and the public relations debacle, the University had to offer me the one semester transition option I had requested, while still keeping the buyout. At the same time, they offered to pay me that final spring semester's salary if I didn't return.

Now I had a decision to make. I could just take the buyout and get out, or I could reject the buyout and stay. After all, I was still a tenured faculty member. And since I could still teach my class that made it a lot more attractive. If I were 45 I'd definitely have done that. But I wasn't 45 and I had been starting to think about retiring. Staying for the long term might not be good. Maybe I should take the modified buyout. My husband and I tossed and turned. Should I just take the retirement agreement and leave, or should I take the risk and come back? How would these decisions affect others? Would I make the University look good by coming back, letting them say that they had given me academic freedom? Or would I make them look bad by coming back, forcing them to retract their decision? There seemed to be good arguments on both sides.

On the one hand, there were several reasons why I was afraid to return. First, the threats against me still stood that if anyone came forward to complain, I could be fired for cause and lose both the retirement deal and my future health insurance. And since the situation had gone viral and they had made fools of themselves, I thought CU would be motivated to pull people out of the woodwork to support their claims, even though they still hadn't found any actual complainant. Second, my department was roiling, torn apart between the chair who had pushed me out, the people who had stood behind me, and the junior faculty who were too scared to take a stand. Threats, intimidation, yelling, and cursing were being thrown around through the faculty email list and in person. I would definitely be going back to a hostile working environment. Would going back be even more stressful?

Despite this, I wanted to return. First, I didn't want to feel like I was being pushed out on a moment's notice. I thought that one more semester there would help me adjust my life and my identity. Second, I was devastated by the sadness I would feel of losing my classroom and my students. I wanted to experience the joy and passion I felt for teaching one more time. Third, many people and organizations had supported my rights of academic freedom and due process, and I felt that if I was given the chance to return, I ought to take it for them. Finally, I was motivated to stand up for principles. I didn't want the University to be able to just push me out, or to set this as a precedent for what they could do to other people. And the Boulder Faculty Assembly was forming a "Patti Adler Committee" to look into how my case was handled by the University.

In the end, I decided to come back, even though I knew it would be more stressful. I felt that whatever anxiety I had to undergo, it was important for me to fight. I ended up taking the early retirement deal, but on my own terms and on my own time. I retired at the end of this next semester, and my husband, shaken to the core by this stress as well, did the same.

The last semester was as awful as I had imagined. I had to pass people in the hall who averted their eyes from me. The University's legal counsel told my colleagues not to talk to me for fear of a lawsuit, and so many of them were scared to interact with me. I got stalking and scary emails from creepy people who were religious fanatics, birthers, and right-wingers. I got anonymous notes of support passed under my office door from colleagues within and outside my department saying how scared they were. Legions of sex worker activists crawled out of the woodwork to tell me how I should teach the course, which now felt like a powder keg. Naturally, they did not agree with each other. I felt afraid to make a joke in my classroom, which I think is a by-product of this contretemps that continues to this day. Even though I tried as hard as I could to keep the skit, the chilling effects on the participants and me made it impossible and I ended up dropping it at the last minute. So the victory was small and ultimately Pyrrhic.

Conclusions

What are some of the take-aways from all of this about developments in the academy for the 21st Century?

The Culture of Fear

There was a time when universities, in a free society, were ideally centers of learning, places to experiment with new ideas, and centers of exploration and growth. Universities existed to challenge people's beliefs and assumptions, including on controversial subjects such as sexuality. We have not always achieved that ideal, but threats to it are currently on the rise. That has changed. The *corporatization of the academy* is now well-known. Email missives hail the "business model" under which universities now operate and unabashedly refer to students as "clients." Since the economic downturn in 2008, liberal arts colleges and universities across the country have reshaped their curricula. They have narrowed the fields of study to prepare students for vocational work geared toward quantification and statistical analysis, shearing away the arts and humanities from the intellectual model that has underpinned students' critical thinking in the United States over the past century. As many as 50 percent of private universities may be out of existence in the next 15 years and these institutions have turned to anything they can do to stay alive, including dropping departments or colleges and pampering to whining students and over-involved parents. *Risk-aversion* and *fear of lawsuit* now dominate decision-making, and the role of university counsel has grown. Administrative decisions are commonly made that violate core principles of academic freedom, autonomy, and policy in naked attempts to placate irate students and their tuition-paying helicopter parents. We have come to an age when campus administrators view unhappy students as consumers who are always right and faculty are seen as potential lawsuit risks whose careers can be threatened without due process.

Learning and Comfort

Does a discussion of uncomfortable topics constitute harassment? Many students come to universities, especially large state institutions, from sheltered home environments where few challenges to the existing norms and values are present. Many disciplines, but especially sociology, have the potential to offer new and possibly disturbing perspectives. Sociology was, is, and always should be an unsettling field of research. My friends and colleagues, perhaps people reading this book, research some very discomforting topics, and many work to humanize the dehumanized, normalize deviance, question the powerful, give voice to those without a platform, and challenge the everyday assumptions that we all have held at one time or another. Sharing research like this is often difficult, but education about uncomfortable issues is not "harassment." Teaching about white privilege, racism, and deviance present a pedagogical challenge to everyone who teaches these topics. And yet, these things should not be avoided because they are unsettling; they should be tackled precisely because they are unsettling.

The trend among college campuses across the country, coming from the Left, especially from students, is pressure on faculty to give "*trigger warnings*" if they will be discussing sensitive topics in their classes. The trigger warning signals not only the growing precautionary approach to words and ideas in the university, but a wider cultural hypersensitivity to harm and paranoia about giving offense. Issuing caution on the basis of potential harm or insult doesn't help us negotiate our reactions; it makes our dealings with others more fraught. Trigger warnings reinforce the fear of words by depicting an ever-expanding number of articles and books as dangerous and requiring of regulation. The question then for us is: Do we dare to be uncomfortable?

Administrative Bloat and Overreach

We have recently been witness to the greatest increase in administrative hiring in academia. This is well documented in the report by the Delta Cost Project on labor trends in higher education.[4] Drawing on data collected between 2002 and 2010, Desrochers and Kirshstein found that the growth in administrative jobs has been widespread across higher education, but most of these jobs have gone to mid-level administrative management positions (business analysts, human resources staff, counseling, and admissions staff), rather than professional executive and managerial positions. The percentage of new faculty hires that went to full-time, tenure-track (FTE) positions declined, while part-time, adjunct, and instructor jobs increased. The ratio of faculty and staff to administrators decreased by over 40 percent, as more administrative units were created while departments and programs were curtailed and merged. Across all educational sectors, wage and salary expenditures for student services were the fastest growing salary expense. While faculty salaries remained relatively flat, increasing portions of university and college budgets have been allocated to student services and dramatically rising administrative salaries. While college tuition has skyrocketed, this has not been due to the cost of actual education, but rather to administration. This "administrative takeover" of academia has gone hand-in-hand with several related trends.

Mission creep has become commonplace, as a number of entities within universities today can now be recognized to have expanded their domain beyond what was originally intended, including institutional review boards (IRBs), offices of discrimination and harassment, learning disabilities centers, athletic departments, and legal departments.

IRBs

In 2003 Peter and I wrote an article about IRBs in which we asked if university lawyers defined our research value system.[5] This question is even more apt now. The reach of IRBs has grown every year since their inception. While they were once tasked with monitoring the exploitation of human subjects in medical research and protecting people from experimental research, they have extended their tentacles into the social sciences and humanities, applying an experimental/medical model of research that is not an appropriate fit for these fields. Rules and policies change regularly, expanding their purview and demands. Enormous variability exists horizontally, as the rules and policies are unclear and differ widely between institutions. Members of institutional review boards serve for mainly three year periods, and there tends to be little institutional memory over time. To members of the social sciences especially, the demands of these boards often appear capricious and ignorant.[6]

Offices of Discrimination and Harassment

Though founded with the ideal of protecting women and students from the exploitation of male privilege and power, these administrative units have continuously redefined their purpose, increasing their jurisdiction and power. They strike fear into the hearts of faculty and administrators alike. To be accused has come to be assumed guilty. Investigations have taken on a witch-hunt quality, with questions asked that lead respondents, presume unproven accusations, and distribute stigmatizing judgments. These bodies claim a disproportionate amount of power and have no corresponding checks and balances, answering to no higher body. Academic principles get trampled. This situation has veered so badly away from a neutral presumption of innocence, that male graduate and undergraduate students have been getting railroaded. Not surprisingly, this has provoked a backlash from the Right, and was one of the many factors propelling Donald Trump into office. Once there, his Secretary of Education, Betsy DeVos, set about unwinding the avenues of redress available to women on college campuses. In 2017 the Department of Education formally rescinded Obama-era guidelines on how schools should handle sexual assault reporting and investigations under Title IX federal law. Criticizing these as having gone too far, they raised the standard of proof for school disciplinary proceedings, undermining protections for victims of sexual harassment and assault. Many view this as the beginning of a larger assault on Title IX.

Offices of Disability Services

Although established to level the learning environment for students with differential learning abilities, these entities have come to offer enhanced privileges for those whose parents can afford to acquire the expensive documentation required to support diagnoses of learning disabilities. Once students are accepted as clients of disability services units, they are often offered a laundry list of services for which they can ask, a menu that continues to grow each year. Initially, the required accommodation was for faculty to provide documented students with extended time for exams. Added to this have been mandates that faculty provide "distraction reduced environments" (no more than three students in any exam room), note-takers, tutors, laptop computers for test-taking, and to turn over their own notes and PowerPoint slides, among many other things. All of this is demanded of faculty without providing them the necessary support resources. A backlash has begun from non-disability students, who then come to complain about the greatly enhanced privileges of their classmates, which they view as exceeding reasonable benefits. This puts professors in a bind and, once again, impinges on their ability to teach what and how they want.

Athletic Departments

Although athletic programs once struggled to gain the academic help necessary to aid their struggling student athletes, the educational services provided to athletes have similarly expanded. The academic support division of athletic departments are huge domains, employing several full-time coordinators and administrators. They hire undergraduate and graduate students to assist athletes with course preparation, exam preparation, and writing papers. They come to professors and ask for differential accommodations for athletes, such as oral exams, take-home exams, and amnesty from exams. Some schools place athletes in different sections of required classes where faculty (and especially graduate student teaching assistants) are pressured to "dumb down" the curriculum and standards. Sadly, it has become commonplace for scandals to emerge documenting the extent to which such programs bribe, coerce, and sidestep the *educational* principles and academic freedom of the scholastic side of universities.

Legal Departments

Finally, the offices of university counsel extend their tentacles into every corner of the university. They guide decision-making. They encourage administrators to cut more and more secret deals. They dispatch people with threats and intimidation. They silence people with gag orders and non-disclosure agreements. They represent an intractable force for bureaucracy.

Ultimately there is a much bigger story to be told here. My case was not isolated; it just received more publicity because of how ludicrous the decisions were, because I was a respected, internationally-recognized senior scholar with strong professional support, because I was a popular teacher on campus with enormous student support, and because I didn't shut up. Since my time the media has reported on many people whose stories are scarily similar, and the number of stories that go unreported are significantly greater. While I was able to fight, and at that, only win back one semester, I know that those with less experience, especially junior faculty, do not get even that. Most cases get swept under the rug, as faculty are intimidated and disempowered.

This, sadly, has been the harbinger of things that continue to deteriorate. The academy in which many of us have fruitfully spent our careers is changing dramatically and rapidly all around us in frightening ways. Threats to academic freedom come not only from the Left and the Right, but also also from institutional authority, as university counsel is neither leftist nor rightist but institutionalist, in a very limiting, reactive sense. In many respects the greatest dangers come from "establishments" that are motivated not by ideology but by more mundane concerns with "risk" and "brand." These trends will have ripple effects globally, as some of our worst trends domino overseas, and become exacerbated in the Post-Covid era as institutions increasingly turn toward online and computer-mediated teaching, as they fight for their very existence.

We have argued that issues that were initially well-intended, such as sensitivity to language, to students' abilities, their roles, and their identities, have a tendency to propel themselves to extremes where they become destructive and threaten both the integrity of education and academic freedom. It is dangerous to be lulled into complacency because something's original purpose appeared beneficial. If one little skit on one day of a class is going to get a full professor in effect fired with no due process, something more seriously problematic will be treated worse.

Classrooms have ebbed in their role as centers of exploration, and faculty find themselves increasingly fearful of being victims of student challenges, complaints, and lawsuits. Potentially sensitive topics are being eliminated from the curriculum, humor as a didactic device is under seige, and professors find themselves much more guarded in their self-expression. Faculty have become disposable, as administrators, guided by lawyers, do their cost-benefit analyses and realize that their financial interests do not lie with them. This represents a power shift from once autonomous faculty to administrators, students, and their parents.

Increasingly, conservative state legislatures are stepping in, implementing loyalty oaths, disciplinary committees, and subjecting faculty behavior and social media postings in individuals' private lives to scrutiny. Firings have occurred based on tweets, Facebook postings, civil disobedience, and political activism. The Wisconsin legislature (under republican governor Scott Walker) instituted policies that weakened tenure protections and gave administrators greater flexibility to close programs and eliminate faculty jobs. Left-leaning faculty and programs have become threatened, as well as those that show a less direct tie to financial benefits for both students and university budgets.

It is important to be sensitive to students, of course, but it is also imperative to be able to address important and diverse topics and to have freedom of expression. At stake are critical issues in the war against academic freedom. That is the purpose of tenure, and that is what is being ultimately threatened.

These trends are tied to the increasing *loss of power and autonomy of faculty* in universities. We see this in the institutionalization of the lumpenprofessoriat, what Alan Greenspan lauded as the class of "insecure laborers" that would inject health into society by not asking for wage benefits or increases. We see this in the rise of Internet courses, which have been characterized by some as a means of replacing faculty with cheap online education. We see this in the plethora of "new rules" about absence from campus, conflict of interest, post-tenure reviews, bureaucracy, and accountability.

Faculty senates have become reticent about representing the voices of their faculty; department chairs' role as advocates for their units has declined. They become lackeys, marionettes of the administration and not defenders of their colleagues. It is surprising how quickly many of them step over to the other side and leave their professorial perspective behind. They become the "office" and protect their institutions. They listen to lawyers whispering in their ears, they sidestep political controversy, and have learned that it is easier to dispose of us faculty rather than to stand up and advocate for us and what is right.

While we were dozing, no one was paying attention. If we allow these trends to continue unchallenged, the power and position of faculty erode and due process and academic freedom die.

Endnotes

[1] This chapter was originally published in Hermanowicz, Joseph C., ed. *Challenges to Academic Freedom.* pp. 25-48. © 2021 Johns Hopkins University Press. Reprinted with permission of Johns Hopkins University Press and the authors.

[2] American Association of University Professors. 2015. "The History, Uses, and Abuses of Title IX." *Bulletin of the AAUP.* American Association of University Professors: Washington, D.C. Media accounts of the episode include Ferner, Matt. "Patricia Adler, CU-Boulder Professor, Allegedly Forced Out Over Prostitution Lecture [UPDATE]." *The Huffington Post*, January 24, 2014. Available at http://www.huffingtonpost.com/2013 /12/16/patricia-adler-deviance_n_4454652.html (accessed January 24, 2014); Schmidt, Peter. "U. of Colorado's Response to a Gritty Lecture Worries Sociologists." *The Chronicle of Higher Education*, December 17, 2013.

[3] Lubin, Joann S. January 10, 2005. "Travel Expenses Prompt Yale To Force Out Institute Chief." *Wall Street Journal* https://www.wsj.com/articles/SB11 0532423531621358. Downloaded February 3, 2014.

[4] Desrochers, Donna M. and Rita Kirshstein. 2014. *Labor Intensive or Labor Expensive?: Changing Staffing and Compensation Patterns in Higher Education.* Washington D.C.: Delta Cost Project.

[5] Adler. Patricia A. and Peter Adler. 2003. "Do University Lawyers and the Police Define our Research Value System?" In Will C. van den Hoonaard W (ed.), *Walking the Tightrope: Ethical Issues for Qualitative Researchers*, 34-42. Toronto: University of Toronto Press. 2003.

[6] van den Hoonaard, Will C. and Ann Hamilton A. (eds.). 2016. *The Ethics Rupture.* Toronto: University of Toronto Press.

The Scandal of Being Woman:
The Ejection of
an Uppity Woman from a Southern University

Teresa K. Buchanan

You can't get fired when you have tenure. You have to work hard to get tenure. The college wants to ensure that you are doing notable scholarship before offering that sort of job security. Tenure ensures that professors who teach controversial material won't have to worry about the consequences of, say, introducing the theory of evolution to the innocent daughter of a wealthy, well-connected Christian family.

That's what I heard in graduate school, and it might well be true. But when a couple of good old boys decide they want to get rid of an uppity woman, there are ways. Even if that woman is a tenured professor and about to be promoted to full professor, you can find a way around tenure protections. This is a story of how that happened to me. It is a strange story, and even ten years later, as I write this, it seems like the theater of the absurd. When possible, I've quoted documents that tell the story, and I have tried to stay as close to the facts as possible to avoid the defensiveness that naturally occurs when one has been attacked.

My story starts with an invitation to lunch. I developed and ran a nationally recognized teacher certification program that prepared students to teach preschool, kindergarten, first-, second-, and third-grade. We called it the "PK-3 Program." A nearby school system superintendent asked if he could take me to lunch because he wanted to discuss partnering with my university. My faculty team and I met him for lunch at our faculty club. He brought along a high school principal and administrative assistant. During the elegant lunch (which he paid for), my team and I listened to him describe problems he had in his school system. He wanted us to send student teachers to work in his system to help improve the annual district report card they receive from the state Department of

Education. I should have known by his emphasis on the state accountability system that he wasn't interested in improving the schools. He just wanted to raise his scores. I also should have listened to the members of my team, who thought this was a bad idea.

Ours was a "teacher-leader" program. We were preparing teachers to be change agents, so this seemed like an excellent opportunity for them to learn skills they'd use after graduation. Also, the superintendent said he'd pay stipends for the student teachers to commute to his district. At that time, many students had to commute an hour to work in a different school system, one we considered exemplary. They student-taught for two full semesters in their senior year. So I decided to let them work in the superintendent's troubled school system, supported by a stipend, for one semester and work in the "model" system in the other semester. In retrospect, that was a terrible decision.

At about the same time, our college was assigned a new dean. I use this language intentionally. Some administrators in our institution were more political appointees than qualified academic administrators. This new dean came to the college with minimal experience. He knew next to nothing about teacher education, and it showed. During his first semester, he made some proposals that many faculty opposed. He wanted faculty to begin teaching in an online graduate program administered by an outside for-profit entity, above and beyond their normal teaching assignments, with no additional compensation. He wanted to restructure faculty promotion evaluations by implementing simplistic quantitative metrics. When he came to the faculty requesting feedback on his ideas, I made another poor decision. I was one of the few tenured faculty members and I felt secure in my job, so I tried to act as a spokesperson to communicate faculty concerns. Many people were reluctant to speak freely to this relative stranger, and it turns out they had the right idea. This relatively young and inexperienced new dean would have preferred a subservient faculty that offered no dissenting views.

In the meantime, our students were struggling in their new placements. We supported them as they tried to employ good pedagogical practices. To be considered "failing" as a district in a state with the lowest-performing educational system in the country is a remarkable accomplishment. The reason for this soon became apparent. The district administration had expectations that made it difficult for teachers to offer effective instruction. Our students were doing an outstanding job negotiating those expectations, and were slowly beginning to see results.

But the superintendent did not like what he was hearing—we said the curriculum his friend sold to the district didn't reflect sound educational practice. We said the new smart boards—touch-sensitive interactive whiteboards—they bought for their beautiful new magnet school might as well be overhead projectors because they weren't being used to enhance learning. He heard that our student teachers used Common Core, a national set of educational standards first implemented in 2010, to teach children critical thinking and problem-solving skills, and that student teachers wouldn't be allowed to stay in the district for a second placement.[1] Finally, he was hearing that I thought he was crazy (which I did).

The superintendent called me in for a one-on-one meeting in his office. It felt like I was being called into the principal's office. The tone of his request was so odd that I reached out to my department chair for guidance. My department chair had heard bad things about the superintendent from other people. He told me not to meet with the superintendent alone, advice I was happy to follow. I responded to the phone call from the superintendent with an email seeking clarifications of his concerns and cc'd my chair on the message.

At the time, I was living out in the country in my grandmother's home. I'd moved there after I got divorced, and stayed there a year and a half. The internet and cell service were unreliable at home, so when I went to town I'd check my messages and catch up on digital tasks.

It was early evening on the last day of the semester before the winter break and I wanted to catch up on work before Christmas. I had a grocery list with the ingredients to make my traditional cookies. I was feeling relaxed, and was anticipating a good holiday season. When I opened my email, one of the messages was from our new dean. That was unusual, but I thought it was notice news about my promotion to the rank of full professor. He had recommended me for promotion to full professor earlier in the semester, so I was anticipating the notice that my promotion had moved forward. I found out later that the university committee had approved my promotion, and my promotion papers were on the desk of our Provost that day, awaiting his signature. In 2011 and 2012, I did the best teaching of my career. The athletes, honor's college, and booster club gave me teaching awards during these years. So I had gone up for promotion the fall of 2013 and had glowing letters of support from both inside and outside the university.

But my dean's email wasn't about my promotion. I sat stunned in my car, reading and rereading the document. This occurred over a decade ago, and I still have trouble reading this email. Unacceptable performance? What had I done? The memo came with no preceding meetings, memos, or notice. I had 19 years of good annual performance evaluations, had never been "written up" and was just recommended for promotion to full professor. It was bewildering. I did not know what he was referring to and because the university was closed, I had no way to contact him.

The Xmas Email from My Dean

Teresa Buchanan

From:	Damon P Andrew
Sent:	Friday, December 20, 2013 7:55 PM
To:	Teresa Buchanan
Cc:	A G Monaco; Earl H Cheek
Subject:	Unacceptable Performance

Importance:	High

ORIGINAL TRANSMITTED VIA US POSTAL SERVICE
COPY PLACED IN FACULTY MAILBOX IN SCHOOL OF EDUCATION

December 20, 2013

To: Teresa Buchanan

From: Damon Andrew, Dean

Re: Unacceptable Performance

There have been multiple serious concerns brought to my attention regarding your performance both in the classroom and in the field. These concerns center around inappropriate statements you made to students, teachers, and education administrators.   Most recently, as you know, you were banned from the Iberville Parish campuses by the superintendent. This behavior is completely unacceptable and must cease.

In light of this information, you are being removed from the classroom for the Spring 2014 semester while these issues are investigated further. The Office of Human Resource Management will conduct an investigation for any violation of university policies, including the university Sexual Harassment policy. You are expected to cooperate fully with them to resolve the matter. During this period, the effort that you would normally apply toward your teaching should be applied to your research accordingly.

Regarding the recommendation for your promotion to Full Professor, this additional information is being communicated to the Executive Vice Chancellor and Provost for consideration in his review of your packet. Should you wish to withdraw your packet from any further consideration, you may do so by writing to me through the director, Earl Cheek.

Please note that this behavior will be reflected in your annual review and will be considered unsatisfactory as defined under Policy Statement 109.

Cc: A.G. Monaco, Associate Vice Chancellor for Human Resource Management
        Earl Cheek, Director

Damon P.S. Andrew, PhD | Dean
Dean E.B. "Ted" Robert Endowed Professor
Dean's Office | 221 Peabody Hall | Baton Rouge, LA 70803
O:(225) 578-1258 | F: (225) 578-2267
Email: damonandrew@lsu.edu | Website: chse.lsu.edu

1

The dean said I wasn't supposed to discuss this email with him, or anyone for that matter. First, I was concerned for the students in my spring courses. None of the faculty assigned to teach my courses reached out to me, as the dean had instructed them not to talk to me. I felt helpless. For the next 18 months, I didn't know what I was supposed to be doing. Was I allowed to continue serving on student committees? Was I supposed to continue my university service? What was I supposed to do for work? I had no idea and no one to ask because at the dean's direction I was ostracized. No one in my department, except two stalwart friends who supported me personally but not professionally, even spoke to me until June 2014.

In mid-January, I received an email from the executive director of the Equal Employment Office from Human Resource Management that instructed me to meet with them the following day. A friend told me I shouldn't go alone, so I looked for someone to accompany me. I knew about the American Association for University Professors, and looked on their website for people who could help me. That night, I emailed another professor who had been treated poorly by my university and asked her for advice. She agreed to cancel her previously scheduled meeting and accompanied me. Later, she said it was the most hostile meeting she'd ever attended. The assistant H.R. manager fired interrogatory questions at me, one after another, in an angry and harsh tone that was unlike anything I'd ever experienced. I'd been advised only to answer their questions, so I kept my replies short and focused, but his questions and tone were bewildering.

Looking back to try to find the answer to the baffling *why* question, I've come to the same conclusion my attorneys reached. It could have been administrative incompetence. It could have been a bad case of misogyny. It could have been a power play. But probably it was just this: I was a pain in the ass, and they were going to find a way to get rid of me, one way or the other. The faculty handbook said a tenured professor can only be fired for some grievous cause like sexual harassment. Perhaps the dean latched on to those words and then decided to use them to "rid me of this meddlesome professor" (to paraphrase Henry II).

The dean's office and human resource department spent months building a case against me. They accused me of things that never happened, like being kicked out of schools and school districts. Once a principal had objected to my comments during a student evaluation and asked me not to do so in her school again. But no one banned me from their school.

They accused me of true but irrelevant things, like cherry-picked negative student evaluations. I taught 100 students per semester, and some of them, usually low-performing students, did not like me, so they sometimes disparaged me in their course evaluations. The dean's office assigned a staff member to review my evaluations (almost 20 years of them) and highlight the negative comments. There were many more positive evaluations than negative evaluations and the majority of the negative comments came from low-performing student teachers, but that was not factored into their review.

I had high expectations of students, and some didn't like that. A few years before I lost my job I was trying to raise the grade point average required for admission to my teacher-education program to 2.5 (out of 4). An administrator asked, "What degree program would those students be able to go into if you have such high admission requirements?" High? How well can someone teach mathematics and history and science and literature if they haven't mastered the subjects? In my mind, educators should have at least a C average in their core courses. Unfortunately, in a state that regularly falls at the bottom in all education metrics, I was in the minority in my demand for academic rigor.

Last, they accused me of trivial but true things. For instance, I sometimes used profanity at work. The example my inquisitors provided was a time when I said "fuck no" to a colleague in the hall. I occasionally used profanity when teaching, but it was intentional, purposeful, and not directed toward anyone. Another example: in a discussion about clothing for student teaching, I joked that my children once told me not to wear brown pants because, in their words, "people might think you are gay." That was a joke in poor taste, but it was not sexual harassment.

Another example they included was something that happened while I was teaching students how to prepare their classrooms for a new school year. I'd said it was a good idea to start fixing their rooms in the summer before they were required to be at school because it takes a lot of time to prepare a classroom for young children. A student interrupted me mid-sentence and said, "That won't be a problem for me because my fiancé will help." I said, admittedly irritated, "They might do that for a few years while the sex is good, but you are going to need to learn this for later." That was unkind and unwise, but I was also speaking from an academic knowledge of family relations, and that, as one might say, is "what the research shows."

This was the nature of the evidence they gathered against me. The reporter who first wrote about my case, who read all the documentation produced by the university, kept asking me, "But how is this sexual harassment?"[2] I just shrugged. The university subjected me to a few brief meetings during what was, for me, a 15-month sojourn in hell. They can be summarized as follows:

- May 26, 2014: I met with the Employee Relations Coordinator, Human Resource Management and the Academic Policy Consultant. They gave me a memo written by the Executive Director of the Equal Employment Office that said I was found guilty of sexual harassment and violating the Americans with Disabilities Act That was the first time I heard anything about a violation of the ADA, and I was given no details or information regarding such a violation.

- June 12, 2014: I met with the Dean, Assistant Dean of Finance and Administration, and the Faculty Senate Vice President, who was by then my peer advisor. I was given another memo at the beginning of the meeting, which said I had been found guilty of sexual harassment and violating A.D.A. The dean asked me for "my side." I tried to explain the context of the statements they found objectionable, but neither were listening. They gave me disapproving looks, and I could almost see the thought balloons above them saying, "Not ladylike." The dean had difficulty keeping his eyes open during the meeting, having just returned from a trip to South America.

- July 24, 2014: I arrived at 1:00 for a meeting with the Provost, briefly preceded by our dean's office secretary delivering a packet of material to the Provost. The Provost's secretary frowned at me and said my meeting was not until 1:30. I showed her a copy of her email from my iPhone, which said 1:00. She said he was not ready for me, and told me to return at 1:30. At 1:30, I met with the Provost, the human resources executive director, and my peer advisor for approximately 30 minutes. The Provost said he proceeded with the dismissal for cause process because the dean had requested it. As he opened the dean's packet of materials and glanced through it, he asked the human resources director questions that indicated he had yet to read the material and knew nothing of what was happening. Again, I tried to provide some context and clarity. My comments were ignored.

Finally, in March 2015, we had a hearing in accordance with university procedures. It resembled a trial. My attorney and peer advisor sat next to me. I could ask them questions, but they were not allowed to speak on my behalf. I could call witnesses, and I did. I called undergraduate students from the classes my accusers were referring to, as well as a student who had nominated me for a teaching award. I called colleagues who co-taught those classes with me and a graduate student from one of the classes being described as a "hostile learning environment" by the administration. This student had come to graduate school for the express purpose of working with me. All of the witnesses called by the university representative were administrators who read from the memo prepared by human resources, then answered my questions. At the same time, a jury of my peers—fellow faculty members from other departments—listened. We met from 8:00 am to 7:30 pm—that is, eleven and a half hours, with an hour lunch break. I went through an entire roll of Tums. After some deliberation, the jury agreed that, given the language of our sexual harassment conduct code, I was guilty but should not be fired. The president decided to fire me for sexual harassment anyway, on the grounds that I'd violated Title IX.

Since then, the American Association of University Professors (AAUP) and the university's faculty senate have thoroughly reviewed all the materials from my case, including the transcript from the eleven and a half hour hearing. Both came out with solid statements supporting me and censuring the university for its actions.[3] Another organization, the Foundation for Individual Rights and Expression (FIRE), took up my case, and we went to court.[4] FIRE argued that my speech was protected under the First Amendment, but the court disagreed. In the midst of this, the Provost took a position at another university. The H.R. executive director resigned a year or so later after an investigation into his activities. The dean left shortly after I did after an investigation into his use of college finances. The president took another position after my legal actions concluded. He resigned from that position after an investigation of the way he had handled Title IX at my university.

You may have wondered why I mentioned the school superintendent at the beginning of this story. It turns out that he was a well-connected fellow who knew some influential people. He was on the college's advisory board. During their fall 2013 meeting, something interesting happened between the time the dean wrote his letter of support for my promotion and the time he wrote the email accusing me of unacceptable performance. The dean was reporting on the college's international work when he was stopped in the middle of his presentation. The superintendent interrupted and blurted out a question, "So what are you going to do about Common Core?" Being new to education (he had a degree in kinesiology), the dean stuttered a bit and then asked a department chair to field the question. It put the blushing, seemingly embarrassed dean off balance for the remainder of the meeting.

After the board meeting, an attendee was surprised to see the dean cornered by that superintendent. As this person passed them, she heard my name being spoken. It's easy to picture two southern good old boys sitting cross-legged in an office and the dean, leaning back and saying in a soothing tone, "Now, don't you worry about a thing. I'll take care of that Buchanan woman." It's speculation on my part, but given how things work in Louisiana, something like that may well have happened. And what happened to the superintendent? He left the school district under a cloud a year or two later.

As I write this, I'm listening to my former university's football team play a bowl game with a sense of detached and surreal nostalgia. That football team played an outsized role in my life for most of my adult years. The loyalty I still feel, and my love for my alma mater and former employer are bone deep. In the midst of all these events, I was desperately worried about the damage short-sighted outsider administrators seemed to be doing to my beloved school.

I told my attorneys we would need to frame the lawsuit in a way that showed we were trying to protect this institution. That didn't happen, because they had a different agenda. They were, admirably, attempting to create a legal precedent related to free speech in higher education. I believe they will ultimately be successful. And if I had the resources to hire my own legal team and we had sued for discrimination and wrongful dismissal, we might well have won.

With hindsight, I realize my connection to the university was probably not healthy. My physician says I have significant post-traumatic stress disorder, and there are times when I experience problematic cognitive distortions that have emerged from those events. But I have strong support networks that help me manage the symptoms. Maybe it is more important to focus on the fact that I've grown and learned since being forcibly ejected from what was, after all, just a job. I hope that growth has been toward becoming a more whole person. It's said that to become truly free, you need to detach from worldly things. Maybe being able to tell my story with some objectivity indicates some degree of positive personal growth.

What did I learn? That life will crush everyone at some point. Maybe that's a good thing. An acorn has to break and come apart before it grows into a tree, and we, members of the human species, as a category of nature, also need to break and come apart at least once. As awful as this sounds, the sooner that happens, the better. My life path was reasonably smooth until this episode occurred. Unfortunately, because I was 50 years old, my experience generated a lot of collateral damage, impacting my family and friends in ways that I am sad about. But as for me? Well, it's probably been for the best. I'm at peace, and I'm always happy. I can see the Divine in every living thing, which gives me great joy. It is unlikely that would have happened without that devastating experience.

Now I'm confident that things will be okay. Even when our most essential sense of self is destroyed, when we are utterly lost and floating in a sea of uncertainty and absolute despair, "all shall be well, and all shall be well, and all manner of things shall be well."[5] We can live through the awful things that happen to us and come out stronger. It strikes me as interesting that before all of this occurred, one of my research projects concerned post-traumatic growth.[6] The experiential lesson for me was this: the path through hell is acceptance and gratitude. Being able to live in the present moment, to accept things and people as they are, and to focus on the infinite myriad of things available to enjoy and appreciate? Well. That is real magic. Also, in case you were wondering, my former university's football team won their bowl game.

> To live in this world
>
> you must be able
> to do three things:
> to love what is mortal;
> to hold it
>
> against your bones knowing
> your own life depends on it;
> and, when the time comes to let it go,
> to let it go.[7]

Endnotes

[1] Common core, a national set of educational standards, had become a political football by this point, with the Republican Party renouncing it in 2013. Bidwell, Allie. "The Politics of Common Core." *U.S. News*, March 6, 2014. Available at https://www.usnews.com/news/special-reports/a-guide-to-common-core/articles/2014/03/06/the-politics-of-common-core#:~:text=As%20the%20issue%20of%20Common,our%20children%20so%20they%20will (accessed May 24, 2024).

[2] Lussier, Charles. "LSU Professor Fired for Using Salty Language: Committee Suggested Keeping 20-Year Veteran." *The Advocate*, June 30, 2015. Available at https://www.theadvocate.com/baton_rouge/news/education/lsu-professor-fired-for-using-salty-language-in-classroom-claims-shes-witch-hunt-victim-plans/article_eaf46e12-8995-5602-b688-cfabb8994589.html (accessed May 20, 2024).

[3] American Association of University Professors. "Academic Freedom and Tenure: Louisiana State University, Baton Rouge, A Supplementary Report on a Censured Administration." September 2015. Available at www.aaup.org/report/academic-freedom-and-tenure-louisiana-state-university-baton-rouge-supplementary-report (accessed June 19, 2024); Louisiana State University faculty senate. "Resolution 15-15: Regarding the Case of Dr. Teresa Buchanan." October 6, 2015. Available at www.lsu.edu/senate/files/15-15resolution.pdf (accessed January 29, 2024).

[4] Morey, Alex. "Teresa Buchanan Uncensored: How an Innovative Educator Created Top Teachers and Got Fired for It." Foundation for Individual Rights and Expression, January 22, 2016. Available at www.thefire.org/news/teresa-buchanan-uncensored-how-innovative-educator-created-top-teachers-and-got-fired-it (accessed January 29, 2024).

[5] Julian of Norwich. *Showings*. Translated by Edmund Colledge and James Walsh. Paulist Press, 1978.

[6] Kilmer, Ryan P., Virginia Gil-Rivas, Richard G. Tedeschi, Arnie Cann, Lawrence G. Calhoun, Teresa Buchanan, and Kanako Taku. "Use of the Revised Posttraumatic Growth Inventory for Children." *Journal of Traumatic Stress: Official Publication of The International Society for Traumatic Stress Studies* 22 (2009):248-253.

[7] Oliver, Mary. *At Blackwater Pond*. Beacon Press, 2006.

Committing Philosophy

Robert Frodeman

1.

I missed the call.[1] But the fact that it came on a Saturday morning—September 29, 2018—was cause for concern. Why was the dean, who never phoned me, calling on a weekend? When I rang back his voice was tense. I was being removed from my classes "effective immediately." I was no longer allowed on campus, nor was I permitted to contact any faculty member, staff, or student "on pain of termination."

I was given no explanation for any of this. I only knew this much: 12 days earlier I had received a letter from the University stating that I was the subject of a Title IX investigation. The letter said that an inquiry had begun three months earlier, in June of 2018, prompted by an anonymous complaint about two departments on campus, one of which was mine. That inquiry uncovered an allegation that I had sexually harassed a graduate student in 2006, some 12 years earlier. No information was given about the source or content of this allegation. The letter, dated September 17th, 2018, had also said nothing about disciplinary action. What had changed between then and my removal on the 29th? The emailed notice that arrived after the phone call provided no clarification.

I've never discovered what prompted my sudden expulsion from campus. There was, however, a notable intervening event: on September 27th, 2018, Brett Kavanaugh and Christine Blasey Ford testified before the Senate Judiciary Committee. The country was in an uproar about sexual assault. I later learned that the chair of my department had been pulled out of a bar on the afternoon of Friday the 28th for an emergency meeting to sign the paperwork for my removal.

Yanked from my classes, barred from campus, and disallowed from contacting anyone at my university except the dean—who would not talk to me. All I knew was that at some point I would be contacted by a law firm that had been retained to investigate me. Until then, silence. I was told that the investigation would take 40 days. Instead, I found myself in the midst of a 14-month odyssey. In the end, I—a tenured full professor, a former departmental chair, and the founding director of a million-dollar university center on campus—was forced to resign under threat of termination. Even though I was *cleared* of the sexual harassment charges.

Given no real opportunity to defend myself throughout these proceedings, I resolved to write up an account of my experience. The result was 'Ordeal by Title IX,' published in *Quillette* in August of 2020. It described a process that was dishonest, shambolic, and without accountability, with rules applied without explanation and changed without warning. Every step of those proceedings—including that letter of September 17th—was filled with distortions. I was kept in the dark about the nature of the charges for months, even as these allegations changed over time to fit a predetermined result. The safeguards that should have protected me, of due process and tenure, were swept away.

The *Quillette* piece was written in the aftermath of a searing experience. With time, however, I've realized that the essay missed part of the picture. I had been too close to the events. For now it is clear that it is not only the story of someone caught up in the contradictions of Title IX at a time of heightened cultural tensions. It is also a chronicle of the power of the oil and gas industry and its interference in higher education. Finally, it is also a case of score settling, where a colleague used the tools at hand to strike out at someone who had uncovered their own misdeeds. Certainly, there were people motivated by Title IX concerns. But the sexual tensions of the Age of Trump also provided a powerful means for others to pursue personal and political ends.

2.

In retrospect, there were warning signs of what was to come. A year before my troubles began, my department met to discuss the two new faculty positions we were filling. Our new chair opened the meeting by announcing that "we will be in deep shit if we don't hire two women." I replied:

> We agree on the goal, but this can't be our sole criteria. Only 27 percent of new PhDs in philosophy are women, and many places want to hire them. If two candidates are close in our evaluation, let's hire the woman – or person of color. But our central goal has to be to hire the best candidates.

The looks around the room made it clear that these remarks were not well received. Other attempts to introduce dissenting viewpoints drew a similar response. For instance, it was announced that an upcoming departmental workshop on feminism would only be open to female faculty and students. Was this desirable? I asked. Or even legal? Would it be acceptable to hold a workshop that was limited to men?

Inconvenient inquiries have traditionally been central to the philosopher's trade. I put pointed questions to liberals and conservatives, believers and atheists. My colleagues, however, now viewed matters differently. A growing number of issues were now closed to debate. Rather than embodying a philosophical attitude, my questions stamped me as the defender of repudiated points of view.

Departmental life was becoming less congenial. But professors largely operate on their own, and I had a sabbatical coming up. The department met as a group on only a couple of occasions in the fall of 2017, and I would be out of town for nine months beginning in December. Perhaps things would be better by the fall of 2018.

It turned out that other plans were afoot. Seven months into my sabbatical, in June of 2018, I was contacted by the University Office of Equal Opportunity (OEO). Someone in the department had filed a sexual harassment complaint against me. Since I was out of town the interview would be conducted over the phone. I wasn't allowed to see the complaint, but I was expected to answer a series of questions.

The interviewer began by asking if two years before I had invited a newly hired departmental lecturer to a local coffee shop. Yes, I had. Why? To welcome her to the department, as senior people are supposed to do with new colleagues. The interviewer then asked if we had discussed why she had been hired in the department, and if I had replied "I have no idea."

Correct on both accounts. What had I meant by my statement? I was perplexed: I told the interviewer what I had told her—that I hadn't been on the search committee, or looked at the candidate's files, and was not part of any of the deliberations. But my comment had been seen as being dismissive of the candidate's qualifications rather than a simple statement of fact.

The questions continued. Some months later, had I asked this same lecturer for recommendations for readings on feminist approaches to film noir? Yes I had: I was teaching aesthetics and wanted feminist perspectives on movies like *Double Indemnity*. She had recommended a couple of essays and I had used one in class. The interviewer somehow saw this interaction as nefarious. The interviewer had nine such questions: in each case, innocuous interactions were interpreted suspiciously.

I spent the summer waiting for the result of the investigation. It arrived in August—the OEO had reached a determination of "no violation." Good news! Except an allegation of sexual harassment was now a permanent part of my record. I would eventually learn that three such charges were on my record, all of which had been filed within days of one another in late May, 2018 while I was out of town. I had not been contacted about the two other complaints. I only learned about them months later, after the law firm's investigation was complete.

These other complaints involved another of our new faculty members, who claimed that I had made her feel "potentially unsafe." This was curious, since we had only met a couple of times, at faculty meetings and at her job interview. Her complaint was that a year and a half earlier, during the faculty dinner for her on-campus job interview, I had asked what her husband did for a living and how her parents were employed. The third complaint had been filed by a male colleague, after another faculty member claimed that she had seen inappropriate conduct 12 years earlier, in March of 2006. He told me later that he felt compelled to turn in a report lest *he* be fired for overlooking an allegation of sexual harassment.

Even though all of these cases were dismissed, they implied a pattern of harassment. The other possible interpretation that the investigators could have drawn—that this was an organized campaign to damage my reputation for reasons that had nothing to do with sexual harassment—was not considered.

3.

In the meantime, matters were also proceeding on another timeline. In 2008 the university approved my proposal to create the nation's first center for the study of interdisciplinarity. The provost declared the center to be her top new priority, and as director I was given a three year budget of over a million dollars to identify best practices in inter- and transdisciplinarity. For the first few years the work went well. In 2010 much of the administration attended the celebration of our publishing the *Oxford Handbook of Interdisciplinarity*. We funded workshops and conferences at home and abroad, and there were discussions about hiring faculty to be housed in the center.

The center's focus on concrete outcomes meant that most of our research was done via interdisciplinary projects and case studies. Thus when a local town councilman came to us in 2011 with concerns about fracking we embraced the idea of a local case study. The community was troubled by the 250 fracking wells sited within city limits, many of which were near playgrounds and schools. Positioning ourselves as honest brokers, I and a colleague convened a series of public meetings where all parties (industry, environmentalists, politicians, citizen groups) could come together to discuss the challenges of fracking within city limits.

Here is where our troubles began. My colleague and I took no position on fracking. Nonetheless, the meetings soon became an occasion where scientists and environmentalists exposed the misrepresentations of the fracking industry. Other presentations by parents described the health problems of their children—unexplained nose bleeds and other illnesses, seemingly caused by proximity to fracking sites.

I soon received a call from a vice provost. She suggested that the center and university logos be taken off the posters advertising these public meetings. Treating these as suggestions made in good faith, rather than as a warning, I argued the opposite: this was precisely the role that the center and the university should play in the community. We kept the center and university logos on the poster.

Over the next few months the troubles mounted. The local Republican Party posted a letter on its website accusing us of being communists and followers of the radical activist Saul Alinsky. And the vice provost was now questioning the relevance of our center. Why do we need to study interdisciplinarity? Doesn't everyone already know how to do it? The center was put through a program review, after which its budget was cut. We were also moved out of our spacious offices to a smaller location across campus.

A few months later I received a call from the provost on Friday afternoon. I was asked to attend a meeting with the university president at nine a.m. the next Monday morning. The president had just come from his semi-annual meeting with the university board of regents. That hour-long meeting was mostly taken up with complaints concerning the center's work on fracking in Denton. Some of the regents demanded that my untenured colleague be fired. We were assured by the president that no such thing would occur, but we were asked to be more sensitive to the political dimensions of our work.

At this point, however, the local fracking debate had taken on a life of its own. A referendum to ban fracking within cities limits was placed on the ballot. Despite being outspent 10-1 by industry groups the ban passed in November 2014 by a 59-41% margin.[2] The victory, however, was short-lived: the very next day the Texas State legislature introduced House Bill 40, which gave the state government sole jurisdiction over the oil and gas industry. In other words, the State was instituting preemption legislation, a ban upon local bans. Shortly thereafter I ran into the university president in the student commons. His comment concerning these happening was quite striking: "in [Texas capital] Austin, [my untenured colleague's] reputation is lower than whale shit." It was dawning on me that the same was true for my own reputation.

Things continued to go downhill with the center. Our funding was cut again, and then eliminated entirely. We still had support coming from federal grants that allowed us to keep the center open. But this was not enough to sustain us: the university initiated another review, the result of which was the decision to close the center as of September 1, 2014. In my last posting on our soon-to-be defunct website, I speculated on the possible reasons for its elimination. I mentioned our work on fracking as one possible cause. In retrospect, I should have named this as the primary cause.

4.

The OEO investigation into the charge of sexual harassment was completed in August of 2018. I thus had only a one-month respite before the September 17th Notice of Investigation. The Notice described "an anonymous complaint of sexual harassment by faculty members in the Department of Biological Sciences and the Department of Philosophy and Religion. Based on the investigation to date, you have been identified as a Respondent based upon an alleged inappropriate relationship with former graduate student beginning in approximately 2006."

The Notice was incorrect. The next spring I received the original complaint, heavily redacted, after the investigation was over. It's clear that it was a complaint against an individual, not two departments. The redacted names are short, only allowing for a person's name or pronoun (e.g., "he") rather than the name of a department. And the details that were legible matched details of my career.

The challenge I faced was to prove a negative, demonstrating that I hadn't done something 12 years earlier, when I did not even know the specifics of the charges. I would have no information about the allegations until being interviewed by the university's lawyers. During the six weeks until that interview I was unable to contact or reply to colleagues and students—leaving projects hanging, student questions ignored, and letters of recommendation unwritten. I was forbidden to even tell people that I could not communicate with them under threat of being fired.

I spent this time learning about Title IX. I found that I had no right to see the specifics of the allegations against me. Nor would I be allowed to confront my accusers. I would walk into the October 30th interview blind, to be asked questions on unknown subjects for an unknown amount of time. I would not have access to files in my office to check dates or refresh memories, opening myself to charges that I had lied. Finally, the university ombudsman position was empty and requests to the faculty senate for help—I dared that much contact—went unanswered.

I learned that my experiences were far from unique. Laura Kipnis, Nick Wolfinger, and later Sarah Viren had detailed how faculty across the nation have been swept up in arbitrary investigations that were ruining careers.[3] I sought legal representation. Even a city as large as mine had no attorneys specializing in Title IX law, so I hired a New York firm that had made the front cover of the *New York Times* Magazine, and who had represented both students and faculty. The firm estimated that their representation would cost me $10,000. This was a significant amount, but I thought of it as insurance: the one thing I couldn't afford was to lose my job. The bill eventually came to $27,000.

The October 30th interview with the university-hired law firm began with the two lawyers stating that they were simply seeking the truth. But their neutrality did not last through the first question: had I ever been charged with sexual misconduct in my time at previous universities? I had not, but how was this relevant to allegations concerning my time at this University? I was asked questions about my marriage: did your wife know about your relationship with a graduate student? This was a complex question that assumed something that had not yet been established. I was interrogated about my entire professional life—relationships with colleagues, undergraduates, graduates, and staff, from the beginning of my career to that morning. This was not an interview. It was an inquisition.

Eventually the lawyers focused on my relationship with a particular graduate student. The outlines of the charges became apparent as they zeroed in on events in March of 2006 in New Orleans. I was there to run a National Science Foundation-funded workshop that examined the Hurricane Katrina disaster from an interdisciplinary point of view. Thirty researchers from around the world came for three days of work, with our meetings running from morning into the evening.

The federal grant supporting this work included money for a research assistant. The lawyers asked whether I had shared a hotel room with my assistant (no), and whether I had held hands with her during the meeting (no; in the midst of a professional meeting?). I was asked whether I'd had a sexual relationship with the student during the meeting. All these allegations were false. But because I had not been informed of the allegations ahead of time, I wasn't able to call upon workshop participants to attest to the fact that there had been no improper behavior on anyone's part during the workshop.

The questioning then moved from the March 2006 workshop into 2007 and beyond, after the student had graduated. They continued up through 2018. The interview lasted nearly two hours. I returned home to wait for the results of the investigation.

On October 21st, 2018, nine days prior to my interview, I had written the Title IX officer asking for the details of the allegations against me. I received no reply. I sent follow-up requests on October 24th and 29th, November 27th, 28th, and 29th. No reply. On December 3rd, my attorney contacted the University's General Counsel demanding a response. On December 6th, I finally received an answer: The University now claimed there was no complainant:

> The current investigation in which you are a Respondent was initiated by the University in response to information collected during the investigation of a separate matter. As such, there is no complainant, nor is there a specific person who identified you as a Respondent. Title IX requires postsecondary institutions to promptly investigate incidences of suspected sexual harassment. The University therefore initiated this investigation without a complainant.

Set to one side that this is an inaccurate account of the original (redacted) September 17th Notice of Investigation, which I would later discover had made specific claims about me. I was charged with sexual harassment, but no one was doing the charging, for there was no one claiming that they had been harassed. The investigation was generated by hearsay: someone was claiming that someone else had been harassed by me *12 years earlier*. I was removed from the classroom and campus and suffered grave professional harm based on an anonymous surmise made about someone else's experience more than a decade before.

5.

In September I had been told that the investigation would take approximately 40 days, but it took that long just to be interviewed by the University's hired lawyers. I heard nothing in November. On December 6th, 75 days in – or 160 days, counting from the June OEO interview – I was interviewed again. The investigation would not be completed until the end of February, 265 days from its inception the previous June. The final resolution—my resignation—occurred in August of 2019, 14 months from the beginning of the investigations.

In the second interview (conducted over the phone), the lawyers broke little new ground. But I changed my approach. I now acknowledged a relationship with the graduate student, which had begun in the fall of 2007 – a year and a half after the March 2006 workshop, and several months after she had finished her thesis, left the area, and had begun a PhD program in another state.

I revealed this now because in the meantime I had uncovered an email the 33-year-old former student had written to her parents years later, in 2009, which she had shared with me. It described the history of our relationship, which had begun at a conference in Canada in October of 2007. Her letter emphasized that there had been no romantic involvement with me during her time at the University, and that she had initiated the relationship. I sent the letter to the law firm, hoping that it would settle matters. They contacted the former student, and she confirmed the contents of the letter.

My lawyers expected the investigation to conclude by the end of the fall semester. Instead, in mid-December the dean wrote that the investigation was ongoing, and I would not be teaching in the spring. The taxpayers of the state were now paying me to stay out of the classroom for nearly an entire year on the basis of an anonymous rumor contradicted by the alleged victim.

It was by chance that I looked at my campus email account on the night of December 30th. That's the least likely time to get an email from a university, since universities shut down between Christmas and New Year's. Nevertheless, at 5pm that evening an email arrived from the Title

IX officer. The law firm had completed a draft report; I had until end of business on January 2nd, 2019 to say if I wanted to respond. The timing seemed chosen in the hope that I would miss the deadline.

Yes, I wanted to respond. The Title IX officer said that I would have to come to her office to see the draft. I was out of town for the break. She refused to send me the draft, but after some haggling, she said that the report would be made available to me on a secured website for 24 hours. I asked why I was not being given a copy of the draft, and why I had only a limited amount of time to review it. I was told that I was being belligerent. When I asked if university officials would also be similarly constrained in their viewing, the Title IX officer hung up on me.

In mid-January I was given access to the draft report. It was nine single-spaced pages. I used my phone to snap pictures of the document. Now I had access to, if not the original charges, at least some of the evidence and a summary of the conclusions being drawn. This was when I learned of the two other complaints of May 2018.

The draft report hid identities by using locutions (e.g., "Faculty 10"), but I was able to identify the source of some of the allegations. I had invited only one of my departmental colleagues to the New Orleans workshop, someone with whom I had difficult relations. In fact, the invitation was an attempt at rapprochement. My efforts were unsuccessful, and over the years the relationship had been strained. Matters had gotten worse two years earlier when I was on the departmental committee evaluating her possible promotion to full professor. Reading her file, I found that she listed the same book as "in press" that she had listed ten years earlier when she had first come up for tenure. I raised the point with the other committee members, but they refused to discuss the matter. I have little doubt that my comments got back to her.

I eventually learned more about this person's role in my case. In March, at the conclusion of the Title IX investigation, I was sent a batch of documents concerning my case. One was seemingly sent in error—a video of her testifying about alleged Title IX violations in our department. Time-stamped August of 2018 and fourteen minutes in length, it was mostly concerned with faculty other than me. Providing no evidence, she accused the male members of the department of sexual harassment, comparing them to abusive Catholic priests. The audience for this testimony wasn't visible, and of course no one had the chance to respond to these allegations. I was also told by a colleague that this individual had organized the three sexual harassment charges of 2018, and had brought those individuals to the provost's office to complain about me.

In my response to the draft report, I complained that it buried the central outcome of the investigation—that I had been exonerated. No evidence was found to support the allegations against me, and the supposed victim had testified that I had always acted appropriately with her. Instead, the draft slandered me. It claimed that "numerous individuals raised concerns" about issues unrelated to the investigation, that I was:

> Combative, abusive, harassing, and generally difficult to work with. Although these additional allegations do not rise to the level of sexual harassment and are not the subject of this investigation, we felt it important to communicate in this Report that many of the Respondent's colleagues share these concerns...

It was a classic case of poisoning the well. I had been asked to provide the names of faculty and graduate students who could describe my behavior. Three of them had reported to me that when interviewed they had emphasized my collegiality, integrity, and propriety. None of these comments made it into the report.

6.

The law firm turned in their final report on February 25th, 2019. The slanders remained, and while the report noted that I had been cleared of sexual harassment, it did its best to bury the point in the middle of the document. Rather, and to my perplexity, the document now shifted its focus to events after the graduate student had left campus.

In early March I received a letter from the dean. He noted that the outside investigation was now complete, and said nothing about me being cleared. He then added that the University's own internal investigation "was only beginning." This was news—there had been no prior mention of another internal investigation. Up until now the law firm's investigation *was* the investigation. Attention would now concentrate on whether I had violated the University policy on consensual relations. This policy states that relationships between faculty and students are not permitted. For cases such as mine where there are no elements of sexual harassment three remedies are listed:

A. Instruction to the parties to terminate the relationship;

B. Transfer of one of the parties to a new department or job responsibility; or

C. Other disciplinary actions, including demotion or termination in severe cases.

Since the graduate student had left campus six months before our relationship had begun, and the entire matter was now 13 years in the past, I was at a loss as to what there was to investigate.

On March 7th, I received a letter from my department chair. It stated that he was considering recommending revocation of my tenure and termination of employment. The reason: I had a relationship with a graduate student while I "served as the student's thesis advisor, including submitting her degree plan and providing her a grade in her thesis course." The ostensible seriousness of this violation was compounded by the fact that I was departmental chair at the time.

He was in error. The student's degree plan (the final document recording that all work had been completed for the Masters) had been turned in months before the relationship began. But eventually the real point became clear. Even though the former student had moved out of town in May, only returning to defend the Masters in July, had matriculated in a PhD program at another university in August—which was only possible because she had completed her Masters—and had turned in her revised thesis and degree plan to the graduate school in September, the chair still considered her a University student because she had not walked across the stage to receive her diploma. And this, apparently, was the "violation," and one that was worthy of termination.

The law firm's own investigation had demonstrated that by the time our relationship began in October 2007 there had been no supervision of the student for some months. The chair focused on the fact that I had given her a grade that fall for thesis hours. This was true, but he knew that this was merely an administrative requirement required by the graduate school until a student "walked." At my grievance hearing, the graduate school confirmed that such grades were *pro forma*, involving no assignments, and were simply the means for the University to keep the student's file active until they were handed their diploma.

When I made these points to my chair, I was told that I was not taking my violation seriously, thereby compounding the gravity of the offense. I now faced a dilemma: should I treat talk of my violation as sincere, and address the details of documents and timelines in a logical manner? Or should I call out this whole business for the absurdity that it was? For it seemed clear that when the administration couldn't find justification for firing me via the Title IX process, they were now pursuing the point via internal policy.

I met with my department chair on March 13th. I expressed remorse for not being more attentive to policy guidelines in 2006 while pointing out the marginal nature of my violation. To no avail—the chair's March 19th letter to the dean and provost recommended my firing. The matter now sat on the dean's desk. On April 5th, I received the dean's letter saying that he was considering his own set of penalties. He noted that my violation did not merit firing. He called instead for a $5,000 reduction of salary, no merit increase for a year, and no teaching graduate courses or working with graduate students for three years. In my response I pointed out that this penalized graduate students (some of whom had come to the University to work with me) for something that had occurred more than 13 years before.

I thought that I had escaped the worst. But on April 25th, I received a letter from the provost in which she stated her intention to revoke my tenure and terminate me. We met in her office on May 3rd. I brought documents, charts, and timelines that showed that by the time the relationship began neither I nor anyone else could have affected the student's Masters degree. The next day the provost sent me a letter saying she was recommending to the president that I be fired.

Now only the faculty senate, the president, and the board of regents could prevent me from losing my job. I asked for a senate grievance hearing. I had been assured by the previous provost (who thought the whole business outrageous but was unwilling to say so publicly) that the faculty senate was biased toward protecting the rights of faculty. I found a professor to serve as my advocate at the hearing, and we met several times to strategize.

The hearing was held in June 2019. I discovered that the provost herself would be prosecuting my case. Members of the grievance committee said this was unprecedented, and noted that it placed committee members in the position of standing in judgment of their own supervisor. I had also been told that both I and the provost would have to turn in our presentations a week beforehand so that the arguments would be available to all. I sent in my PowerPoint presentation, but when I asked for the provost's I was told that she had no prepared remarks. On the day of the hearing she walked in with a printed document from which she read.

It became clear that the provost had studied my PowerPoint: her argument was now different from the rationale for firing she had offered in the letter of May 4. Rather than discussing the minutia of thesis hours, she now focused on events in late May of 2008. This is when the former student had gone to Chile to participate in a field class run by the University. She transferred the credits back to her new university in Arizona to count as work toward her PhD.

I was also in Chile at the time. I was there to do my own research and had no involvement in the class she was attending. And in any case, her presence in the class was irrelevant to my case, for in the meantime she had "walked," ending her last association with the University that was in any way connected to me. The provost, however, claimed that my presence there was outrageous, for it had made other faculty uncomfortable (although she produced no evidence of this). Nor did she explain how this constituted a violation of any University policy.

At the first break a committee member pulled me aside. "This is a bunch of bullshit. You're being railroaded." He was also angry about being asked to stand in judgment of his superior the provost, even though he had the protection of tenure. In the next session the provost called the lawyer from the firm that had investigated me to attest to the seriousness of my transgressions. After the lawyer had summarized his investigation, the provost asked: "Did you hear of any other rumors that you didn't put in the report?" The lawyer was happy to relate additional gossip.

When it was my turn, my advocate and I pointed out the marginal nature of the allegation, and noted that the offense, 12 years ago, had not been repeated. We also pointed out that there were faculty currently employed at the University who had broken the consensual relations policy. Finally, we noted that University disciplinary policy listed 13 levels of sanction, beginning with an oral reprimand, the loss of summer teaching, etc. Only the last of the 13 called from revocation of tenure and termination. We asked how this marginal violation merited firing.

I returned home that night shaken but believing that at least one person on the committee would rebel at the proceedings. Two days later I received the notice: the committee had supported the provost's call for revocation of tenure and termination.

The university president was well aware of the events of the previous 12 months. I had contacted him on a couple of occasions, asking if we could meet. He had replied that we should hold off meeting until the entire process was over. Now, however, he refused to meet with me, and simply deferred to the recommendation of the provost.

I had a last opportunity of appeal—going to the next meeting of the board of regents. They had final say on firing in the case of tenured faculty. But at this point the writing was on the wall. After all, it was the board of regents who had complained to the university president about the activities of my center concerning fracking. Finally, even if I were successful in keeping my position I would be *persona non grata*. And I hoped that by resigning I might preserve some viability for future employment. It was time to live another life.

7.

Cleared of the Title IX charge of sexual harassment, I was driven from my job because of a supposed violation of the university consensual relations policy. But the fact that my violations were either minimal or non-existent suggests that there was more going on.

So did the prejudicial nature of the investigations. The university-hired lawyers were obviously biased, and profited by their pursuit of me. The administration refused to explain the details of the allegations and denied me an opportunity for a timely response. My accusers were allowed to remain anonymous, generating rumor and innuendo with no obligation to defend their words. I was simply a bad actor who had to go.

Surely there were parties to this process who thought it correct to pursue these allegations. 2018 was the height of the #MeToo movement, itself an understandable response to the election of a president charged with (and now convicted of) serial cases of sexual assault. But the enormous gap in time, as well as between the nature of the possible infractions and the severity of the punishment, makes it clear that more was involved.

There are two additional explanations to add to this. One is the personal animas shown by a senior member of my department. I was told by a colleague that she had visited the provost's office on several occasions with younger female faculty during my investigation to press the case against me. The other is the criticisms that the university administration had received concerning my center from the board of regents and from elected officials in the state capital. 'Academic' is often used as a pejorative in order to emphasize the abstract and irrelevant nature of faculty research. The fate of my center illustrates the dangers of trying to make that research relevant to the wider world.

Five years on I have now reconstructed my life. I still have some contact with academia, publish some, and receive invitations to speak. I have also become a member of a vibrant community in the American West. I use my background and training to help improve the quality of my community. I still bear my scars, but in the end, things have worked out.

Endnotes

[1] This is a modified version of an essay published in *Quillette*, "Ordeal by Title IX." August 13, 2020, available at https://quillette.com/2020/08/13/ordeal-by-title-ix/ (accessed May 29, 2024).

[2] See Adam Briggle, *A Field Philosopher's Guide to Fracking: How One Texas Town Stood Up to Big Oil and Ga*s (W.W. Norton), 2015.

[3] Jeannie Suk Gersen. "Laura Kipnis's Endless Trial by Title IX." *The New Yorker*, September 20, 2017, available at https://www.newyorker.com/news/news-desk/laura-kipniss-endless-trial-by-title-ix (accessed May 29, 2024); Nicholas H. Wolfinger. "How I Survived the Title IX Star Chamber." *Quillette*, August 24, 2017, available at https://quillette.com/2017/08/24/survived-title-ix-star-chamber/ (accessed March 7, 24); Sarah Viren. "The Accusations Were Lies. But Could We Prove It?" *The New York Times Magazine*, March 18, 2020.

The Perils of Teaching while Male

Dennis Gouws

This chapter examines three occasions when some faculty members and administrators at my college took exception to me because I disagree with the current women-centered orthodoxy in higher education. The first concerns a December, 2013 meeting with senior administrators upset about my teaching on men and masculinity; the second, an October, 2017 petition critical of me, composed and circulated by some of my coworkers after my hostile workplace treatment was widely publicized; and the third, the February, 2019 punishment doled out to me by the provost for once again drawing media attention to my poor treatment at work. None of my antagonists faced workplace consequences for their actions.

My 2013 began well: I was tenured, recently promoted, and I had been asked to join the editorial board of *New Male Studies: An International Journal*, founded by John A. Ashfield and Miles Groth. Ashfield is the author of *Doing Psychotherapy with Men: Practicing Ethical Psychotherapy and Counseling with Men* (2011), the first book I read that uncompromisingly dignified men's experiences (and remains the best book on the subject); Groth is the coauthor of *Engaging College Men: Discovering What Works and Why* (2010), a helpful resource when I started a men's group on campus.[1] By this time, I had also read *Spreading Misandry: The Teaching of Contempt for Men in Popular Culture* (2001), the first book in a series that presented groundbreaking research by Paul Nathanson and Katherine K. Young, arguing that men were disadvantaged because of the gynocentric (women centered) and misandrist (anti-male) assumptions about them embedded in Western popular culture.[2] I had introduced this argument to the students in my men's group and classes, and they were receptive to it. Students also critiqued Nathanson and Young's argument and discussed what men might need to live well. My department chair at this time asked me to propose a Men in Literature course to complement the Women and Literature course offered by the department. I gladly did so.

I had heard from a few coworkers that some of the women on campus were unhappy about what I was doing. The dean of students had contacted me to let me know that some people were concerned about our men's group and its social media page. When I told him that we had done nothing wrong and that I had no intention of changing what we were doing, he complained to the student leader of the men's group. (He once told the student leader that our group aimed "to keep women in chains.") The director of human resources met with me to express her misgivings about male well-being posters on my door (she triumphantly spread copies someone had made of them out on her desk for me to see and seemed surprised that I saw nothing wrong with them). Naively believing that our meeting was about solving problems, I agreed to remove some of the posters from my door that had apparently upset someone. Then I was summoned to the abovementioned December, 2013 meeting with the director of human resources, the provost, the dean of students, and the dean of my school. I was informed by the director of HR in a November 27, 2013 email "we have received complaints and have been reviewing them" and "we would like to meet with you to discuss the matter." In my response I asked for confirmation that those who had complained would be present: "I would like to address their actual complaints directly and want to find out their reasons for not discussing their complaints with me personally— as is the suggested protocol [in the faculty code]." The HR director promptly responded, "The faculty member(s) who lodged the complaint will not be in attendance. As you stated it is the 'suggested' protocol with the key word suggested. Every situation is different and is reviewed on a case by case basis." This was my first indication that the college's administrators only used established rules and protocols when it suited them. For their friends, everything; for their enemies, the law.

The meeting was a serial monologue: the administrators took turns telling me that they and other unnamed people at the college were not happy about my teaching and my men's group. I remember being unsure and afraid: ours is a private institution with no union representing the faculty. Who knew what these administrators would do now they had voiced their disapproval? What they did was write me a letter, dated December 17, 2013. On behalf of the administrators present at the meeting, the director of HR composed a document which "summarized the actions that were agreed upon and [their] expectations for [my] conduct moving forward." Believing me chastened, they wanted to document what a bad professor I'd been and to tell me how to be a better one. Their expectations were threefold: they wanted to monitor what I was allowed to post on my office door and on the men's group social media page; they wanted to oversee the activities of the men's group; and they wanted me to consult the feminists in the social science department about my research.

On a few occasions after my abovementioned meeting with the director of HR, I had shown her some pictures that I had intended to post. I was hopeful that in the spirit of open academic inquiry, we would be able to introduce heterodox ideas on campus without upsetting anyone. The December 17 letter stated: "You agreed [with the administration] and subsequently removed posters" and "we encouraged you to seek clarification from myself for any poster you wish to post going forward but have questions about its suitability." Yes, I had agreed, but I was amused by this: "We discussed posting male positive topics on your door as well as on the Facebook page of The Men's Group." The administrators had no idea what *male positive* meant. They had used the phrase during the meeting as a catch-all for what they did not like about my work, but they refrained from putting in writing precisely what their objection to it was.

The letter also asked me to remove a non-student from the Men's Group Facebook page and to add, on the recommendation of the student dean, "two additional members of [the college] community who would like to join the group." These additional members—both college administrators—had no prior interest in the men's group. In the letter I was encouraged to speak with the dean of students or his subordinate—a man who subsequently warned me that the senior administrators had placed "a target on my back"—for "clarification related to my responsibilities as advisor [of] the group, the administrator of the group's Facebook page, or any questions related to the student group." The objective seemed to be administrative monitoring of all of the group's activities.

Most troubling, I was informed that the provost and the dean discussed my "responsibilities as a faculty member " and my "responsibility to present data and research results in a balanced manner with the highest critical standards." I was "encouraged to consult with trained Sociology faculty, for example, on this campus [if I was] involved in the assessment of research results outside of [my] academic training as an English professor." This suggestion infringed on my right to free inquiry; moreover, it required my compliance with compelled speech because the sociology faculty only adopted a feminist approach to sex and gender issues.

The letter ended thus: "We look forward to working together to resolve any concerns moving forward." I did happen to have concerns, and after consulting friends I wrote a January 23, 2014 letter that asked for "written confirmation that [the college] is responsible for providing me a safe working environment that is free from harassment and bullying." Given my prior interactions with the dean of students and the HR director, and my concern about the letter's stifling directives, I wanted the college to reaffirm its commitment to academic freedom and open inquiry. I was most troubled by what was written about my work, so I stated that "I stand by my research record and invite [the college] to consult my peer-reviewed publications for evidence of their balance and critical standards." I also "welcomed any sociology faculty who wish to collaborate in qualitative research concerning men to contact me."

During our meeting I'd been alarmed that the dean mentioned a partisan special-interest group, the Southern Poverty Law Center, as a reliable source for information concerning men's issues, so in my letter I cited a November, 2013 *Forbes* magazine article that criticized the Center's false "hate-group logic"—summarized as "I disagree with you. You hate me"—when discussing men's groups.[3] I wasn't destined for fair treatment if the SLPC is where my dean learned about men's groups. I asked the dean "to provide me with written assurance that if her personal and political opinions influence her assessment, [the college] would intervene to make that transparent." I finished by asking for an indication in writing as to how the college would respond to such a situation.

The college was obviously surprised by my letter. On January 30, 2014, they send a brief response assuring me that the college would follow its own rules. The text of their letter left little doubt that lawyers had been involved: "[A]ll conduct of the College directed toward [me] or any other employee of the College, has been and will be, administered in a similar manner and will be consistent with the College's legal obligations, its policies and procedures and the . . . philosophy of the College." In a February 11, 2014 letter, I pressed my case again:

> Many of the questions I raised in the letter were not addressed in your reply and surely must be dealt with if the conversation is to go on upon a steady foundation and with absolute clarity and transparency. I am sure you would agree that precisely that is necessary to resolve the proximate and underlying issues.

They, however, disagreed, noting in a brief February 24, 2014 letter that "The College understands your requests and has responded in a manner that it believes is appropriate for the circumstances. The College will not be responding further to these or similar requests." I had pressed them for specifics, and they had declined to engage.

My department chair, who was sent a copy of the December 17 letter, offered me no support. In retrospect, I should have expected her to sit on her hands: she had offered no support to an untenured male colleague who was fired (instead she went around urging us not to talk about the matter), yet when the provost expressed reservations about granting tenure to a female colleague because of concerns about her teaching (more on her later), the chair strongly advocated for her. When the chips were down, the department chair only supported women.

Soon after this incident she stepped down and was replaced by another woman. My new chair was a former high school teacher. Her years in the trenches teaching in a public high school had instilled in her uncritical obedience, so I imagined she too would raise no objection to any mistreatment I experienced. Not long afterwards, the college welcomed a woman president, who promptly replaced the woman provost—and hired (you guessed it) a woman to replace her. One of many "inclusion" gestures that followed the arrival of the new president involved converting only men's restrooms to all-gender restrooms, despite protests from some male faculty. (Our dean tactlessly said of the converted men's room in her building, "The good news is: the bathroom is open to any who wish to use it—its [sic] fully inclusive by design.... I popped into the gender neutral room myself.")

The dean had her underlings distribute an article, "This is a Trigger Warning," to all faculty in the school of arts and sciences.[4] Our obedient department chair wrote to us that "some context for the article would be helpful," that the dean "felt the article offered useful information—a reminder to faculty that when choosing readings and assignments, sensitive topics could create a 'trigger' effect for some students 'with invisible disabilities' and those who 'come to our class with severe traumas.'" Using this article about a woman's pain as a pretext, the dean and the department chair were encouraging us to censor our course materials to avoid offending students. (A recent study found that trigger warnings don't work.[5])

In this censorious environment I submitted my application for a sabbatical to prepare for publication a collection of essays by various contributors to *New Male Studies*. My application received lukewarm support from my department chair and no support from the dean. I appealed the denial of my sabbatical via the college's grievance procedure, but the grievance-committee chair refused to answer my request for an explanation of their decision to deny my appeal. I was informed, "We now "terminate all business on the matter, forwarding its decision to the grievance [sic] and the President of the College." When I again requested an explanation, I was told the committee "has completed its role and responsibility in handling your grievance."

My Men in Literature course was cancelled because of complaints the dean claimed she received about it, but did not disclose. The materials on my office door were twice vandalized in October of 2015. When I reported this incident, the college's lawyer predictably suggested that I report it to the college department of public safety, and that there was no need to notify the city police department. The lawyer also advised me against speaking out publicly about my treatment, saying it was "unclear of the benefit or purpose of contacting any media." The public safety officers conducted a cursory investigation, and the captain assured me she would contact me once the investigation had been completed. She never did.

The compliant language arts chair retreated into retirement from the cluster-*foutre* she had made of our department, and the woman coworker whose tenure decision concerned the provost was made department chair. She had once committed an act of workplace violence that was hushed up by HR, so she knew she would likely face no unpleasant consequences for her conduct as chair. She and the dean became an abusive tag team, making it very difficult for me to do my job. Sometimes their abuse was absurd. The chair once complained that the students in my class were silently reading when she walked past our classroom. The dean once scolded me for being unfamiliar with a certain department policy—until I pointed out to her that I wrote the policy as one of my service tasks. I had to attend many pointless meetings with them during which they berated me for apparent missteps they would not put in writing (more about that later). The bullying stopped for a while when I approached the National Association of Scholars in 2016 for help. The NAS not only wrote to the college on my behalf, questioning my workplace treatment, but also published articles about my situation that attracted the attention of other news outlets. I probably kept my job because of the publicity given to my case in 2016 and 2017.

After my workplace treatment had received extensive media attention, a petition denouncing me—identified as a "statement of concern" by its original signatories—was circulated among my coworkers in the fall of 2017. The December 10, 2013 meeting had apparently been occasioned by concerns expressed by some members of the college community, and the petition included similar criticism of my work about men.

Friends told me that a link to the petition had been sent from a college administrator's email account to the college faculty. The pretext for the petition was a video sympathetic to my situation made by Professor Janice Fiamengo for her *Fiamengo File* series; the petition expressed concern about my work and the possible public exposure those who opposed it might face. The cover letter to the petition, authored by one of the college's two female sociology professors (the partner of the administrator whose email account was used), urged the prospective signatories to watch Professor Fiamengo's video, adding,

> . . .the [college] faculty member highlighted in this video is part of a small so-called academic field that calls themselves 'male studies.' 'Male studies' is NOT the same as 'men's studies.' The field of men's studies involves a substantial number of scholars (of all genders) who study men and masculinity within the context of the larger field of gender and women's studies.

The distinction the petitioners draw between the two fields might seem trivial, but it accurately describes the problem they have with my approach to discussing men. Male studies and gender studies represent two distinct schools of research. Male-studies scholars do not defer to those feminist assumptions about men that inform gender studies (assumptions about male privilege and toxic masculinity, for example); instead, they build on the male-oriented research by people like John Ashfield, Miles Groth, and Paul Nathanson and Katherine Young. Rather than teaching "within the context of the larger field of gender and women's studies" representing "all genders," I was unapologetically teaching while male, and as will become apparent, the petitioners found that perilous. One would think my coworkers would celebrate work that approaches a subject from a different perspective, but they saw it as a problem that needed solving.

"There is a group of concerned faculty" the cover letter continues, "who have drafted a statement of concern we will present to the Provost and President of [the college] because the problem goes beyond the video." How so? "The faculty member's public airing of his grievances has motivated some of us to generate a statement to express our concerns." The cover letter then states its purpose: "In short, we are asking [the college] to address the troubling affiliation of this faulty member with a misogynist hate group, and the ongoing negative impact on our students, colleagues, workplace, and [the college's] reputation." Yes, there are misogynous hate groups focused on men's rights (just as there are misandrist hate groups focused on women's rights). But the cover letter mentions neither the name of the hate group, nor my alleged affiliation with it. Its hate-group logic seems to be *we disagree with his work, so he's a member of a misogynist hate group*. In addition to teaching while male,

I had gone public about how I was treated on campus by those who disagreed with my work: those in the media wrote about my situation described how the institutional processes I adhered to and the people in charge of them had failed me. I already knew this publicity (and possible accountability) alarmed my colleagues: After the National Association of Scholars contacted the college on April 4, 2016 about my treatment, the college's senate president emailed me, on April 6: she was "checking in to confirm" that I was pursuing my grievances through the appropriate administrative channels.

The petition itself was more strident:

> As faculty at [the college], we are concerned that another member of the College's faculty, Professor Dennis Gouws, has been a party to a YouTube video titled 'Professor Dennis Gouws: A Case Study in Feminist Harassment,' in which [the college] is depicted as restricting his academic freedom....We find the video's public attack on [college] administrators and another faculty colleague, all of whom are female, and, ultimately, the College, to be a form of intimidation and harassment by the video producers. The video's target audience includes followers of the pseudo-discipline calling itself 'Male Studies' and members and followers of misogynist websites, such as *A Voice for Men,* where Professor Gouws has been an active member for years, and which has been named as a misogynist hate group monitored by the Southern Poverty Law Center.

There are four noteworthy points here: first, the tacit acknowledgment that female employees at the college were primarily responsible for what was done to me (the actors and their actions mentioned in the video are not disputed); second, the absurd claim that I had "been an active member" of *A Voice for Men* (websites don't have members); third, the claim that *A Voice for Men* had been identified as a misogynist hate group by the SPLC (it had not); fourth, the fact that the whole petition was a clumsy effort at guilt by association. As with the subsequent claims made in the document, no evidence is presented. (It is amusing that male studies has been promoted from "a so-called academic field" in the preamble to a "pseudo-discipline" in the statement.) But the ten authors of the document were just hitting their stride: "While the [Fiamengo] video, in our view, constitutes a form of intimidation aimed at Professor Gouws's colleagues, supervisors, and other senior administrators, it is also his long-term membership in groups such as *A Voice for Men* that deeply concerns us for the following reasons."

The reasons fall under three headings: students, college, and workplace environment. Here are the highlights from each:

1) Students

> We are concerned that the anti-female propaganda informing Professor Gouws's teaching and scholarship creates a hostile climate for women in his classes, curtails students' rights, discourages a plurality of viewpoints, presents a poor model of intellectual integrity and academic responsibility, and contradicts [the college's] . . . philosophy and mission.

As in the cover letter, the petitioners provide no description of what I was actually teaching; they give no examples of what made the class a hostile environment; they don't explain how I supposedly curtail students' rights; they present no evidence of how my teaching goes against the college's mission. The petitioners merely resort to smearing me using hate-group logic to suggest I was creating a classroom climate that was perilous to students.

The paragraph concludes,

> Further, some of the statements made by Professor Gouws are widely disputed by the majority of research findings in behavioral and social science. His continued dissemination of unsubstantiated claims in the classroom and online sends the message to students that the overall research findings that they learn in other classes or sources are inaccurate.

Once again, no details are given; the same smear tactic is used. The concern that students might question the "behavioral and social science" research they encounter in "sources" taught in "other classes" at the college seems odd. Surely the whole goal of taking college classes is to learn to question what you hear in college classes. Why are the petitioners against that? Moreover, they're demeaning their own students in the process, assuming that the students are too dumb or impressionable to decide what's right and what isn't. This concern is more sinister when one reads testimonies from students who have taken these "other classes:" for example, a graduate student told me that she had taken a class with the sociology professor who wrote the cover letter. This professor told students they were only allowed to use research she had provided because these articles were "the facts." The student noted that these articles were all written from a point of view that accorded with the professor's point of view. By insisting that students only refer to her sources, this professor "curtails" those "students' rights, discourages a plurality of viewpoints, presents a poor model of intellectual integrity and academic responsibility" mentioned among the petitioners' concerns.

2) College

> We are concerned that the YouTube video, the articles posted on National Association of Scholars website, including entire folders of internal correspondence and documents, and Professor Gouws's advocacy of misogynist propaganda presents a distorted view of the College, which can harm the future recruitment and retention of students and faculty particularly women and people of color.

For the first time the petitioners provide evidence of what upsets them: the mention of "internal correspondence and documents" confirms their concern about public exposure of their conduct. Their characterization of what I do merely rehearses their tired hate-group logic trope; however, their assumption that all "people of color" and women are similarly impacted by so-called "misogynist propaganda" defies logical explanation.

Chillingly, the paragraph continues, "We are also concerned that College resources—administrators' time and energy—are diverted from the main focus of the College in order to monitor and document the online presence of Professor Gouws." I knew that administrators and faculty members were visiting my pages, but I was unaware that this was being done when they should have been attending to their work. The petitioners' claim of college-sponsored monitoring and documenting was perhaps a lie intended to impress potential signatories that this scurrilous petition enjoyed the college's imprimatur. The documenting I had noticed was sometimes comical. When one of the English-professor composers of the petition attended a conference presentation of mine, she spent most of it almost doubled over frantically trying writing down everything I said on a notepad. Had she asked, I would gladly have sent her a copy of my paper.

The climax of this paragraph is startling: "We are concerned that Professor Gouws's public support for ideas and groups promoting such reprehensible ideas as rape denial leaves the College vulnerable to accusations of gender discrimination and possible legal action." A "rape denial" smear? This outrageous claim, presented without evidence, suggests that in my case, the perils of teaching while male were experienced by the teacher—that is, myself—rather than the taught. This claim, written in a document that was not sent to me, suggests the petitioners' fecklessness in their stifling of dissent.

3) Work Environment

Four points are made here:
1. "We are concerned that professor Gouws's affiliation with *A Voice for Men* and his continued public smearing of the College and his colleagues and women administrators creates an atmosphere of intimidation and fear on campus. The YouTube video creates an atmosphere in which colleagues may be publicly attacked without prior contact or invitation to a civil dialogue." Once again the petitioners falsely state that I am affiliated with *A Voice for Men*. Their use of "may" demonstrates the flimsiness of their claims: to my knowledge, nobody had been attacked; nor had I fomented a hostile mob. A reasonable person would agree that I am only responsible for my own conduct. I was pleased that they too were concerned that no "civil dialogue" had occurred concerning the complaints about me and my work; of course, they had not initiated one before they wrote their petition.
2. "We are concerned that some faculty have been asked to take on workload that would normally have been undertaken by Professor Gouws, i.e., search committees, advisee meetings, and even

course assignments, but is not assigned to him out of concern for his impact on students and the effective running of the … department." I had noticed my attempts to volunteer for service on college committees was routinely denied. Presumably, the administrators thought my ideas rendered me untrustworthy for helping with college service. Because my failure to do college service would adversely impact my annual performance review, I began noting on my annual report those service opportunities for which I had volunteered but had been denied an opportunity to undertake. In her first meeting with me, the new department chair threatened to give me a bad evaluation unless I stopped including these in my annual report. As described below, she seemed determined to give me a bad performance review.

3. "Given that Professor Gouws has decided to pursue his grievances against the College through social media and the internet, we are vulnerable to the actions of unknown consumers of these media, potentially in real life as well as on line." Of course, I had tried pursuing my grievance through official college channels, but that had not worked out. What's more, the petitioners disingenuously suggest I am somehow responsible for the conduct of others.

4. "While we recognize the need for confidentiality related to personal matters, we are concerned that we may not be aware of any change to Professor Gouws's employment status at the College and we fear the possibility of retribution should that status change." This sentence implies that the idea of firing me had been raised. My insecure employment status and the possible grounds for dismissing me were also established in this document: the suggestion that my decision to publicize my treatment somehow made the perpetrators feel "unsafe." The target on my back had become much bigger.

The ten original signatories of the petition included three English professors, three sociology professors, two psychology professors, one history professor, and one music professor. The petition was sent to all faculty members at my college. On January 17, 2018 I emailed the three signatories who taught in my department, asking for a copy of the petition and its cover letter. Having received no reply from them I renewed my request in a February 11, 2018 email, adding the following to the original message: "I have included the Office of the President in this email because I believe [the president] was an intended recipient of [the petition]. If this be the case, perhaps someone in the Office of the President could sent me a copy." I received no reply.

By this time the dean and the department-chair had settled into the aforementioned tag-team routine of harassing me. My chair claimed in her review of my annual report that my teaching was unsatisfactory and needed remediation—whereupon I pointed out to her that my quantitative and qualitative teaching evaluations indicated I was a good teacher. In March of 2017, the dean had put me on official warning status—what normal people call probation—a step possibly leading to my termination. After I questioned the college's treatment of me, my chair justified "because of several instances of insubordinate conduct."

Not long after I was removed from probation, my chair demanded I meet with her about a student complaint, I declined to meet because she refused to tell me in advance, in writing, what the meeting was about. I had tried to defend myself against the college by routinely asking my chair and my dean to justify their disciplinary actions in writing and to heed the academic grievance policy (the protocol for dealing with student complaints, which that the chair and the dean had ignored) and those policies given in the faculty handbook.

In a November, 2018 letter, the dean notified me that I once again was "being placed on 'Official Warning Status' [sic]" for "substantial and manifest neglect of professional duties associated with" my role as a faculty member. In the letter the dean demanded that I "desist from sending e-mails that refer to the Academic Grievance Policy as justification for my "refusal to meet;"" that I "desist from sending accusatory e-mails to [my] chair that express [my] judgments of her behavior"; and that I "desist in sending demands for Faculty Handbook citations to justify requests made … regarding the placement of [my] content in [my] annual self evaluations [sic]." (The dean liked to instruct faculty to arrange the content of their self-evaluations in ways that might expose them to criticism for not fulfilling all of their job requirements.) Predictably she then stated, "If you do not comply with the above, I will recommend to the Provost your termination of employment at [the] College." I had been advised by one of my mentors to write a strident letter in response to the dean's letter to in order to elicit a written response from her. I did so, but I also decided to reach out to a lawyer. He advised me that the situation was serious and that if I wanted to remain employed, I would have to do what my employer wanted me to do. The most startling of my employer's dictates was that I would be held responsible for anyone on campus feeling "unsafe," not because of what I had done, but because of what others had written about me. I was advised that this "safety responsibility" nonsense probably wouldn't prevail in court, but that the college seemed prepared to drag me through an expensive and exhausting legal ordeal. The following excerpts from the provost's February 21, 2019 letter described what they had in store for me.

The provost asserts, "you have been intellectually dishonest and you have fostered harassing behavior of colleagues." Where was this going? Here:

> On multiple occasions you have made baseless claims knowing that your actions could harm the status and reputation of campus citizens. You have purposefully threatened to and followed through on, providing incomplete and misleading materials to cause others to publicly criticize, discredit, harass and intimidate members of the campus community. You have omitted relevant facts and information that, to a reasonable person, would provide a more complete and unbiased perspective.

I had let the dean know I was going to talk to the media. And, of course, the article that appeared in *The Federalist* on December 4, 2018 was a problem for the provost. My prior contact with the media resulted in much negative commentary about the college. She continued, "As a result and while under official warning status for substantial and manifest neglect of professional duties [declining to attend the abovementioned mystery meeting with the chair], your actions caused concern of harm to campus citizens." Read that last bit again: "concern of harm." What harm?

There's more: "*The Federalist* blog that references materials you provided portrays your supervisors in a negative light and caused a firestorm of vitriolic responses and actions that have further heightened concern about the safety of individuals on this campus." Note the change in the provost's language: now her concern is no longer harm—it's safety. She was suggesting that I was somehow responsible for people on campus feeling unsafe because of what someone wrote about how I was treated. Some people who read *The Federalist* article might have made threats, perhaps vile threats, to the college's administrators. That's how things work in the social media era. This is a shame, but academic freedom means protecting my right to talk about issues of public import, like my college. It's a pity someone felt threatened, but it's not my fault. The provost's comments reveal her attempts at abrogating her duties and my right to open inquiry.

There's even more from the provost:

> I have counseled you that the faculty grievance policy is the appropriate means for adjudicating your concerns regarding actions taken by College administrators. Your recent threat to the dean to knowingly present biased views of her publicly to the world, your follow-through after being told again that the appropriate avenue to pursue your concerns was the faculty grievance policy, your subsequent follow-through to cause misleading information to be made public via an internet blog, and the resulting comments from members of the public leading to heightened concern about the safety of campus employees are all unacceptable and in violation of faculty and College policies.

I was once again being offered the faculty grievance policy as a remedy for what had been done to me. This policy had successfully insulated my detractors in the past; I had no doubt that it would do so this time. Apart from that, the provost was turning up the tonal heat, but not shedding much light—until the final paragraph of her letter:

> Although I believe your continued actions and violations of the above policies warrant your immediate dismissal under Article 11, Section C. 1 of the Faculty Personnel Policy, I am choosing not to exercise that option at this time. Rather, I am placing you on a one-week unpaid suspension. . . . Additionally, I am placing you

on official warning that any future violation of institutional policies will likely result in termination of your employment with the College.

Yes, dear reader, that's how your employer screws you. But there was an added twist: "I am hopeful that our discussion and this intermediate action will cause you to reflect on your behavior and conform your actions in the future to the expectations of the College." According to her, I had been a very bad professor. As with the petition, there are no specific allegations, just vague aspersions. Would the people who created the petition also be punished by the university for taking extra-administrative action against one of their colleagues? Would the people who created the petition also be punished by the college for going outside official channels? Of course not.

The following excerpt from my March 4, 2019 response to the provost's letter, along with her response, suggests that filing a grievance in this instance would not have been a good idea:

> You said that "the faculty grievance policy is the appropriate means for adjudicating [my] concerns regarding actions taken by College administrators;" however, during both our January 28, 2019 and February 20, 2019 meetings you conceded that this policy deals with procedural matters only and would be of no use in my case. This concession of yours accords with what I was told by your predecessor. . . about the limited scope of the faculty grievance policy when I was preparing a grievance of [the college's] decision to deny me a sabbatical. During our February 20, 2019 meeting, you also mentioned that [faculty] members were working to correct this limitation of the grievance procedure.

Here is her March 13, 2019 response:

> I have repeatedly encouraged you to use the grievance policy. While I agree that the policy deals primarily with procedural issues, I gave you one example of where it would not. The example I gave you was that if you believe that an administrator (including me) has been arbitrary or capricious in their treatment of you, then that would be considered under the policy. I have no recollection of saying the policy would be of no use in your case.

The written policy does not stipulate what she claims, and of course she has no recollection of any actions or utterances of hers that are not in writing. That's how plausible deniability works. This did not really surprise me: she had done something similar before. In 2017, the provost gave a convocation address strongly defending free speech , and I emailed her asking for a transcript of it. Just over a week later she replied, "Public speaking is not my forte and it is not my practice to share my remarks beyond the moment for which they are intended." In both instances, she would not provide written evidence that might be used to hold the college and its administrators accountable for conduct limiting my speech. I had no further recourse.

What became of the people mentioned in this chapter? The provost left rather unexpectedly halfway through the 2021-2022 academic year. Her legacy achievement was allowing one of the sociology professors mentioned in this chapter to oversee the radical reorganization of the college's curriculum during the summer when most of us were away and off contract. The dean left to become the provost of a remote state-university campus; she stepped down from that role after three years. My department chair was not chosen to serve another term, but overseeing the implementation of the new curriculum—which she left rather suddenly after a year. She's back teaching undergraduates. Three of the ten authors of the petition denouncing me—a sociology professor, her English-professor male partner, and a male sociology professor—retired with emerita /emeritus status[6] as are the two women English professors, one of whom was chosen to run the college's honors program (with predictable results: very few men are enrolled in the program). The other was put in charge of one of the college's annual publications. The male history professor was awarded tenure and promotion, and the woman music professor is still listed on the college website. One female psychology professor was appointed to chair a department; the other is now an associate vice president at our college.

That was my perilous experience of teaching while male. There is much more to this story, and I will tell the rest of it in the book I am currently writing. A scholar-friend astutely observed of my experience, "all of this happened because you simply wanted to discuss men's issues on men's terms."

Endnotes

[1] Ashfield, J. A. *Doing Psychotherapy with Men: Practicing Ethical Psychotherapy and Counseling with Men.* CreateSpace Independent Publishing Platform, 2011. Kellom, G. and M. Groth. eds. *Engaging College Men: Discovering What Works and Wh*y. Harriman, Tennessee: Men's Studies Press, 2010.

[2] Nathanson, P. and K. K. Young. *Spreading Misandry: The Teaching of Contempt for Men in Popular Culture.* Montreal and Kingston: McGill-Queen's University Press, 2001.

[3] Reilly, Peter J. "SPLC Calls Family Research Council Hate Group - Should IRS Take Action?" Forbes, November 2, 2013, available at https://www.forbes.com/sites/peterjreilly/2013/11/02/splc-calls-family-research-council-hate-group-should-irs-take-action/ (accessed 4/6/24).

[4] Shaw-Thornburg, Angela. "This is a Trigger Warning." *The Chronicle of Higher Education*, June 16, 2014, available at https://www.chronicle.com/article/this-is-a-trigger-warning/ (accessed 4/6/24).

[5] Bridgland, V. M. E., Jones, P. J., & Bellet, B. W. (2023). A Meta-Analysis of the Efficacy of Trigger Warnings, Content Warnings, and Content Notes. *Clinical Psychological Science*, 0(0), available at https://doi.org/10.1177/21677026231186625 (accessed 4/6/2024).

[6] Emeritus status provides various benefits on retired faculty members, including library access and office space. At some schools it's conferred automatically on retiring professors, while at others it requires a faculty vote.

A colonel of truth by Dave Porter

Prelude

In 2000, after 34 years of military service, I was considering retirement. The academic department I headed at the Air Force Academy was packed with excellent educators. The Academy's approach to assessing learning outcomes had received national acclaim.[1] My work with others in establishing Western Governors University's "competency-based" approach to higher education was nearing inter-regional accreditation.[2] I had been invited to speak about assessment at a national conference.

My Air Force career had been a success.[3] Had I stayed at the Air Force Academy another five years, I would have been promoted to Brigadier General upon retirement. However, the officer corps of the military was becoming increasingly conservative, and as a life-long liberal, I was weary of swimming against the current. It irritated my colleagues when I suggested it was unfair to blame cadets for "playing the game" we, as faculty members, created. My dedication to the educational mission as well as cadets and junior faculty members was recognized and appreciated, nonetheless. In addition to my selection as a Permanent Professor, I had served as Officer-in-Charge of the Freethinkers Club and was known to some as the Diversity Colonel and to others as the Colonel of Truth. The U.S. Air Force Academy PrayerNet, however, in reference to my professed agnosticism, had referred to me as "the spawn of Satan."

I confided my uncertainty about retirement to a vice president of the American Association of Higher Education (AAHE). She told me she knew a college looking for a provost where I would be a good fit: Berea College. It had great students and a unique mission, she said, but cautioned that it also had a rather "bombastic" president and a "beleaguered" faculty. I didn't tell her I was born in Berea while my father was a sophomore at the college.

In 2001, I retired from the Air Force and accepted Berea College's offer to become their Academic Vice President and Provost. Berea College is an extraordinary institution; the first school south of the Mason-Dixon to educate Black and White, men and women, together. It charges no tuition and has an income cap for eligibility. All students work for the college for at least 10 hours a week throughout their enrollment. Its unique mission, distinctive history, and the extraordinary contributions of its graduates have earned worldwide acclaim. However, both the faculty and administration suffered from many of the petty maladies that plague other liberal arts colleges. Low stakes do not diminish the fervor (or venom) with which organizational politics are played.

An incident occurring soon after my arrival as the new provost captures the ambivalence of my relationship with the College president. At the end of one of our private conversations, he asked me to oversee a short documentary about the college. He opened his *Faculty and Staff Directory*, and it was decorated with hundreds of red and green felt tip tick marks next to nearly every picture. He explained that the green marks were instances of support and the red marks were negative. He wanted the documentary to feature the "good people" and avoid the others. I was stunned.

Complying with the President's wishes was easy: the film crew was only on campus for a day and had a clear idea of the scenes they wanted. The President's directory provided quick solutions. Nonetheless, I was stunned he was keeping score. I would later learn that he had a network of informants who regularly provided inputs for his color-coded catalog. He was proud of maintaining a continuous evaluation of Berea's entire faculty and staff of nearly 500. As I would later learn, some individuals referred to him as "the neutron bomb" because, despite destroying the campus community, he left our buildings in good shape.

My approach to leadership involved decentralization, diversity, and development.[4] The President's was just the opposite: centralized authority, "viewpoint alignment," and continuous competitive selection. Despite our different approaches, our administrative efforts were often complementary; during my first four years at Berea, the graduation rate increased from 45% to just over 60%, a progressive program of providing each student with their own laptop was successfully implemented, the *Entrepreneurship for the Public Good* program was established, and a comprehensive academic assessment program including standardized student evaluations of teaching was developed and deployed.[5] Despite having faced probation as a result of their previous SACS accreditation visit, the college passed its 2005 re-accreditation visit with no adverse findings and many laudatory comments.

In 2005, because of our different leadership styles, the president and I parted ways. He asked that I relinquish my administrative position to become a tenured professor of psychology and general studies. This was an appealing prospect—spending my time in the classroom rather than endless administrative meetings was well worth a reduction in salary.

Back in the Classroom: Educational & Organizational Contexts & Pedagogical Propensities

I loved Berea's students and I loved teaching. I developed two new courses: Questioning Authority; Skepticism & Science as Antidotes for Oppression and An Introduction to the Behavioral Sciences. In my first few years back in the classroom, I was recognized as the college's Outstanding Academic Advisor and, the following year, the Outstanding Student Labor Supervisor. My post-tenure review showed that my student ratings were consistently in the top 10% of our faculty. Having developed a distinctive integrated approach to teaching senior research, my approach had helped students earn 30 competitive regional awards for the quality of their research.[6]

I focused on my own courses, striving to improve my students' learning by revising my syllabi and finding new ways to pique their interest and increase their engagement. I took responsibility for overseeing the development of the department's adjunct faculty members we relied on pending approval to replace several tenure-track positions. These worked out well. In fact, one of my teaching protégés went on to win the Teacher of the Year award at a nearby public university.

The President retired following a period of campus conflict, and a new, somewhat less aggressive, president was hired.[7] Calm and patient, the new president was a good listener; if he had opinions, he seemed less inclined to impose them on others. He asked me to co-facilitate a faculty book group examining Derek Bok's *Higher Education in America* (2013). In the following years, I was invited to join several academic assessment committees and I developed seemingly cordial relations with the administration.

Nonetheless, in 2018, my development of a survey of perceptions and judgments relating to hostile environment protection and academic freedom for my Industrial/Organizational Psychology class, evoked an impassioned response from grievants in a prior Title IX case. The administration sided with the grievants, removing me from my classes, banishing me from campus, and prohibiting me from communicating with students. Following my 10-week suspension and without any formal investigation, a Faculty Appeals Committee recommended I be dismissed and the President agreed. My appeal to the Board of Trustees executive committee was unsuccessful, my tenure was terminated, and I was dismissed from the college.

How did this happen? This question has vexed me for the past six years. Being branded as "dangerous," "unprofessional," and "incompetent" by colleagues and administrators was painful. In discussing a settlement, the college demanded I agree to never "enter any College building that contains a classroom." Given my high ratings from students, numerous publications, and other professional successes, the surprise attack for apparent political and personal reasons ending my academic career felt like an assassination. I now realize that the survey itself was merely a trigger the administration used to rid itself of a persistent, annoying critic and perceived threat.

I know that I am not alone. As Lukianoff and Schlott (2023) wrote in *The Canceling of the American Mind*, in the past 13 years, there have been more than a thousand attempts to censor, discipline, or punish college professors for perceived speech infractions.[8] A national survey of students rated Berea College's free speech environment as being about average among 251 colleges and universities.[9] Unfortunately, I am one of over two hundred faculty members, mostly old white guys, whose cancellation meant an end to tenure and dismissal.

Let's come back to my departure from administration, when I returned to classroom teaching. I spent a sabbatical year developing two new general studies courses. I saw this as an opportunity to use what I had learned about teaching and learning to develop student-centered courses that would enhance motivation and achievement and provide a foundation for students' academic success.[10] What follows is not an argument for "how good was I as a classroom teacher?"; it is an inquiry into the question of "how was I good?" In what way might my style have come to be seen as a threat by my colleagues and college administrators?

Questioning Authority: Skepticism and Science as Antidotes for Oppression was a first-year course designed to be challenging and enlightening. There would be daily quizzes, weekly interactive postings of personal insights, and a final reflection. Students considered three types of oppression: intrapersonal, interpersonal, and systemic. The basics of cognitive behavioral therapy were introduced to acquaint students with beliefs related to anxiety, depression, and self-censorship. A simple version of Eric Berne's *Transactional Analysis* (1979) helped students consider relationships and the ways they might lead to interpersonal oppression, like bullying. A sociological perspective provided the framework for considering systemic aspects of oppression. Although similar to some facets of *critical race theory*, this was presented as only one of three types of oppression, and as the one over which a person would have the least control. I embellished the course with activities, videos, provocative readings, and projects from my previous three decades of teaching. Some of my colleagues labeled this "edutainment."

The other general studies course was Introduction to the Behavioral Sciences; Anthropology, Sociology, and Psychology. This course used a Venn diagram as a framework to examine these three overlapping behavioral sciences, what they had in common, and distinctions among them. The course began with the claim that the scientific method and evolution were the two core concepts from which the scientific study of human behavior in each discipline advanced. *Psychology* studied individuals and relationships; *sociology* focused on groups and demographic categories; *anthropology* was concerned with the evolution of species (physical anthropology) and cultures.

We also identified portions of each discipline that were not scientific. In psychology, psychodynamic therapies involving recovered memories, facilitated-communication, or eye-tracker training lay beyond the pale due to their lack of supportive objective evidence. Similarly, portions of sociology and cultural anthropology relying heavily on conflict theories, and ideologically motivated scholarship involving political and social grievances and activism deviate from the strictures of the scientific method. This course also included daily quizzes, weekly interactive reflections, and an integrative final project and learning reflection.

The psychology department, already with an unfilled faculty position, had lost its two most senior faculty members shortly after my return. About half the departmental teaching load involved general psychology classes, but there were also over a dozen specialized courses offered to accommodate the 100 undergraduates majoring in psychology. Departmental faculty members' advising loads were about twice the campus average. The research capstone course was where I was most needed, but laboratory courses in industrial/organizational psychology and cognitive psychology also became my responsibility.

I was excited by the opportunity to teach these courses. My doctorate was in experimental cognitive psychology and the field was exploding with new insights and discoveries after a decade of focused examination of the brain had transformed many areas of inquiry.[11] As for industrial/organizational psychology, my Air Force Academy experiences as an equal opportunity and treatment officer, supervisory and command experiences in a variety of leadership positions, as well as my role as Berea's academic vice president and provost provided experiences and insights students found interesting.

I had learned how assessing and adjusting administrative processes could enhance organizational effectiveness. The aircraft maintenance unit in which I served as an organizational maintenance officer and chief of quality control had earned the Daedalian Award for the best aircraft maintenance in the Air Force in the mid-1970s. The rescue squadron where I'd served as a rescue helicopter pilot and executive officer earned the distinction of "best in rescue" in 1983. The Department of Behavioral Sciences and Leadership I headed at the Academy achieved consistent success and launched its graduates and faculty colleagues into careers with abundant professional distinctions and accolades (e.g., college deanships and presidencies, vice presidencies, and directorships in large organizations and corporations, and, in one case, promotion to major general). One of my students jokingly suggested my approach to teaching our core leadership course might be entitled "Bullshit, Buzzwords, and War Stories."

Students at Berea were very receptive to research and assessment activities that addressed topics they found to be personally relevant. I developed and refined capstone activities for courses as I learned about students' interests. Our senior capstone course required each student to identify an important research question, then design and conduct an experiment and report the results.[9] The class was very collaborative; I wanted students to learn that research was a team sport. In addition to research and assessment in my courses, I used summer research funding to engage small groups of interested students with more elaborate research and assessment projects.

The first such project involved the question of predicting student retention. At Berea College, SAT, GPA, and family income did not predict retention (i.e., students returning for their 3rd semester.) Thus, my first summer research team used available first semester information to predict retention and GPA in students' third semester. Much of the information we used was confidential due to FERPA restrictions, but I carefully scrubbed the data base to prevent disclosure.[12]

Since nearly all first-year students took an introductory course in composition and critical thinking, we wondered if this course might contain predictors of retention. With relatively few constraints, each faculty member designed and taught their own section(s). Some teachers required extensive reading and writing while others made only minimal demands. Some courses had daily quizzes, others had only a mid-term and a final. We collected syllabi and, after developing qualitative rubrics, assessed each syllabus on ten subjective dimensions, including workload, form and frequency of evaluation, explicit emphasis on liberal arts, competitive versus cooperative reward structures, and faculty availability and support. We also had comprehensive student grade information.

Our hope of finding "the one best way" to structure this course was unsuccessful: none of the dimensions we guessed might be important predicted students' retention or GPA. What mattered was the grades the students received in the course. Somewhat surprisingly, the actual grades were a better predictor of student retention and subsequent GPA than were the student's relative grades within his/her section. While we didn't identify course characteristics predicting success, we found a potent predictor of academic disengagement. Of the 36 sections of the course we examined, all but four had filed syllabi. The third semester GPA of the students in the 32 sections with syllabi on file was very close to 3.0. In contrast, nearly 60 students who had been randomly assigned to sections with no syllabus on file, had an average 3rd semester GPA of 2.3.

I did not share the identity of these sections with the student researchers, but I accessed the information. Three of the four sections without syllabi had been taught by faculty of color. One of them was a first-year teacher who would leave the faculty at the end of the semester, having decided that college teaching was not for him. The other minority faculty member, someone notoriously disorganized and often unprepared for class, also did not continue her duties in the classroom; she was "promoted" to become the director of diversity and subsequently its vice president.

We presented our retention study at James Madison University's (JMU) Center for Assessment and Research Studies (CARS) as well as the Kentucky Academy of Sciences and the Mid-America Undergraduate Psychology Research Conference. One of these students, after earning her doctorate in quantitative psychology at JMU and serving as Auburn University's director of academic assessment for several years, became the executive director of CARS. Another student in this research group also earned his doctorate from JMU, and now serves as research manager at *IXL Learning* and is the past president of the New England Educational Research Association.

Several experiments in my senior research course also addressed academic questions. *Stereotype threat* is a phenomenon identified by Claude Steele & Josh Aronson.[13] Reminding minority individuals of their membership in groups that perform poorly can depress their performance.

While most experiments of this phenomenon have focused on race and/or gender, Berea College's distinctive student body containing only financially disadvantaged students might also suffer from this phenomenon.

Poor kids are not expected to excel academically (and they know it). Some past administrators have exaggerated their own contributions to the academic success of Berea College graduates by accentuating our students' deficiencies. One of my senior students used these administrators' words as an independent variable to examine stereotype threat.

As predicted, students who read administrators' lamentations about poor students' deficits performed worse on a subsequent GRE practice math test, than those who reviewed a brief article on the academic success of Berea College graduates. Even more interesting was the significant interaction between subjects' own EFC (a measure of family income) and the effect of stereotype threat. The performance of the most impoverished students was hurt the most by reading the negative messages. I shared this with the senior academic administrators as a reminder of the potential negative impact of our narratives about our students and their capabilities.

Earlier, I referenced my participation on committees assessing organizational effectiveness and learning outcomes. Despite expert advice cautioning against reorganizing the faculty (especially by adding an additional layer of administration between the academic dean and department chairs), the former president had pushed this change through with promises of budgetary savings and increased faculty engagement. The implementation resolution passed by the faculty stipulated that after five years, the new structure would be evaluated.

I was a part of this assessment committee; we developed a survey of faculty members' perceptions of our academic administration. Of those who had experienced both academic structures, there was a slight preference for the prior organization. It was also apparent that the promised budgetary savings never occurred and interactions among faculty were unchanged. The Dean was disappointed in these results, but since they were equivocal, he resisted calls to return to the former, less hierarchical (and less expensive), academic structure.

Shortly after this committee concluded its work, new faculty committees were assigned to assess Berea's eight Great Commitments. I had argued that the College needed a mission statement. As great as its Eight Commitments were, in promising to be all things to all constituencies (e.g., championing interracial education, gender equality, Appalachian regional commitment, plain living, environmental awareness, and providing a top-quality liberal arts education), they did not constitute a succinct institutional mission statement. Multiple commitments could be used to justify nearly any initiative but did not distinguish among them. I co-chaired the committee that reviewed the college's commitment to provide a high-quality liberal arts education.

Course grades were related to educational quality. The committee was pleased that the rate of grade inflation over the previous 20 years was less than one third the national average for private colleges. However, looking at these data more closely revealed some awkward facts. Considering all the grades given in upper division courses over the previous 10 semesters, the overall college average percentage of A grades was about 33%. However, when results were compared across academic departments, large differences emerged. The basic sciences and political science awarded A grades less than 25% of the time. In contrast, several other departments (Education, English, and Theater) had awarded A grades over 50% of the time. Students' perception of the quality of their major's program were correlated with the proportion of A grades the program awarded, but the relationship was negative ($r_{27} = -.38$, $p < .05$): the academic programs that gave the most As were judged as being of the lowest educational quality.

Many students who come to Berea have limited educational experience—many did not expect to attend college, especially not a private liberal arts college like Berea. As first and second year students consider their choice of academic major, they are warned by classmates and some faculty members against playing "GPA roulette" (i.e., enrolling in a rigorous major might jeopardize one's GPA). Students of color and those with the greatest financial needs are the most susceptible to these warnings. Consequentially, many of the students who would benefit most from getting into challenging majors opt out and select what they consider to be softer (and safer) options. I shared these results with the Dean and the division chairs at one of their weekly meetings. They showed interest, but, in the end, took no action – some claiming that grading was a matter of academic freedom and not an administrative concern. I disagreed, but was to learn that I was in a relatively small minority.

In 2011, the AAUP's *Journal of Academic Freedom* featured several articles demonizing outcomes assessment as a threat to academic freedom. Along with these essays was a challenge daring anyone to argue for academic assessment. My essay the next year, "Assessment as a Subversive Activity" accepted this challenge:

> We cannot improve unless we are willing to accept the fact that we are imperfect—and our blots and blemishes are what assessment, when done well, can show us. Used in this way, assessment has power; one might even consider it the ultimate subversive activity. It provides a mechanism through which the authority of the institution might even contribute to the kind of transformation and liberation most valued in the liberal arts tradition. . . .[14]

My most recent essay submitted to the AAUP, "We have met the enemy, and they is us!" was not selected for publication but posted on Lawrence Krauss' Substack, *Critical Mass.*[15] I argue that by suppressing viewpoint diversity, the faculty itself has created a culture more inclined toward cancellations and is facilitating its own demise.

Madeleine Albright distinguishes fascism, with a small "f," from the National Fascist Party of Italian dictator, Benito Mussolini. In *Fascism, A Warning,* (2018) she suggests the danger of fascism is not its alignment with a political extreme but rather the propensity of autocrats to suppress the critical speech of others. The illiberalism we witness on campus is often benign; however, Albright warns that normalizing the suppression of divergent viewpoints is a harbinger of dire consequences.

Woodie Guthrie famously painted a warning on his guitar in the 1930s: *This Machine Kills Fascists.* I think of academic assessment similarly: it kills organizational oppression. As a subversive activity, assessment provides the evidence needed to hold autocratic administrators accountable. Administrative politics without principle and no evidentiary constraint inclines toward authoritarianism and institutional oppression, fascism's handmaidens. This is not unique to Berea College. Comedian

Bill Maher's critique of higher education characterizes the consequences of intellectual oppression in higher education:

> [H]igher education has become indoctrination into a stew of bad ideas, among them the notion that the world is a binary place where everyone is either an oppressor or oppressed. . . . [Students] don't know much of anything actually, but it doesn't deter them from having opinions. . . . If ignorance is a disease, Harvard Yard is the Wu Han wet market. . . . Elite colleges are the mouth of the river from which radical left and illiberal, yes illiberal, nonsense flows. . . . [expressing divergent views] is riskier than shooting the shit in Scientology. . . .[16]

"No good deed goes unpunished…"
Berea College General Counsel & Secretary

In 2012 our Psychology Department contained three male professors. We relied on postdoctoral teaching positions and adjuncts to accommodate growing student enrollments. Eventually, we were allowed to fill three tenure-track positions. We hired with a desire to increase our diversity: all three new hires were women, two of them openly lesbian.

Unfortunately, performance issues with the new faculty members soon emerged. Despite his efforts to provide support, the department chair was blamed by our new female faculty for their classroom difficulties and less than glowing tenure reviews that had been written by the academic division chair. Consequently, they filed a formal Title IX complaint against him for discrimination in hiring, discrimination in promotion, and retaliation, and enumerated ten incidents allegedly creating a hostile work environment. This fire hose of grievances was facilitated by the campus Title IX coordinator, who had recently been pilloried by students for her lack of success in "prosecuting" the alleged perpetrators of sexual assaults on campus.

There was no evidence of discrimination, retaliation, or that the incidents cited were either serious or pervasive. However, after a cursory investigation and sham hearing which selectively excluded contrary evidence, the department chair was found guilty of having created a hostile environment (based on the validation of three of ten alleged events), removed as department chair, and relocated to a newly created basement office near to the college herpetarium—a punishment that seemed rather biblical (even if inappropriate).

I served as the "faculty advisor" for the chair during his hearing but was prohibited from speaking during the proceedings. I was appalled by the lack of due process. Several false claims and exaggerations by the grievants were simply ignored by the administration, as was the defendant's subsequent ADHD diagnosis. I expressed my concerns in an essay I sent to the Dean, the President, the college counsel, a visiting Title IX investigator, and several other senior faculty members and administrators but received no response. The president later claimed he had not read the essay because "it was an attachment."

Despite a clear obligation to provide education and training relating to Title IX standards and nothing prohibiting disclosure of Title IX proceedings, the administration released no information about this case. In the absence of any official word, the grievants filled social media with their version of events. The former chair was labeled as being so racist, homophobic, and misogynistic that faculty in a nearby department concluded that he should be prohibited from entering their departmental area. There was a lot of heat, but very little light concerning this case.

In the Spring of 2018, I engaged students in my Industrial Organizational Psychology course in the development of a survey to examine the college community members' perceptions about academic freedom and Title IX protections from hostile workplace environments.[17] The survey contained approximately 20 realistic (and ecologically valid) scenarios and asked the respondents to decide whether the behavior described created a hostile environment, then whether the behavior described would be protected by academic freedom. Although hypothetical, some of the scenarios described behaviors by faculty or administrators that might be considered unethical or dishonest.

I sent drafts of the survey to a dozen senior faculty members, and received written feedback from half of them. None of them expressed concerns about breaches of confidentiality or privacy. None of them suggested the survey should be reviewed by the IRB, including the current IRB chair. The Institutional Review Board is the college's human subjects committee. I addressed concerns two of the six colleagues raised about potential campus backlash against the survey, and adjusted the survey items to minimize it. I posted the survey with extensive technical assistance from the IRB chair.

Some of the scenarios presented classroom situations in which teachers suppressed student speech, even just asking questions. In my opinion, in classrooms where anyone's freedom of expression is abridged, everyone suffers.

Two of the three incidents for which the chair had been convicted of creating a hostile environment were included in the survey. This is one:

> 37. A department chair, greatly distressed by the repeated disruptive behavior of a student in one of his classes, discusses the issue at a department meeting. Frustrated by his colleagues' repeated efforts to suggest that his own behavior was part of the problem, he blurts out that he thinks "militant lesbianism" is the basis of the difficulty since the disruptive student had privately accused him of "not being an ally to the LGBT community." Two junior faculty members who identify with the LGBT community are offended and file a grievance against the department chair. Please express your agreement that the department chair, by using the words "militant lesbianism" in anger created a hostile environment for his junior colleagues.

Here is the other scenario that related to the hostile environment charges in the Title IX case:

> 43. In an interview on National Public Radio, Chrissie Hynde, a former rock star, suggested that getting drunk and showing up at a biker party in her underwear contributed to her gang rape 20 years earlier. Many feminists decried the interview and harshly criticized Hynde, claiming that expressing her views contributed to "rape culture." A male department chair sought to find out what a junior female faculty member thought about this issue. When it became apparent to him that their conversation made her uncomfortable, he stopped the conversation and left her office. Two years later, this incident was cited as evidence that he had created a hostile environment based on gender. Please express your relative agreement that the department chair violated college policy by creating a hostile environment by introducing &

attempting to discuss the Chrissie Hynde interview with a junior female colleague.

The survey responses to these items were interesting. For the first scenario, two thirds of the respondents agreed that this behavior contributed to a hostile environment and that the behavior would not be protected by academic freedom. The hearing committee's decision reflected this view. However, in the second case, the result was just the opposite: 85% of respondents did not feel that the chair's action created a hostile environment and 77% believed academic freedom protection was appropriate. Unfortunately, the college president forbade me using or sharing any of the results from the survey at my hearing.

I did not anticipate that the survey would become the instrument of my termination. Even if I had, I'm not sure what I would have done differently. Although unaware of a need to defend my decisions concerning the survey, I wanted the survey to show my students how a behavioral scientist might collect relevant data in an emotionally and politically fraught situation. The scenarios were objective descriptions focused on the behaviors relating to academic freedom and hostile environment protection. Respondents were asked to focus on the actions described in each scenario. Descriptions of the actors were limited to race, gender, and role (i.e., student or faculty member) and some of these descriptions were changed to prevent respondents from identifying the individuals involved. The survey instructions explicitly made no claim about any relationship between the scenarios and actual events.

In the past, similar surveys in this course were praised by both students and administrations. It was only when the Berea College administration felt threatened, that they decided to grant a *heckler's veto* to protect themselves and past grievants from potential criticism. I am a pretty good classroom teacher and researcher; however, I'll confess to my deficiencies as a politician; I was no match for what was about to transpire.

Soon after the survey was posted, one of the Title IX grievants posted a hyperbolic condemnation of the survey falsely claiming it was devoid of any academic purpose and simply retaliation against her and the other grievants in the previous Title IX case. A few students enthusiastically joined the ensuing social media melee. The administrative response was swift: I was removed from my classes and banished from campus, forbidden from communicating with students, and prohibited from using or sharing the results of the survey. The Dean was to assume the roles of proxy grievant (since the primary grievants had not signed a formal complaint), investigator, prosecutor, and was also the supervisor of the four Faculty Appeals committee members who would consider my case 10 weeks later.

In our initial conversation about the survey, the Dean promised to forward me the complaints about the survey he'd received from several faculty members and identify particularly problematic items. However, a short time later, he posted a public announcement condemning the survey and calling on me to take it down and apologize to the campus community for the harm I'd done. I drafted a three-page apology and sent it to the President and Dean, but the President rejected it almost immediately, claiming I was blaming others. The Dean met with me and my academic division chair as required by the faculty manual. However, when I asked to discuss the grounds for my suspension (also required by the faculty manual), he refused, saying that the time for discussion ended when I did not immediately remove the survey and unequivocally apologize to the community.

The Dean met with the Faculty Status Council to gain their support for my dismissal. When one of the council members asked if a less severe consequence might be considered, the Dean claimed that I was "unrepentant and unapologetic." Two of the female council members, allies of the grievant, chimed in that they feared for their physical safety, suggesting I might come to their homes and "get in their faces." (There was never any evidence to support these bizarre claims.) A member of the Council who did not concur with the dismissal for cause was invited to depart the meeting while the others drew up the charges against me. These charges contained many counts that alleged the negative impact the survey had on my students and others in the campus community. One charge alleged that I had undermined confidence in the College's Title IX Program. Ultimately, the charging document concluded that my "personal conduct" had "demonstrably hindered fulfillment of my professional responsibilities."

Several of my students rushed to my defense. Inspired by *The Hunger Games*, they began referring to the Dean as "Dean Snowberry." They printed small stickers with the three-finger salute of the 12th District Resistance with the inscription #FreeDave (see below). However, two of the instigators of these activities were identified and summoned to appear before the dean of students. They were told that their activities constituted "retaliation," and would be investigated and subject to expulsion if found guilty. They were advised ten weeks later that the charges had been dropped.

During my suspension, several students nominated me for the annual Student Service Award. I was selected to receive the award by the Student Government Association (SGA) executive committee and subsequently endorsed by the SGA student senate. However, when a faculty advisor to the SGA learned of this, he composed a vicious attack on my competence and character, echoing the false claims from social media postings. His message was presented to the SGA House of Residents by the SGA VP but no one was allowed to speak on my behalf. The House declined to endorse my selection for the award.

After my dismissal, I sued this SGA advisor for defamation, and the court affirmed that his e-mails contained potentially defamatory statements. However, the court also accepted the College's assertion that his was an individual act and did not reflect the College's position. Thus, the court rejected my defamation claim against the College under the doctrine of *respondeat superior*. Nonetheless, the court would later accept this individual's defense of qualified immunity because he claimed he was acting in his role as an advisor to the SGA. Due to the restriction regarding my communicating with students during my suspension, I had not learned of these events until after they were concluded.

I have heard there was considerable administrative conversation about my case during this period. However, since any message relating to the case was copied to college counsel, all of these messages were excluded from our subsequent discovery as being privileged communication. However, one message from the Dean to the Chair of the IRB with the subject of "Mea Culpa" (the title of my draft apology that was rejected) was produced; it was simply a notice that an *encrypted* message had been sent earlier. From the beginning, the college appeared to be preparing its legal defense.

The case against me presented to the Faculty Appeals Committee was composed of a parade of faculty members asserting that the survey itself was "a dismissable (*sic*) offense." Other than two sobbing sociologists, who falsely claimed that using any actual events in organizational assessment surveys was inherently unethical, none of the College's witnesses had conducted or published research relating to perceptions or attitudes. As the survey results might have predicted, all those who testified against me were women.

Although several counts against me were for the negative impact my survey had on my students, no students testified against me. A recent graduate, a non-traditional student who had also served time in prison, testified that the scenarios depicted in the survey were so transparent "even Ray Charles could see the participants' identifies." He then identified two scenarios in particular, claiming they referred to students and faculty he knew well. However, he was mistaken: both scenarios were based on events that had occurred before he was admitted to the college. Unfortunately, my efforts to introduce this information was rejected by the Committee.

The Faculty Appeals Committee recommended I be dismissed and the President accepted this recommendation. I appealed this decision to the Board of Trustee's Executive Committee who unanimously supported the

President's decision. I've taken the case to court and have two able attorneys who accepted my case on a contingency basis. Nonetheless, Berea College, with its nearly 2-billion-dollar endowment, is a formidable foe.

Post Traumatic Recovery Efforts

I was naïve to think that Berea College would not be affected by national trends, or to expect it to keep its promises concerning academic freedom. Yet, I should have realized that Berea College was not the Air Force Academy, and assumptions I had made in my past academic life were no longer tenable. As I would discover, all that was needed to end my tenure and dismiss me were the claims that: 1) I was dangerous and incompetent and 2) the survey was an instrument of retaliation rather than a valid academic endeavor. The college claimed it was not obligated to protect my academic freedom or provide due process despite the explicit promises in the faculty manual.

I requested that my suspension be lifted while I awaited my faculty hearing; however, the president made a "plenary decision" that the suspension would continue because my presence on campus was "a danger to the well-being of faculty and students." A more detailed account of the ways in which my treatment deviated from AAUP guidelines (and the College's own Faculty Manual) can be found in an article I published later in *Minding the Campus*.[18] The results of a subsequent independent investigation by the National Association of Scholars are contained in an open letter to the college President, which concludes:

> [M]any of Porter's peers believed the survey was academically sound and in no way contributed to a hostile environment. Porter's work is publicly available and clearly is academically sound. . . . I would unhesitatingly affirm Porter's professional competence. . . . Berea College's judgment that Porter engaged in "unprofessional" behavior was plainly unfounded. Moreover, the ensemble of evidence strongly suggests that Dr. Porter was harassed rather than harassing, and that the claims that he was the perpetrator are badly supported... All these circumstances, ably summarized in *Porter v. Sergent and Berea College* (2019), argue that Berea acted unjustly.[19]

Within weeks of my dismissal, I had contacted state and federal government civil rights offices and received permission to sue the college for discrimination and violation of their promises of academic freedom and due process. Two local attorneys accepted my case and filed suit, first in state, then in federal court. Finding lawyers was difficult; over time, the College had engaged most local law firms and practices with small matters which nonetheless posed conflict of interest exclusions against them taking my case. Based on the college's claims that I was both dangerous and incompetent, I became a pariah in this small Appalachian town. A few former colleagues would cross the street to avoid encountering me. I suffered a minor stroke a month after my dismissal but recovered quickly and fully.

The process for bringing a civil suit in federal court is complex and expensive. Despite two lawyers' taking my case on contingency, my personal legal expenses have exceeded $65,000 and I recently learned that the court is awarding the college an additional $11,000 in copying costs. The process of discovery provided literally tens of thousands of pages of the college's disorganized and often mislabeled documents, and I was deposed by the college's attorney for nearly 30 hours over six days. In addition, we deposed six witnesses. Both my deposition and those of the other witnesses supported our claims that 1) I was neither incompetent nor dangerous; 2) the survey was a valid academic study directly related to my industrial and organizational psychology course; and 3) I had been mistreated by the college. Nonetheless, a federal judge granted the college's motion for summary judgment in its favor. Due to the many factual errors in the judge's opinion, my lawyers filed an appeal to the 6th Federal Circuit Court. In November 2024, the 6th Circuit partially reversed the district judge's summary judgment; a jury will be required to consider my defamation claim.

Most of the primary participants in my case have now left the college. The original Title IX coordinator was replaced by a well-qualified lawyer; to the best of my knowledge, there have been no more hostile environment prosecutions. Despite having been granted tenure, the two primary grievants in the initial Title IX and *ghost grievants* in my case subsequently left the college due to what students described as classroom behavior concerns. The defendant of the Title IX complaint was removed from the department and is nearing retirement; he has a new office no longer near the herpetarium. The VP for diversity, equity, and inclusion was hired as provost at a liberal arts college in Pennsylvania. The President retired and was replaced by Berea College's first woman president. The Dean was replaced after the Board of Trustees support for the president's decision to dismiss me included a comment that they would have handled the case differently than the Dean had. He became the VP for Alumni Relations, and later also responsible for communication and development with an annual salary near $200,000 with additional travel and entertainment accounts. He has raised tens of millions of dollars for the college's already immense endowment.

Despite Berea College's efforts to suppress the results of my study, it has been presented more widely than any research I've ever done. Our analysis of the survey data contained several noteworthy results: there was considerable disagreement among respondents concerning which scenarios reflected hostile environments and deserved academic freedom protection; gender, sexual orientation, and political identity and beliefs influenced the perception of hostile environments; the perception of a situation as being a hostile environment predicted that the action involved would be judged *not* to be protected by academic freedom. These results could have been used by the college to engage the community in considering important issues underlying hostile environments prevention and academic freedom protections, and improve its Title IX program. Alas, this never happened.

The real victims in this debacle were our students. I regret not meeting and engaging the hundreds of students I would have encountered had my tenure continued over the last six years. More importantly, one of Berea's most effective academic departments has been destroyed. Enrollments are down; faculty searches for adjuncts as well as tenure-track positions have ended in repeated disappointments. Departmental chair duties are sometimes assigned to faculty in other departments. Almost no undergraduate students are presenting research either locally or at state or regional conferences; no one receives awards for research excellence. No alumni are praising the quality and rigor of the academic program. Few, if any, students make it to graduate school; no one seems to know… or care.

In Rodriguez v. Maricopa County Community College System (2010), a Federal Circuit Court, which included the former Supreme Court Justice Sandra Day O'Connor, asserted:

> Without the right to stand against society's most strongly-held convictions, the marketplace of ideas would decline into a boutique of the banal. . . . The right to provoke, offend, and shock lies at the core of the First Amendment. This is particularly so on college campuses . . . [T]he desire to maintain a sedate academic environment does not justify limitations on a teacher's freedom to express himself on political issues in vigorous, argumentative, unmeasured, and even distinctly unpleasant terms.[20]

This decision by a federal circuit court did not distinguish between public and private colleges. All educational institutions exist to discover and disseminate the truth. Freedom of speech, academic freedom, and due process are essential in higher education; hopefully greater judicial support for higher learning will yet emerge as my appeal is considered.

Postscript: The Words Out about
My Study and My Firing from Berea College

Despite Berea College's efforts to suppress the results of this study, it has been disseminated more widely than any study I've ever done. A student undergraduate research poster at the *MidAmerica Undergraduate Psychology Research Conference* received a dozen "thumbs up" ratings in 2019. In 2021, I spoke at an open hearing conducted by the federal Department of Education regarding the implementation of Title IX on college campuses.[21] Two presentations to the Social Sciences Division of the Kentucky Academy of Sciences Annual Conference received laudatory comments.[22] I am grateful to the Canadian Society for Academic Freedom who published a synopsis of the results (and hosted a two-hour presentation by my students and myself). *Minding the Campus* has published several essays pertaining to my case.[23]   The school's underground student newspaper (with support from theFIRE.org) has also published an article about my case and an essay about the survey results.[24]

Two graduate students produced a two-hour podcast about my case.[25] Finally, the Heterodox Academy hosted a presentation of our study and my treatment by the College.[26] I am naturally pleased that our study has achieved such extensive validation.

Endnotes

[1] Porter, David, and Sandra Eisenhut. "Educational Outcomes Assessment: An Integrated Approach." A collection of papers on self-study and institutional improvement. Chicago, IL: North Central Association of Colleges and Schools Commission on Institutions of Higher Education, 1996); Porter, David, and Sandra Eisenhut. "An Integrated Approach to Educational Outcomes Assessment." The Best of Adult Assessment Forum 1991-1997. The Phoenix Institute, 1998.

[2] Porter, David, Thomas Hilgers, A. Regan, William McGregor, and Peter Ewell. "Challenges to Re-envisioning Liberal Arts through a Competency-Based Model." Paper presented at American Association of Colleges and Universities Annual Conference, Seattle, WA, January 22, 2009.

[3] An official account of my time at the Academy appears in Head, James, and Erlind G. Royer. *A History of the Permanent Professors of the United States Air Force Academy.* Fulcrum Group, 2018.

[4] Over the years I've written extensively about my leadership style. Porter, David B. "Total Quality Transformations." 34th Mountain Plains Management Conference: Diversity and Complexity as Organizational Assets. USAF Academy, CO: Dept of Management, 1992, 192-199.; Porter, David B., and Deanna G. Sergel. "Institutional Assessment: The Indispensability of Diversity." Proceedings: Sixteenth Applied Behavioral Sciences Symposium. USAF Academy, CO: USAFA-TR 98-1, 1998.; Porter, David, and Tom Angelo. "Learning Organizations as a Model for Successful Self-Studies." Collected Papers. North Central Association of Schools and Colleges, 2001.

[5] Porter, Dave, Joe Bagnoli, Janice Blythe, Donald Hudson, and Deanna Sergel. "Organizing Student Services for Learning." In *Fostering Student Success in the Campus Community*, edited by Gary Kramer, 262-301. Jossey-Bass, 2007.

[6] My articles about my pedagogy include Porter, Dave. "Senior Research: Scholarship – Discovered, Integrated, Applied, and Taught." In *It Works for Me as a Scholar-Teacher*, edited by H. Blythe and C. Sweet, 112-114. Stillwater, OK: New Forums Press, 2008; Messer, Wayne, and Dave Porter. "The Capstone Research Course: A Case Study in the Evolution of Educational Efficacy." In *Best Practices for Beginnings and Endings in the Psychology Major*, edited by Dana Dunn, Bernard Biens, Maureen McCarthy, and G. William Hill IV. Oxford University Press, 2009.

[7] I called for the president to resign in the student paper. Porter, Dave. "Mr. President, the Time Has Come. . . ." *The Pinnacle* (Editorial), Vol 155, Issue 10, November 19, 2009. His departure was covered by *Inside Higher Ed*. Stripling, Jack. "A President's Last Stand." Inside Higher Ed, March 24, 2010. Available at https://www.insidehighered.com/news/2010/03/25/presidents-last-stand (accessed April 21, 2024).

[8] Lukianoff, Greg and Rikki Schlott. *The Canceling of the American Mind: Cancel Culture Undermines Trust and Threatens Us All—But There Is a Solution*. New York: Simon and Schuster, 2023.

[9] In fact, FIRE's survey of colleges placed Berea College 146/251 in their support for freedom of speech. However, the college was in the bottom quintile in "disruptive behavior," "self-censorship," and "willingness to discuss controversial topics." Fortunately, for students there is an alternative; Eastern Kentucky University, only 12 miles north of Berea and serving many of the same kind of students was rated 4th out of 251 on this national survey of support for free speech. Foundation for Individual Rights and Expression (FIRE). 2025 College Free Speech Rankings. Available at 2025 College Free Speech Rankings | The Foundation for Individual Rights and Expression , available at https://www.thefire.org/research-learn/2025-college-free-speech-rankings (accessed September 13, 2024).

[10] Porter, David. "A Perspective on College Learning." Journal of College Reading and Learning 24, no. 1 (1991): 1-15; Darley, John, and David Porter. "Learner Centered Education." In *Education in the Information Age*, edited by Carl Pletsch and Randy Stiles. USAF Academy, CO: USAFA Publication, 1997; Porter, Dave, Megan Rodgers, and Kaleigh McCoy. "Using the Scholarship of Discovery to Enhance Classroom Teaching and Student Learning." In *It Works for Me as a Scholar-Teacher*, edited by Charlie Sweet and Hal Blythe, 94-96. New Forums Press, 2008.

[11] Porter, David. "Computer Games and Cognitive Processes: Two Tasks, Two Modes, Too Much?" *British Journal of Psychology* 82 (1991): 343-357.

[12] FERPA is the Family Educational Rights and Privacy Act.

[13] Steele, Claude, and Josh Aronson. "Stereotype Threat and the Intellectual Test Performance of African Americans." *Journal of Personality and Social Psychology* 69, no. 5 (November 1995): 797-811.

[14] Porter, David. "Assessment as a Subversive Activity." *Journal of Academic Freedom* 3 (2012): 1-28. Available at https://www.aaup.org/JAF3/assessment-subversive-activity (accessed April 29, 2024).

[15] Porter, David. "We Have Met the Enemy, and They Is Us." Guest post in Critical Mass, edited by Lawrence M. Krauss, October 12, 2023. Available at https://lawrencekrauss.substack.com/p/we-have-met-the-enemy-and-they-is (accessed April 29, 2024)

[16] Biagini, William. "College 'Makes You Stupid': Bill Maher Slams Elite Universities for Indoctrination." Campus Reform Blog, November 7, 2023. Available at https://www.campusreform.org/article/college-makes-you-

stupid-bill-maher-slams-elite-universities-for-indoctrination/24319 (accessed April 29, 2024).

[17] Porter, David. "How Hostile Environment Perceptions Imperil Academic Freedom: The Effects of Identity & Beliefs on Perceptions & Judgments." Researchers.One, 2022, available at https://researchers.one/articles/22.11. 00007v1 (accessed April 20, 2023).

[18] Porter, Dave. "Why Did a Christian College Fire a Tenured Professor?" The James G. Martin Center for Academic Renewal: Academics, July 9, 2021. Available at https://www.jamesgmartin.center/2021/07/why-did-a-christian-college-fire-a-tenured-professor/ (accessed April 21, 2024).

[19] "Open Letter to Lyle D. Roelofs, President of Berea College." The National Association of Scholars blog, July 24, 2020. Available at https://www.nas.org/blogs/article/an-open-letter-to-lyle-d-roelofs-president-of-berea-college (accessed April 21, 2024).

[20] Rodriguez v. Maricopa County Community College District, No. CIV 04-2510-PHX-EHC (D. Ariz. Jan. 12, 2006). Available at https://casetext.com/case/rodriguez-v-maricopa-county-community-college-district (accessed April 29, 2024).

[21] A transcript of my comments appears here: https://www2.ed.gov/about/offices/list/ocr/docs/202106-titleix-publichearing-complete.pdf (pg 73-76; accessed April 30, 2024).

[22] Porter, Dave, Deshontanae Davis, Jenifer Fidela, Aaron Clark, & Yabsira Ayele. "The Effects of Identity & Beliefs on Perceptions & Judgments: How Hostile Environment Perceptions May Imperil Academic Freedom." Kentucky Academy of Science Annual Meeting, November 5, 2021 and Porter, Dave, Jennifer Fidela, Janae Davis, Aaron Clark, and Yabsira Ayele. "Flies in the Ointment: How Distortions, Discontinuities, & Dissonance Thwart Cancel Culture's Promises." SAFS Newsletter, October 6, 2021, 37-43. Available at http://safs.ca/newsletters/issues/nl89.pdf (accessed October 28, 2024).

[23] Porter, Dave. "Due Process is Essential to Higher Learning." Minding the Campus; Reforming Our Universities, June 14, 2021. Available at https://www.mindingthecampus.org/2021/06/14/due-process-is-essential-to-higher-learning/ (accessed October 28, 2024); Porter, Dae. "The Catechism of the Woke." Minding the Campus; Reforming Our Universities, June 25, 2021. Available at https://www.mindingthecampus.org/2021/06/25/the-catechism-of-the-woke-a-cautionary-tale/ (accessed October 28, 2024); Porter, Dave. "The Baffling Bull Behind Title IX." Minding the Campus; Reforming Our Universities, April 16, 2024. Available at https://www.mindingthecampus.org/2024/04/16/the-baffling-bull-behind-title-ix/#respond (accessed October 28, 2024).

[24] Gitaliyev, Ülvi, and Lily Barnette. "Professor in Exile: How a Former Provost and Professor Was Fired for Incompetence at Berea College." The Berea Torch, April 19, 2019.

[25] Hartman, Rachel, and Paul Conner. "Berea's Dave Reckoning." More of a Comment than a Question podcast, December 4, 2021. Available at https://moreofacomment.buzzsprout.com/1207223/9662481berea-s-dave-reckoning-with-dave-porter (accessed October 28, 2024).

[26] Porter, Dave. Presentation at Heterodox Academy's Heterodox Communities, November 27, 2023. Available at https://heterodoxacademy.org/events/guest-speaker-dave-porter-from-berea/ (accessed May 27, 2024).

Weaponizing Title IX
at the Oregon Health & Science University
Buddy Ullman

This is a story about the weaponization of Title IX, the transformative federal civil rights law that prohibits gender discrimination in federally funded educational institutions. Enacted in 1972, Title IX has provided opportunity, fairness, and justice for the powerless and vulnerable among us, particularly for girls and women, whose access to educational programs and activities had been traditionally hindered because of gender. Unfortunately, the application of Title IX has become distorted, exploited, and misused. My story describes how a cabal of powerful administrators at the Oregon Health & Science University (OHSU) in Portland, Oregon hijacked and misappropriated Title IX to attack and sabotage the career of a prominent faculty member who was powerless to defend himself. That faculty member was me.

Let me be clear: there was plenty of wrongdoing and misconduct—but just not on my part. Faced with multiple frivolous and false charges, all formulated surreptitiously by OHSU administrators and their minions, I endured five investigations over the course of three years, and lost them all. The upshot of my ordeal was suspension from the university, the destruction of my academic career, the loss of all my professional files, and a coerced involuntary resignation from a faculty position that I had held for 32 years. My students, of which there were hundreds at any given time, as well as my faculty colleagues, were collateral damage.

This is also a story of retaliation, harassment, and abuse, of me and a thousand others. These experiences provided an impetus for the 2020 federal reforms on how Title IX is enforced on college and university campuses.[1] Throughout this chapter, I will allude to past, present, and potential future federal regulations that govern the enforcement of Title IX on college and university campuses.

About Me

I was hired as an assistant professor in the Department of Biochemistry (eventually renamed the Department of Biochemistry and Molecular Biology) in the School of Medicine at OHSU in 1985. As a faculty member at OHSU, I headed a laboratory-based research program in molecular parasitology that was continuously funded for 34 years by the National Institutes of Health. My research focused on the dissection of unique transport, metabolic, and organellar targeting pathways in protozoan parasites that cause devastating diseases in humans. I trained dozens of graduate students and postdoctoral fellows. Many went on to prominent positions in universities, research institutions, or clinical medicine.

Context

I was a major contributor to OHSU's many instructional programs, for which I was accorded 51 teaching awards and honors over 29 years. I was devoted to my students—there were several thousand of them over the years—and nearly all were appreciative of me. Of course, there were exceptions. Most of my educational efforts were directed toward the first-year medical education program, where I taught metabolic biochemistry, enzymology, molecular biology, genetics, nutrition, and parasitology.

In 2004, I was appointed to be the course director for the first-year medical curriculum course called Cell Structure and Function (CSF). CSF was widely considered to be the most taxing course of the entire medical curriculum, and my job was to shepherd students of diverse academic backgrounds through the gauntlet. The CSF directorship required hundreds of individual meetings with students annually, many of which were both tense and intense. The meetings were typically held in my office, and my office door was always left open unless the student asked that it be closed.

Almost all the students completed CSF, but every year there were stragglers, generally students who were ill-prepared for medical school because of poor undergraduate training. Those few students who failed to pass CSF were required by the School of Medicine to pass a comprehensive summer remediation exam.

At OHSU, I was perceived as a faculty leader because of my vocal advocacy for students and faculty, and for my outspoken views about academic policy. This brought me into occasional conflict with some of the deans and associate deans in the School of Medicine. I would come to pay a price for championing students and faculty.

One incident was particularly noteworthy: my vigorous defense of six first- and second-year medical students who had been threatened with expulsion and forced to plead to save their academic careers by the recently appointed Associate Dean of Undergraduate Medical Education (AssocDean) and the new Senior Associate Dean of Education in the School of Medicine (SrAssocDean), just because of their participation in a video skit that had been presented at the annual Medical School Follies in 2014. The video was a clever parody of Idina Menzel's "Let It Go" from the movie "Frozen" and innocuous in content and language. I'd made a brief appearance in this skit.

It was clear to both faculty members and other students that the threat of expulsion was unjust. The SrAssocDean, who was not my administrative superior, demanded a meeting with me for my cameo in the skit. I declined to take the meeting. The whole imbroglio was brought to a close a few days later by OHSU's top administrators. I had played a vocal role in defending the six students, and I have always suspected that the root of this entire episode was due to my participation.

In 2014, after the aforementioned SrAssocDean and AssocDean had been hired, a new medical school curriculum was implemented. This curriculum excluded my Cell Structure and Function course, and henceforth the Biochemistry and Molecular Biology Department would play only a minor role in training medical students. My own participation was minimal, perhaps a couple of lectures or small group discussions per year.

That same year, I had the misfortune of becoming a Title IX respondent. I was investigated, presumably under the vague and imprecise Title IX guidance that the Obama-era Department of Education issued in 2011.[2] This guidance was, thankfully, rescinded in 2017 by the Trump

Department of Education, and replaced in 2020 as noted above by Education Secretary DeVos. Unfortunately, the Biden administration plans to replace the DeVos rules with new guidance that is much worse.[3] Full disclosure: I am a liberal democrat and an ardent supporter of both the Obama and Biden presidencies, but the DeVos rule is far more progressive and enlightened than Title IX guidelines that were devised by the Obama and Biden administrations.

The following pages describe my Title IX ordeal. Because OHSU administration has denied me access to my professional files, this account is based on my recollections and hard copies of documents that I made throughout the ordeal.

My Title IX Experience

The details of the five investigations that destroyed my career and cost me my job are myriad, convoluted, and complex. Because these investigations involved multiple campus administrative units, voluminous written and recorded materials, and profoundly compromised logic, I can only outline the adversities that I faced over a three year period. There is documentation for everything that I assert, much of which also ended up at the Office for Civil Rights in the U.S. Department of Education. The ostensible purpose for these investigations was to punish and silence me for my student and faculty advocacy, and to deny me access to the educational programs and activities of the university. The multiple inquiries eventually morphed into a mechanism to destroy my thriving research career and to fire me.

The initial investigation for which I was named respondent was a fraudulent sexual harassment complaint that was launched on May 16th, 2014 by the AssocDean on behalf of one single medical student out of a class of 135 who had failed CSF and, therefore, faced a remediation examination and potential expulsion from the medical program. Thus this student had ample motive to retaliate against me. The student had falsely claimed in an email to the AssocDean written earlier that day, 3 ½ months after the CSF class had concluded, that I had kissed her on the forehead in my office and that I had made a harassing and "pseudo-predatory" comment on a Facebook photo of ten of her female classmates, all my former students. She was not pictured.

The alleged kiss was a fabrication, later embellished by additional mendacious accusations that I had put my arms around her and touched her with a "weird romantic energy disguised as paternal like in a sugar-coated way." To be clear, I never touched the student. She and I did have two uncomfortable conversations in my office during CSF, each lasting about 5-10 minutes, about her academic struggles. I would only learn about her emails to AssocDean over a year later, nine months after the case against me was closed. I would never be offered an opportunity to contest the accusations.

The Facebook comment this student alluded to was warm and sentimental, but not of a sexual nature. None of the ten students pictured in the screen shot were aware of the student's email to the AssocDean, and they would have been mortified to have been included as unintended participants in a sexual harassment complaint against me. The student had taken the liberty to represent her classmates in what would become a formal sexual harassment complaint about which these ten students and I knew nothing. In addition, the email had stressed that my Facebook comments were "directed toward female students exclusively." This claim was demonstrably false.

The student's motives were obviously retaliatory, as were those of the OHSU administrators. Whether she hoped to sidestep her obligation to take her remediation examination, or to complain that she was a victim of sexual harassment in case she failed to pass the exam, I cannot know. Motives aside, her email was the excuse that OHSU administrators were seeking to launch an investigation against me. Over the next three years, OHSU administrators would lob many more grenades from its armamentarium. Given OHSU's propensity for bending the truth, an exemplary 32-year academic career offered OHSU plenty of ammunition.

A few hours after receiving the student's email, AssocDean forwarded it to the Affirmative Action and Equal Opportunity (AAEO) office, which handled discrimination, harassment, and Title IX complaints at OHSU. The AAEO investigator christened the complaint a sexual harassment complaint and designated the student as the complainant—although this was a third-party grievance launched by the AssocDean. I was named the respondent. Neither the complainant nor I, the two parties in the Title IX dispute, were aware of the formal sexual harassment complaint at the time of instigation, and there would never be anything remotely resembling fact-finding or an investigation.

By the next business day, the SrAssocDean, the AssocDean's immediate administrative superior, had expanded the scope of the investigation. Multiple emails in my possession establish complicity between the Dean's and AAEO Offices at the inception of the investigation. The SrAssocDean's two allegations were pure retaliation, and completely irrelevant to the complainant's accusations. The first pertained to my ten second cameo in the aforementioned Student Follies skit. The second concerned a humorous, self-deprecating email that I had sent to all the first and second year medical students about my role, or lack thereof, in the newly designed curriculum. The Dean's Office was copied as courtesy. The email described a fictitious conversation with an unnamed female faculty colleague with whom I was quite friendly and who had read and pre-approved the email prior to transmission. The students appreciated the farcical nature of the email. The SrAssocDean responded the next day by sending an email to all of the first and second year students admonishing me for my email and accusing me of undisclosed policy violations. The students were livid at this admonition.

A couple of weeks later the SrAssocDean consulted with the Dean of the School of Medicine about summoning the human resources and the information technology offices to join in the crusade against me. I remain unaware whether the dean responded, but he and representatives of HR and InfoTech would all join the fray at later dates. This was going to be an unconventional Title IX complaint.

I first learned about the existence of the harassment/discrimination complaint against me from an email that the investigator sent me on August 14th, 2014, three months after the investigation had been initiated (although there were nebulous leaks emanating from the Dean's Office). Federal Title IX guidelines, as well as OHSU policy, are unambiguous that Title IX investigations, and in particular sexual harassment complaints, must be conducted and completed promptly, usually within 60 days, and I hadn't even been informed of the complaint until 90 days after the complainant's email was shared with the Dean's office and AAEO. More importantly, federal Title IX regulations and OHSU policy are emphatic that universities must immediately remedy any sexual harassment detailed in a complaint. That never happened.

The university's failure to comply with this directive is obvious. Of course OHSU couldn't substantiate any inculpatory harassment, discrimination, or offending behavior on my part, but OHSU had a complainant, two other female medical students to provided "testimony," and a cadre of powerful administrators with a lot of tools in their arsenal—and zero oversight. The two student witnesses merit further mention. First, their identities were kept from me throughout the investigation. Second, both were among the complainant's closest friends at OHSU and may well have conspired with her. Third, their testimony was provided over the telephone, an obviously inferior way to collect evidence. One testified that I had hugged her and expressed romantic aspirations, while the second claimed that I had requested to see a hematoma on her butt she'd acquired from a fall. Their assertions were fabrications, yet they remained unknown to me for the entirety of the investigation, so I never had the chance to refute them. The investigator would conclude that both the complainant and the student witnesses were credible. They were not.

The investigator would follow her email with telephone calls, one to me and one to my department chairman, who at the same time was being harassed out of the university around by the Dean and his minions. The investigator reiterated to both of us that I was a respondent in a harassment/discrimination complaint but refused to provide details. She also informed me that I would be interviewed, and she issued a gag order: I was not allowed to talk about the case.

I was fully aware that discrimination and harassment were extremely serious accusations, especially in an academic setting, but I also knew that I had never harassed or discriminated against anyone in my life. Because I did not deal with OHSU administration on a regular basis, I was unaware of the machinations behind the scenes, and naively believed that the investigation would be fair. My chair was more than familiar with the intrigues in the Dean's Office and would have defended me had he not resigned from the university a few months later. He was replaced with an interim chairman, one of my departmental colleagues who was purely interested in establishing a good working relationship with the Dean's Office. He would never lift a finger to help me.

Since I could not consult with colleagues for advice, I sought legal assistance. I hired a prominent Oregon employment lawyer who charged around $500 an hour to represent me. She proved to be less than useful.

Prior to my so-called interview with the university's "civil rights" investigator, I had received written instructions to be honest, open, and forthright. That is my nature, but it would prove to be a huge tactical mistake, especially with a disingenuous university gumshoe on the case. Although the Title IX investigators and coordinators masquerade as fair, dispassionate arbiters, they are functionaries primarily tasked with protecting academic institutions and their administrators from personal and institutional liability (i.e., lawsuits, the loss of federal educational funds). And at OHSU, Title IX and its derivative school policies had been weaponized to target faculty and employees that have incurred the displeasure of powerful administrators. I was paramount among several faculty victims.

I met with the investigator on September 5th, 2014 for 90 agonizing minutes. Also present were my attorney, who never said a word and did not defend me, and OHSU's Legal Counsel. Unbeknownst to me, September 5th, 2014 was also the date that the investigator would close the investigation, ensuring that I would never be able to respond adequately to the allegations against me (which I was never informed of anyway).

The interrogation did not go well. I was completely unprepared, because I lacked knowledge of the charges, and the investigator harangued me with salacious questions about everyday academic activities. She also seethed with hostility. I beseeched her multiple times to disclose the specific allegations against me and to tell me names of the complainant or witnesses, but she refused. It was obvious that the investigator had no interest in fact-finding. Despite my naïveté, I sensed a trap.

I was particularly devastated that my attorney made no effort to support me during the harangue. She urged me after the interrogation to beseech OHSU for mercy in exchange for a promise to reform. The problem was there was nothing to reform and no bad behavior to ameliorate. The lawyer was not interested in advocacy, and we had no further contact. I suspect that the high-powered attorney just didn't see enough dollar signs in defending me.

There was a total lack of fairness and due process in the proceedings. Here is a summary of the procedural lapses in my ordeal. Vladimir Putin would have been proud.

1) The charges against me were never discussed in my presence, precluding any semblance of a defense.

2) The named complainant appears to have been unaware of the filing of the civil rights complaint with the Affirmative Action and Equal Opportunity office at the time the complaint was filed. The Title IX complaint against me was initiated by a third-party surrogate, the AssocDean, who had her own agenda.

3) There was no formal or written complaint. I asked to see the formal complaint multiple times, and was never informed that it did not exist.

4) The scope of the complaint shifted and expanded throughout the investigation.

5) I was not allowed to know the identities of the complainant or the witnesses (i.e., the Associate Deans and other students). OHSU wanted to conduct its accusation under anonymity for understandable reasons—but also because I would have immediately recognized the retaliatory nature of the Associate Deans' and specific students' allegations.

6) I was not offered any opportunity to present evidence on my behalf, while the "prosecutors" were given four months to collect and submit evidence.

7) I was not offered an occasion to bring forth witnesses, of whom I would have had thousands. The complainant side had four witnesses: the two Associate Deans and the complainant's two friends/housemates, each of whom had concocted novel untruths.

8) Witness testimony was taken over the telephone.

9) All exculpatory evidence collected by the AAEO investigator was withheld from me.

10) The inculpatory "evidence" that the investigator collected (or made up) did not involve wrongdoing and was, without exception, frivolous or baseless.

11) The investigative report, identified as the "Closure Memo," was not provided to me. I only became aware of the Closure Memo's existence ten months after the case against me was concluded. It was replete with falsehoods and distortions, and lacked context throughout. There was no opportunity provided to rebut the Closure Memo, as is currently mandated by federal Title IX regulations.

12) I was not informed in a timely matter about any aspect of the investigation against me. Every step of the investigation was a revelation.

13) I was muzzled throughout the proceedings (and presumably afterwards). The gag order prevented me from recruiting witnesses, getting help within the institution, and otherwise organizing a defense.

14) I was continually threatened with termination. This was intimidating, to say the least.

15) The outcome of the "investigation" was seemingly predetermined, but it took me a while to arrive at this conclusion.

After the meeting with the investigator, I would wait almost four months for her findings. She then produced the Closure Memo (see point 11 above), which summarized the "allegations" and "findings." The "allegations" weren't actual allegations of wrongdoing, and the "findings" were without exception both untrue and out of context. I could have made this clear to her if she had bothered to share the allegations and findings with me.

I received a summary of the investigator's findings, designated the Letter of Closure (different from the Closure Memo) on November 25, 2014. The Letter of Closure was both prejudicial and farcical. The investigator concluded that I had engaged in sexual harassment of female medical students for the entire 29 years I had been teaching at OHSU. Although the case against me had already been ongoing for six moths, this was the first time that I had any inkling that I was being "investigated" for sexual harassment. This revelation was flabbergasting, since there had never been any sexual harassment, and categorically no behavior of a sexual nature on my part toward any OHSU student or employee during the three decades I served on the OHSU faculty. The investigator also found that I had engaged in gender discrimination and inappropriate, unprofessional, and disrespectful behavior toward female medical students, perhaps to ensure that I had been found in violation of almost every single institutional policy that supports Title IX. I had never engaged in gender discrimination or inappropriate, unprofessional, or disrespectful behavior toward female medical students, or for that matter toward anybody else.

The Dean of the School of Medicine stated in a separate Letter of Caution to me, also dated November 25, 2014, that I had "violated OHSU's Code of Conduct, the Equal Opportunity Policy, and the Sexual Harassment Policy through unwelcome hugging, wrist-grabbing, cheek kissing and forehead kissing of female students." This was news to me, because I had never engaged in unwelcome hugging, wrist-grabbing, cheek kissing, or forehead kissing of female students. What's more, these allegations were never mentioned to me during the investigation. My Dean also rebuked me for two inoffensive jokes that I made in class about a protozoan pathogen that differentially affected men and women. Each joke emphasized an important educational point, brought the house down, and constituted protected free speech according to written OHSU policy (which the Dean ignored). This hardly constituted behavioral transgressions or policy violations, but that did not matter. I was duly punished, and there was never any effort on the part of the institution to get me to change my behavior, as mandated by institutional policies and federal statute.

The Title IX investigation was not fair, impartial, nor legitimate, and it was most certainly not well-intentioned. Not only had the investigator functioned as a prosecutor throughout the inquiry, but she also served the roles of investigator, plaintiff (it was she who made the specific sexual harassment accusation), judge, jury, and executioner. Because there was not one iota of legitimacy to any of the investigator's or the Dean's conclusions, it was obvious that the OHSU administration had hijacked

Title IX in order to retaliate against me for my activities and views. The shortcomings in the AAEO investigation were not an accident. Title IX was wielded as a weapon, a strategic tool that the Dean's Office subsequently employed to clobber other faculty. Former Department of Education Secretary Betsy DeVos' new guidelines for Title IX enforcement on college/university campuses address every single one of the investigative shortcomings in my case, which is why I enthusiastically endorse them.[4] The new regulations do not, however, address the competence and integrity of Title IX investigators, nor the ability of bad actors to manipulate the outcome of Title IX proceedings.

My subsequent request for an appeal based on erroneous conclusions and lack of due process was denied by OHSU's legal counsel, the same person who played a role in the original AAEO investigation. But I was granted an internal grievance procedure, effectively a second investigation, that was distorted almost beyond recognition by the university's legal council. It was a sham. The grievance panel, consisting mostly of bureaucrats beholden to the university's top administrators, concluded that my due process rights had not been violated because I could have presented a defense after my case was closed (to whom was I supposed to do this?). The panel also averred that I didn't need to have been informed about the specifics of the allegations, because I should have been able to figure them out by the line of questioning. That's a tall order when the alleged misconduct never occurred! Although the outcome of the grievance procedure was predetermined, it did enable me to learn the nature of the charges against me and the names of the complainants and witnesses who testified against me. This was cathartic.

After losing the initial Title IX case and the consequent internal grievance, I filed an appeal with the Seattle branch of the Office for Civil Rights (OCR) of the federal Department of Education. The OCR took the case, investigated OHSU's AAEO office, and apparently compelled substantial changes: the AAEO Director was subsequently fired. Still, OCR concluded that OHSU had adhered sufficiently to the Obama-era Title IX guidelines, noting that OHSU's grievance process constituted an adequate response to my due process concerns and, thus, took no further action on my behalf. In other words, neither the lack of due process nor the erroneous outcome in my case was of concern to OCR. The OCR decision was disappointing, and it left me exposed to further retribution.

Once the OCR had completed its review of OHSU's AAEO Office and Title IX compliance, the OHSU administration, blasting through any OCR whistleblower protections, retaliated against me repeatedly. The administration filed at least five more frivolous charges against me, most of which were Title IX-related. The Title IX Office punted on these, but it didn't matter. Thereafter the administration launched two new investigations, the fourth and fifth overall. The outcomes were predetermined, and ultimately succeeded in denying me access to the medical education programs at my institution.

The first of these latter two investigations was filed with OHSU's Integrity Office by the SrAssocDean and AssocDean. It arrived on the heels of their vindictive last-minute attempt to cancel my upcoming medical school lecture. Their plans were foiled by the new Interim Dean of the School of Medicine, and their subsequent attempt to bar me permanently from the med school teaching faculty was forcefully rejected by a faculty committee that the SrAssocDean had appointed.

Human Resources was tasked with this investigation. The Human Resources investigator initially refused to inform me of the accusation or the names of the complainants, but considering that this wasn't my first rodeo, I informed her that I would not participate in her inquiry unless she provided the information that I requested. She duly relented and informed me that the SrAssocDean and AssocDean were the complainants, and the accusation was retaliation. This is a grave offense in academia, but there had been no retaliation. The very idea that a subordinate faculty member can retaliate against a dean is preposterous.

During the 30 minute interview with the Human Resources investigator, I explained that there was no basis to the Associate Dean's charge. I easily refuted the retaliation allegation. However, she must have had her marching orders, so the allegation was revised after our discussion. She would conclude that I violated the institutional Code of Conduct's "professionalism and respect" expectations because I had used the exclamation "yuck" in an email to a colleague. I mocked her for this conclusion, precipitating the investigator herself to launch her own complaint against me.

The administration continued to retaliate me in other ways. I was banished from the medical school classroom on three separate occasions for no reason except the deans' animosity. This denied me access to the institution's other educational activities. I was then made the subject of a nasty, disparaging email sent by the SrAssocDean and AssocDean to the entire 600-person medical student body, many of whom did not know me, in response to my cameo at the 2017 Medical Student Follies. This email deserves special mention, not only for the uproar that it caused among the medical student body—who valiantly came to my defense—or because it was the last straw that precipitated my firing, but because it was emblematic of the tribulations that I had endured at the hands of the OHSU administration for the better part of three years.

I had been invited by the medical school class of 2019 to give the "keynote" address at the 2017 Medical Student Follies in which students (and selected faculty) have an opportunity to poke fun at themselves, their professors, and the curriculum. A week later, the SrAssocDean and AssocDean sent an email to the entire student body that began like this:

> We write to you today with heavy hearts and a great sense of disappointment. This past Monday, we learned that Professor Buddy Ullman addressed the students, staff and faculty who attended the Follies on June 17, 2017, making derogatory remarks about the MD curriculum and program, and boasting that he blatantly disregards the OHSU Code of Conduct. While we know the event is designed to be light-hearted and entertaining, joking about and showing pride in unprofessional behavior is not something we find amusing. To us, there is nothing humorous about an attack on the tenets that underlie the medical profession in any setting.

Although the intent of the email was to humiliate me in front of the students, the email backfired: the students went ballistic. Let me be clear: neither the SrAssocDean, AssocDean, nor any of their staff were present at the Follies, and their email was factually incorrect. I did not make "derogatory remarks about the MD curriculum and program," did not boast that I "disregard the OHSU Code of Conduct," and did not "attack the tenets that underlie the medical profession," all of which were covered by multiple student skits. My sin was to commit satire at a satirical event.

A few days later, I was placed on administrative leave, exiled from campus, and had my email deactivated and my access to my work computer barred permanently. These actions effectively ended my 47 year career in biomedical research. Furthermore, when the Interim Dean of the School of Medicine and the Vice President of Human Resources came to my office to place me on administrative leave, it was because of three new charges that had been filed against me. They removed me from campus, even though they not tell me why I was being placed on administrative leave. I asked what the new charges were, but they told me that they themselves didn't even know!

Another sham investigation was about to ensue, this one organized by the OHSU legal department. I was well aware that the outcome was inevitable, and that OHSU was going to fire me. There were now four charges, one of which, that nonsense about the Follies, was eventually dropped. The names of the complainants, obviously senior administrators abetted by subordinates, would never be divulged. This last investigation was conducted by an outside investigator, an attorney in Portland who proudly advertised on his website that he specialized in helping large organizations get rid of problem employees (e.g., me). The attorney, hired and remunerated by OHSU, did not even make a pretense of being impartial. He determined that I was guilty of two counts of retaliation: one, for writing an email to one of the original witnesses after she had graduated and was no longer associated with OHSU, informing her that I knew of her false accusations against me; the other for telling the Human Resources investigator that it was preposterously comic that "yuck" constituted a violation of the Code of Conduct.

After the outside lawyer had finished his witch hunt, I was given a letter on plain paper (not on letterhead) initialed by the new permanent Dean telling me that she was initiating termination proceedings against me. I officially resigned a few days later with the administration's loaded gun pointed at my head.

Epilogue

Many of my colleagues, friends, and family members have inquired over the years why I refrained from filing a lawsuit. There were many reasons. First, I am not litigious by nature, and I wouldn't accept remuneration that I didn't earn. Second, when I was axed I was close to retirement and had no desire to remain at OHSU because of the way I (and others) had been treated. Third, I signed a termination agreement, clearly under duress, that would provide me with a salary equivalent and medical insurance for another nine months if I promised not to sue. Fourth, I already had two lawyers: the first, whom I had hired three years earlier for the first investigation, who was unhelpful, and a second who afforded me advice during the fifth and last investigation. He thought it would be best for me to retire, mainly for mental health reasons, rather than endure a prolonged court proceeding. He was right. Fifth, I am a pensioner on a fixed income, and I would have been taking on a multi-billion dollar organization with effectively unlimited resources. Sixth, OHSU would have fought me tooth and nail. The entire administration all the way up to the university president had targeted me—and could have been implicated in wrongdoing. And finally, I was exhausted. After three years of continuous harassment and discrimination at the hands of OHSU administrators, no channel to achieve fairness or justice internally, and concerning blood pressure measurements, continuing as a faculty member at OHSU was untenable. I am delighted to be gone from OHSU and have devoted much free time in retirement helping other aggrieved faculty members nationally who have been victimized by Title IX or similar proceedings.

Endnotes

[1] Anderson, Greta. "U.S. Publishes New Regulations on Campus Sexual Assault." *Inside Higher Ed*, May 6, 2020. Available at https://www.insidehighered.com/news/2020/05/07/education-department-releases-final-title-ix-regulations (accessed March 22, 2024).

[2] Department of Education, Office of the Assistant Secretary. "Dear Colleague Letter." April 4, 2011. Available at https://www2.ed.gov/about/offices/list/ocr/letters/colleague-201104.html (accessed March 22, 2024).

[3] Eckes, Suzanne, R. Shep Melnick, and Kimberly J. Robinson. "Reactions to the Biden Administration's Proposed Title IX Changes from Education Law Scholars." The Brookings Institute, June 30, 2022. Available at https://www.brookings.edu/articles/reactions-to-the-biden-administrations-proposed-title-ix-changes-from-education-law-scholars/ (accessed March 22, 2024). R. Shep Melnick is a leading scholar of how the 2011 Obama-era guidance distorted the original intent of Title IX and shredded due process on campus.

[4] Ullman, Buddy. "Title IX Reforms Will Restore Due Process for Victims and the Accused." Newsweek, June 12, 2020. Available at https://www.news week.com/title-ix-reforms-will-restore-due-process-victims-accused-opinion-1510288 (accessed March 30, 2024).

Me Too Far: A Title IX Story
David C. Wiley

I was fired from my tenured professor position at Texas State University after nearly 30 years for "violations of the sexual misconduct policy." As I will recount below, these charges were either baseless or complete misunderstandings of the situations and context of relationships between the parties. One key element should be noted: I was terminated based on "violations of the sexual misconduct policy," yet all parties agreed that at no point was sexual misconduct actually involved.

I spent most of my professional life as a faculty member at Texas State University. My research was focused on adolescent health, specifically in sex education and teenage pregnancy prevention programs. Personally, I am opinionated and often spoke up regarding academic standards, rigor and other issues facing the department and the University at large. I also admit to having a dry sense of humor and a sarcastic streak. Such a personality attracts supporters and critics alike, and I know that my style could offend some people. Such behavior can be seen as "leadership" when successfully used to advance a faculty member's career but can be redefined as "bullying" when it suits a university to do so.

The Beginning of the End

In August of 2017 a new chair of my department was named. Our problems began within two weeks after she assumed her new position. Though she and I had been friends for almost ten years, she embarrassed me at a faculty meeting in August. In October she falsely accused me, in writing, of violating Texas State University System Regents Rules (and included some colleagues and staff members in her email) and notified me in December that she was removing me as a program coordinator. It was at the December meeting that I learned she had contacted at least three different offices/people on campus to "apologize" on my behalf for some emails I had sent—but had never told me she had issues with those emails. At this December meeting she made personal comments to me, with a witness present, that I "would never change" and that my reputation on campus "wasn't what it once was."

I filed a grievance against her, and we agreed to an informal mediation session on January 9. 2018. At this meeting she began crying and admitted that she had "mishandled" the situation and I was being reinstated as a program coordinator. She later followed with an email in which she said she looked forward to continuing our work together and learning how to be a better supervisor. That afternoon I stopped by her office about another matter, and she came from behind her desk, initiated a full chest-to-chest hug with me in her office, and apologized again for the situation. I assumed our dispute had been resolved.

Initial Notification

On Friday, February 2, 2018, I received a phone call and an email from the Texas State Interim Title IX Coordinator, asking to see me later that afternoon. When I arrived, I was told that "several of my colleagues" had complained about my behavior. Given that I had no idea what he was talking about, I actually thought he had summoned the wrong person. He assured me I was the correct person and showed me the names of two of the four complainants. I had considered these two women to be good friends and colleagues with whom I enjoyed professional and personal relationships. We would joke back and forth and would exchange non-sexual side hugs and an occasional kiss on the cheek. At no point had anyone ever communicated to me or exhibited any overt physical cues indicating discomfort in my presence or with my behavior. Instead, they complained to the Title IX office and requested that I be fired. I later learned the names of the two other complainants whom I also thought were personal friends as well as professional colleagues.

The Title IX Coordinator told me that he did not think the complainants were after my job, but they just wanted the behavior to stop. When I asked him "what specific behaviors?" he said "I don't know, but we will try to have a quick investigation to try to resolve this issue." He closed with, "I don't think this is serious."

He then told me I could no longer maintain an office in the building, Jowers Center, I had been in for almost 30 years, because the complainants were "scared" of me. I was mystified at why anyone would be scared of me. I had never threatened anyone in my department and, in fact, had helped some of the complainants with work issues over the years. I was given until that Sunday night—one weekend—to vacate my office, even though I already had plans to be out of town that weekend. I was told I could teach my classes in Jowers but could not use my office.

That evening, February 2, 2018, I wrote a detailed email to the Interim Title IX Coordinator asking for guidance on several issues. For example, could I still meet with colleagues in the building? Could I still manage my seven graduate assistants in the building? Could I still attend faculty meetings? My goal was to avoid adding any fuel to the situation and to honor the spirit and intent of the "do not contact" orders. He never responded to my queries, which eventually resulted in my being banned from the building entirely. When I did exactly as I was told the following Monday, November 5, 2018, by teaching my classes in Jowers, I was reported for "violating" the no-contact order and my classes were officially moved across campus. I later learned the complainants were incorrectly told I was banned from Jowers Center and could not be in the building in any capacity.

Being banned from the building alerted my colleagues and graduate assistants that I was now under investigation. Even if I survived the allegations and investigation, my reputation was irreparably damaged. My ban from the building also facilitated the complainants' ability to meet and coordinate their stories. In addition, one complainant reported during her interview with the Title IX investigator that she went to every female faculty and staff member in the building to learn if anyone else had ever had an issue with me (none did). She later denied having said or done that in an appeal hearing, at which she was under oath.

Texas State Title IX Protocol

At Texas State, Title IX complaints are investigated by the Title IX office and a final report is issued to the dean of the college where the faculty member works. The dean decides (with input from the department chairperson) and the decision is delivered to the faculty member.

The lowest level of evidentiary burden ("more likely than not") is used to determine guilt in a campus hearing/ proceeding. A 50.01% undefined finding of "more likely than not" can result in severe sanctions while the 49.99% of "not likely" finding is ignored. The administration then has an array of punishments available ranging from a private reprimand to termination. At no point is a faculty committee involved in determining the original guilt or innocence. The only way to have any faculty involvement in the process is to appeal, which can be extremely expensive and protracted.

I was also not allowed to see the final report or question any witness statement before the final decision was made. My attorneys were not allowed to cross-examine the complainants or witnesses prior to a decision being reached. In short, I was not allowed to face my accusers before being terminated. This process would be analogous to a trial where the prosecutors present their case to a judge without revealing all evidence to the accused person (i.e., respondent) and a decision is rendered. This was the first of many violations of my due process rights.

I reached out to the American Association of University Professors to notify them of my situation, and they contacted the President and Provost of Texas State to alert them that their procedures were not considered best practices. Both letters were ignored.

The Title IX Interview

On February 20, 2018, I was interviewed for three hours by a Title IX investigator about the allegations. Per Texas State University rules, I had my attorney present, but she could not speak, or address the investigator in any way. In a cartoonish twist, she was allowed to whisper to me what she wanted to ask, which I could repeat verbatim. Also in attendance was the university's general counsel, who listened quietly for approximately three-fourths of the interview. I later learned she was meeting with the complainants to help organize their respective statements. My attorneys were not allowed to attend the interviews of any of the complainants or witnesses. I was interviewed this one single time and was never re-interviewed to provide additional information based on the interviews with witnesses and the complainants. Eventually, the University attempted to subvert the Freedom of Information (FOIA) process by claiming legal privilege over the transcript of the proceeding. The University also claimed that their attorney was not functioning as the complainants' attorney; a point that was disproved later in the process.

I was asked about several incidents, some of which I remembered and others I did not. One constant was that all the incidents were presented without context or understanding of the situation and relationships. On virtually every comment that I remember making it would be plainly obvious to an observer that I was joking or being sarcastic. For example, I was personal friends with the university provost, and we would meet once a semester for happy hour to shoot the breeze about a number of subjects; usually the state of our sports teams. The complainants used this personal relationship to claim they were "scared" I was going to have them fired if they spoke up. Provost Eugene Bourgeois responded in writing to questions my attorneys posed and wrote that he and I never talked about departmental personnel, and we discussed almost exclusively college athletics and/or the strategic plan/future of the University.

In addition, it was not uncommon for one of the complainants to joke around with me. Any comment presented without context, tone/facial expression of the speaker, or understanding of the relationship between two persons can be presented as being sinister and menacing. For example, the full, chest-to-chest hug the Department Chairperson gave me on January 9, 2018, could have been interpreted as sexual harassment and I could have filed a complaint against her. She also once gave me a kiss on the cheek at a happy hour, which could be interpreted as sexual harassment. Hyperbolic language was used to describe the interactions as well. A friendly pat on the shoulder became "a massage." One complainant who had sent me two handwritten thank you notes for helping her with a work issue was now "terrified" of me.

The incidents were reported without full and explanatory details. For example, I invited one complainant to a faculty happy hour in 2009 and she claimed in 2018 (yes, nine years later) that she felt harassed because of that incident. This person was the Department's instructional support specialist and failed to note that she had been in my office approximately once a week for the past nine years and never asked me to leave the office while she worked, and never asked for a witness to be present, but I always made sure the door was open to the hallway. This same complainant testified that I had texted her on a weekend and that mere act in and of itself had offended her. What she failed to reveal in her testimony was that her mother had died the previous day, and I was checking on her as a friend to see if she or her father needed anything. Those types of selective recall and cherry-picking of details were common in the testimonies provided to the Title IX investigator and during the appeal hearings that were to come later.

Throughout this entire episode, not once was any documentary evidence ever presented. There were no inappropriate text messages, emails, photographs, or voicemails in the record. All that was presented were their beliefs, perceptions, and opinions about our interactions, interactions that often occurred in open hallways and with witnesses present. Imagine trying to defend yourself from beliefs and perceptions that were never spoken about and with no hard evidence to explain or refute. It is impossible to disprove a complainant who said she felt harassed ten years earlier by an invitation to a group happy hour. All the complainants "believed" I could have them fired, even though an individual faculty member has no authority to hire or fire anyone. It did not matter what the reality of the situation was; what they believed to be true was what was true.

Some of the information marshaled against me was both false and unsubstantiated. For example, one complainant testified that I had told a colleague that "I am guilty of everything they are accusing me of." That colleague was interviewed by my attorneys and reported that statement was "absolutely false and did not occur," yet the Title IX investigator never followed up with that colleague or the complainant to research this false statement. The complainants all agreed that I had never asked any of them for sex, to meet for sex, offered a quid pro quo for sex, touched them in a sexually sensitive area, or anything of this sort. Their entire set of complaints centered around jokes, comments/office banter, and non-sexual touching they objected to, but had never mentioned to me.

Regardless of how the Title IX officer made his case, I had considered all the complainants to be friends and was upset they had felt harassed. That was certainly not my intent, and I wanted the opportunity to apologize to each of them individually. I asked if we could participate in mediation, but all four refused. The case against me then escalated. The Title IX investigator's documents were initially being withheld from me, so it was only ten months later that I learned that all four complainants indicated termination as the "desired remedy" when they first filed their respective Title IX complaints.

The Title IX investigator did note in her final report that I was "credible" in my claim to be unaware that I had done anything offensive. Her conclusion matches exactly my claims from the very start of the investigation. I had no idea the complainants felt harassed, and I wanted to apologize and find a path forward to continue working together. Unfortunately, I was never given that opportunity.

The Termination Meeting

I continued to teach my classes in the new classrooms and remained absent from Jowers Center while the investigation continued and a final report was prepared. I was contacted by the Dean of the College of Education and told to report to a meeting in his office on March 20, 2018. This meeting was scheduled to discuss "internal College of Education matters." I asked to bring my lawyer and was told that she could not attend. This order by my Dean violated the university's rules regarding Title IX meetings. in which legal counsel is allowed to attend. I audio recorded the meeting for my attorney to hear later, and as evidence of a clear policy violation

The HHP Chair attended this meeting and sat quietly while the Dean spoke. He told me the final report "wasn't ready yet, but he was going to recommend termination." He gave me until the following Monday at 5:00 pm to resign and "all of this goes away." I refused to resign and noted that the entire investigation came after the problems I had experienced with the Chair. The Dean then said that I was being placed on paid administrative leave, but I was not given any indication as to what that meant. I soon learned that it meant I no longer had access to my email or voicemails, and my name was removed from all HHP websites that day. The next day I returned my two university-issued laptops and keys. By locking me out of my email, I had no method to contact colleagues who were looking for me, nor did I have access to potential emails that could help exonerate me. Even though I was appealing the Dean's decision, the University's response was to treat me as if I had already been fired.

I was asked to resign before being shown the evidence against me and the deadline for my resignation (March 26, 2018) occurred one day before we were given a copy of the final report. We were shocked when we read it. Approximately 40% of the report contained information I was never asked about. It included various witness statements and hearsay that I could have easily impeached had I been asked about. However, the greatest shock was the fact that the Chairperson had served as a hostile witness while still serving as my immediate supervisor. She voluntarily testified that she was "intimidated" by me and found me to be a "bully." She never revealed this conflict of interest and did not recuse herself from her role in advising the Dean about faculty employment. It should be noted that the faculty flow chart clearly indicates that the faculty work for the Chair, not the other way around.

We later learned the Chair's original report to the Title IX office on January 29, 2018, asked that I be fired. University policy notes that the Chair "advises the Dean in employment decisions" and she remained in that role even though she wanted me fired before I was even notified of the complaint (February 2, 2018) and before the investigation had begun. Her conflict was real and convincing. It was at this point I began to realize that these complaints were being used to remove a faculty member whom the Chair found difficult to control.

It was in reading the final report that I first became aware that rules for evidence in Title IX cases are nothing like those in civil or criminal proceedings. For example, witnesses really do not have to witness anything. They were allowed to report second and third-hand information and speculate without any proof of what they were reporting. It soon became clear that my case had started somewhat of a feeding frenzy in the department in which anyone with whom I had ever had a cross word or dispute with was now serving as a "witness." Given that I was banned from my department and cut off from university email, it made it virtually impossible for me to recruit witnesses myself or to defend against the ongoing smear campaign. In addition, anonymous comments/emails were allowed in the record. Absolutely none of this would be allowed in a courtroom, but the University procedures allow for it and then refer to this hearsay, innuendo, and slander as due process. The appeal hearings are also structured to make certain witnesses and complainants were not cross-examined, thus allowing anyone and everyone to speculate with little concern for responsibility and recourse.

The Appeals Process

At Texas State there are two appeals permitted in cases involving tenured faculty. The first is considered a "due process hearing" in which a five-member faculty panel hears testimony to determine if due process was provided. This form of due process should not be confused with the legal definition of due process. This first hearing was designed to determine if Texas State followed their definition of due process. The second hearing also considers due process but is in essence a tenure revocation hearing. I was the first faculty member to be fired and have his tenure revoked using the Title IX process, so there was no precedent for my legal team to study.

In the Texas State protocol, no one could be compelled to attend hearings. Unlike legal proceedings where witnesses can be subpoenaed, participation was voluntary. In addition, the witnesses would be "sworn in" by a court reporter, but there was no penalty for perjury.

"Due Process" Hearing #1: Off to State Court, Twice

Once the University was informed that I was appealing, they required me to file requests for documents using the Texas Public Information Act (TPIA), the state's law mirroring the Freedom of Information Act (FOIA). This quickly became cumbersome and costly. They also began withholding documents, claiming legal privilege between the university attorneys and the complainants, while also making a conflicting claim that they were not serving as legal counsel for the complainants. As an example, they required that I submit open records requests for their old Title IX policies, which had been electronically archived. I had to FOIA their own policies, forcing me to spend more money to defend myself. This sort of thing is a hallmark of defending oneself in a campus sex case. Another example: at the first hearing my lawyer was required to make 11 print copies of over 1,100 pages of documents—for a total over 12,000 pages—when scanned copies would have been more convenient for everyone. Instead, I incurred hundreds of dollars in photocopying fees, and everyone hauled around these massive binders. The University also sets the cost for obtaining these FOIA documents and I never once challenged a fee, even though some were clearly unreasonable.

By law, the University has ten business days to provide documents to a requestor (with some exceptions). The pattern was for the University to wait until the tenth day to respond or ask for additional information. In one instance we asked for 32 separate documents, and the University requested a legal opinion on one document from the Texas Attorney General's office but withheld the other 31 documents until receiving the approval from the AG's office. The other 31 documents could have been released. This created the appearance that the goal was to overwhelm my legal team with documents at one time (i.e., a "document dump") so that we could not properly prepare a defense.

It is important to note that once a state university is sued in Texas, the Texas AG's office takes over the case and represents the university in all legal matters. The result is that plaintiffs are now fighting the multibillion-dollar entity known as the State of Texas. The State's resources are unlimited and can outlast most any private citizen seeking legal remedies from the court. As an example, each of these court appearances cost me thousands of dollars while we waited to be seen by the judge. All the while the meter was running on the hourly rates for my attorneys. On the other side, the University's expenses were essentially zero.

The original hearing date was scheduled for early March of 2018, but we were still lacking so many documents to prepare for the hearing. So I sought a temporary restraining order (TRO) against the University in state district court to postpone the hearing. State District Court Judge Bruce Boyer granted the TRO and commented from the bench that he was "concerned this gentleman is being railroaded." The University rescheduled the hearing for August of 2018.

Over the late spring and summer of 2018, requested documents would be provided periodically, but I still lacked the documents to hold a hearing that August. As a result, I returned to state district court and Judge Bill Henry granted a second TRO against the University. Judge Henry questioned the University about providing free legal counsel to the complainants but not me and was told by an attorney representing the AG's office they were not providing free legal counsel, but "the interests of the university and the complainants are the same."

After I won two legal proceedings against the University in state court, the State of Texas successfully moved all future litigation to federal court. They were able to do this unilaterally because they are the State of Texas and have the power to determine the venue for legal action. The respondent has no ability to impact these decisions as the State of Texas determines the playing field.

Appeals Hearing #1: Off to Federal Court

In October of 2018 I filed suit against the University in federal court in Austin, TX, asserting the University's appeals procedures were unfair and were designed to support the decisions of the University and were, in essence, a waste of time. Judge Robert Pitman dismissed the case but "without prejudice," meaning I had to participate in the Texas State University appeals process but could re-file my case in the federal system if I felt my constitutional rights had been abridged. During the oral arguments by attorney from the AG's Office, Judge Pitman also expressed concern that the University was providing free legal counsel to the complainants while I was having to pay my own legal fees. He noted, "Dr. Wiley is still employed by the University. Why isn't he receiving free legal services as well?" The attorney for the AG's office again noted that they were not providing free legal advice to the complainants and again stated the legally dubious claim that the complainants' and University's "interests were the same."

December Document Dump

At the beginning of December of 2018, my attorneys received a letter from the AG's office that did not clearly acknowledge that the University's legal office had been providing free legal advice to the complainants but noted that if there "was that perception" that any and all claims of attorney/client privilege were being waived. After that letter was received, the University began providing a great deal more documents that we had been requesting for months. Specifically, we were able to see multiple email exchanges between one of the University attorneys and the complainants. In one exchange, the University attorney helped a complainant write her statement, but during one of the appeal hearings lied by denying helping any of the complainants. Other email exchanges referred to scheduling group meetings between complainants and University attorneys to organize their complaints and respective testimonies during the appeal hearings.

In January of 2019 (one full year later) we finally received copies of the original Title IX complaint forms from the four complainants and my department chair. They were all dated January 28 or 29 of 2018 and all of them indicated "termination" as the "remedy sought." None of them were willing to mediate and all wanted me terminated before an investigation had begun. However, they all later testified in depositions they did not discuss or collude with each other regarding their respective complaints. In short, with Texas State's Title IX procedures, the complainants can file their allegations and are allowed to recommend the penalty.

"Due Process" Hearing

Once documents began arriving the first hearing was held on March 5, 2019. A five-member faculty panel was selected to hear the case and render judgment. These hearings are not considered legal proceedings, and therefore no one involved in the case can be required to attend. Witnesses were "sworn" by a court stenographer, who has no legal standing. In addition, my attorneys were not allowed to conduct live cross-examination but instead had to submit written questions in advance based on guesses as to what the witnesses might say. The Chair of the Tribunal would then select questions she felt were appropriate. We submitted 48 questions for the Chairperson, of which she was asked just two.

The complainants and all the witnesses also claimed to be scared of me. Therefore, I was forced to watch from another room via a closed-circuit video feed. I had never threatened anyone, never made any disparaging comments about any of them, and no evidence was ever provided as to why they were scared, but they were allowed to poison the process and possibly taint the committee's judgment by having me excluded from my own defense. As was the pattern throughout this case, the complainants have substantial influence over the process while I had virtually none.

The testimony of several witnesses focused on my bullying, with no mention of sexual harassment. Each person was allowed to decide what his/her definition of bullying was, but my attorneys were not allowed to cross-examine. As an example, one person said she felt bullied because I made a joking comment ("Don't we pay you enough to buy a Texas State shirt?") to her about wearing a shirt with the logo of another college to a faculty meeting. As had been the case from the beginning, all information was presented without information on context, tone, facial expression, understanding of situations, and so on. Remember that I was being terminated for sexual harassment, not bullying. Still, these witnesses were allowed to cast aspersions on their perception of my personality rather than on allegations of sexual harassment.

One complainant's stepfather had been the HHP department chairperson for seven or eight years and she admitted she had never said a word to him about my behavior, even though he and I were close friends. She said that she never said anything to him because she thought she "wouldn't be believed" and didn't want to "ruin our friendship." She also said she sent an RSVP to my wedding eight days before filing charges against me because she was afraid I would "get her fired" if she didn't come to the wedding. I attended her wedding years earlier and she later claimed that she felt that she had to invite me, or I would have her fired. These were the types of allegations I had to respond to.

One administrative assistant testified he was concerned because I always learned the student workers' names each semester. Most of the faculty never took the time to learn their names, but I did to be polite and avoid awkward situations by saying "hey, student worker." Somehow that was turned around on me in that I was potentially "recruiting" these students for sex when all I was trying to do was be kind. Every single exchange between me and the student workers occurred in the main office in the presence of full-time staff. The person who testified to his concerns is someone I had worked with for over ten years and had known for close to 15 years. He and I would have one to two casual conversations per week in one of our offices. In all those years he never once made a comment about his concerns—but was willing to testify to it when my career and livelihood were on the line. Because university rules prohibited live cross-examination, his comment went unchallenged because we were unable to guess in advance that he might say something so outrageous.

The committee's task was to determine whether any significant procedural errors or omissions occurred during the investigation as defined by Texas State. The judgment was not whether Texas State's protocols were fair or reflected due process, but whether they followed their rules, no matter how flawed or insufficient. To no one's surprise, the committee found in the University's favor by a 5-0 vote.

Within weeks of the ruling by the committee, I was notified that I had been suspended without pay (May 3, 2019) even though I was still appealing my termination and had not yet completed the process. The American Association of University Professors (AAUP) contacted the President of Texas State to inform her that I deserved to continue to be paid because I was still technically employed by the University and suspending me without pay was not in line with their best practices. That letter went ignored.

Each of these court hearings and due process appeal hearings cost me thousands of dollars a day, and I now was forced to find a way to continue paying my legal team while no longer receiving a salary. Such practices are common when faculty appeal rulings against them. Most universities have effectively unlimited resources, and control faculty access to salary to limit legal action. In fact, during a 2023 deposition of the university president (now retired) she admitted there was no policy or budgetary reason to stop paying me. To my legal team, the decision seemed completely arbitrary, with the goal to eventually starve me of funds until I was forced to abandon my appeals. To date, I have spent in the low-to-mid six-figure range to defend myself.

Tenure Revocation Hearing

Because I was a tenured professor, the University had to revoke my tenure to terminate my employment. This hearing took a full two and a half days and was the most excruciating experience of my life. The rules for this hearing were different than the first hearing in that my attorneys could cross-examine the complainants and witnesses. However, just like the first hearing, no one could be required or compelled to attend and there were no penalties for those who were not honest in their testimony. And unlike civil or criminal proceedings, there was a time limit on the process. All four complainants attended the hearing and were required to sit for cross examination. This second and final hearing was the first time I was truly allowed to face my accusers, more than two years after I had been recommended for termination.

Both sides exchanged witness lists, but many on the University's list did not show for the hearing. A few of the no-shows were notable because they could have shed light on many of the claims by the complainants and witnesses. As an example, one complainant was a staff person who was often difficult to find during the workday, so she gave me her cell phone number to text her. When I told her that I really didn't want to make her use her personal phone, her response was "It's not a problem." At that time, a former chair of HHP had told faculty to contact this staff member using her personal cell phone. However, during testimony this staff person said she had "no idea where I got her cell phone number" and that I was "the only person who ever texted her about work issues." The former chair was on the witness list, but did not show up for the hearing, thus denying my attorneys the opportunity to question him about these inconsistencies. The department chair at the time the hearings started was also on the witness list but did not attend. She was a key player in my case from the beginning but was never subjected to live cross-examination.

I was able to recruit four people to speak on my behalf. But it is very difficult to garner much support from my colleagues because a) I was banned from the building; b) I was hesitant to contact too many people because I did not want to be accused of trying to intimidate my colleagues; and c) the handwriting was on the wall about my termination, and not many people want to join a losing team. In addition, I did not want to put people in the position of possibly being harassed for supporting me. As an example, my wife was verbally abused in a hallway one day by one of the witnesses, but she chose not to report it to the chairperson because of her role in my termination. My wife left her position at Texas State shortly thereafter.

At the same time, the complainants had easy access to work colleagues and all the time needed to gin up whatever support they could secure. Several former students were willing to testify on my behalf, but all of them worked full-time and lived out of town. I chose not to upend their lives to testify in the fruitless Texas State appeals process, but they did provide supportive statements to our investigator early in the case.

For the most part, this second hearing was primarily focused on painting me as a bully. Because the legal definition of sexual harassment includes "unwanted" comments, language, or touch, the complainants/ university attorneys had to develop a strategy to explain why no one ever said a word about my conduct until they filed charges against me. They decided to make me out to be a bully to explain why the complainants had never mentioned any concerns to me whatsoever.

Much like the first hearing, "witnesses" were allowed to report first, second, or third-hand information that may or may not have had any relevance. Without providing context, most of their reports about me painted me as someone to fear. The most minor and insignificant interactions were now being presented as major conflicts. The building manager testified that I was seen in the building after the initial meeting with the Title IX office and that I had been "banned" from Jowers during that meeting. When shown documentation from my lawyer that I had in fact, not been banned, and was allowed to teach my classes in the building, he had no answer.

This is when I learned that my assertive personality was seen as "leadership" when I was helping people but was recast as "bullying" when I wasn't. For example, the handwritten thank you notes referenced earlier were referring to my assistance to one of the complainants in having her job upgraded from lecturer to clinical professor, a significant upgrade in pay and job security However, within two years this person was now "terrified" of me, although she didn't provide single example or reason for her changing views of our relationship.

There were several inconsistencies in the complainants' respective testimonies. Their stories changed or facts were altered from their original statements. When cross-examined by my attorneys, they claimed not to remember details or became frustrated with being questioned. One complainant perfectly summed up the entire case by saying in an agitated tone, "I don't know what I said; I just know how I feel." Imagine having to defend oneself against shifting facts based on people's feelings.

The complainants told their stories selectively and left out any details that might create questions about their own behavior. One complainant had the habit of wearing black outfits to work and we had a running joke that black was her "uniform." When she didn't wear black, I would comment that she was "out of uniform" or she would come by my office to jokingly show me what she was wearing. However, the story changed when she testified by noting that I would "comment on what she was wearing" with no mention of her role in our dialogue. This complainant had once been comfortable enough with me to tell me that she once dated a guy but "liked chicks more than dicks." This comment was completely voluntary and unsolicited by me. Of course, that comment was never referred to her during her interview with the Title IX investigator or during her testimony.

Another complainant sobbed throughout her testimony and said that she still thought I was "going to have her fired." Her husband is a staff member at the University in an office that has nothing to do with academics and she testified she was concerned I was going to have them both fired. All of this occurred at a hearing where I was being fired. All the complainants returned to the "he was going to have me fired" defense when asked why they never mentioned any concerns to me. However, not a single complainant could identify a single incident where I had hired or fired anyone.

There was one consistent element in their statements: they all agreed that I had never asked any of them for sex, to meet for sex, and so on. In short, I was being fired for "violations of the sexual misconduct policy" when all parties agreed sex was not involved. Imagine sitting in a room for 2 ½ days listening to people who you thought were your life-long friends completely trash you personally and professionally. It was the most disheartening experience of my adult life.

Much like the first hearing, the committee voted 5-0 to support the revocation of my tenure. Absent unexpected intervention from the Board of Regents, my 30-year career at Texas State had ended.

Unwanted Publicity

I went through the cursory process of appealing to the board of regents and as expected, they unanimously supported the decision of the University, and I was formally terminated in February 2020. The good news about the university process being over is that we could return to federal court and file a lawsuit, since Judge Pitman had dismissed our earlier case without prejudice.

As anticipated, the case made local and national news outlets like Inside Higher Education, so my humiliation was no longer contained. I had tried to talk to as many friends as I could in advance to let them know this was coming, but it was impossible to reach out to everyone. Of course, my immediate family had been aware of everything since the beginning of the case, but they were still subjected to seeing someone they loved publicly embarrassed.

I had secured a part-time consulting job with a local healthcare provider, and I was immediately suspended when the news became public. The CEO knew of the situation from the beginning, but the publicity of the case was now creating an issue for him and his leadership team. I was eventually released from that contract in March of 2020. I had never been fired before in my life, but now had been terminated twice in four weeks.

With all that happened, I still feel as if I had to challenge the university's decision. I could have skulked away in silence by resigning and saved myself embarrassment and hundreds of thousands of dollars in legal fees, but that would be a de facto admission of guilt. I just could not walk away, and my friends and family supported my decision without wavering.

Final Legal Steps

My case file was assigned to Magistrate Mark Lane for review. Like judges, magistrates preside over trials, rule on objections, consider the evidence, and make decisions on a case. Despite being a court authority, magistrates are not judges, and therefore cannot sign court orders. At the end of January 2021, we received the magistrate's recommendation to Judge Pitman. The magistrate upheld most of the major claims in my lawsuit and rejected the state's motion to dismiss. Thus it was recommended that the lawsuit be allowed to go forward. It is relatively rare to survive a motion to dismiss by the state, so this recommendation to Judge Pitman was certainly good news. Pitman accepted this recommendation in March 2021.

Once Judge Pitman had denied the motion to dismiss, we reached out to the Attorney General's Office to gauge Texas State's interest in discussing settlement options. We were told "those overtures would be welcomed." Per their request, we developed a "demand letter" which would serve as a starting point for settlement negotiations. After two weeks of silence from Texas State, we were contacted and told the University had "decided not to make a counteroffer." They added, "because we feel that we have provided Dr. Wiley with an extraordinary level of due process," apparently ignoring Judge Pitman's denial of their motion to dismiss and allowing our lack of due process claim to survive. Therefore, there are no ongoing settlement discussions.

The trial was set for a date in 2024, but the deposition of the former university president took place on January 23, 2023. The former president was deposed for almost eight hours and revealed a few interesting facts. In particular, she had no answers as to why three other people who we learned had committed Title IX violations (including one faculty member who committed a sex crime) were still employed by the University. The recorded deposition could have been quite damaging to their case.

Three weeks before the former president's deposition, the State of Texas subpoenaed me, my doctor, and my wife to be deposed. My doctor knew nothing of the case, and I tried my best to keep my wife out of the situation. The only reason they subpoenaed her was to try to embarrass me and scare her. We ultimately decided to drop the case on January 27, 2023, because I refused to put her through that nightmare.

In addition, the State never proposed mediation or offered a settlement. They also made it clear that they would appeal any negative finding from the trial in the Fifth Circuit Court of Appeals, adding hundreds of thousands more dollars to my expenses, as well as another 5-10 years of litigation. When we formally dropped the lawsuit, we were five days short of five years in fighting the University and State of Texas.

Closing

I would not wish this experience on my worst enemy. And even if I were to have survived the allegations and remained in my job, I would have been painted with the scarlet letter of being an accused bully and sexual harasser by my colleagues.

I was fortunate to have the ceaseless support of my family, and, in some respects, they were more outraged than I was. Many people accused of sexual harassment do not enjoy the same familial support that I have and, as a result, end up quietly resigning to avoid embarrassment to the family.

I am very saddened that people who I thought were my friends felt as if filing formal complaints were the only way to address their issues. All any one person had to do was mention their concerns to me and everything would have changed instantly. I was never given a chance to address their concerns and I feel a great sense of loss over losing their friendship and the respect of my colleagues. There is no court that can return friendship and the respect that I spent a lifetime developing and cultivating. The damning comments made during the hearings by people who I thought were my friends have not faded from my memory.

I am also grieving over the way my career ended and the loss of my relationship with Texas State University. I was a loyal employee for 30 years who was very proud to represent the University in any way possible. To have everything cave in around me in a matter of six weeks is still beyond belief, and very sad to think about. I loved the University, my job, and colleagues and to have it end like it did was never in my wildest nightmares. There were so many other ways this situation could have been handled, but I was never given that opportunity.

Dreams from My Father

Nicholas H. Wolfinger,
University of Utah

1

I was a late bloomer, with mediocre grades and few discernible interests when I started graduate school in 1990. It was a less competitive era, and you could squeak by with a comparably weak academic record. I didn't quite know what I wanted to do with my life, but if college is a four-year vacation, grad school might be good for a ten-year vacation. A four-year college degree had taken me six years, so I was already off to a good start. And it was clear that a Ph.D. in sociology would prepare me for a career in higher education, so I'd be spared any further decisions about my future.

I knew little about either scholarship or academia but was familiar with the lifestyle: my late father, Raymond Wolfinger, taught political science at Stanford and UC Berkeley for 45 years. I didn't quite know what he did, but he was home all the time and didn't seem to work very much. He also seemed happy with his job, at least once he moved to Berkeley in 1971.[1] This all looked good to me, so I was sold on academia as a career choice.

As I progressed through graduate school, I was motivated to learn from my dad what a career in academia entailed. He was one of those scholars who'd been anointed, deemed to be smart and relevant by his peers. He taught me that the only thing that mattered was producing quality science, unimpeachable and consequential findings about how the world worked. No theory, no speculation, no bullshit, just rigorous empirical scholarship. Teaching was just something you had to do well enough that you could live with yourself.

This is the understanding I took in 1998 to my assistant professorship at the University of Utah (my graduate vacation turned out to last eight years). My job, I thought, was to do research and teach. I also hoped to have colleagues. This last point was appealing: many of my parents' lifelong friends were my father's fellow assistant professors at Stanford in the early 1960s. So I socialized with my peers, but it wasn't a great fit. They all had young children, while I never had kids. They were all married, while I've spent more time single than any male academic I know.[2] Like all academics, they loved hiking and nature; I do not. It's boring. More broadly, it dawned on me that I was. . . different. This point is easily made: Do you own a potbellied pig? If not, you should get one. They're great pets. I've spent decades doing jiu jitsu, a sport popular among engineers and bench scientists, but not in the social sciences or humanities. And so on.

All of this mitigated against close social relationships with many of my colleagues, while my received understanding of academia would soon cause decades of professional problems. I knew it was better to be on good terms with my colleagues, but I didn't think it was a prerequisite for a good academic career. For this I looked to my experience in grad school: most of my professors, while good scholars, could best be described as bastards.[3] So it was my understanding that you didn't have to be likable to get tenure, only that you had be a good researcher and a minimally competent teacher. And besides, I'm more agreeable than my grad school professors were, and was on pleasant speaking terms with all my colleagues.

Things got better when I helped recruit a new professor to my department. Let's call her Portia. She and I were to become about as close as platonic friends could be. She was my "work wife," especially when we attended conferences together. We jogged together. My then-wife and I socialized with her and her husband. And since Portia and I were about the same age and at the same career stage, she brought to mind all those enduring friendships my parents formed in the early 1960s.

Does this sound like a troubled tenure case in the making? What I failed to understand were the local professional norms. For instance, my department had a culture of publicly fretting about your tenure prospects. I'd witnessed Portia abasing herself in a faculty meeting as she voiced her unfounded fears about a negative tenure decision. Why would she do this?

Why would I do this? I'd published more than any tenure candidate in my department's history, with a book and many articles in well regarded peer-reviewed journals. And my teaching evaluations, while never stellar, were reliably good. That's what I understood the tenure qualifications to be at a research university like mine: produce a lot of good scholarship, with teaching distinctly less important. And so this is how I spoke about the job with my colleagues.

I also questioned the frequency of faculty meetings. Through my decades in academia and my research on higher education, I've learned there's an inverse relationship between the quality of an academic unit and how many meetings it holds. Top faculties don't meet a lot, because most of the time the only reason to meet is to hire and fire people (that is, deciding whether to grant them tenure). It's also understood at good schools that bureaucratic make-work takes people away from their research. In contrast, small state school faculties sometimes meet weekly. I pointed this out to my colleagues, suggesting there was no need to meet to read out loud memos from myriad university offices, or to have a social worker visit to show off her therapy dog (yes, this really happened in my department). All these meetings, I was told, were part of the department's tradition. What's more, I should be glad the department didn't meet weekly on a regular basis, as it had into the early 1980s.

But I hadn't thought any of this mattered too much in the big picture. It was therefore a considerable surprise when I received the seventeen-page, single-spaced evaluation of my tenure bid in 2004, hashed out over an astonishing *nine* meetings between my senior colleagues. My research record was deemed impeccable, but in evaluating my teaching I ran into trouble. My department had a lot of dead wood, faculty who'd gotten tenure and stopped doing research. At one point, I had six colleagues (out of a total faculty of around fifteen) who'd languished at the rank of associate professor for an average of eighteen years. When they stopped doing research, they purported to care more about teaching. Some were indeed award-winning teachers, leaving my department with the best teaching evaluation scores of the whole college. Back in grad school at UCLA, a teaching award was viewed with suspicion, perhaps a sign that you weren't spending enough time on research. Now my colleagues were poised to judge me on the basis of my teaching.

And to judge me on a whole lot more. One of my colleagues obtained my emails via a Freedom of Information Act request, then added them to my file after the official close date, when no new information was to be added. A University of Utah vice president was dragged to two of those nine meetings to consult about the rule violation and decided *factum valet* to keep the emails in my tenure file. Another colleague complained about my inappropriate language (remember this one, as it pops up more than a decade later). Colleagues groused that I had publicly stated that research is more important than teaching—as, by all accounts, it should be at a research university. In other words, my tenure evaluation presumed to judge me about what I *said* about teaching, not whether I was good at it. Finally, the folks reviewing me for tenure had cherry-picked negative comments from my teaching evaluations to impugn my teaching. All of this appeared in that seventeen-page tenure evaluation written by my colleagues.

The report can easily summed up: some of my colleagues just didn't like me very much, and lobbied hard against me. I was to learn later that only three of them were actively opposing me.

My senior colleagues voted six-to-five in favor of tenure, but three-to-six with two abstentions against promotion to the rank of associate professor. This is a virtually unheard of determination in higher education, where tenure and promotion go hand in hand. The presumed intent was to retain me at Utah, but still inflict punishment (promotion to the rank of associate professor generally comes with a decent pay bump).

None of this stuck, as my colleagues' vote was reversed at every stage up the food chain: department chair, dean, college committee, provost, university president. I received tenure and promotion, but at a cost: any disputed tenure-and-promotion case is tremendously time-consuming. At each stage of the process, I had to write a response memo. When your career is on the line, these memos take a lot of time. As of this writing, the University of Utah has inflicted over 50 pages of memos on me.

2

Many positive tenure decisions are unanimous. Some faculty members
are tormented for years about the identity behind a solitary no vote. I had.
. . more than that. Perhaps I could have moved past the tenure ordeal, but
the next decade produced more frustrations. I was offered a tenured
professorship at another university for a much higher salary, and Utah
didn't make a counteroffer (The outside offer had its own problems.) I was
denied promotion to the rank of full professor the first time I sought it. The
department chair who engineered this result was part of the dead wood, a
permanent associate professor who became chair because no one else
would (A year later the university removed him as department chair.[4]) My
dean supported this decision, rejecting me for promotion on the specious
grounds that my file didn't include my H-index (a quantitative measure of
scholarly prominence). No one in my department knew what an H-index
was; I contacted the three faculty members promoted that year in the
College of Social and Behavioral Sciences, and none of them had included
an H-index either.[5] Meanwhile, my salary was frozen below $70,000 for
six years.

Finally in 2014 I was promoted to full professor and given the
commensurate raise. I was now a senior faculty member, and beyond the
reach of my colleagues. Or so I thought.

3

Between 2016 and 2021 I was investigated three times by my
university. Each time I wrote about the experience for a popular audience.[6]

Since I've already recounted my investigations in some detail, I won't
fully recapitulate them here. Instead, I'll touch on the lowlights, and how
they accord with the whole—the whole of my 25 years at the University
of Utah, and faculty investigations as a whole.

My first visit to the star chamber was the product of a Title IX sexual
misconduct case. When this episode started, I figured that the university
had just found an innovative new way to torment me. I had no inkling that
my case was part of a national trend until a friend told me about Laura
Kipnis's accounts of her own investigation.[7]

I remind readers of a couple of details I'd shared about my early years at Utah. Upon arriving in 1998, I socialized with the other assistant professors in my department, most often at the Pie Pizzeria over slices and beers (or Diet Cokes, in my case). One of these colleagues took a dislike to me and was the instigator of both my difficult tenure case and my Title IX case.

The story I always repeat about the Title IX case is the one about the strip club, which is where I proposed to my ex-wife. I had no other answer to give about where my wedding proposal took place, because it indeed occurred at the Crazy Horse in Las Vegas. Yet somehow this was one of the allegations against me in the complaint: that I'd told my accuser that I'd popped the question at a strip club (true) during a lap dance (false). My accuser just didn't think this sounded "very romantic" (which is what she recalled saying in the statement she provided to my Title IX investigator nearly twenty years later).

Adult entertainment was very much on the mind of my accuser. Here's another of the allegations against me, in the words of my Title IX inquisitor:

> Witness One says that on at least one occasion, also in the "early 2000" [sic] Wolfinger requested that [Portia] meet him at his home to collaborate with him on a project. Witness One says that Wolfinger used the desktop computer located in his bedroom/office, and when he turned the computer on to work, pornographic images appeared on the display.

The true part of this allegation is that Portia, a frequent collaborator in those days, and I sometimes worked together at my house. This wasn't particularly strange; Portia and her husband sometimes came over for dinner, or vice versa. But she and I worked in the living room, and I don't have a computer in my bedroom.

The question, of course, is how Witness One knew about the porn on my home computer. It almost sounds like she was part of a ménage à trois with me and Portia that went bad. But I've never slept with any of my colleagues, serially or in parallel, and I suspect she only knew Portia and I sometimes worked at my house because Portia or I told her in passing. The legal name for Witness One's allegation is hearsay, since she wasn't at my purported porn house, but such evidentiary concerns don't matter in Title IX cases. Ultimately this allegation didn't matter, as Portia directly refuted it.

This was also true for what I saw as the most disturbing allegation: a reporter contacted the University of Utah to say I'd been "inappropriate" with her. What reporter? I study marriage and divorce, and have done hundreds of interviews for newspapers, magazines, blogs, TV, podcasts, and radio. What had I said to her? Was it potty mouth? In heavily Mormon Utah, it's easy to offend someone with the d-word, the f-word, or even the s-word (in class I've issued trigger warnings for the most innocuous of content, to forestall complaints and investigations). Was that it, or had I said something truly diabolical? Come to think of it, was she (or he?) even a reporter? Who knows. It's not great for academic freedom when anyone can contact your university to complain about anything, and in doing so cause problems for a faculty member. The University of Utah even lets you do it anonymously, via a web form.[8]

And on the allegations went in this vein. Since I'd long been attuned to trouble from the university, I was instantly cautious when first informed about the complaint against me. I retained a lawyer right away. I refused to come in for a meeting, since I was already out-of-state indefinitely. I demanded to see the allegation in writing, ignoring the protestations of my inquisitor that written allegations weren't part of the process. I never even talked to the Title IX investigator after the initial phone call.

These turned out to be good choices. I later learned that most accused faculty members are invited to open-ended meetings, where they're encouraged to talk freely and thereby handed the rope to hang themselves. As it was, my Torquemada had more than enough data to go on: he interviewed every one of my colleagues. He also tried to interview our grad students, although none of them could be bothered to talk to him. The same holds true for the aggrieved "reporter." It took the investigator four months to do all this, after which he exonerated me of sexual misconduct.

But I wasn't out of the woods. Perhaps I wasn't guilty of sexual misconduct, but the investigator's report went out of its way to depict me as a troublesome colleague. Most of his maledictions had a grain of truth to them but were exaggerated in ways that didn't flatter me. I'd once said "fuck" in a faculty meeting; on another occasion I'd theatrically rested my head on the table for a moment. Here's how the report had it: "When other faculty members wanted to discuss the issue further, he cut the conversation off and yelled "Fuck!" repeatedly, and slammed his head against the table." "To yell" seemed to be the only verb my inquisitor knew when attributing an utterance to me: e.g., "Wolfinger yelled 'I feel vindicated! This is exactly what I've been saying all along!'"

Another theme was the high status I accorded to being an active researcher. Apparently I hadn't learned from my tenure review that I should refrain from articulating this fact. More than one colleague attributed to me statements like this: "[Wolfinger] look[s] down on anyone who he sees as doing more teaching/service and less research." It's indeed true: I'd articulated this as a standard for personnel decisions. Is it so wrong to think that faculty at research universities should do their jobs and conduct research?

If you, reader, are wondering what any of this has to do with strip club wedding proposals, colleagues laboring together in porn houses, and other allegations of sexual misconduct, you're not alone. I protested to my Title IX magistrate, but it was no use.

The other shoe dropped three months later. On the basis of the Title IX report, my new dean informed me that she was initiating her own sanctions, this time for violating university standards of "professionalism." Let's call her Dean Ratched. Her report reprised the fucks, the head-on-the-table incident, and so on. "[H]ostile body language . . . [is] unacceptable in a professional setting," she said. For these transgressions, Dean Ratched informed me that she would be fining me a month's salary—about $5,000 after taxes—and issuing me a formal reprimand. After pleading extenuating circumstances, she agreed to cut the fine in half.

Part of me wanted to pay Ratched her $2,500 and be done with it. After all, I was already out almost $15,000 in attorney bills, so the proposed fine didn't seem like as much money as it otherwise would. But the louder voice in my head wanted to fight back, so I explored how I might contest my dean's dictate. At this point I was used to tussling with my university, and I was offended by both the investigation and the penalty.

Hadn't I just been exonerated of sexual misbehavior? It turns out that Dean Ratched was following a common playbook: the Title IX complaint just opened a door to more arbitrary disciplinary torment. Along with a generation of academics, I learned that "collegiality" and "professionalism" are bits of academic code that let universities punish faculty at will. Indeed, the exact same thing happened to a long-time friend at a university in North Carolina about the same time it was happening to me: she was exonerated of sexual misconduct, then arbitrarily punished for purported lapses of professionalism.

A fine from a dean was outrageous on its own merits. I've never heard of such a thing in higher education. Nor had any of my friends in the professoriate. Having had one of the roughest tenure cases among my academic friends, I wasn't prepared to be the only one fined.

I've been a member of the American Association of University Professors my entire career. One of the things the AAUP has long done was to shine a spotlight on institutions that undermine academic freedom, via its "censured institutions" list. AAUP model guidelines stipulate that academics facing disciplinary action are entitled to a jury of their peers. At Utah, this is known—for reasons that defy both institutional memory and common sense—as the Consolidated Hearing Committee. I duly called the relevant campus administrator to inquire about the possibility of a hearing. She didn't have a clue about how the committee worked, or when it had last been convened (or, I guess, consolidated). Nonetheless, I declared my intention to have a hearing.

At this point the vice president for faculty, who outranked my dean in the academic food chain, recognized that fining me thousands of dollars for "hostile body language" was nuts, and made the whole thing go away. I agreed to de jure half-time status, which was fine by me as I was already on de facto half-time status (mostly on the basis of grant money).

Like Richard Nixon in 1960, my dean had lost the battle but not the war. She disappeared, also like Nixon, into several years of quiescence, at least as far as I was concerned. I imagine she wasn't happy when my accounts of the two investigations appeared in *Quillette* later that year. The *Wall Street Journal* helped to rub it in a little more when it reprinted part of my second *Quillette* article, and the world learned that the University of Utah was the kind of place that tried to fine faculty thousands of dollars for their body language.[9] And I myself gave the knife another twist when I published a guest editorial in a local paper making the point that frivolous investigations like mine were an insult to students and faculty who'd actually been sexually assaulted or subjected to sexual harassment.[10]

By this point I'd learned that I wasn't unique, that an untold number of faculty members across the country had been subjected to investigations like mine. I started volunteering for Families Advocating for Campus Equality, a nonprofit that provides peer counseling for students and faculty falsely accused of sexual misconduct, and lobbies for better policies at the state and federal level. I became FACE's faculty coordinator, the person who talked to all the faculty who reached out to us. Twice I provided commentary at federal Department of Education open hearings on proposed revisions to guidelines on how universities should adjudicate allegations of sexual misconduct.[11]

To its credit, my university never responded to the five or so articles I'd written about my first two investigations. I'm not surprised at this, as objecting to a piece of written work cuts to the core of academic freedom. Yet it happens, as scholars like Laura Kipnis can attest to (her Title IX investigation resulted from an article she wrote).[12]

4

A twice-investigated professor with decades of conflict with his university. The year 2020, with its surging ideological passions and lockdown-inspired flurry of social media activity. What could go wrong? Viewed in these terms, my third and last investigation seemed inevitable. And it started the way trouble often started in 2020, with a tweet.

As with my first two trips to the star chamber, I've published a detailed account of how my third and last investigation unfolded. Here are the basics. What distinguished this go-around were the new lows in institutional bad faith.

I'd disparaged an article whose authors happened to be women. In response, someone said that I was more or less a sexual predator. This someone turned out to be a masters student in another department at my university. I took the bait, tweeting about my research on gender equity in higher education, research that's produced real changes in how universities treat their female faculty. I then suggested that students shouldn't speak of their professors in the way this masters student had: "Finally, NAME, here's some free ex cathedra advice: you should avoid publicly antagonizing the tenured faculty at your own institution, or elsewhere." Twitter somehow construed this as me threatening her, and I was mobbed. Faculty from around the world demanded that I be punished for "punching down," with some announcing their intention to alert my university about the monster in its midst. It was disheartening to see that one of these people was a younger departmental colleague, with whom I'd previously had a good relationship. None of these people stopped to think exactly how I might make good on my "threat" to a student in another department.

Two days later I received an email signed by both my department chair and Dean Ratched (i.e., the scourge of hostile body language). Replete with passive voice—"have been interpreted as threatening a student with retaliation"—I was informed that I had misbehaved. Without admitting to anything, I promised to do better. In a normal world, that would have been the end of it. Certainly I wasn't given any indication at the time that matters hadn't been resolved.

Based on the history I've described, I should have known better. The very same day I posted my tweet, Dean Ratched had sent the "threatened" student this email:

> I have just been made aware that you were the subject of a threatening exchange on twitter with Nick Wolfinger. I wanted to check in with you to make sure that you are OK and also let you know that I am happy to talk with you over the weekend or next week (your choice) about this matter. My cell # is 801-XXX-XXX and I'm happy to talk at any time.

I'm the one who'd been mobbed, with scores of people threatening my career, but subsequent emails indeed confirmed that the student was OK, albeit "stressed" over her upcoming exams. I suppose I could be reassured that Dean Ratched was concerned with at least one of her charges.

Two months later, a formal complaint arrived. Once more I was to be reprimanded for my "unprofessionalism." Termination would follow if I didn't straighten up and fly right. As before, I instantly secured an attorney. Last time I'd gone with a local recommended by a lawyer friend; this time I retained out-of-state counsel who specialized in higher education cases, Samantha Harris. She and I had become acquainted through my Title IX advocacy. It was immaterial that she wasn't a member of the Utah bar, since she would be representing me in a university hearing. I was finally to learn how the Consolidated Hearing Committee worked.

Samantha and I began by poring over the relevant university documentation. One of the things we learned is that the rules stipulate informal mediation. Dean Ratched had skipped over this part. When I protested, the vice president for faculty proposed to mediate. Unfortunately, it wasn't the same VP who had saved my bacon back in 2017. I had two Zooms with the new VP, where I proposed several specific suggestions for reconciliation and restitution. The VP made no counteroffers, and most of the second Zoom was taken up by the allegation that I'd appeared intoxicated on this and other remote meetings. This was preposterous, as I haven't had drink or drug since I was a teenager (I have other vices.)

Sometime after the second Zoom, I was informed that informal mediation had failed. What's more, the VP for Faculty, who had presented herself as a neutral arbiter, had added her name to the complaint against me. I was headed for the Consolidated Hearing Committee, apparently being convened for the first time in living memory.

The CHC rules, once the university finally figured out what they were, turned out to be advantageous to me. Aside from a carefully rehearsed three-minute opening statement, my attorney could do all the talking on my behalf. This was especially beneficial given that Dean Ratched's strategy was to lure me into an intemperate outburst in order to confirm to the jury of my peers what a bad colleague I was. And the hearing went on for over three hours, demonstrating something I already knew: for faculty investigations, the process is part of the punishment. Ratched spent a lot of time talking about all the harm I'd done, all the dishonor I'd brought to the good name of the University of Utah, and so on. The colleague who denounced me on Twitter appeared as a witness, where he idly speculated that my presence on the faculty had reduced the number of applicants for an open faculty position in our department. Dean Ratched upped the ante, claiming that my tweet had reduced graduate student and faculty applications to the university. Ratched also denounced me for "chilling" student speech.

Ponder that one for a moment. Because of an intemperate tweet, I spent $10,000 more on counsel, had a hearing that lasted over three hours, and eventually received an official reprimand. Just whose speech was being chilled?

In the end, the Consolidated Hearing Committee failed to deliver a consolidated verdict on my case, instead deciding to reprimand me by a split vote. The official report made no mention of a threatening tweet, instead deciding I had failed to be collegial. It's in the spirit of the book you're reading that I was accused of one thing and then "convicted" of something else.

Even as the Committee was reprimanding me, it didn't hold back about what it saw to be Dean Ratched's true motivation:

> During the hearing, the complainants indicated that their goals were to change behavior and have Dr. Wolfinger take responsibility for his actions; however, their apparent unwillingness to negotiate toward informal resolution suggest that their true objective is to set the stage for termination rather than seek to change Dr. Wolfinger's behavior.

That was in 2021. Four years later, I remain a tenured faculty member at the University of Utah. And those four years offer some perspective: my case began in 2020, during COVID, just after the murder of George Floyd, in a moment of madness in which twitter mobs, investigations, cancellations, and firings seemed ubiquitous. Sitting at home, Dean Ratched and her collaborators had time on their hands to work up a case against me. It must have been a welcome respite from wiping down their groceries and bleaching their mail. Would this investigation have happened today? Given my history with the university, the answer may well be yes, but another faculty member might have been shown greater leniency.

Finally, it's worth considering the position of the student I purportedly threatened. Assume she really was intimidated by my tweet, even though she gave no indication of such a reaction in her email response to Dean Ratched. If we accept this premise, is a $10,000 legal bill, a three-hour hearing, and an official reprimand really a commensurate punishment? Perhaps a more fitting response would have been an informal meeting and an apology.

5

Things have been quiet for the past four years. I have a new chair and a new dean, neither of whom has shown any inclination to cause trouble for me. And for over a decade, I've lived out of state and commuted to teach. It turns out that living out of state is a great way to avoid your colleagues. Three years ago, I took a couple of new professors out to lunch; otherwise, I haven't been in a room with one of my colleagues for five years. My mother once told me that people become academics because they want to be left alone, and she wasn't wrong.

My only contact with my new dean was exceedingly propitious: ten years ago, long before she came to the University of Utah, I'd autographed her copy of my 2013 book on gender equity in higher education. It would be hard to think of another small thing that would leave a dean better predisposed to, um, not investigate you. As for my new department chair, it helps that she lived through the Cultural Revolution in her native China. This experience has left her unusually suspicious of moral panics and persecutions.

Several years after campus discipline, I continue to uphold my father's legacy by spending most of my time sitting around the house. Like dad, I'm free to conduct rigorous empirical research on things that interest me. I'll continue to do so until I get tired of commuting to work. Maybe I'll never have to see my colleagues again?

Including Portia. She was department chair during my three investigations, and our friendship didn't survive them. By the third investigation, the one over the tweet, she was one of the complainants, participating in the marathon Zoom hearing. I'm pretty sure my father, who died in 2015, couldn't have made sense of, let alone foreseen, any part of that.

6

It is a privilege to be editing this volume and contributing a chapter to it. For all its faults, academia is the only profession that allows its members to publicly criticize their employers with virtual impunity. This is part and parcel of the rightful objective of the social sciences, which is to make sense of the world human beings have created. It's what I've done in my scholarship, relying primarily on national data to better understand trends in sex, marriage, and divorce, and how these basic human activities interact with larger social institutions. This book seeks to shine a spotlight on how universities have failed both their faculty members and their broader mission through their arbitrary and capricious imposition of kangaroo courts and harsh justice.

The experiences of my fellow authors, many of whom suffered far more than I have at the hands of their institutions, strike at the heart at the academic ideal of open inquiry. I can imagine our best and our brightest forsaking academia as a career choice if they anticipate only star chambers and intellectual blinkers. What kind of universities will we have when our faculty can't speak, write, or teach the truth? Who would want to work at universities like that?

Let's not find out.

Endnotes

[1] Dad hadn't been happy at Stanford. My parents talked about Stanford political scientist Heinz Eulau the way other people's parents talk about Hitler. Post-Eulau, my dad's job satisfaction was normal for academia: the vast majority of professors are happy with their jobs. For recent data, Cengage Group. "Faculty Satisfaction up 31% as Many Embrace the 'New Normal' in Higher Education." September 28, 2023. Available at https://www.cengagegroup. com/news/press-releases/2023/cengage-second-faces-of-faculty-report/#:~: text=Faculty%20report%20high%20levels%20of,down%20from%2026%2 5%20in%202022 (accessed April 21, 24).

[2] This is a question of professional expertise, given a line of research on gender equity in higher education that culminated in my 2013 book, *Do Babies Matter? Gender and Family in the Ivory Tower*. Unmarried male academics are very few and far in between; this is far less the case for women.

[3] I'll make an exception for my dissertation advisor, the statistician William M. Mason.

[4] My chair had spent the department into six figures of internal debt. How is this even possible in academia? The guy gave graduate students fellowships even though the university hadn't allocated the money to the department.

[5] My current H-index is 31, meaning that I have 31 publications that have each been cited at least 31 times. And if you think this is a good way of evaluating academic research, I have some prime lunar real estate you may wish to purchase.

[6] Investigation #1. "How I Survived the Title IX Star Chamber." *Quillette*, August 24, 2017. Available at https://quillette.com/2017/08/24/survived-title-ix-star-chamber/ (accessed March 7, 2024); Investigation #2. "Pursuit of Injustice: Further Adventures Under Title IX." *Quillette*, November 17, 2017. Available at https://quillette.com/2017/11/17/pursuit-injustice-adventures-title-ix/ (accessed March 7, 2024); Investigation #3. "The New Dirty War Against Faculty." Arc Digital, November 1, 2021. Available at https://www.arcdigital.media/p/the-new-dirty-war-against-faculty (accessed March 7, 2024).

[7] Kipnis, Laura. "My Title IX Inquisition." *Chronicle of Higher Education*, May 29, 2015. Available at https://laurakipnis.com/wp-content/uploads/2010/08/My-Title-IX-Inquisition-The-Chronicle-Review-.pdf (accessed March 7, 2024); Kipnis, Laura. *Unwanted Advances: Sexual Paranoia Comes to Campus*. Verso Books, 2018.

[8] If you, dear reader, take umbrage at something in this chapter, you can file a complaint against me at https://utah-advocate.symplicity.com/public_report/index.php/ (accessed November 13, 2024). This webpage relies on pull-down menus, so you won't have to work too hard.

[9] Wolfinger, Nicholas H. "Notable & Quotable: Adventures in Title IX." *Wall Street Journal*, November 24, 2017. Available at https://www.wsj.com/articles/notable-quotable-adventures-in-title-ix-1511559938 (accessed March 2, 2024).

[10] Nicholas H. Wolfinger. "Op-ed: Frivolous Title IX Investigations Are an Insult to Real Sexual Assault Victims." *The Deseret News*, October 24, 2017. Available at https://www.deseret.com/2017/10/14/20621493/op-ed-frivolous-title-ix-investigations-are-an-insult-to-real-sexual-assault-victims/ (accessed March 2, 2024).

[11] The second time occurred via Zoom during the pandemic. My three-minute remarks can be viewed here: https://www.youtube.com/watch?v=tnjCZkgjXWg (accessed March 2, 2024).

[12] Kipnis 2015.

Race
and
Ethnicity

Weaponizing the Academic Bureaucracy

Lee Jussim and Nathan Honeycutt

Rutgers University

6/14/24

American universities have ostensibly robust protections for academic freedom. Free speech is supposedly protected by the First Amendment at public institutions. Nevertheless, academic bureaucracies have increasingly been enlisted to silence academics speaking out on a variety of controversies, as well as those who offend the sensibilities of special interest groups. Academics have been punished for advocating students take personal responsibility for their Halloween costumes, criticizing the notion of micro-aggressions, and arguing that sex is biological.[1] Indeed, the president of The Foundation for Individual Rights and Expression (FIRE) has reported that, since 2014, more faculty have been fired for what was supposedly protected expression than during the McCarthy era.[2] The weaponization of academic bureaucracies to silence expression goes well beyond a handful of infamous cases.

In this essay, we describe two encounters with academic discipline we've had, neither of which would ever have been disclosed had the editor of this volume not invited us to share them. We can only wonder how many more stories like these there are out there.

Part I: White Women White Womening

Lee Jussim

Back in 2019, someone I regularly interact with on Twitter, a blogger named Gretchen Mullen (@SkepticReview1989), posted a tweet that deplored the impulse to coddle working women (indeed, a recent meta-analysis shows that since 2009 there has been more job discrimination against men than against women, so Gretchen's assertion had some merit).[3]

This was retweeted by someone named Abeba Birhane, whose Twitter profile states that she now works for Mozilla and is an adjunct professor at Trinity College Dublin. Back in 2019, she was either a grad student or postdoc somewhere in Ireland. Her commentary when retweeting Gretchen was this:

"White woman white womening in action."

I then referred to Birhane's (misspelled here as Burhane) tweet as a "racist sneer:"

Birhane then took to Twitter accusing me of "harassing" her, and denounced me as a "real danger" to women of color, diversity, and so on:

These tweets unleashed a Twitter mob, my first experience with such a thing. Hundreds, maybe thousands of people were denouncing me and calling for my head. These next tweets are just a small sample of the endless accusations, denunciations, and attempts to report me to Rutgers.

Nathan Oseroff-Spicer
@nathanoseroff

Solidarity with @Abebab—as someone that has
experienced being targeted for harassment by tenured
old white regressive men in academia, it's a horrible
experience. You feel very alone, and it feels like the
entire institutional structure is against you.

Jim Thompson @jimthommo · Jul 22   ⌄
If anyone needs a case study of punching down, the example provided by
@PsychRabble has been textbook

> 🐸 **Abeba Birhane** @Abebab · Jul 21
> These are not trolls you disagree with, block and move on. These are the
> people who gate-keep and make academia a hostile place for
> underrepresented people. These are powerful people that need to be
> exposed for their bigotry.
> Show this thread

  💬 2   ⇄ 4   ♡ 17   ⬆

Then there was the gaslighting. *Before* accusing me of harassing her,
Birhane seemed to seek out a discussion (see the Birhane tweet below that
begins "What exactly do you want from me?"). I replied, "an apology for
the racist "White women white womening tweet."" Shown below is Lisa
DeBruine, a psychology professor at University of Glasgow, who then
accused me of harassing and bullying Birhane, and of being an online troll.

Perhaps these wild accusations make sense upon learning that
Professor DeBruine, a neuroscientist, received a graduate certificate in
women's studies from the University of Michigan. Women's studies
programs often teach an ideology that reduces interactions to identity
characteristics and Manichean power relations.

The mind-boggling thing here is that for any of these denunciatory tweets to be at all coherent they require believing that referring to @SkepticReview89 as a "white woman white womaning" is just fine and dandy but calling "white women white womening" a racist slur constitutes harassment.

But then it escalated beyond a mere mobbing on Twitter. People started calling on Rutgers to investigate me for this incident. Here are two examples.

Dr. T 🎗️ 🏳️
@SciSwany
...

Hey Abeba, I'd like to bring @AlertStem and #STEMTrollAlert to your attention! They're a band of male allies that will pop in and take out the trash for you!

@RutgersU, looks like you've got some trash to take out yourselves.

3:36 PM · Jul 21, 2019

Christopher Jackson @seis_matters · 3h

Yep. @bat_go and I contacted Rutgers about his conduct. Sorry you've been put through this.

Q 2   ↻   ♡ 3   ⬆

Dr Bat
@bat_go

Replying to @seis_matters @PsychRabble and 5 others

Yeah sent an email to the dean - never got any answer

5:07 PM · Jul 23, 2019 · Twitter for iPhone

In the "Andrew & Sabina" (@PsychScientists) and "Dr. T" (@scisSwany) tweets above, they contacted Rutgers by including @RutgersU in their tweets. This was probably little more than moral grandstanding and virtue-signaling because most academics know that tweeting to a university is not likely to produce a response. Jackson and "Dr. Bat" (@bat_go), however, reported having contacted Rutgers directly. In the Andrew and Sabina sub-tweet, Abeba Birhane (@Abebab) has simply lied about me. To this day, I have never seen a tweet—or any other media—from Birhane claiming that "academia is biased against black women." She may have posted such tweets, but I did not see them, reply to them, or comment on them. I was mobbed simply because I referred to "White women white womening" as a racist sneer. There is no sane universe in which accusing a nonacademic (@Skepticreview89) of "White women white womening" means "saying that academia is biased against black women."

Many people denounced me on Twitter and called for my head. Some claimed to have contacted my dean. It was my first time experiencing such an online attack. One of the rules that I later learned for coping with Twitter mobs was to document everything, for use later in either defense or counterattack. But at the time these things didn't occur to me. I was naive to how online mobs worked. I wasn't aware of the twisted nature of some people on the far left, especially but not exclusively academics. I didn't know that they seemed to actually believe in the oppressor/oppressed binary, that sexist and racist insults are fine as long as they are directed at the "oppressors" —but that publicly calling them racist and sexist insults constituted "harassment," "bullying" and "trolling." In retrospect, I wish I had saved more of the hostile tweets directed at me. There were a lot of them.

Everything I've described so far is consistent with broader sociopolitical developments. Innovative psychological research has documented that there are White far-left extremists who endorse Hitler's rhetoric if applied to White people rather than Jews.[4] The twitter posts presented thus far show how vile statements about White people are acceptable to some on the far left, perhaps because Whites are seen as oppressors. But pointing out that vile rhetoric is, indeed, vile, will itself be interpreted as oppression if its source is a Black person.

The complaints about me to Rutgers registered with my deans. At the time, I was chair of the Psychology Department. A few days into my mobbing, the associate dean for the Social and Behavioral Sciences contacted me for a meeting. After some regular business, he brought up the complaints from the Twitter mob. After first assuring me that neither he nor anyone in the dean's office saw anything racist in my posts, he said that the Rutgers administration really preferred not to be drawn into these sorts of controversies. Then he went a step further and said—and here I paraphrase—"You can post anything you like as a professor. Academic freedom protects that. It means that no one will come for your job. However, academic freedom does not mean that the Dean must keep you on as Chair. Also, do you really want or need to court this type of public controversy?"

The "does not need to keep you on as Chair" comment was an obvious threat. I began to get angry about it, and I almost pushed back. What stopped me was the Associate Dean's final question. He made a good point. I really did not need the nonsense and was not accomplishing anything worthwhile by engaging with toxic academics on social media. In hindsight, I realize I had two blind spots that had created a vulnerability to these types of attacks: 1. I did not at first really understand that these individuals actually believed their own rhetoric (or, if they didn't believe it, they did such a good job at pretending to do so that there was no practical difference); and 2. I had labored under the misimpression that reasoned dialog and facts could bridge most differences. I am no longer that naïve.

Returning to the conversation with my associate dean, I concluded that I did not need the Sturm und Drang of Twitter wars, and agreed to avoid these types of confrontations in the future. That settled things down with the Deans, and I completed my term as Chair without further incidents involving social media controversies.

Where are They Now?

My denouncers have had an interesting array of experiences after the mobbing. Abeba Birhane has proven herself to be a serial mob instigator.[5] Petra Boynton is the author of a book titled *Being Well in Academia: Ways to Feel Stronger, Safer and More Connected.* Andrew & Sabina fled Twitter after Elon Musk bought it. Lisa DeBruine is prominent in the movement to improve the methods and practices of psychological scientists—presumably because making claims that are actually true is important. Jim Thompson is a full professor at George Mason University; he occasionally publishes some neuroscience. He hasn't tweeted much since October, 2023, but reported being very disappointed that the Australian people (in a landslide) rejected an amendment to have indigenous peoples have special representation in parliament. SciSwany (who is anonymous) has protected her tweets, meaning only people she approves can see them. Christopher Jackson (@seis_matters) is a prominent geologist in the United Kingdom, but his account is no longer on X (formerly Twitter).

Epilogue

It wasn't an easy way to learn how to deal with social media mobs, and I'm a slow learner, but learn I did. White Women White Womening was my first exposure to toxic academics seeking to impose their "values" through public shaming and punishment. But it was not my last. I had learned how to fend off online mobs, and how to come through with my professional life *actually improved by the experience.* What's more, I turned the experience into a productive area of scholarship on academic illiberalism, authoritarianism, and endorsement of censorship.[6] Being mobbed wasn't fun. Still, coming through it has improved my life in ways

I would never have dreamed. As Winston Churchill once said, *There is nothing quite as exhilarating as to be shot at with no effect.*

Some might find it hard to believe how good life can be after being mobbed, but it's true if you play your cards right, I say this not to brag, but for the benefit of others who might otherwise be intimidated into silence by social media mobs. Here is the short version of what happened to me: I was subject to a second mob in 2022, instigated by different people but with the same ideological components.[7] In the aftermath of this attack, my work was reported by the *New York Times* and the *Washington Post* and my collaborators on one paper published a *Wall Street Journal* op ed about it —that is, rather than being ostracized, my work has gotten more public attention after these attacks than it ever had previously. This attack and others like it inspired two forthcoming edited books. *The Free Inquiry Papers* is on academic freedom and free speech; the other, titled *The Poisoning of the American Mind* is on the prevalence of delusional and toxic beliefs and attitudes on the political left and political right in the U.S. The first publication listed in footnote 7 appeared in *The Proceedings of the National Academy of Sciences,* one of the most influential, widely-read, and prestigious outlets, not just for psychology but for all of academia. I have also published three papers based on large-scale collaborations since 2023, which means that, to the extent that the mob had intended to banish me from academia, it failed. And, most deliciously, the same associate dean who threatened to remove me as chair for the White Women White Womening episode invited me to be chair of another department. This department was having difficulties electing a chair acceptable to the dean, so it was facing the appointment of an outside chair (in the academic world, this means your department is going into receivership.) This is an inherently fraught situation, so my consideration as outside chair was a huge vote of confidence in me. When he offered the job, my dean said something like, "We know you have tough skin and could handle difficulties graciously." The appointment came with the largest raise I have ever received, and the first thing I did with it was take a trip to France with my wife.

Part II: Wrestling With the IRB

Nathan Honeycutt and Lee Jussim

In the White Women White Womening mobbing, it was the dean's office that sought to silence Lee, through a threat of punishment. In a second series of incidents, the Rutgers Institutional Review Board (IRB; sometimes also called the human subjects committee) was weaponized. From 2016-2022, when Nathan was Lee's graduate student, we collaborated on many projects, including some surveys of university faculty. This work was connected to Lee's Twitter mobbing, because it addressed manifestations of political bias and the radicalization of higher education faculty (this was also the subject of Nathan's dissertation). Some of our questionnaires included measures on campus climate. Others included measures of left-wing authoritarianism.

In most survey research conducted by psychologists, participants are given a general sense of what the study is about. The descriptions are often broad and vague, to avoid biasing the survey responses. That said, it isn't always possible to disguise a study's purpose. That we were studying aspects of campus climate, or of the far left and its dysfunctions, may have been apparent to some survey respondents.

In 2022 on three separate occasions, we were subjected to audits initiated by the Rutgers Institutional Review Board. This involved an outside investigator appointed by the Rutgers IRB, who was charged with performing a for-cause review of our research. As we understand it, "for-cause" means the IRB received at least one complaint about the study. We were told the audits entailed reviewing study processes and their administration to provide appropriate study oversight, as well as looking to see if any ethics violations occurred.

This may all sound technical and bureaucratic to non-academics, so here is a brief explanation of what the IRB is supposed to do. All colleges and universities that have faculty conducting research on human or animal subjects have an IRB. Typically, an IRB is a committee made up of seasoned scholars. The committee is charged with reviewing all proposals for research involving human or animal subjects to ensure that research is conducted in an ethical manner, in accordance with voluminously documented policies and procedures, and in a way that minimizes harm to participants. "Ethical" means things like not mistreating participants and obtaining their consent to participate. At larger institutions like Rutgers, IRBs have paid staff that assist in reviewing submissions and ensuring compliance with IRB protocols.

Back to the audits of our studies. For the first audit, we were caught by surprise—neither of us had experienced, let alone even knew, that IRBs ever retained outside investigators to conduct reviews. We complied with the audit, even though the IRB largely kept us in the dark about the precise nature of the complaint(s) lodged against us. We knew we had nothing to hide because everything in our studies was done completely by the book.

Upon notification of a second audit, concerning a completely different study, warning bells went off. And when we learned of the third audit of yet another one of our studies, alarm bells rang loud. How, for the first time in both of our careers, over the course of only a few months, could three separate research projects we were conducting be subjected to audits? Was the IRB grossly incompetent, or were they potentially complicit in targeting us, using frivolous complaints as a means of impugning our research?

It sure seemed like someone had weaponized the Rutgers IRB against us. Of course, we can't know this for certain. But if one knows about how IRBs often work at large universities, we can certainly make a strong case.

What does it mean to weaponize an IRB? Our IRB, we came to find out, received some bizarre complaints about the scientific validity of our survey designs, and about our survey questions being "biased" or "offensive" or being used to "draw conclusions or to support a political agenda." All complaints and allegations were anonymous to us—the complaints were either submitted anonymously to the IRB, or the IRB masked the complainants' identities. Furthermore, we were never told which questions in our surveys were supposedly biased or offensive.

At Rutgers, formal complaints such as these always trigger a full investigation. Although we never saw the rule mandating such investigations in writing, we were repeatedly assured by the Rutgers IRB Chair that such a rule indeed existed. But that's not the point. Rather, the rule is ridiculous. Some complaints should be dismissed out of hand, with no investigation because even if they are true, they constitute no ethical violation.

More importantly, researchers have every right to ask biased questions. For example, some of the most trusted and widely used measures of political extremism are, in some sense, inherently "biased" because they're designed to measure extremist beliefs. The social sciences are filled with questionnaires assessing people's endorsement of conspiracy theories, derogatory views of various social groups, and political violence. Furthermore, even "biased" or "offensive" questions violate no known standard for the ethical conduct of research. No participant was ever coerced into answering any question; if they found anything offensive, they were free to move on or not complete the questionn·ˈe—which of course had already been approved by the IRB.

All study participants are provided with a form asking for their consent to complete questionnaires. Academics are not permitted to field surveys without first soliciting respondent consent. Obviously, because the Rutgers IRB had approved the study, our *questionnaire been had already deemed ethical.* Complaints about it should have been simply ignored.

For each of the three different audits, the outside investigator required us to produce documentation for *everything.* Specifically, we first had to provide all materials, including research protocol documents, informed consent forms, recruitment materials, survey instruments and questionnaires, and anything else used in our data analysis. For some materials, explainer documents also had to be generated. Then we had to provide access to any data we had collected. Next, we had to produce records of all communications with the IRB, including IRB approval documents, all IRB study modification approvals, and all emails received from, or sent to, the IRB. Following, we had to produce records of all communications with participants. This included emails we sent to participants to solicit their participation in the studies, emails sending gift cards in exchange for their participation (where applicable), and any email we received back from a participant. This included, but wasn't limited to, emails critiquing the study, emails where participants just wanted to say they found the study interesting, or emails where participants inquired about the findings of the study. Finally, we had to submit administrative documents, including records of Human Subjects Certifications, CVs (i.e., our academic resumes), delegation of authority logs (details of our responsibilities and length of time on the studies), and post-approval monitoring self-assessments. All said and done, across the three audits, this resulted in over 3,300 pages of documentation and records.

In addition to generating reams of documentation, many phone calls ensued. Over five hours of meetings to discuss the work and review some of the documents took place. All in all, the audits—which started in February 2022 and concluded in July 2022—comprised hours upon hours of mind-numbing effort for no constructive purpose that we could ascertain. By the time the second audit started, it felt like a witch-hunt, though not a witch-hunt initiated by the auditor—the auditor was always cordial and was simply complying with a mandate from the Rutgers IRB. Was the IRB using the audits to dig around for an excuse to nail us to the wall? Or was the IRB bureaucracy simply following its internal rules? It hardly mattered. The upshot was the same: a horrendous and unnecessary waste of our time and effort.

The outcome of all this time, work, and effort was zilch: all three "investigations" turned up nothing. Each time, the auditor reported that, "there were no regulatory findings discovered during this review, as the study followed the approved protocol." After six months of being under a microscope we were finally done, or so we thought.

Despite the clean bills of health from the auditor for all three of the audited projects, the Rutgers IRB was still not satisfied. For one project, the IRB initiated a review to evaluate the validity of the study design and the methodology of the study. And for all three audited projects, the IRB changed the review classifications from "exempt" to "expedited" to formalize mandated annual IRB reviews and thus perpetual oversight— thereby creating additional administrative work for us. Despite our repeated requests, the IRB refused to provide any justification for these penalties. Granted, the penalties were minor. But given that the three audits unilaterally vindicated us, there should have been absolutely no penalties levied, and we should have received an apology. But the IRB at Rutgers is granted wide latitude to regulate research, and faculty subjected to its capricious rulings have no recourse but to appeal to some higher authority at the university (such as a provost or president, which we did not do because we expected that to be another waste of time and effort).

Looking at the big picture of what we experienced, it was bizarre that there is seemingly no mechanism in our IRB to dismiss frivolous complaints out of hand. Instead, there was a serious consideration of whether we were guilty, though guilty of what is to this day unclear. Perhaps guilty of conducting research that some participants didn't like? Such a dynamic permits malevolent actors who know how this system works to game it in order to cause consequential problems. If we had not kept meticulous records, even if we had done nothing wrong, our projects might have been shut down on a technicality.

From the standpoint of the malevolent actor(s) filing the complaints, it was worth taking a shot at us because there was nothing to lose. There is no system for punishing people for completely spurious complaints. Our research projects were at risk, not to mention our standing with the IRB for conducting human subjects research in the future. An inability to conduct research would have jeopardized Nathan's ability to complete his Ph.D.

This didn't happen, but the costs to us were still substantial. The time and productivity burden each of the audits created meant that countless hours were lost that could have been put toward other research projects, getting papers published in academic journals to enhance Nathan's CV in preparation for the academic job market, or literally anything else. Plus half a year's worth of unease fretting over the potential consequences to our scholarly research—the lifeblood of success in academia.

The Rutgers IRB is, from what we have heard, not necessarily more intrusive than other IRBs. We have heard other stories like ours from our colleagues. The original mandate for IRBs was to ensure ethical treatment of research subjects. This mandate is appropriate and justified: researchers should not be allowed to do harmful or risky things to participants without their consent. But, with rare exceptions, for the type of social science research we conduct—which mainly involves asking questions in online surveys—it is nearly impossible to cause any harm greater than annoyance (a poorly worded or offensive question can indeed be annoying). When an IRB exceeds this mandate, it is, in our view, a clear violation of academic freedom. But until some sort of intervention is conducted to rein in runaway IRBs, nothing is likely to change anytime soon. Indeed, we suspect things will get worse.

Conclusion

There are some simple solutions to the type of bureaucracy weaponization described here:

1. Faculty expression as private citizens, whether in op-eds or social media, should be beyond the jurisdiction of academic bureaucracies.

2. IRBs need an "off ramp," a system for summarily dismissing frivolous complaints, without burdening the researchers with "investigations."

This is not hard, or, at least, it need not be.

---

[1] Hooven, Carole K. "Academic Freedom Is Social Justice: Sex, Gender, and Cancel Culture on Campus." *Archives of Sexual Behavior* 52, no. 1 (2022): 35–41; LaChance, Mike. "Prof's Lawsuit Alleges He Was Fired for Calling Handout on Microaggressions 'Garbage.'" Legal Insurrection, April 18, 2020. Available at https://legalinsurrection.com/2020/04/profs-lawsuit-alleges-he-was-fired-for-calling-handout-on-microaggressions-garbage/ (accessed November 15, 2024); Morey, Alex. "One Year Later, Erika Christakis Breaks Her Silence on Yale Halloween Controversy." FIRE, October 28, 2016. Available at https://www.thefire.org/news/one-year-later-erika-christakis-breaks-her-silence-yale-halloween-controversy (accessed November 15, 2024).

[2] Lukianoff, Greg. "The New Red Scare Taking over America's College Campuses." *Washington Examiner*, September 25, 2023. Available at https://www.thefire.org/news/new-red-scare-taking-over-americas-college-campuses (accessed November 15, 2023).

[3] Schaerer, Michael, Christilene Du Plessis, My Hoang Bao Nguyen, Robbie C. M. Van Aert, Leo Tiokhin, Daniël Lakens, Elena Giulia Clemente, et al. "On the Trajectory of Discrimination: A Meta-Analysis and Forecasting Survey Capturing 44 Years of Field Experiments on Gender and Hiring Decisions." *Organizational Behavior and Human Decision Processes* 179 (2023): 104280.

[4] Jussim, Lee. "Who Agrees with Hitler?" Unsafe Science, edited by Michael Bernstein and April Bleske-Rechek, April 16, 2023. Available at

https://unsafescience.substack.com/p/who-agrees-with-hitler   (accessed November 15, 2024).

[5] Inbar, Yoel and Michael Inzlicht. "Facing a Social Media Mob (with Stefan Uddenberg)." Two Psychologists, Four Beers Podcast, August 24, 2022. Available at https://www.fourbeers.com/93 (accessed November 15, 2023).

[6] Clark, Cory J., Lee Jussim, Komi Frey, Sean T. Stevens, Musa al-Gharbi, Karl Aquino, J. Michael Bailey, et al. "Prosocial Motives Underlie Scientific Censorship by Scientists: A Perspective and Research Agenda." *Proceedings of the National Academy of Sciences* 120, no. 48 (2023): e2301642120; Jussim, Lee, Nathan Honeycutt, Akeela Careem, Nathan Bork, Danica Finkelstein, Sonia Yanovsky, and Joel Finkelstein. "The New Book Burners." In press. To appear in J. Forgas (ed.), *The Tribal Mind: The Psychology of Collectivism*. New York: Taylor & Francis; Stevens, Sean T., Lee Jussim, and Nathan Honeycutt. "Scholarship Suppression: Theoretical Perspectives and Emerging Trends." *Societies* 10, no. 4 (2020): 82.

[7] Jussim, Lee. "My Vita of Denunciation." Unsafe Science. May 19,2024. Available at https://unsafescience.substack.com/p/my-vita-of-denunciation (accessed November 15, 2024).

How Does a Chemistry
Professor Nearly Get Canceled?

Patanjali Kambhampati,
Professor of Chemistry, McGill University

Introduction

"I am not against free speech, but…" Those comical words appeared in my teaching evaluations. They're from an undergraduate student taking my course on physical chemistry, thermodynamics, for non-chemistry majors. It was a required course for students majoring in biology but intimidated by physical chemistry. The content was often a tough sell to the students, but there was never any room for politics or social thought. Or so I assumed.

The only exception to the rule of not discussing politics in the classroom was made for the Trump election and presidency, even though I teach at a Canadian university. I know about this "rule" from undergraduates who have informed me. I am proud of the fact that students have found me to be open to discussion and dissent outside of classroom content in physical chemistry. Indeed, this impression is an accurate rendition of reality, as I have demonstrated in my outreach on social thought in the past decade of the Great Awokening.[1] Chinese scientists see the parallels when I have invoked their history to discuss the present. For any number of reasons, I wanted to be able to mentor students and do more than teach them physical chemistry, but to get them to think about nature, critical thinking, and how they can contribute to society.

On one such instance I exhorted the students to join in the great adventures of the day by working hard and contributing their acquired knowledge, rather than expressing grievance and complaint with moralistic posturing. Today's strident and shrill protests were in stark contrast to the sober scientists I know who have worked on this issue for decades. Much to my surprise and pleasure, my students gave me a standing ovation. Perhaps due to that exhortation, my teaching evaluations that year (2019) reflected some unusually glowing comments. Students seemed inspired by me in person as a university professor who was, well, professing. This was in stark contrast to the professors who were whining about Trump.

When I saw the phrase "I believe in free speech, but. . ." I knew it was about to get bad. I had this sinking feeling before, which is partly why I'm contributing to this volume. Having seen much hatred levied at me on social media, and then having much of that come back to me on campus, I knew to be alarmed by this student comment. In 2024, students wield much power over their professors. According to the student evaluation, this student was looking me up on the internet, where I am easy to find by virtue of my name.

I was easily found on Instagram where I maintain a low-profile account only to archive photos for myself, mostly of my pets. On my Instagram account I also had memes saved. In previous years I had participated in online debates between libertarians, classical liberals, and modern Anglophone leftists. Apparently, this student was so offended by the fact that I posted memes to a nearly private account, an account that never mentions my professorship, that she suggested in her evaluation that I should not be teaching college students. The student wrote that I was especially unsuitable for teaching females since I did not believe in the "patriarchy" nor in "male privilege" as invoked by modern Anglophone feminists.

My great transgressions were that I mocked modern Anglophone leftists and had the gall to question feminism as a man, and a "colored" man at that. It was as if a caste system inhabited this student's mind that ranked the importance of one's feelings and of different people's value as human beings. That idea hit home with me, as hard as the physical violence and name-calling that I used to experience as the rare brown boy in Minnesota in the 1970s. This was the familiar terrain of being dehumanized. I can trace a through line from my childhood experience to my experiences with cancel culture as a university professor in STEM (science, technology, engineering, math for the uninitiated).

As a chemistry professor, why did I get involved in cultural commentary?

Independent of my employment as a chemistry professor, I maintain a longstanding interest in politics, culture, and social thought. Having been interested in politics and culture in addition to chemistry and physics in my day job, why would these worlds ever collide? In teaching undergraduates their basic science courses, there is absolutely no role for politics or social commentary in the classroom. That is a policy that I have strictly maintained in my twenty years as a professor. So how does cancel culture intersect with my career in academic chemistry?

In 2010 I first heard the phrase "check your privilege." It had taken root among the student group leaders who tend to be leftist activists at all universities. This term of "checking" implied some moralistic posturing. And this term of "privilege" immediately implied some level of both grievance and human hierarchy. Both terms were very troubling to me, and I had a bad feeling that things were about to get much worse. I could immediately tell that the students in 2010 were aping the words of my undergraduate peers in 1990, albeit with much more focus and intensity. Nowadays we know that the rise of this current culture really came back in 2010 and truly exploded in 2014.[2] The point is that it seemed to me that a long-growing problem had finally metastasized.

Cancel culture warning bells

I had lived through the rise of political correctness around 1990, and I could tell that that culture had festered for years and had emerged as a powerful new force. I vigorously debated these ideas on Facebook. I especially debated internet feminists/genderists as a long-standing egalitarian libertarian across all possible axes in life.

In particular, I refused to let human equality and rights and responsibilities be a topic to be discussed only by wealthy white women. I wanted the voices of people like my father and my sons to be heard, for the first time. How often do you hear Asian men who do STEM (science, technology, engineering, math) discussing their thoughts about race and gender?

To borrow from my understand of the Hindu caste system, there now seemed to be a universal caste system based upon a matrix of race and gender and class. And it was clear that in this caste system, I and my father and my sons were low in status or privilege, to use the parlance of our times. There is an anthology of chapters written by regular men called *Sons of Feminism*, edited by Janice Fiamengo.[3] I contributed the opening chapter, and my experiences inspired her to produce a video on the "empathy gap," to parallel all the gaps feminists are happy to discuss.[4]

In 2014, it seemed as though people all over Facebook and the internet were all of a sudden questioning feminism/genderism. That year, I saw the YouTube videos of Warren Farrell and Janice Fiamengo discussing both gender from a male perspective, and feminism from a critical perspective that was rigorous and intellectual. At the same time, speakers and events, and sometimes even attendees were being canceled, and a few university lectures ended in what we now know to be student-led riots. By 2024 those extreme events are now history, but they still loom large in the prevailing academic environment—this environment which gave rise to cancel culture and still fosters it. At least we finally see the mainstream reporting on these activities

Those riots of 2014 very much reminded me of the experiences I had as a Carleton College freshman in 1988, with people actually hissing when they encountered ideas or people they disliked. Based upon my experiences with early political correctness and my lifelong involvement with both debate and the internet, I was naturally headed towards a conflict. And those conflicts would result in numerous cancellation threats on social media, cancellation attempts by students, and formal procedures levied against me by university administrators at McGill.

What did I do to trigger the ire of the university administration?

What did I say that so "problematic," to use the language of our times? As a student of history, human behavior, and evolutionary psychology, I like to observe patterns and to draw meaning from them. One such pattern I see is the conviction of one's virtue. Everyone is a hero in their own narrative. I always imagined what it might be to be an aspiring young Fascisti studying in Milan a century ago. Or to be a young Communist anywhere a century ago. Or to be an academic eugenicist a century ago. This last one was key to my analysis as it showed that awful practices and awful people are often the cartoonish end game of some grand scheme hatched by progressive intellectuals aiming to "make the world a better place." As a student of how grand schemes generally end poorly, I have reprints of some of those old racist academic monographs.

One aims to learn from history. So I compared critical race theory, efforts to "decolonize STEM," and especially women's/gender studies to the academic racists of the late nineteenth and early twentieth centuries. And those racist scholars informed the Ku Klux Klan of the 1920s, the Nazis, and eventually Maoist China. In hindsight everything is clear. I compared women's/gender studies to the academic racism of the Progressive Era, and considered what feminism/genderism had in common with racism and communism. This proved to be the linchpin of the attempts to cancel me.[5]

On social media between 2014 and 2019 I had shared my thoughts and experiences on the topics of race and gender. It may sound trivial, but I believe men and women should have equal rights and responsibilities and freedoms and liberties. The same holds true for race or social class or caste or sexual orientation. Based upon my personal "lived experience" as well as my intellectual understanding, I saw many parallels between a century of racism and a century of feminism/genderism. For doing so as an egalitarian father of sons, comparing my experiences and intellectual analysis of racism and genderism, I was treated poorly. Much has been written about online misogyny. It surely exists. In contrast, little has been said about online misandry. As noted in the online presentations of Jordan Peterson, behavior is often gendered and women sometimes pursue reputational destruction, especially in groups.[6]

Professors who get canceled or survive cancellation attempts are often severely traumatized by the experience. I have unfortunately experienced this trauma as a brown boy bullied in Minnesota in the 1970s. I have drawn on this experience to strive for tolerance of others, in the spirit of Martin Luther King Jr. and Gandhi. Being called terrible things on the Internet did hurt, especially from friends, but it did suggest to me that I was onto something.

Having survived both sticks and stones, I could survive people calling me names on social media. The problem arose when they looked up my name and found out that I was a professor of chemistry at McGill University. Then the threats came to my livelihood and what defines me as a person: being a scientist. Some people, all women, would not just take offense at my ideas and data, they would not just insult me or threaten me, but they would threaten to report me to my employer. That scared me and caused much emotional pain for me, which then overflowed to my family.

Between 2015 and 2023 I have been contacted by many members of the McGill administration from chemistry department chairs to the dean of science, to the dean of diversity, to the provost, to the principal (what Americans would call the provost), to the acting principal regarding my discussions about women's/gender studies and feminism/genderism as analogues of racism. It is notable that these administrators have never received objections from people regarding critical race theory, "decolonization," or diversity, inclusion, equity (DEI,DIE,IDE). I have had students write in my teaching evaluations that I have criticized feminism/genderism. I have had random people on the Internet write to complain that I should not be allowed to teach students or to be a professor.

The Dean of Science takes it upon himself to "fix" me

According to McGill University records, many professors have contacted the dean of sciences and have asked how can I still be a professor after I have questioned feminism/genderism as an egalitarian man of color and a father of sons? All of these contacts come from people complaining about what I said as a private citizen, with no mention of my status as a McGill faculty member. I am not pleased to have to live with the fact that all this correspondence is documented in university records, due to the diligence of the dean of science. But at least I can live with myself by following the edict of saying what you mean and meaning what you say, always with consistency. I stand by my lifelong pursuit of being egalitarian beginning with caste-ism. Race and gender and orientation followed suit in my personal cosmology of egalitarianism.

In addition to my forays into public debate as a private citizen, and my invitations to other academics to discuss their historic intellectual parallels, I have openly questioned women's/gender studies professors who were lecturing at the McGill University physics department, and the dean of diversity that lectured to the entire McGill science faculty. On my personal record, it is noted that I had the gall the question the very ideas of the dean of diversity. I thought questioning ideas is what we did in academia? In science we do not just question ideas but attack them with vigor, to see how they stand up. During the course of two women's studies professors arguing their ideology to physics students and researchers, I had questioned them vigorously. This led them to report me to the Dean of Science for being a "threat to their well-being."

What has happened to me as a result of these efforts to cancel me? I have had my normally staid chemistry department chair ask me, "is everything OK," which is something of a kiss of death. It got far worse once university deans were involved. The dean of science had conducted a years-long campaign to harass me, seemingly on account of political motivations.

From 2014 to 2019, I had meetings with the Dean where he would say that he would get asked about me and complaints about me due to my questioning feminism and genderism as a private citizen on the internet. In all, I have had a half dozen formal letters and meetings with the dean of science. I have never refrained from questioning feminism and genderism, and I have been vocal on the Internet since its pre-1995 beginnings. Why should I stop now, at this point, when it seems my ideas are gaining broader traction? The Dean cited complaints that I should not be allowed to teach at a University due to my views on gender as a private citizen.

The dean also mentioned that the dean of diversity had complained about me. This dean had presented to the faculty a seminar on hiring "best practices" and commenced with a discussion of the implicit association test (IAT). The IAT has been questioned in both scientific and public writing.[7] I sat there with my arms crossed, just as I did in 1976 at age six with the United States Pledge of Allegiance.

Apparently, the Dean of Diversity was so bothered by me that she refused to speak to me after the meeting, and then reported me to the dean of science for "questioning her ideas." I was talked about behind my back for having "incorrect" thoughts. I did not even aggressively attack her ideas as I would in a science conference. I merely disagreed with her in public. And indeed, the complaint was duly included by the Dean of Science in his allegations against me over the past five years.

Our physics department had an EDI presentation on women in physics. The presenter was a caricature of a women's studies professor. Her presentation was a collection of anecdotes. Some of those anecdotes included girls complaining about all the Asians present. That seemed racist to me. The professor was also very misandrist and gynocentric. So, I decided to engage with this professor as a colleague, and challenged her talking points. In addition to questioning the field of women's studies, I questioned critical race theory and the movement to "decolonize" STEM. In this case she ran to the Dean of Science and cried foul. Now the dean of science has one more example of me being "problematic."

Perhaps the clearest demonstration of the ideological biases espoused by the Dean of Sciences concerned his reaction to a handwritten note I'd posted on my office door. The picture on the right shows the note. I had written that note in a moment of frustration in having to write a diversity statement for a grant proposal in 2019. I was asked about how I would address things like "microaggressions," a point which deeply offended me as someone who experienced actual aggressions in my youth in Minnesota in the 1970s. I could not abide by their discussions of equity, when I had come from the developing world myself. So I wrote this for my diversity statement: "We will hire the most qualified people based upon their skills and mutual interests." The episode caused me such angst that I responded with a satirical note on my office door (see photo).

The attentive reader might note that I changed the EDI acronym to DIE, not just for obvious humor but to reference a gag from the Simpsons.[8]

Things soon got worse for me. The story of my refusing to play along with the request for a diversity statement in my grant proposal and then not even making it to scientific peer review made the national news.[9] Since then, I have become more vocal about my opposition to EDI/DIE/ DEI. I decided that DEI might really stand for "Didn't Earn It."[10]

My opposition to EDI/DIE is merely one more thing that sets the stage for the witch hunt by the Dean of Science. He once complained me about some statement of mine as being "against EDI," as if this presented a problem. Indeed, I struggled to understand why a single faculty member's opinions about EDI was part of his job description.

The day I had posted the DEI DIE! note outside my office was the anniversary of a 1989 mass shooting in Montreal. As a college student in the United States at the time, I didn't know about it. Apparently this day of remembrance looms large in the Canadian psyche. I only learned this from the Dean's actions.

It was already known that I was a critic of modern feminism, instead favoring classical liberal-based egalitarianism. When the DEI DIE! note was posted outside my office on the anniversary of the Montréal Massacre, McGill University concluded that I was somehow a "threat." So the Department Chair took a photo of the note on my door and sent it to the Dean of Science, who immediately told me to have it removed. The Dean of Science then began a furtive campaign of harassment against me.

When the Dean met with me, he discussed the Montreal Massacre and how I was a "credible threat" (his words) given my views (a threat to what, exactly?). I truthfully informed him that I had barely heard of the Massacre, and I certainly did not remember the date (I can barely remember a handful of birthdays and Christmas.) He said he did not believe me, that I was lying. He said that to me in person, and in formal reports in my personnel file. The Dean of Science also thought I view the loss of life flippantly, notably when it resulted from a mass shooting. This is offensive to me, as someone who was raised as a Gandhian pacifist and remains a deeply committed egalitarian across all axes of life. So now the Dean of Science is telling me that I'm indifferent to mass murder?

This interaction during the anniversary of the Montreal Massacre became much more inflamed, again by his seeming need to protect women from me—as he has intimated to me in a handful of meetings. My newest transgression was that I had hurt the feelings of a woman, a white woman. And me, a colored man!

McGill gets involved in an email flame war

I was on a Heterodox Academy email group, and a garden variety flame war ensued. A woman that I had only met once in real life wanted to be removed from the email list and sent a rude reply-all. So, I called out her shortfall of etiquette and suggested she should have emailed me directly as the sender, or the admin of the group. I did the thing one cannot do on the Internet in modern times: as a Colored man, I scolded a White woman. This caused a handful of other women to join in the fray and pile on me and move to personal insults and name calling. Interestingly more people came back to defend me and to question the folks attacking me.

The reader may be taken aback at my reference to "White women." The Dean of Science and the HR lawyer were taken aback. My view is that we have spoken of the racism of White men ad nauseam and have paid less attention to racism and xenophobia from White women, especially upper-caste White women. Indeed, the majority of racism I experienced as an adult was from White women. Rather than let it go, the woman on the listserv, who occasionally writes for outlets in the heterodox space, proceeded to report me to the McGill Dean of Science. Now the dean had more than just angry emails: he had a real-life woman in distress. The dean went for this like a shark goes to meat.

The Dean of Science claimed that I had a history of bad behavior that culminated in my insulting some woman in an email. The woman in question is neither a McGill employee, nor a professor anywhere else. This random woman with negligible connection to McGill had hurt feelings after she'd lashed out at me in an email group unrelated to McGill. Yet with this tenuous connection to McGill activities, the Dean of Science decided to go into action against me.

The Dean concluded that I should be suspended from McGill for two weeks, without pay. What's more, there should be some permanent letter in my file describing my transgressions. The Dean sent this recommendation to the university Provost , along with confidential details I was not permitted to see. The Provost then met with me to hear my side of the story. The Provost immediately sided with me, stating that academic freedom was paramount. I remain unpunished for my perceived transgressions per the Dean of Science. While I was pleased that the Provost sided with me and invoked academic freedom, I was concerned about the years of harassment by the dean of science for reasons seemingly political and personal.

After the dust had settled from the Dean's effort to bar me from work for two weeks, I wanted to meet with him. During the meeting he became flustered and defensive and began to yell at me. He once again defended his assertion that I was a liar for saying I did not know about the Montreal Massacre. He was simultaneously defensive and aggressive throughout the meeting. I told him I have needs that were not being met, not the least of which was my not being harassed. The meeting ended without him getting up from his desk. I subsequently sent him a long letter setting out my grievances.

The Dean replied to my letter, stating that there is nothing he could do for me despite my documentation of rampant mistreatment. If I want to be "left alone," then fine. Is his admission to "leave me alone" an admission of guilt? The Dean did not in fact leave me alone, and continued to harass me.

The Dean of Science remains my administrative dean. Hence all my concerns and grievances go upstream to this office. I think it is unlikely to find sympathetic ears in the Dean's office, and suspect that he won't assist in my professional advancement. All these dealings with this Dean been very stressful and unpleasant. Academia is a place of intellectual wars, but it is supposed to be collegial. Now my intellectual home was anything but collegial. In fact, it was outright hostile.

Conclusions

What sins did I commit? I spoke out about culture on the internet as a private citizen, never mentioning my McGill professorship. I did act as a professor in emails to other professors, in which I explained that I vigorously disagreed with them. While I have broadly criticized a wide variety of modern cultural phenomena, including Black Lives Matter, critical race theory, decolonization, and modern leftism, the only serious problems arose when I questioned feminism/genderism. That was the foundation of the decade-long process of trying to cancel me for being a university professor who is fiercely egalitarian. Indeed I was recently interviewed by Canadian academic Gad Saad for his YouTube channel, wherein I was introduced as the "Anti-Woke Chemistry Professor."[11]

What I experienced from 2014 to 2019 resulted from the rise of cancel culture in Anglophone society. It is not purely American, as some mistakenly believe. One sees more of this culture in Australia than in Quebec, for example. These modern ideas seemed to emerge from academia decades ago but lay dormant for years, only to return in young people's social media feeds from 2010 onward. It also appears that there is a gendered quality to this modern day witch hunting, just like there is a gendered quality to bar room brawls. The gendered dimensions of the current culture was recently discussed by Jordan Peterson and the British academic Eric Kaufmann.[12]

I first experienced so-called hate speech from my classmates and former friends. It then expanded to civilians on social media. Then the civilians found out that I was a university professor and reported me to the university for Wrong Think. Many members of the university administration saw me as a problem to solve, rather than supporting me in the spirit of academic freedom. Members of the university administration tried to punish me for my protected speech about human freedom and equality as a private citizen and as a professor.

All of these experiences were painful to the point of being traumatizing. Having said that, I have experienced many traumas and much hatred in my life from boyhood to adulthood, and what I expected from the dean of science was no different. It was merely par for the course. Perhaps that made it easier for me.

I defer to other public intellectuals who have written extensively on this phenomenon, from Jonathan Haidt and Greg Lukianoff in their more broadly palatable work, to Jordan Peterson and Gad Saad in their deeper and harder-hitting work found on YouTube.[13]

In the process of directly emailing professors with whom I vigorously disagreed on intellectual grounds, I also took the trouble to email professors who I thought were on the right track and living up to the spirit of my intellectual heroes, like Bertrand Russell and Carl Sagan.

I contacted Jordan Peterson, thanking him for his stand on behalf of free speech (and against compelled speech) when he first burst onto the public scene in Canada. I have sent similar letters to other academics who I thought were brilliant and courageous thinkers, including Gad Saad and Janice Fiamengo. Interestingly Peterson, Saad, and Fiamengo are all Canadian, notable given that Canada seems even more woke than the United States. I offer this comparison as someone who has been a citizen of India, Canada, and the United States.

Peterson, Saad, and Fiamengo were bravely leading the charge to criticize cancel culture and wokeness. As a result of all this emailing, I created an email salon. After some discussion we agreed on the name Dissident Herd of Cats (DHOC), because whilst we are all dissidents from the prevailing orthodoxy, we are all independent thinkers who embrace free speech. We aim for freedom of thought and human freedom—and it's impossible to herd cats.

Jordan Peterson has written about the virtues of stopping to pet a cat when you see one in the street. I can strongly attest to this practice. Another member of the DHOC is the Ukrainian-American chemist Anna Krylov, who has written brilliantly against DIE (She's also an avowed fan of cats.)[14] The DHOC continues to discuss ideas in a free and unfettered way among a group of people who perceive no value in collectivism or shaming or moralization. The DHOC is also a group of people for whom cancel culture has no place, and we take issue with its roots in academia. Hopefully there will be the natural re-growth of other dissident cats to stand up to the current culture of academia.

Endnotes

[1] Goldberg, Zach. "How the Media Led the Great Racial Awakening." *Tablet*, August 4, 2020. Available at https://www.tabletmag.com/sections/news/ articles/media-great-racial-awakening (accessed February 1, 2024); Yglesias, Matthew. "The Great Awokening." *Vox*, April 1, 2019. Available at https://www.vox.com/2019/3/22/18259865/great-awokening-white-liberals-race-polling-trump-2020 (accessed February 1, 2024).

[2] For a superb discussion, see Ellis, John. *The Breakdown of Higher Education: How It Happened, the Damage It Does, and What Can Be Done.* Encounter Books, 2020.

[3] Fiamengo, Janice, ed. *Sons of Feminism: Men Have Their Say*, 2nd edition. Little Nightingale Press, 2017.

[4] "The Empathy Gap." Fiamengo Files, episode 4 (podcast). Available at https://www.youtube.com/watch?v=YKXfv_8qCRU (accessed September 22, 2024).

[5] Rather than articulate my views in full, I refer readers to the excellent works of Janice Fiamengo, who has evaluated feminism, genderism, women's studies, and gender studies from a rigorous egalitarian perspective.

[6] Jordan B. Peterson Clips. "What is the Relationship Between Cancel Culture and Toxic Femininity?" Video, October 22, 2022. Available at https://www. youtube.com/watch?v=HVpJskHzlwo (accessed November 20, 2024); PhilosophyInsights. "Jordan Peterson: Why Cancel Culture is Feminine Bullying." Video, June 5, 2021. Available at https://www.youtube. com/watch?v=KrXDzFlyzx0&t=174s (accessed November 20, 2024).

[7] Jussim, Lee. "12 Reasons to Be Skeptical of Common Claims About Implicit Bias." *Psychology Today*, March 28, 2022. Available at https://www. psychologytoday.com/us/blog/rabble-rouser/202203/12-reasons-be-skeptical-common-claims-about-implicit-bias (accessed September 25, 2024).

[8] Mostly Simpsons. "The Simpsons – Die Bart Die." Video, December 15, 2015. Available at https://www.youtube.com/watch?v=gaXigSu72A4 (accessed November 22, 2024).

[9] Higgins, Michael. "Minority Professor Denied Grants because He Hires on Merit: 'People Are Afraid to Think'" *National Post*, November 24, 2021. Available at https://nationalpost.com/news/canada/minority-professor-denied-grants-because-he-hires-on-merit-people-are-afraid-to-think (accessed June 8, 2024).

[10] Higgins 2021.

[11] Saad, Gad. "My Chat with Dr. Pat Kambhampati, Anti-Woke Chemistry Professor." The Saad Truth podcast, episode 1342, November 26, 2021. Available at https://www.youtube.com/watch?v=mkTAeiRan9w&t=55s (accessed September 27, 2024).

[12] Peterson, Jordan. "Why Young Women Are More Woke." Podcast, June 5, 2024. Available at https://www.youtube.com/watch?v=grNLfzFwPpg (accessed September 27, 2024).

[13] Lukianoff, Greg and Jonathan Haidt. *The Coddling of the American Mind: How Good Intentions and Bad Ideas Are Setting up a Generation for Failure.* Penguin, 2019; Lukianoff, Greg and Rikki Schlott. *The Cancelling of the American Mind: Cancel Culture Undermines Trust and Threatens Us All— But There Is a Solution.* Simon and Schuster, 2023.

[14] Krylov, Anna I. "The Peril of Politicizing Science." *The Journal of Physical Chemistry Letters* 12, no. 22 (2021): 5371-5376. Available at https://pubs.acs.org/doi/pdf/10.1021/acs.jpclett.1c01475 (accessed November 22, 2024).

Expurgated Slurs, Heart Palpitations, and Gaslighting: My Journey Through the "Access and Equity" Meat Grinder

Jason J. Kilborn,
Professor of Law,
University of Illinois Chicago School of Law

On Sunday, December 20, 2020, at 8:54 p.m., my dean emailed me, "A couple of issues regarding your fall courses have come up over the weekend, and we would like to discuss those with you." She wanted to talk at noon the very next day, Monday, four days before Christmas. I thought my fall courses had gone exceptionally well, so I was taken aback by the suggestion to the contrary, let alone the urgency of a conversation.

I had been among a handful of faculty who had agreed to come physically to campus in fall 2020, the first full semester of the COVID-19 pandemic, to try to maintain some sense of normalcy for the students. At the same time, I constructed an entirely new hybrid-remote-electronic approach to serve those students who preferred to stay at home. I thought the effort had succeeded marvelously, so I couldn't imagine what these "couple of issues" might be.

Little did I know how my life would be upended over the next several years in the long-lingering aftermath of a sham investigation of a contrived transgression. My dean, associate dean, and I met electronically (due to COVID restrictions, all meetings at this time were held by Zoom) on Monday, December 21, 2020. At this meeting, my dean revealed that she had been told I had "used a racial slur" on one of my exams, upsetting some students. I was actually relieved, as this seemed to indicate a serious but simple misunderstanding that could be cleared up quickly. Little did I know.

The Infamous Exam

Earlier that month, I had administered the final examination in my Civil Procedure II course at the University of Illinois Chicago (UIC) School of Law. The course explores the rules for how lawyers guide cases through the court process. Because anti-discrimination law is among the most frequent substantive bases for federal litigation, the course had frequently explored civil rights and race discrimination in the civil litigation process. I therefore included on this exam a hypothetical employment discrimination scenario in which a woman sued because she suspected she had been fired on the basis of her race and gender.

One question challenged students to put themselves in the position of the employer's lawyer who at great effort and expense had discovered a devastating piece of evidence: an account from a former manager that she had "quit her job at Employer after she attended a meeting in which other managers expressed their anger at Plaintiff, calling her a 'n____' and 'b____' (profane expressions for African Americans and women) and vowed to get rid of her." The question appeared exactly like this, with respectfully expurgated references to the race and gender slurs to make the point clear while avoiding gratuitous disruption and anxiety.

The question asked if this former manager's identity and location must be disclosed in response to a formal "discovery" request from plaintiff. This question was designed to test the rule that, no matter how damning the evidence might be, and no matter how expensive it was for the employer-defendant to find it, this manager's identity and location are not "work product" that generally can be shielded from the opponent, but must be revealed precisely because they are so directly relevant to the plaintiff's precise claims. The extreme nature of the hypothetical testimony offered by this manager was a crucial part of the question, intensifying the employer's (and the student-lawyer's) desire to withhold the information. The question powerfully challenged the students to resist their natural desire to give their client only the answers the client wants to hear.

This same question had appeared on my Civil Procedure II exam for the previous ten years, administered to at least a dozen classes (averaging between 50 and 90 students each) that included numerous African American students. No one had ever suggested the question was objectionable. So it came as quite a shock that, in late December 2020, my law school's Black Law Students Association (BLSA) initiated a campaign of petitions and protests of this question and its expurgated references to racial and gender slurs. BLSA alleged in a widely disseminated online petition that reading this question had caused one student to have "heart palpitations," and it decried the "Inexcusable Usage of _____ on a UIC John Marshall Law School Civil Procedure II Exam."

I explained to my dean that I had not, in fact, *used* the word, as she and many others had mistakenly understood from BLSA's petition; rather, I had simply included a respectfully expurgated reference in the context of an employment discrimination litigation hypothetical. Nonetheless, I spontaneously offered to send a note of regret to my class if those oblique references had caused anyone any distress. My dean agreed, and I sent such a message to my class, additionally offering to talk to anyone who might have concerns about the question, my intent in using it, or anyone's negative reaction to it.

No Good Deed Goes Unpunished:
My Ill-Fated Meeting with the BLSA Student

While many students in the class who took the examination (including Black students and members of BLSA) responded to me to express that the exam question was unobjectionable, only one student—who was *not* in the class—eventually arranged to speak with me about BLSA's concerns. A friend and colleague, who's Black himself, had heard the misleading story, and when I explained things to him, he suggested I speak with a member of BLSA to set the record straight and assuage concerns about the exam. The student and I scheduled a remote meeting for 5:00 p.m. on Thursday, January 7, 2021. Despite the late hour and the intrusion on my personal family time, I agreed to this. In retrospect, it was a foolish decision.

To set the stage, I shared with the student recent correspondence I had had with a reporter from the legal education commentary website AboveTheLaw, in which the reporter had explained, "When I initially read the student petition, I thought the exam had written out the full word when the reality was very different. . . . I do intend to write a story about it, though my take will very much be that using the euphemism for the slur is exactly what we've asked professors (who have used the full word in academic settings) to do in order to engage with the ideas and still be sensitive to the harm the word does." I suggested the student take this measured perspective into account in preparing for our conversation.

With both of us comfortably seated before our computers in our respective homes, the conversation proceeded in a generally cordial and constructive manner. It rambled and ranged among various tenuously connected topics, one of which, I distinctly recall, was an extended conversation about the fact that I resembled the student's pastor, and we wondered aloud what Jesus would do in a situation like the one we found ourselves in. When the hour mark approached, and the student seemed disappointed to break off the conversation, I reassured him that I was willing to talk as long as it took to find some understanding and healing, so the conversation continued. I allowed the conversation to stretch well into the evening, a total of four hours, until 9:00 p.m. Many of my colleagues have since told me I was foolish to allow this to drag on for so long, but I was determined to show this student that I genuinely cared about finding a mutually acceptable resolution.

At one point a little more than an hour into the conversation, the student asked why the law school dean had not shown me the BLSA petition criticizing my exam question (I had heard about but had not seen the petition at this point). Having developed what I thought was a friendly rapport with this student after an hour into our Friday evening conversation, I let my guard down and said something that would turn my life upside down. I responded that perhaps my dean had not shared the petition with me because maybe she feared that if I saw the hateful things said about me in that petition, I might become homicidal. I clearly used that phrase in jest, and the conversation continued with no indication that the student felt in any way distressed, much less actually threatened. When the conversation wrapped up after four hours, on a Friday evening at 9:00 p.m., we seemed to part on cordial if not friendly terms, and that seemed to be the end of it.

I later learned that, during a planned meeting the following Monday, January 11, 2021, between several BLSA students and the law school dean and other UIC administrators, the student with whom I had spoken on Friday misreported that I had exclaimed that I "was feeling homicidal" or "would become homicidal." In light of this politically charged situation, the dean and university officials used this purported threat as a pretext to invoke UIC's Violence Prevention Plan to convene a Behavioral Threat Assessment Team (BTAT) to assess this purported threat of imminent physical violence. Without communicating with me or undertaking any other investigation, the BTAT authorized my dean to take the most extreme measures.

I Enter the Rabbit Hole: Summary Suspension #1

The next day, at 6:39 am on Tuesday, January 12, 2021, my dean summoned me to yet another electronic meeting at 8:15 am. This was the first morning of the spring semester, and I was preparing for another pair of large classes. At this point, the COVID pandemic had reached a new peak, so no classes or other university activities were being held on campus. Neither students nor faculty were coming onto campus for the foreseeable future, and none of the BLSA students in particular was required to come into contact with me for any reason. Nonetheless, my dean summarily announced that I was being placed on "indefinite administrative leave," all of my classes were cancelled for the entire semester, and I was forbidden from coming onto campus or from engaging in any university activity, including remote electronic activities.

Shocked, I asked what the basis could possibly be for such a rash action. I was told only that the basis was "additional complaints and concerns brought forth by students regarding possible violations of University policies, including the nondiscrimination statement," and that UIC's Office for Access and Equity (OAE) would explain more "in a few days." The entire electronic meeting lasted only a few minutes.

I was dumbfounded. For the next hour, I walked feverishly through my neighborhood, repeating over and over the mantra, Let It Go. I was trying to convince myself to abandon my usual *fight* reaction and instead, for once, opt instead for *flight*. But I was not about to let this go. I fired off dozens of emails to various people and listservs, describing my unbelievable predicament and asking folks what they thought I should do.

A member of one of the listservs suggested I contact FIRE, which I later learned was an acronym for Foundation for Individual Rights in Education, and which has since expanded its mandate and changed its name to the Foundation for Individual Rights and Expression. I filled in their online "tell us your story" box, and within hours, I received a call from a FIRE representative, who explained that my kind of story had become worryingly common in recent years. They were there to help. I would not have made it through this ordeal without FIRE's support.

Meeting with OAE

After several agonizing days with no answers, I hastened to meet electronically with OAE on January 15, 2021. At the very outset of this meeting, the OAE Associate Chancellor asked me if I recalled having a conversation with a student about my exam question and BLSA's petition. Of course I did—it was just a few days prior. I was further asked if I recalled the student asking me why my dean had not shared that petition with me, and how I had responded. Without hesitation, I reported the story recounted above. Finally, the OAE Associate Chancellor revealed for the first time that the "homicidal" comment was actually the sole basis for my summary "indefinite administrative leave."

I immediately suggested that this outrageous ordeal could have been avoided had anyone taken a few minutes to discuss the situation with me. I obviously did not represent a threat of physical violence of any kind to any person, especially in light of the COVID lockdown. I offered to work with OAE to modify its approach to UIC's Violence Prevention Policy, which clearly called for a more incremental, common-sense approach involving communication and compassion for all involved.

In retrospect, it is fairly clear that the purported threat was a mere pretext, offering UIC officials cover for their politically motivated actions. In one of a series of articles published by Northwestern University law professor Andrew Koppelman in the *Chronicle of Higher Education*, Prof. Koppelman posits, "It is hard to believe that [the dean] would have reacted the same way if Kilborn's exam had not already provoked controversy. The complaints about the exam were apparently not sufficient to trigger the sanctions that might mollify the complaining students. The purported threat, however, offered that opportunity."[1]

I immediately reached out to my dean and offered to resume my university duties and get my classes back on track for the benefit of the more than 70 registered students, as I clearly represented no threat of any kind to anyone, especially in light of the fully-electronic remote teaching environment at the time. This offer was summarily rejected. All my students were curtly instructed to quickly rearrange their class schedules.

To be cleared of this "indefinite administrative leave," I was required to meet physically, on campus, with university health officials. Recall that the world was then in the throes of a horrific pandemic, so coming to campus—to the health center in particular—represented a serious threat to one's health and safety. Nonetheless, I capitulated. In anticipation of the meeting with health officials, I sent them one of the Koppelman articles mentioned above. In it, Prof. Koppelman observed, "The university cannot possibly suspend and bar from campus everyone who uses the occasional violent figure of speech. Such metaphors are common in casual conversation. In context, no reasonable person could take his language literally …. Even if one did take it literally, his statement was a speculation about the dean's state of mind, not a statement about his own."

Ignoring these neutral third-party perspectives, on January 21, 2021, UIC health officials forced me to come physically to campus and sit for two hours of examination regarding my Civil Procedure II exam, the ensuing outcry from BLSA, and the electronic conversation with the BLSA student. They subjected me to drug testing and extended meetings with a nurse, a social worker, and a doctor. It was one of the most surreal experiences of my life. It was around this time that I truly and deeply learned the meaning of the term "gaslighting," as these people so earnestly probed the depths of the plainly idiotic notion that I represented a grave physical threat to the lives of goodness knows what people.

On February 1, 2021, my dean approved my final return to unrestricted duty, just in time for me to undertake several days of service as a member of the university Promotion and Tenure Committee. I had no other duties to return to, however, as my classes had been cancelled, and no one would consider revisiting that decision. I would soon have other things to occupy my attention.

Further Gaslighting via an Official Investigation

Two weeks later, on February 17, 2021, another phase of the inquiry began. OAE notified me that it had commenced an investigation into "allegations of race based discrimination and harassment" in that I had allegedly "created a racially hostile environment for ... non-white students between January 2020 and January 2021, particularly during your Civil Procedure II course." OAE's notice of investigation indicated a list of vague allegations from unidentified sources, offering virtually no detail or context. Among the few clear allegations were the December 2020 exam question described above, along with the conversation described above with the BLSA student concerning that exam and what OAE referred to as the "comment from you would become homicidal" [sic].

The other allegations were so vague as to make it impossible for me to respond meaningfully:

> Making racially insensitive comments during lectures including: referring to racial minorities as 'cockroaches,' metaphorically referring to media stories that expose the negative behavior of White men as 'being lynched' or are 'lynchings' and denouncing racial minorities' participation in civil rights claims; Engaging in dismissive and demeaning conduct toward non-White students during the Spring 2020 Civil Procedure II course; [and] engaging in racially biased conduct toward non-White students by specifically addressing minority students when discussing topics about Black, Latinx, or Middle Eastern culture.[2]

I objected that expecting me to respond to such vague allegations from unknown sources violated any fair sense of due process, but I attempted as best I could to respond, at first in writing, and eventually at an electronic "investigative interview" on February 26, 2021. The sole instigator of this complaint was a male African American student whom I had been forced to drop from my spring 2020 Civil Procedure II course due to his excessive absences. I personally oppose this childish policy and would have preferred to just allow the student to remain in the course, take the exam, and most likely fail on the merits, but my dean was exceptionally demanding about our enforcing American Bar Association and law school policies on student attendance.

I offered OAE a long chain of email communications to respond to the most disturbing allegations of race-based discrimination. My extended correspondence with the chronically truant student ultimately satisfied OAE that I had committed no racial discrimination. As for "harassment" from my teaching and exam-related speech, I communicated to OAE a letter to UIC from FIRE pointing out UIC's obligations under the First Amendment and calling for no discipline and an immediate end to UIC's investigation. I also conveyed many other similar analyses from legal commentators on the internet concerning the exam question and the misreported and obviously metaphorical "become homicidal" comment. I shared additional student email communications on the basis of my speculation as to what the other allegations might refer to, though at this point I was fumbling through the dark as to what the allegations were even about.

Three months later, on May 28, 2021, with no further attempt at clarification or any opportunity for me to respond, OAE delivered its "findings letter." In a vague and ambiguous four-page letter, the original allegations were enumerated again, now for the first time with a specific date for a specific class in which several of the allegedly problematic comments had allegedly been made: January 23, 2020, now more than 16 months prior, and almost an entire year before the infamous "n_____ b____" exam question. Had I known this date earlier, I could have referred to my class notes and the recordings of the class, as discussed in detail below, but OAE gave me no such opportunity.

After determining that the single student complainant's allegations of racial discrimination had not been substantiated, OAE concluded that I had nonetheless violated the "harassment" aspect of UIC policy because of my final exam question referencing a racial slur. What's more, my "responses to criticism of the final exam question" had "interfered with Black students' participation in the University's academic program and therefore constituted harassing conduct. . . ." This statement was all but impossible to understand on either facts, law, or university policy (as racial harassment was not defined in a way that could possibly pertain to my conduct in either the school's harassment policy or any state or federal law).

Indeed, the details of OAE's findings remained obscure, hidden behind this four-page letter, until six months later. In November 2021, UIC released, for the first time, a 24-page OAE "investigative report" dated May 28, 2021, in response to a Freedom of Information Act request to UIC from a newspaper reporter. I received this investigation report "as a courtesy" from UIC counsel's office on November 11, 2021. The UIC Chancellor also posted the document on the internet and emailed it to the tens of thousands of students, faculty, and staff at UIC in an attempt to tamp down the still raging campaign by BLSA to get me fired. It did not have the desired effect.

The investigation report revealed substantial new information about OAE's investigation and findings which had never been provided to me and to which I never had an opportunity to respond. It made clear that OAE expressly did not find any evidence that I had targeted non-white students "when discussing topics about Black, Latinx, or Middle Eastern culture," nor did I "diminish or dismiss the perspectives of an African female student because of her race as a Black woman and based on her accent." As to the allegations that OAE purported to substantiate, all were misunderstood and misconstrued, divorced from their appropriate context, and misreported in the findings letter and the investigation report. The OAE investigator had selectively quoted single words from email correspondence and audio recordings of a single class session, actively concealing immediately adjacent words and context that reveal her conclusions to be demonstrably false and misleading.

Cockroaches

The most incendiary assertion from the findings letter was that I had "referred to racial minorities as 'cockroaches' and denounced racial minorities' participation in civil rights claims as part of a discussion of modern-day extortion theory. . . ." The letter went on to find that the allegations referring to "cockroaches" had been "substantiated." OAE never offered me any explanation of the basis for the obviously ludicrous allegation that I had "referred to racial minorities as cockroaches." Only in the secret "investigation report" did OAE reveal the degree to which it was prepared to avoid due process and pervert the truth to arrive at a desired conclusion.

OAE conceded that I "did not explicitly call a racial minority a 'cockroach.'" Nonetheless, it stretched to preserve its preconceived notion of a racial slight by asserting that I "referred to plaintiffs who file egregious claims as 'cockroaches' in the context of discussing a legal case that involved a racial minority plaintiff." This description of the remark is wildly inaccurate, but OAE made no attempt to clarify its misimpression with me.

The audio recording of my January 23, 2020, class session reveals that the remark arose in a discussion related to my attempt to get the students to place themselves in the unfamiliar mindset of defendants who were company directors making a cost-benefit assessment of settling what they considered frivolous litigation. A student asked if it wouldn't *generally* be more cost effective, over time, to maintain litigation teams to defend, and wouldn't plaintiffs with frivolous cases be deterred if *any given* defendant-company racked up a sufficient number of wins. My response, placing the "cockroaches" remark in context, was as follows:

> The fact that other plaintiffs see that one other plaintiff lost isn't a disincentive. If it were, frivolous litigation would have ended long ago, because lots of plaintiffs have been pushed to the wall and lost. You don't hear about those stories in the media. You hear about idiot people winning $1 million verdict against Subway for having 11.5"-long sandwiches. That's what makes the press, right, that Subway lost. Not that they win against this ridiculously frivolous case. That wasn't in the media, only in the legal media, maybe, if you were paying attention. And that's the problem. If they win, no one hears about this. They only hear about it if they lose, and God forbid that, then all the cockroaches come out of the walls, they're thinking, right?

The Subway litigation had been in the popular and legal press in recent weeks, and it was of special interest in our region. The U.S. Court of Appeals for the Seventh Circuit is immediately across the street from our law school, and that court had recently held that Subway's settlement agreement, conceding a loss to the plaintiffs, should be rejected and the case dismissed as frivolous. That report appeared only in the legal press, however; the popular press had reported only on Subway's original capitulation to this lawsuit.

The proper context of my reference to cockroaches was not only ignored but concealed in both OAE's meeting with me and in its investigation report and findings letter. First, the reference to cockroaches arose in the context of the Subway litigation, which involved no identified minority parties. Second, the discussion was about someone else's mindset about settlement strategy, not my own. I was simply putting the students in the mindset of a company, like Subway, facing frivolous litigation, suggesting that "they're thinking" (i.e., Subway's directors are thinking) of the parade of horribles that might flow from losing a frivolous case. Third, I was not characterizing *any* person as a cockroach; rather, I was simply using a colorful and vivid expression to describe all manner of hidden ills that might suddenly stream out into the open, like in the classic horror movie scene in which cockroaches stream out of the walls of a house. In order to offer this explanation, however, I would have needed notice of the particular contention, which was for the first and only time revealed in OAE's private investigation report, released only several months after our meeting.

African American Vernacular English

Another of OAE's recriminations even more clearly reveals the bias within the investigation. Recall that OAE offered me no factual detail or context for any of the allegations against me, either in its original notice to me or in a meeting we had in February 2021. They did not allow me to confront their purported evidence against me, and did not even disclose some of their allegations that eventually became their "findings."

The OAE investigator claimed to have listened to an audio recording of my 23 January 2020 class. But she never confronted me with the evidence she thought she had found, and she never allowed me to mount or present a defense. My favorite example of this is in the findings letter, asserting for the first and only time my alleged "using African-American

Vernacular English ('AAVE') accent when referencing a Black artist's lyrics.'"

In our discussion of the U.S. Supreme Court case of *Ashcroft v. Iqbal*, I tried to distinguish the case (involving a Pakistani Muslim who claimed discriminatory treatment in prison) from the common social problem of racial profiling stops of young African American men by police on the South Side of Chicago. I thought it would make the discussion more vivid and acknowledge the ongoing struggles of African Americans in a similar yet distinct context, and I had heard a particularly apt line in a song that morning. In that song, Jay-Z describes just this sort of racial profiling, in which a police officer explains why he stopped a young Black man, asserting, "You was doin' 55 in a 54." That's all I said, pronouncing it as Jay-Z does in the song, because it would have been ridiculous if I had pronounced "doing" and "four" in the Queen's English and corrected the grammar to "you were," and it would have undermined my effort to connect with students and make my lesson about pretextual police stops vivid and accessible to them.

The class tittered with delight when I quoted this line, in a context that recognized the injustice of police profiling. I remember that even the student who submitted the February 2021 complaint to OAE laughed. OAE made no attempt to understand any of this. That this phrase was now for the first time brought to my attention by the OAE a year-and-a-half later and cited as an example of something problematic was and remains confounding. Notably, no student had ever raised this issue. Neither the complaint nor the notice of investigation mentioned a word about it. The OAE investigator came up with this on her own, and with no mention to me or any attempt to appreciate (or even reveal) the context.

Lynching

Another word game the OAE played involved a fleeting reference to "lynching" in that same January 23, 2020, class. We considered how an executive at Citibank would likely strategize about the *Swanson v. Citibank* case (involving allegations of racial discrimination in lending). I challenged the class to put themselves in the shoes of a bank executive considering whether to settle with plaintiff Swanson, even if (as the dissenting judge suggested) her case lacked merit. I suggested that the executive might be concerned about biased media reporting on such an incident, which if the story were not true and the bank had done nothing wrong might be resented by the executive as a "public lynching" of the bank by the media ("I'm not subjecting my corporate bottom line to that public lynching.").

This was a poor choice of words on my part, and I apologized for the remark. I recall the complainant himself responding "thank you, I appreciate that," and I pointed this out to OAE. Nonetheless, the OAE report noted but did not credit this apology. My use of the words "public lynching" in class was deemed "harassment."

Painful email to white former student

A final example of how OAE trumped up support its conclusion of "harassment based on race" was an OAE accusation, leveled for the first time in its findings letter, that I "responded in early January expressing anger and displeasure with students' objections in a manner that created retaliation concerns for Black students with a January 4, 2021 email that verbally chastised a student for signing the BLSA letter that you referred to as a 'horrible, horrible letter,' and 'attack letter,' that was 'vicious' and 'cruel,' and that led you to feel and to write that your 'hand of help had been bitten off.'"

The OAE investigator misrepresented the content and context of this email. I had provided this email to OAE after our meeting, thinking that it might provide some explanation of the misunderstandings reported in the notice of investigation.

I sent the email to a white female former student of mine from an earlier Civil Procedure class. In early January 2021, someone showed me only the signature page of BLSA's petition, and I was surprised to see the name of this former student for whom I had done several favors, like writing letters of recommendation on extremely short notice. OAE does not disclose that this student is a white woman with no connection to BLSA other than being a member of law school student government, so she had signed the petition "in solidarity" with her student organization colleagues.

My email expressed no anger, contrary to OAE's mischaracterization. Rather, it opens by expressing how painful it was to see the former student's name on a petition that criticized the same language that had appeared on the very same exam this student had taken years earlier—with no mention of any objection. The very next paragraph in my email, not mentioned by the OAE investigator, contradicts the claim that my email could produce "retaliation concerns" on the part of anyone, much less BLSA students who were not cc'ed on this email: I wrote, "I'm not criticizing you, and it hurts that anyone would even dream that I would seek retribution against anyone about all of this—all of these people are and will always be welcome in my classes." This is not language of anger or intimidation; this is language of pain, reassurance, and attempted reconciliation. It specifically says that no one could reasonably fear retribution, and all BLSA members remained welcome in my classes. This first email concludes, "My heart is absolutely broken by all of this." Again, language of pain, not anger. OAE conveniently ignored all of this and perverted this heartfelt note into a threat to unconnected persons.

OAE also disregarded the language of a follow-up email, which appeared on the first page of a four-page pdf file of the email chain I gave to OAE. I sent this response after the student replied, "I'm sorry that you feel betrayed, that wasn't my intention and it is heartbreaking to think that I caused anyone such pain." Again, consistent recognition of pain, not anger. I replied to this, "I admire your support of your colleagues. I support them too." OAE's suggestion that this email in any way disparages BLSA's mission or might prompt BLSA members to fear retaliation from me is plainly contradicted by this language clearly and explicitly expressing support for BLSA and its members. Once again, one can hardly escape the conclusion that the OAE investigator's own bias led her to not only ignore, but to actively conceal, compelling evidence that contradicted her preconceived conclusion against me.

This preconceived conclusion apparently originated with a person identified in OAE's investigation report as "Faculty A." This is obviously one of my colleagues, a mentor of the disgruntled student whom I had to drop from the course and who subsequently submitted the OAE complaint. This colleague inserted himself into the case and, according to the investigation report, persuaded the OAE investigator that my heartfelt email to a former student was "intimidating and threatening given Prof. Kilborn's position of authority." OAE never asked me about this, but I had no position of authority of any kind over these students, none of whom would ever be required to take any class from me (remember that my classes for that semester were cancelled). OAE fails to identify any way in which I *could* have retaliated against any BLSA student even if I were so inclined,. My colleague's characterization of my "position of authority" is a canard that the OAE investigator included as fact in her investigation report.

School of Law Settlement and Subsequent Punishment

Shortly after OAE released its findings letter, my administration had to decide how to respond. On June 18, 2021, I met (again electronically) with my new interim dean to discuss my case, which I warned would lead to litigation if the administration accepted the OAE's plainly fallacious findings and lack of due process. My interim dean presented me with her tentative "recommendations and requirements" and solicited my feedback. Trying to seek reasonable compromise as usual, I agreed to all but one of her proposed conditions. I agreed that someone from the law school could review my class recordings for four semesters (as all law school classes were recorded at that time, and most still are today). I also agreed to report to the dean before responding to any race-related student complaint, as I had no intention of responding to any such complaint myself in any event.

I strenuously objected, however, to the requirement that I be subjected to sensitivity training by Vantage Solutions LLC on my "white privilege," the importance of "position" in the classroom, and engagement with diverse students on sensitive topics. I was not in need of Maoist-style re-education—a point made exquisitely by Bill Maher when he highlighted my case in a February 3, 2023, segment of his "Real Time With Bill Maker" show on HBO, publicity that ultimately led to the chapter you're now reading.[3] On July 2, 2021, my interim dean accepted my proposed compromise on sensitivity training, which I would be required to undertake only if four semesters of review of class recordings revealed that I had failed to maintain a non-harassing classroom environment.

Then the administration launched yet another phase of its never-ending campaign against me. One thing I have learned in this situation is, once you are marked as an "undesirable," the petty persecution never ends. On July 4, 2021, my interim dean delivered my annual performance review, in which she candidly noted that I had excelled in every category. My "student evaluation numbers were overwhelmingly positive," I "continued to publish at an exceptionally high rate," and I had been "a very productive committee chair" and engaged in "numerous public service activities," including "speaking by invitation at nine different conferences." While she noted the recent OAE investigation, she did not indicate in any way that I had failed to meet any expectations or standards. She encouraged me "to reach out with any questions or concerns that you may have so that we can move forward to address these issues in a collaborative collegial manner."

It turns out that moving forward in a collaborative, collegial manner was not what UIC administrators actually had in mind. Despite my positive performance review, my interim dean tersely informed me on September 6, 2021, that I was "ineligible" for an announced across-the-board 2% standard salary increase. The sole basis for this punishment was OAE's purported finding of a policy violation. UIC administration further exacerbated the dispute by forcing my interim dean to renege on our earlier agreement on sensitivity training. On Friday, November 12, 2021, at 4:15 pm, my interim dean notified me by letter that I would be required to attend sensitivity training despite the fact that I had done nothing to warrant this abrogation of our earlier agreement to the contrary. Indeed, she insisted that this training be completed within less than a month, before December 10, over the Thanksgiving holiday, in a period during which I was scheduled for surgery. She implicitly threatened to bar me from returning to my regularly scheduled classes in January if I failed to complete this training.

This rapid deterioration of the situation seemed to be at least in part the result of BLSA's continually ramping up its very public campaign pressuring UIC administration to fire me. Since the truth had not been strong enough to achieve their goals, why not fudge the truth: Rather than decrying my purported use of the n-word on my exam (eliding the distinction between "use" and "reference," much less the abbreviation I'd used), BLSA members now appeared in multiple public fora claiming that I had called my students cockroaches and racial slurs. This was an outright lie. No one had ever claimed such horrible things, but at the end of October 2021, the new leadership of BLSA began to spread this salacious lie.

Back Into the Rabbit Hole:
Summary Suspension #2 and Maoist Re-education

The implicit threat that I might be barred from another semester of my classes became a concrete action in late December 2021. Disregarding their own arbitrary deadline, UIC administrators delayed for more than a month while purporting to decide what sort of sensitivity training mandate to impose on me. On December 17, 2021, I was abruptly informed that I was to be suspended from teaching for the entire Spring 2022 semester— again with no hearing or prior notice. One of my classes was cancelled entirely, while the other (a key topic for students taking the bar exam) was hastily reassigned to a substitute professor with no experience with the highly technical subject matter.

At that time, UIC administrators finally decreed that I would be subjected to an eight-week sensitivity training course. Only upon satisfactory completion of this program would I be allowed to return to class in Fall 2022. The sensitivity training was structured to be maximally onerous, consisting of three parts: (1) twenty hours of course work and required "self-reflection" papers for each of five weekly modules of an online program from Cornell University, (2) additional readings, writing assignments, and weekly hour-and-a-half-long sessions with a trainer retained by UIC, and (3) three more weeks of "additional supplementary material" and meetings with the trainer. My "engagement and commitment to the goals of the program" were to be assessed and reported to UIC administrators.

Once again, to avoid making waves, not to mention disappointing the many students who had told me they were eagerly awaiting my return to the classroom, I complied with this abusive re-education mandate. The extreme degree of the nonsense involved here was revealed in the very first set of supplemental readings selected and assigned by UIC administrators specifically for my training, presumably as an exemplar of appropriate discourse on these sensitive topics. In an irony that confirms that truth is indeed stranger than fiction, one of their hand-picked readings contained the exact same "usage" of a racial slur that had sparked this entire dispute: The author refers to White people being called "n_____ lover."

The Aftermath

Despite my numerous requests, I have never been informed whether my "engagement and commitment to the goals of the program" were ever deemed satisfactory. Perhaps the administrators are silent because I sued them in January 2022? I have since returned to the classroom without incident, and my lawsuit continues to fester today, with no attempt by UIC officials to find any sort of compromise arrangement, much less to take seriously their stated commitment to academic freedom and free expression.

My colleagues and I now have no way of reasonably predicting what remark in the classroom might be regarded as undefined "harassment" of members of the broad range of social identity groups catalogued in UIC policy. I now fear covering several key cases in future Civil Procedure courses, and I have already felt compelled to remove the *Swanson v. Citibank* case, discussed above, despite the fact that it is an exceptionally good teaching tool. Worse, my attitude toward my students has changed. I am now wary of their motives and their potential Jekyll-and-Hyde transformation, no matter how supportive I have been of them. I fear speaking with students and even voicing opinions in faculty meetings, not knowing what utterance might be misrepresented as "harassment," as defined arbitrarily, retrospectively, and with no advance warning by UIC "diversity, equity, and inclusion" enforcers in their unfettered discretion.

If a tenured law professor is fearful of interference by university administrators with no knowledge of the law, the legal profession, or legal education, then he or she cannot feel free to discuss honestly the evolving landscape of cases involving race and other key social issues. Thus a bedrock aspect of free expression has been dangerously eroded (to say nothing of academic freedom). The chilling effects extend beyond just myself. One of my colleagues has avoided adopting a preferred casebook for fear of UIC administrative repercussions based on a few cases in that book, and another has avoided discussing a recent and important U.S. Supreme Court case for fear of UIC administrative repercussions based on an ethnic slur that is the very topic of that case. Requests from law faculty to UIC administration for explanation and clarification have been entirely ignored. This does not portend well for the future of public legal education—or the rule of law—in our country.

Endnotes

[1] Koppelman, Andrew. "Is This Law Professor Really a Homicidal Threat?" *Chronicle of Higher Education*, January 19, 2021; see also Koppelman, Andrew. "Yes, This Is a Witch-Hunt." *Chronicle of Higher Education*, November 17, 2021; see also Gurkin, Len. "The Review." *Chronicle of Higher Education,* November 29, 2021 (interview with Professor Koppelman).

[2] A supplement containing many of the key files is available at https://drive.google.com/file/d/1woP2U1fXkLCVcLeycAfmOzI_8Io_JkBL/ view?usp=sharing (accessed November 13, 2024).

[3] Maher, Bill. Real Time with Bill Maher, "New Rule: A Woke Revolution," HBO, February 3, 2023. Available at https://youtu.be/yysKhJ1U-vM (accessed November 13, 2024).

Awkwardly Antifascist:
Autistic Social Blindness and Academic Controversy
Liam O'Mara IV

1. The New McCarthyism and American Academic Life

Each era in a country's life has its challenges, and the new McCarthyism at work on social media and in academia is one of ours. It is interesting to be sitting down to write this chapter now, during Israel's 2023/2024 assault on the Gaza Strip, as that issue places me, once again, in the uncomfortable position of speaking out as an antifascist Jew against our government's support for Zionist nationalism and far-right politics in Israel. And this in turn, given application of McCarthyism to many forms of protest, and how heavily politicized is the Israel/Palestine fight in the United States, has brought its share of backlash from university administrators, media, and politicians. This is not what led to the investigation I will discuss in this chapter, but it replicates the dynamics in that both involve criticism of far-rightists and racists that is cynically spun, often by the right themselves, into a form of racism.

I am a professor of history working on Southern California campuses. Like all academics, I am more than my job. In addition to my academic work as a historian of ideas, specializing in extremist movements and Middle East and European history, I am an antifascist activist and, for a time, I was a politician attempting to push Democratic politics to the left. An autistic leftist academic in politics is asking for trouble, and this chapter will discuss one such experience. It briefly threatened my professional life as well as my political activities, even though ultimately I think the university handled it about as well as it could. Yet the experience left me convinced that I was not going to make a difference working from within the political system.

I feel, as I expect do many others, that so long as I am not representing myself as speaking for the university, I should be free to engage in socio-political commentary through my social media and off-campus teach-ins.[1] In my case, that often means critiques of capitalism and of far-right discourses in modern American political culture. Such activities, when using no campus materials, are not the business of my employer, as they take place on my own time, using my own equipment and Internet access, and involve no illegal or unethical methods. Suggestions that academics should avoid political controversy, opinions, and even profanity, as I was recently told, make no sense. I am not representing myself as a spokesperson for a campus, and do not even mention my social media to my students.

Although quickly resolved, that there was an investigation into my online activities is cause for concern precisely for the chilling effect it can have in a world of at-will employment. If I have to worry that my political views and the language I use in my private life are of concern to my employers, then my right to express those views has been stifled, since those of us who need to work for a living will often self-censor. This has been particularly widespread among Middle East scholars in recent years, as a recent poll showed.[2] Intellectual freedom comes with a responsibility to speak out, and some backlash from the public is understandable at times (though of course it should never reach the point of death threats or physical attacks). But higher education depends upon the free exercise of reason, and participation in public debates is a part of that. The university system should be protecting us, not bowing to political pressure to silence us.

2. Who I Am and Why that Matters

By way of introduction, as it is quite relevant to the events in question, I am an autistic savant with ADHD who struggled in early life and school, came from a working class family with no college graduates, and did not start my own university education until I was 30 years old. Prior to that, I worked as a longshoreman, a class-A truck driver, a restaurant fry cook, and a computer network administrator, the latter helping to propel me towards academia. My penchant for tinkering with electronics lent itself to learning about computers, and my career was on the rise until the 1999 tech bubble burst and jobs became scarce. I took the opportunity to enter college, and went straight from BA to MA to PhD, acquiring plenty of student debt in the process. This put me into my dream job: teaching history at the college level.

My discipline is intellectual and cultural history, *i.e.*, the history of ideas, with the Middle East, and Europe as teaching fields. This meant I could easily find work as an adjunct instructor, but my circumstances gave me little chance of securing a tenure-track position. I was in my 40s, in an unusual discipline, and had limited time to write given the lengthy hours I worked. Moreover, I had devoted much time to both my own health issues, and the disabilities of my ex-wife,. All of this wasn't discouraging, as I genuinely loved teaching, and knew that I could continue my own research even if I seldom found the time and energy to publish it. My small home was a library long before college—I have 52 bookcases squeezed into it— as my autistic special interests tend to become all-consuming passions.

One of my biggest interests is identity formation—what makes us what we are. This has led me down a lot of rabbit holes, including many years studying some of the philosophies and movements based on group identity, like fascism and racism. This was not from any sympathy for such thinking—I've always seen myself as an outsider to group dynamics, devoid of a sense of belonging, and have been intensely curious about how and why the world is the way it is. From this study, my natural inclination towards anarchism as a political philosophy matured into a strong antifascist orientation. I ended up studying comparative genocide, worked for a while in a Holocaust library (don't let the name Liam O'Mara fool you: I am Jewish), and taught courses on topics like twentieth century political violence, populist neofascism, and the Israel/Palestine conflict. The deeper I went into understanding reactionary political thought and action, the more convinced I was that we needed to ensure that such views never again achieved wide currency or appeal.

You can perhaps guess, then, how I have felt watching far-right politics reënter the mainstream in numerous countries, from France to Japan, Hungary to Brazil, Germany to India, Italy to the Philippines, Russia to the United States. The evolution of the American right, from

Goldwater to Nixon, Reagan to Trump, has seen a steady increase in the use of conspiracy theories, nativism and xenophobia about migrants, violent bigotry towards the LGBTQIA+ community, deepening Islamophobia, and a resurgent Judeophobia/antisemitism. And all of this has been facilitated by a mix of far-right think-tanks, lobbying, and a for-profit "news" ecosystem spread across talk radio, cable channels, and the Internet.[3] One consequence of all this has been to normalize neo-Nazi and neo-fascist ideals and call them 'conservative.'[4]

One thing I tried a few years back, in my idealistic hope of making some positive change, was to enter politics. After a lifetime as a socialist Green, I registered as a Democrat and entered the Congressional primary in a very conservative Republican district. My goal was to show that authenticity, honesty, principle, and progressive economic policy could sway independents and non-voters, greatly aiding the Democrats' electoral performance. This was borne out in the result: In the 2020 race, my campaign gained 50,000 more votes than any Democrat had received in the history of the district. I had held the mainstream Democratic base while adding youth, leftist, and cross-over votes. And I did so as a long-haired, long-bearded, socialist-anarchist.

Then it all fell apart.

3. Poking Bears: How My Political Activities Were Greeted

Throughout the campaign I had engaged in forceful attacks both on the far right and on the tepid rhetoric of the Democrats in response to it. I believe, both then and now, that such things need to be addressed bluntly and directly, without fear of alienating so-called moderates, because it is exactly the tendency of such voters to enable the rise of fascism that is at issue. So long as people could tell themselves the racism was not a big deal, they could rationalize supporting far-right figures, and decades of the Overton Window taking the country ever farther to the right was something I felt compelled to address.[5] Many of my prior criticisms of the far right used the same rhetoric, and indeed the same image as caused the problem below, which left me rather unprepared for the outcome that time.

In the aftermath of the election, as the votes were being tabulated and it became clear how well a leftist had done in a safely red seat, my house was attacked by vandals and thieves. In total, over a two month period, it was broken into at least 17 times, as evidenced by seeing fresh outside damage and/or a triggered alarm. Early break-ins eschewed obvious valuables and instead rummaged in closets, scattering and rifled through personal papers, and took old laptops and external hard drives. It was hard not to wonder if this was a kind of targeted harassment and not simply bad luck.

Perhaps needless to say, these events caused me a lot of sleepless nights, as well as a couple of huge scares where I thought my cats were dead. In addition, my 80 year old tortoise, inherited from my grandfather, was callously killed by these vandals—something I would not expect of mere opportunistic thieves. I could not help but make a connexion between what I was doing politically and how malicious were these attacks. At one point my framed doctorate was removed from the wall, taken outside, and smashed deliberately into the mud, forcing me to have it reprinted. And my wedding photos from the 1990s were also dumped casually into the rain and mud, and completely destroyed. I lost a bunch of antiques to damage, and about $100,000 in total property losses and damage over the 17 break-ins before I was able to get the rest hauled off into storage while I figured out where to move. I gave up the house and no longer live in the same county.

4. Stepping In It: My Fight with Candace Owens

While all this was happening, I had to keep up my classroom day job, keep up the work to set up my next run for office, and keep up my activism, and the lack of proper rest made it hard for me to make up for my normal autistic social blindness and bluntness. Those on the ASD spectrum know that it takes a lot of energy to make our language fit the expectations of a neurotypical world. And in one 2am tweet on 23 March 2021, I failed to account properly for how my words could be twisted into the opposite of my intended meaning.

And twisted they were. Mind you, I understand now that the pithy way I expressed my point lent itself well to misunderstanding, and was thus flawed. In addition, I ought to have foreseen the way people could misconstrue the image accompanying my tweet. I should have used only my words. Ignoring the way the image could be viewed is an admitted case of white privilege blinding me, but the purpose of the post should not have been so obscure to anyone willing to read it.

On 22 March 2021, far-right political commentator Candace Owens published a tweet that used a 4chan neo-Nazi meme about Jewish control of the media to explain why society supposedly cannot talk about how black men are a violent threat to white and Asian lives.[6] In other words, she used literal Ku Klux Klan rhetoric about innate black violence, and supported her racist attack with an antisemitic conspiracy theory. Being both Jewish and an antifascist/antiracist activist, I was incensed.

My ill-considered response was to borrow an image from a political stunt by Wisconsin Democratic statehouse member Brett Hulsey, who in 2014 planned to hand out cut white napkins to Republicans at their convention to suggest that they are virtual Klansmen.[7] I know of many similar stories, like a Florida Congressman with whom I discussed my response to Owens, who had earlier used images of Klan cross-burnings in his mailers attacking GOP opponents, and hence I did not think twice about borrowing the napkin image for a response tweet. In that tweet I said, "Yikes, you may've dropped this" and placed the napkin image below.

While it may seem odd to link a Black woman like Candace Owens to the Klan's rhetoric, it really should not, since ideas are not biologically determined–anyone can absorb racist ideals, regardless of their own background. This is cleverly addressed by Ibram X. Kendi in his book on antiracism.[8] In fact, arguments frequently made to attack me for the post were themselves deploying racial essentialism in assuming a person regularly using neo-Nazi lines like "white lives matter" cannot be racist because of her skin colour.[9] Owens's language frequently works to normalize and promote the kind of "race realism" that has been circulating on the American far right, by drawing attention to out-of-context statistics in order to suggest white people are right to be afraid of black bodies.[10]

There is nothing particularly new about a fear of black bodies. In part this goes back to tropes from the days of enslavement, when worry over revolts caused a militarization of the young country and the spread of racist rhetoric about black 'savagery.' Such views have been political staples for centuries, but in the politically polarized world born in the desegregation fights it took on new salience.[11] In the decades since, political commentators and politicians have grown more comfortable with explicitly racist rhetoric, and this is perhaps a consequence of the media's sensationalizing of crime and heavy racialization of it.[12] It is unfortunately quite common for white women to cross the street when they see a black man coming up the sidewalk, and such things are a direct consequence of generations of media portrayals of black men as violent and criminal.[13] It is to such stereotypes that people like Candace Owens play.

I argue that far-right propaganda about black bodies, as about the LGBTQIA+ community, migrants, and others, is a form of stochastic terrorism, whereby propaganda and its link to power turns ordinary bigotry into murderous racism.[14] The worry now for the right, as it was in Ku Klux Klan propaganda of the 1920s and again in the 1960s, is that "that African Americans were dangerous because they were organizing to challenge white supremacy."[15] The need to delegitimize the movement for equality in America has led the right back into paranoid racist phantasies that Jews use issues around black Americans as a way to destroy white America, hence the "clown world" reference in her tweet.

My goal in linking Owens's tweet to Klan imagery was to draw attention to her use of literal Klan rhetoric, and to make the suggestion that such garbage belongs in the past and under those hateful hoods. But rather than accept my meaning, numerous people attacked me by saying I had "sent a Klan hood to a black woman as a threat of violence," which in context is absurd. Not only am I known as a pacifist academic leftist, I was calling it *her* hood, and talking about *her* threatening and racist argument. I would, in hindsight, leave off the borrowed image and instead call her out only in words, though the criticism and the association are fair.

But the damage was done, and my intended commentary was lost in a sea of right-wing attacks on "racist Democrats," including a bunch of articles in the far-right press.[16] This caused the Democratic Party to demand that I drop out and sever my links to both state and county bodies, and I was declared persona non grata at all Democratic events by the chair of the county party in an aggressive message that accused me of issuing "death threats" and violating their charter. It is hard for me to believe they could have been sincere in this inane accusation, and I feel they cared more for the way the press cycle worked than for the principles involved or the type of criticism being leveled.

One reason I had been keen to try my hand at politics was to see how voters responded to my principled stands, and the attacks on me didn't seem to hurt me with the voters in my run for Congress. I also received an avalanche of e-mails after the Owens attack expressing support for what I had said. My social media following did not decline at all in the wake of the right-wing vitriol directed at me, and I have every expectation that the affair could have been put to good use in another run for political office. But attacks of this nature in the press gave the Democratic Party the excuse it needed to encourage me to leave politics—it had never been happy about being saddled with a long-haired anarchist as a candidate. Not wanting to lend ammunition to the GOP or help them in another race by dividing the Democratic electorate, I obliged them and resigned my positions in the party.

5. Administrative Overreach: Chapman University Weighs In

What followed this was, if anything, more stressful, at least in the short run. The right-wing media's attacks on me were not pleasant, but since they were partisan in nature it was relatively easy not to give them much credence. And while it bothered me so many establishment Democratic figures were quick to cut me off, that was to be expected—their positions in the party were at risk. One of the central arguments in my campaign is also central to research into these ideologies—*viz.*, that liberals will generally roll over for the hard or far right when they feel threatened from the left. I had thought many of those involved in my campaign understood this, and was disappointed that they accepted the right's identity politics-based attacks, though misjudging people and situations is a personal failing to which I am accustomed. It was frustrating, too, that my tweet was reported to a county Sheriff's department as a violent threat, an absurd reading of my tweet, but since it was entirely the wrong county, I could ignore it (presumably it was reported to this department because the Sheriff in question is in the far-right Oath Keepers militia).[17] What I did not anticipate was complaints to my employers or that any of them would respond to such complaints. This is what most irked me.

Like so many trapped in adjunct life, I work at multiple campuses to make ends meet. One of them ignored the matter completely. Another called me up to say someone reported it. They looked at it, understood the context, and told me not to worry about it. A third, however, received a complaint and opened an investigation. As I said at the outset, I do not think this college was especially unfair in how it proceeded, and I hold no ill will about the matter. But it was still troubling that it was considered worthy of official investigation, given it was done in my private life (which I keep distinct from the colleges at which I teach by not naming them), and was explicitly political commentary (however ham-fistedly done), as was explained repeatedly in the days that followed.

On March 24, just two days after the ill-advised tweet, I received an official notification from the Equal Opportunity & Diversity Officer at Chapman University, letting me know that the campus had determined it was "necessary to conduct an investigation concerning allegations [that] have been made against you." It initially floored me that someone could have complained to the school, but then I remembered how many conservative donors are tied to the campus and understood what I was up against (This was, after all, an institution that had employed far-right lawyer John Eastman, who devised Trump's arguments for overturning the 2020 election results.) One day later, on the 25th, I heard from the assigned investigator, who contacted me to assemble a list of witnesses and to schedule a date for our interview, which was set for the following week. I replied with the requested information and then the waiting began.

But on the same day, I received a message from the Foundation for Individual Rights in Education (now the Foundation for Individual Right and Expression). FIRE said it had noticed the social media backlash against me, and noted that it appeared to concern "protected extramural expression." FIRE observed that some of the online vituperation directed towards me had tagged my employer, and said it would be happy to get involved in my defense. This came as some relief, since all of this was new and confusing to me, having never been involved in any kind of disciplinary procedure before. A flurry of messages followed in which I passed along information FIRE needed and then authorized it to write to the university on my behalf.

A few days later, on the 30th of March 2021, I was informed by FIRE that its letter was ready to go. The letter cited the Chapman University Statement on Free Speech, and that the lecturer's handbook explicitly committed the university to the American Association of University Professor's 1940 Statement of Principles on Academic Freedom.[18] FIRE's letter to Chapman's human resources department made clear that my social media includes no institutional affiliation, and argued that Chapman's stated policies made "clear commitments promising its faculty freedom of expression" and that such "commitments represent not only a moral obligation, but a contractually-binding legal duty on the part of the college."[19]

In addition, the FIRE letter made references to public statements by Chapman's president, Daniele C. Struppa, who had, according to FIRE, "persuasively argued that defending the right to engage in offensive expression—like burning the American flag or yelling 'God Damn America!'—reflects that our country's 'belief in freedom is such that we will defend those who demonstrate their dissent through an act that almost any country outlaws,' proving our 'commitment to freedom of expression.'"[20] Taken out of context and stripped of my accompanying words, the use of the Klan image indeed can be viewed as the sort of "offensive expression" defended by President Struppa. This constituted an effective defence against the university's investigation. Freedom of speech is a right granted to everyone, and I was pleased to see that arguments used to defend offensive right-wing speech also worked for impassioned left-wing speech, and indeed, for that of awkward, bumbling professors like me.

One day after the FIRE letter was e-mailed to Chapman's human resources office, I received notification from the investigator that my interview had been cancelled and that I would receive a communication from the Equal Opportunity and Diversity Officer. As the investigator had, on the evening of the 30th, informed me that our interview scheduled for 1st April at 9am was confirmed, I have to credit the FIRE letter with changing their mind. That having been said, I would like to believe that the university had come to this decision on its own given the absurdity of the claim that I had made a racist death threat. On the 4th I did indeed receive notification that the university had "elected to close its investigation against [me] and plans no further action in connection to the allegations."

6. Dealing with the Fallout: A Personal Coda

This came as some relief to me, as I had been terrified by the whole process and felt in danger of losing a faculty position I had come greatly to enjoy over the previous dozen years. As it happens, a few years later that position disappeared anyway due to a university realignment to employ only full-time faculty, but I had three more years there and I am grateful for them all.

Revisiting this episode has been difficult for me, and not due to any feelings of harm to my reputation or career from it. On the contrary, I have excellent letters of reference from the university and I care little what the far-right press thinks of me. In fact, my presence on Turning Point USA's Professor Watchlist is a point of pride, with its article focusing on my expertise in neofascist and populist movements.[21] The writers of that piece not only included links to my personal pages and to the university, to aid in doxxing attacks on me, they helpfully linked an editorial I wrote addressing the matter and my feelings on it.[22]

The stories in the Chapman student newspaper carried my apology for the use of the image and explained my reasoning, and I am as comfortable as I suppose I can be, given the circumstances.[23] But having to revisit one more in a lifetime of painful lessons brought on by an autistic blindness to how things can be misread has still made this a challenge, and I worry that this chapter may be too personal, and may seek to justify what I did. I should reiterate that I accept the use of the image was wrong. What I will not do is back down in the fight for freedom of expression, both in media and in the university, nor against the racist rhetoric of the far right.

In the end, I am grateful that all three campuses stood by me, and that, despite the unjustified opening of an investigation by one of them, that campus later dropped its enquiry, ultimately handling the matter reasonably well. Once informed I was engaged in legal and protected speech, speech that had been misinterpreted to constitute a political attack on my character, the university cancelled the proceedings and closed the case, all before advancing to a first interview. This was an immense relief, and far from the experience that I expect other contributors to this volume will have, and I am grateful to the administration for recognizing the matter was unworthy of such a process.

Nevertheless, despite the university acting correctly in the end, an investigation never should have commenced. Many people in my position are not so fortunate, so cases like mine deserve scrutiny. This is why, for all the difficulty I faced in returning to this matter to write about it, I feel doing so was important because of my continued commitment not only to free speech and enquiry, but to speaking out against intolerance and hate speech. We may not always do it perfectly, but intellectuals have a responsibility to speak out against injustices, and the new McCarthyism threatens academia's important rôle in the public sphere.

Endnotes

[1] By teach-ins, I mean special events, either held on campus or off, where folks engage in community education. I am a believer that education should be free, or as near to it as possible, and often volunteer my time to help others in their own pursuits of truth and knowledge.

[2] Restrepo, Manuela López. "'Fear Rather than Sensitivity': Most U.S. Scholars on the Mideast are Self-Censoring." NPR, December 15, 2023. Available at https://www.npr.org/2023/12/15/1219434298/israel-hamas-gaza-palestinians-college-campus-free-speech (accessed November 3, 2024).

[3] See, e.g., Mayer, Jane. *Dark Money: The Hidden History of the Billionaires Behind the Rise of the Radical Right*. Doubleday, 2016; Stahl, Jason. *Right Moves: The Conservative Think Tank in American Political Culture since 1945*. University of North Carolina Press, 2016; Huntington, John S. *Far-Right Vanguard: The Radical Roots of Modern Conservatism*. University of Pennsylvania Press, 2021; Miller, Edward H. *Conspiratorial Life: Robert Welch, the John Birch Society, and the Revolution of American Conservatism*. University of Chicago Press, 2021; Muirhead, Russell and Nancy L. Rosenblum. *A Lot of People are Saying: The New Conspiracism and the Assault on Democracy*. Princeton University Press, 2019; Stanley, Jason. *How Propaganda Works*. Princeton University Press, 2015; Donovan, Joan, Emily Dreyfuss, and Brian Friedberg. *Meme Wars: The Untold Story of the Online Battles Upending Democracy in America*. Bloombury Publishing, 2022.

[4] See, e.g., Schoenwald, Jonathan M. *A Time for Choosing: The Rise of Modern American Conservatism*. Oxford University Press, 2001; McGirr, Lisa.

Suburban Warriors: The Origins of the New American Right. Princeton University Press, 2001; Williams, Daniel K. *God's Own Party: The Making of the Christian Right*. Oxford University Press, 2010; Lavin, Talia. *Culture Warlords: My Journey Into the Dark Web of White Supremacy*. Legacy Lit, 2020; Hochschild, Arlie Russell. *Strangers in Their Own Land: Anger and Mourning on the American Right*. The New Press, 2016; Metzl, Jonathan M. *Dying of Whiteness: How the Politics of Racial Resentment is Killing America's Heartland*. Basic Books, 2019.

[5] See, e.g., Berlet, Chip. *Trumping Democracy: From Reagan to the Alt-Right*. Routledge, 2020; Neiwert, David. *The Age of Insurrection: The Radical Right's Assault on American Democracy*. Melville House, 2023; Dunbar-Ortiz, Roxanne. *Not 'A Nation of Immigrants': Settler Colonialism, White Supremacy, and a History of Erasure and Exclusion*. Beacon Press, 2021; Churchwell, Sarah. *Behold, America: The Entangled History of 'America First' and 'The American Dream.'* Basic Books, 2018; Tenold, Vegas. *Everything You Love Will Burn: Inside the Rebirth of White Nationalism in America*. Nation Books, 2018.

[6] Candace Owens's tweet: https://x.com/RealCandaceO/status/13741405983 28954888 (accessed June 11, 2024); on her neo-Nazi meme, 'Clown World.' *RationalWiki*. https://rationalwiki.org/wiki/Clown_World (accessed June 11, 2024); on her far-right politics, Holloway, Kali. "Candace Owens Is a Willing Tool of Republican Racists." *The Daily Beast*, 11 October 2020. https://www. thedailybeast.com/candace-owens-is-a-willing-tool-of-republican-racists (accessed June 11, 2024); "Candace Owens." *RationalWiki*. https://rational wiki.org/wiki/Candace_Owens (accessed June 11, 2024).

[7] DeFour, Matthew. "On Politics: Brett Hulsey Plans to Hand out KKK Hoods at Republican Convention." *Wisconsin State Journal*, 1 May 2014. https:// madison.com/news/local/govt-and-politics/on-politics/on-politics-brett-hulsey-plans-to-hand-out-kkk-hoods-at-republican-convention/article_ba05 39d0-1d24-58d7-882a-415e6715eb95.html (accessed June 13, 2024).

[8] Kendi, Ibram X. *How to Be an Antiracist*. One World, 2019.

[9] Anti-Defamation League. "White Lives Matter." https://www.adl.org/ resources/hate-symbol/white-lives-matter (accessed November 3, 2024); Polus, Sarah. "Ye, Candace Owens Wear 'White Lives Matter' Shirts at Paris Fashion Week." *The Hill*, 3 October 2022. https://thehill.com/blogs/in-the-know/3672606-ye-candace-owens-wear-white-lives-matter-shirts-at-paris-fashion-week/ (accessed November 3, 2024).

[10] On 'race realism,' see, e.g., Saini, Angela. *Superior: The Return of Race Science*. Beacon Press, 2019.

[11] See, e.g., McClellan, Nancy. *Democracy in Chains: The Deep History of the Radical Right's Stealth Plan for America*. Viking, 2017; Perlstein, Rick. *Before the Storm: Barry Goldwater and the Unmaking of the American Consensus*. Bold Type Books, 2001; Kendi, Ibram X. *Stamped from the Beginning: The Definitive History of Racist Ideas in America*. Nation Books,

2016; Lucks, Daniel S. *Reconsidering Reagan: Racism, Republicans, and the Road to Trump*. Beacon Press, 2020.

[12] Sun, Elizabeth. "The Dangerous Racialization of Crime in U.S. News Media." *Center for American Progress*. 29 August 2018. https://www.american progress. org/article/dangerous-racialization-crime-u-s-news-media/ (accessed June 13, 2024).

[13] Onwuachi-Willig, Angela. "Volunteer Discrimination." 40 *UC Davis Law Review* 1895. 2007.

[14] Graves, Joseph L. and Alan H. Goodman. *Racism Not Race: Answers to Frequently Asked Questions*. Columbia University Press, 2022.

[15] Gordon, Linda. *The Second Coming of the KKK: The Ku Klux Klan of the 1920s and the American Political Tradition*. Liveright, 2017, 41.

[16] e.g., Peacock, Alice. "'YOU ARE A PIG' Candace Owens Reports Dem Hopeful to Cops over KKK Hood Pic Sent in Reply to Tweet about Violence against Black People." *The U.S. Sun*, 23 March 2021. Available at https://www.the-sun.com/news/2569176/candace-owens-omara-kkk-racism -twitter-democrats/ (accessed June 13, 2024); see also, "The Professor Watchlist" by Turning Point USA, a group whose leaders have explicitly defended Hitler and Nazi Germany. Available at https://www.professor watchlist.org/professor/williamomara (accessed June 13, 2024).

[17] Neuman, Scott. "California Sheriff Defends His Past Membership in the Extremist Oath Keepers Militia." *NPR*, 8 October 2021. Available at https://www.npr.org/2021/10/06/1043651361/oath-keepers-california-sheriff-chad-bianco-january-6-us-capitol (accessed 6/13/2024).

[18] Chapman University. "Chapman University Statement on Free Speech." Available at https://www.chapman.edu/about/our-family/leadership/provosts -office/statement-on-free-speech.aspx (accessed June 13, 2024); Chapman University. Lecturer Handbook 4 (2018 – 2019). https://www.chapman.edu/ crean/_files/forms/1-3-pt-faculty-lecturer-handbook-2018-2019.pdf (accessed June 13, 2024).

[19] Foundation for Individual Rights in Education. E-mail sent to Dawn White at Chapman University. 30 March 2021.

[20] Daniele C. Struppa. "Beware the Slippery Slope of Censorship." *Orange County Register*, 29 November 2015. Available at https://www.ocregister.com/ 2015/11/29/beware-the-slippery-slope-of-censorship (accessed November 4, 2024).

[21] Turning Point USA. "William O'Mara, Chapman University." Professor Watchlist, Spring 2021. Available at https://www.professor watchlist.org/ professor/williamomara (accessed June 13, 2024).

[22] O'Mara IV, Liam. "Is This Who We Are? Thoughts on the Normalization of Hate, and on Leaving Politics." *Down with Tyranny*. 29 March 2021.

[23] Angelina Hicks. "Chapman Professor Quits Congressional Race following KKK T\eet, Home Invasions." *The Panther*, 12 April 2021. Available at https://www.thepanthernewspaper.org/politics/chapman-professor-quits-congressional-race-following-kkk-tweet-home-invasions (accessed 6/13/2024).

Enforcing Respect in a Canadian University
Mark Mercer

In November 2020, my university initiated disciplinary procedures against me for breaching my obligation "to contribute to a respectful environment for work and study and to help create an environment that is free from harassment and discrimination" as well as my responsibility "to respect the rights of others in the University community and to nurture a climate of respect."[1]

The allegation that I had treated anyone disrespectfully was without merit. My university's president and its academic vice president pursued the complaint to placate the complainant—and, as became clear in my disciplinary meeting, to flex their muscles and intimidate an outspoken professor. On 3 March 2021, four months after being called to discipline, I agreed to send the university president a statement expressing regret that anyone had been upset by the message I had sent, the message that provoked the complaint. Two days later I was informed that the disciplinary procedures against me had been discontinued.

The matter began with events in September 2020 at another Canadian university. Verushka Lieutenant-Duval, a professor teaching on a per-course basis at the University of Ottawa, mentioned the word "n_____" in explaining to her class the phenomenon of *subversive resignification*.[2] "Subversive resignification" is Judith Butler's term for a group's reclaiming a word outsiders have used to disparage the group's members. "Queer" was the first example Prof. Lieutenant-Duval mentioned; "cripple" was another. She spoke the N-word in her course ART 3317, "Art and Gender." The taboo word appeared in the week's reading, a reading Professor Lieutenant-Duval's department had approved.

At the beginning of the next class, Professor Lieutenant-Duval raised for discussion the matter of speaking sensitive words. It was after this class that a student complained to the university.

Without contacting Prof. Lieutenant-Duval or conducting any investigation, the University of Ottawa's dean of arts put ART 3317 on hiatus while determining how to proceed. Ten days later the course resumed, with a parallel section for students who didn't want to continue with Prof. Lieutenant-Duval.

The University of Ottawa failed to uphold academic values and treated Professor Lieutenant-Duval poorly. Ottawa U should have contacted Prof. Lieutenant Duval about the complaint before taking any action. It should not have put the class on hiatus. It should not have opened a second section. The university issued no statement supporting Prof. Lieutenant-Duval's academic freedom to conduct her class as she saw fit; instead, in its official pronouncements, the university took the side of the complainant. ("This language was offensive and completely unacceptable in our classrooms and on our campus," wrote Kevin Kee, Dean of Arts, in a message to students and professors.) Ottawa U didn't explain to those who complained or to the university community generally that Prof. Lieutenant-Duval had done nothing wrong. And the university deprived students of three or four class sessions.

The University of Ottawa may have done damage to Prof. Lieutenant-Duval's career. She has continued to teach on a per-course basis at universities other than Ottawa U, but universities, perhaps fearful of controversy, may well be reluctant to hire her for a permanent position. Prof. Lieutenant-Duval's faculty union was right to object to the university's actions. The grievance the union launched was settled on June 13, 2023, when the university paid Prof. Lieutenant-Duval an undisclosed sum. Since then, Ottawa U has said nothing about the way it handled the complaint or the execrable manner in which it treated Prof. Lieutenant-Duval.

At the time of the Lieutenant-Duval affair, I was president of the Society for Academic Freedom and Scholarship (SAFS), a Canadian professional society. SAFS sent a letter to the president of the University of Ottawa, copied to other Ottawa U administrators, criticizing Ottawa U's decisions to put Prof. Lieutenant-Duval's course on hiatus and to open a second section. The letter also criticized Ottawa U's failure both to uphold academic values and to explain them to students and the university community.[3]

The failure of administrators at the University of Ottawa to support academic values, including academic freedom in teaching, and the academic mission of their institution angered me (indeed, it still does). To bring awareness of the university's abrogation of academic values to a wider audience, I wrote an article for *Minding the Campus*, the blog of the National Association of Scholars, entitled "Bad Words at Ottawa U." This article was published on 9 November 2020.[4] It explains how candor is necessary to university teaching and how deference to sensitivities is inconsistent with respect for intellectual and moral autonomy.

Before this piece was published, I incorporated it in an email message I sent to administrators at my university and at Ottawa U (on 23 October 2020), and then to others who had spoken publicly on the Lieutenant-Duval affair (on 30 October 2020). The email message I had constructed from the article included the N-word, along with arguments about the anti-academic implications of euphemism and indirection. This email message was the basis of a complaint against me initiated by the academic vice president and the president of my university.

I began my email message by saying that past missteps by administrators at my own university made me doubt that our administrators would do any better than Ottawa U's did should something similar happen here. My university's president and academic vice president made my prediction come true.

On 6 November 2020, I received a letter from my university's president summoning me to a disciplinary meeting. The meeting was held on 9 December. These were the days of the COVID-19 lockdown, and so the meeting was conducted by Zoom. The university president, the academic vice president and the university lawyer were together in a room at the university. Present online from their homes or offices were the dean of arts, the chair of the philosophy department, two faculty union executives, the faculty union lawyer, my lawyer, and me.

The university's president and the university lawyer questioned me. They did not answer my questions, whereupon the university lawyer instructed me to stop querying them. I was not told who had complained and I was not shown the complaint. Based on what I had previously heard from the union lawyer and what was said at the meeting, I suspect that the primary complainant was an equity, diversity and inclusion officer at my university. But I do not know for sure.

None of the university's administrators explained how my sending the message violated any university rules. What seems to have happened—though, again, I don't actually know—is that a non-academic university administrator (that is, a university administrator who was not a professor) was upset by seeing the N-word mentioned in my message. Why the academic vice president and the president thought that I had treated a recipient of the email message disrespectfully, I do not know, for they wouldn't say. At this stage of the disciplinary process, they were not required to articulate a case against me. University administrators would ultimately have been required to justify a case against me to an arbitrator some months later, if they had imposed discipline and the union then objected.

I'll note here that in calling me to a meeting, Saint Mary's University failed to comply with the very policies it had accused me of violating. The policies the president cited state that members of the university community who believe someone is treating them disrespectfully are to talk to the person themselves, or to ask a conflict resolution officer to act as an intermediary. I had heard nothing from anyone about my October messages until I received the president's letter summoning me to a disciplinary meeting. Complaints to the academic vice president, most notably complaints that initiate disciplinary procedures, are, by policy, supposed to come last, not first.

I suspect that neither the president nor the academic vice president really cared whether the allegation that I had treated someone disrespectfully was well founded. That the allegation was unsound was irrelevant to their interests in pursuing it. If the complainant was who I think it was—an equity, diversity and inclusion officer—then the president and the vice-president academic would want to show both her and her supporters that they take racism seriously. An EDI officer and her allies could make life difficult for academic administrators at my university if administrators seemed to do little when an EDI taboo was violated.

Administrators at my university, and in other Canadian universities, are interested in appearing to be sensitive to emotional security and identity issues, particularly for members of minority groups.

An underlying reason for calling me to a disciplinary meeting was that my university, along with universities throughout Canada and elsewhere, is seeking to redefine the notion of respect that is to govern personal relations on campus. Traditionally, respect among university people is respect for the ability and willingness of members of the campus community to think and value for themselves. Under this conception of respect, disrespect is when you don't treat people as capable of handling difficult ideas or discussions. The new conception of respect is based on identities and feelings. In this conception, treating people as believers in candor and openness in critical discussion is potentially disrespectful, as doing so might put a person's feelings at risk. Calling me to discipline was my university's way of signaling to those aware of what was happening that senior administrators were enforcing the new conception of respect.

The faculty union officers appointed to the case were consistently unfriendly toward me. They were unhelpful before, during, and after the disciplinary meeting. The union lawyer evinced no understanding of academic freedom or academic culture, but at least he took pleasure in fulfilling his professional responsibilities. I was buoyed somewhat by my sense that he would count it a personal victory to get me off.

Neither the union executives nor the union lawyer had briefed me on university disciplinary procedures, so I was often in the dark. The disciplinary meeting lasted a little over an hour. When it was over, I thought that the university would deliberate and eventually render a decision. I was wrong, for the "meeting" had not ended, despite the fact that we had all left the room and/or exited Zoom. Because the meeting was officially still in progress (as I found out only in late January 2021), the university was under no obligation to decide or settle anything. The lawyer for the university and the lawyer for the union met privately a couple of times, and it wasn't until 8 February 2021, two months after the Zoom disciplinary meeting (and three months after the summons), that I heard anything more about the case. The process, as any faculty member who's been targeted knows, is part of the punishment.

On February 8 I heard from the union lawyer that the university will discontinue "disciplinary procedures" if I sent a statement to everyone who received my 23 and 30 October email messages. The statement would need to express regret that some recipients were upset by seeing a word in those messages. I reluctantly agreed to this deal. I did so because I was doubtful that my union would contest any discipline the university would impose, and I was dispirited by the thought of having to file a complaint with the Nova Scotia Labour Board against my union for shirking its duty of fair representation. I was also on sabbatical that school year and wanted to return to my scholarly research. For those reasons, I prepared a statement, and the union lawyer took it to the university lawyer to see whether it was acceptable.

I felt uneasy about the requirement that I send the statement of regret to everyone who had received either the 23 or 30 October email message. I had sent the message to 38 people and at most two, I believe, had complained. The 36 people not upset by my email message presumably had little interest in learning that I regret having upset the one or two whom I'd purportedly upset. I informed the union lawyer that I would not be sending my statement of regret to all thirty-eight recipients of the original message. Instead, I'd send the statement to my university's president for him to distribute as he saw fit. The university lawyer accepted my proposal.

On 3 March 2023, I received from the university lawyer an extensively re-written version of the statement I had submitted. I was amused to see that the statement now included the phrase "the 'n-word,'" not a phrase I myself would ever use. (My own version had simply said that some people were upset by my message; I didn't say anything about what upset them.) I sent the version re-written by the university lawyer to my university's president.

Two days later, I received from the president a letter entitled "Notice - Disciplinary Process Discontinued." That was the official end of my brush with discipline. In his letter, the president wrote that in my statement, "you expressed regret for your use of the 'n-word.' . . ." But I had not expressed regret for mentioning the N word. I had expressed regret, rather, that some people had been upset by seeing the word. The president went on to say that his view remains that by sending my message, I had violated Saint Mary's University policies on harassment and discrimination. He asked that I "be mindful of this for the future." His letter did not try to explain how I had violated those policies.

I had agreed to send a statement expressing regret that some people were upset by my message, but I was annoyed that the president had twisted my meaning. Moreover, I had not agreed to hear the unfounded and rebutted allegations against me repeated. I certainly had not agreed to be warned.

I sent email messages to my university's president about his misconstruing my statement. I asked him what I was to be mindful of and whether he was warning me, but I received no reply. (The union lawyer told me the president had asked him to direct me not to write to him, the president, about the affair again. The union lawyer, I would have thought, should have told the president to tell me himself.)

I asked the union officials a couple of times to clarify for me whether the last paragraph of the president's notice constituted a formal warning. At Saint Mary's, formal warnings do not count as discipline and cannot be contested by the faculty union (the lowest level of discipline is a reprimand; the faculty union cannot appeal a warning but can appeal a reprimand). Receiving a warning was not part of the agreement, and I was not willing to accept one. I heard nothing from the union about what the final paragraph of the president's letter amounted to until September 2023, long after the faculty union officials who handled my case had stepped down. The 2023 union president assured me that the final paragraph of the letter discontinuing disciplinary processes did not constitute a formal warning. It did not contain the word "warning," she told me, and wasn't presented in the manner of an official warning. It was, then, simply the university's president thumping his chest.

As I said, to bring the disciplinary process to a halt, in early March 2021 I sent to the president of Saint Mary's University a statement, written by the university lawyer, expressing regret for the upset that my email messages from October 2020 had caused one or two of its recipients. My statement was not an apology and it did not imply any wrongdoing or culpability. I don't know what the president did with my statement.

People who over the years have told me about their run-ins with university discipline almost always say that they found the experience surreal. One professor I know came near dismissal for urging that his university's EDI personnel be let go. The professor's call was deemed a case of sexism after an administrator noticed that almost all the EDI personnel were women. One psychology professor was summoned to a meeting with a human resources official for speaking about "boys and girls," rather than "children," in a class. A history professor earned a short suspension for wearing the garb of a 19th century tribal chief—cultural appropriation!—when discussing with his class a treaty that the chief negotiated. Crucial to how surreal these episodes were to the professors was their sense that no one involved in the matter seemed to recognize it as absurd save themselves.

I, too, found the experience surreal. The union lawyer counted the number of times the N-word appeared in my message. Is there a limit, I wondered, that had I stayed under, a complaint would have been deemed unreasonable by the academic vice president?

The union lawyer also suggested at a preliminary strategy meeting that the complainant wasn't a professor serving as an administrator, but a ranking member of the human resources staff. The lawyer explained the relevance of the station of the complainant: if she agreed with me about how the University of Ottawa had mishandled the Lieutenant-Duval affair, he said, she wouldn't be able to say so publicly for fear of contradicting what one of her superiors might think. It took a long series of questions to figure out what the union lawyer had in mind. His meaning was that because she does not enjoy a faculty member's academic freedom, she might have filed a complaint against me so she would stay in the good graces of her superiors, even if she had agreed with my stance on academic freedom. There is no way to make sense of any of this, and yet the two union executives at this Zoom meeting just took it all in stride. I felt I'd materialized in a universe in which the laws of logic don't hold.

Summoning me to a disciplinary meeting for my email message protesting Prof. Lieutenant-Duval's treatment, whatever words that message contained, violated my academic freedom as described in the collective agreement under which I work. That agreement protects both criticism of the university and the exercise of the free expression rights guaranteed by the Canadian Charter of Rights and Freedoms. Even had I violated the policies I was alleged to have violated (which I hadn't), I could not be disciplined, given that the Collective Agreement takes precedence over all other university policies. I made this point at two or three different Zoom meetings with the union lawyer and the two union executives. It was ignored. What is the point of a faculty union, I wondered, if not to stand up for academic freedom when it's threatened?

I hired a lawyer, Carol Crosson, soon after receiving the summons, despite the fact that the faculty union was to represent me in the case. A private lawyer would have no official role, so Carol simply observed and gave me advice. She advised me not to make the case public while it was proceeding. She thought that doing so might stiffen the resolve of the academic vice president and president to punish me. Although I talked freely to friends and to members of the Society for Academic Freedom and Scholarship about what was happening, many of whom disagreed with Carol's advice to stay quiet, I said nothing publicly until the proceedings were discontinued. As soon as they were, I posted everything I had (with phone numbers, email addresses and some names removed) on my website—after checking with Carol, of course.

I enjoyed support from friends and my wife and two adult children during the four months of the case. "It makes me so mad I could spit," said one friend. After I let colleagues and others know what had happened, I received many empathetic messages. Professors at Saint Mary's, some of whom I didn't know well, took me aside to tell me how shocked they were at the news and how well I had dealt with the situation. Strangers sent me email messages castigating my university's president and criticizing my union for its lackluster performance. People also sent me arguments about why no word should ever be banned from discussion. This was edifying for me. I'm a philosopher of authoritarianism, so I was more familiar with the arguments against free speech and open inquiry. All the same, I was disheartened that many presumed defenders of free speech and open inquiry chose to stay silent.

My brush with discipline has not affected my career, at least not in any negative way of which I am aware. My attitudes and practice have not changed. I continue to think that no words are to be forbidden in academic life (or outside it, either). Refraining from violating a taboo just in order to respect that taboo is contrary to sincerity and collegiality. I continue to assume that the people with whom I interact academically prize their ability to think and value for themselves. To engage in euphemism or indirection with them would be to treat them disrespectfully, as though they are unable to hear others express controversial ideas or to express them in their preferred way. I hope I have not begun to censor myself in fear that someone will file another complaint, but it is possible I have.

My relationships with my colleagues have not changed. Many of those who favor equity, diversity and inclusion initiatives have long been hostile toward me, but I don't think their ranks have increased as a result of my case. The new academic vice-president is more committed to academic freedom and collegiality than the old one was. Our president will step down in 2025. One can be cautiously optimistic that governance and collegiality will improve.

I began writing about academic culture, academic values (including, centrally, academic freedom) and the academic mission of the universities in 2006, stimulated by a colleague's own brush with discipline. Philosophy professor Peter March (now retired) was investigated after he posted cartoons depicting Mohammed, first published in a Danish newspaper, on his office door.[5] Because of the Peter March affair, I began to read and to contribute to the scholarly and popular literatures on academic institutions and higher education.[6] I hadn't had much to say about the means and ends of academic discipline, though, until my own case. Since then, I've published two articles on the topic, "The Use and Abuse of University Discipline" and "Is Informality Simply Too Dangerous?"[7]

I also produced an "Instructor's Statement on Freedom of Expression in the Classroom," to which I include a link on all my course syllabi.[8] With this statement, I hope to combat self-censorship among my students. Most students who have mentioned the statement to me approve of it and are glad that it exists. But one student unsuccessfully petitioned my university's academic vice president to order it removed from my syllabi. Another student walked out of the classroom when I was discussing the statement, and dropped the course.

In a recent discussion with my current academic vice president, I learned that no administrator explained to the complainant in my case that he or she had not been treated poorly. In addition, no one in the administration communicated to the complainant about the importance of freedom of expression and respect for autonomy. No academic administrator spoke with the president or academic vice president about their lack of commitment to free discussion. I doubt any administrator advised my university's president against distributing to all 38 people my statement of regret; whether out of fear, indifference, or incomprehension, administrators at my university may have stood aside as the university's president beclowned our institution.

Most significantly, I learned that no university administrators have, in the years since my case, pressed for changes in policies or practices to bring them into line with proper academic values. It remains ambiguous what our policies enjoin us to respect—autonomy or feelings.

In that discussion with the academic vice president, I noted that members of the university community who believe someone has treated them disrespectfully should be encouraged to try to work it out with the supposed offender themselves. After all, informal resolution is the official university policy. Collegiality suffers when administrators step into disputes between members of the university community.

The complaint about my email message gave the two most senior administrators at my university the opportunity to demonstrate their commitment to the concept of respect as deference toward feelings and identities. This is a fundamentally anti-academic concept of respect, one inconsistent with respect for intellectual and moral autonomy. It doesn't much matter for their concerns that in the end I wasn't disciplined. Professors and students who value free and candid discussion will have understood the message that summoning me to a disciplinary meeting was meant to send. It takes courage to ignore that message, but ignore it people must if the academic endeavor is to continue.

Endnotes

[1] Documents and commentary regarding my brush with academic discipline are available on my website at https://professormarkmercer.ca/disciplinary-action/ (accessed November 8, 2024).

[2] My practice is to write the word out, but I am here conforming to editorial standards.

[3] The letter the Society for Academic Freedom and Scholarship sent to the University of Ottawa and other documents relevant to the Verushka Lieutenant-Duvall affair are available on the SAFS website, https://safs.ca/university-of-ottawa-responds-poorly-to-demands-to-censure-professor/ (accessed March 2, 2024). As president of the Society, I signed the letter.

[4] Mercer, Mark. "Bad Words at Ottawa U." *Minding the Campus*, November 9, 2020. Available at https://www.mindingthecampus.org/2020/11/09/bad-words-at-ottawa-u/ (accessed March 2, 2024).

[5] Armstrong, Jane. "Canadian Professor Fans Flames." *The Globe & Mail*, February 6, 2006. Available at https://www.theglobeandmail. com/news/world/canadian-professor-fans-flames/article702987/ (accessed March 20, 2024).

[6] Mercer, Mark. "Report on the Peter March Affair at Saint Mary's University." *Newsletter of the Society for Academic Freedom and Scholarship*, September 2006. Available at https://safs.ca/newsletters/article.php?article=443 (accessed November 8, 2024). This was my first article as a critic of the university.

[7] Mercer, Mark. "The Use and Abuse of Academic Discipline." *Academic Questions*, Winter 2021. Available at https://www.nas.org/academic-questions/34/4/the-use-and-abuse-of-university-discipline (accessed March 3, 2024); Mercer, Mark. "Is Informality Simply Too Dangerous?" *Newsletter of the Society for Academic Freedom and Scholarship*, September 2021. Available at https://safs.ca/newsletters/article.php?article=1157 (accessed March 3, 2024).

[8] Mercer, Mark. "Instructor's Statement on Freedom of Expression in the Classroom," *Minding the Campus*, May 18, 2021. Available at https://www.mindingthecampus.org/2021/05/18/instructors-statement-on-freedom-of-expression-in-the-classroom/ (accessed March 3, 2024).

I Called an Academic Conference
a "Woke Joke" and Ignited a Firestorm

Stephen Porter

I am a tenured full professor in the Department of Educational Leadership, Policy, and Human Development in the College of Education at North Carolina State University, and I teach applied statistics and research methods to graduate students in the College of Education. I also blog on my personal website, largely around issues in education research. When the Great Awokening began in 2014, and white liberals moved far to the left on issues of race and identity and public discourse changed, I began to comment on—and make fun of—issues around education and social justice.[1] Within the next few years, these far-left attitudes would come to dominate campus culture, and my blogging would raise the ire of NC State faculty, administrators, and professional colleagues in my field of study.

Our departmental structure is complex compared to many academic units, but my story will not make sense without some background, especially if you are not in academia. (I spent the first 20 minutes of my grievance mediation just explaining my department structure to the two faculty mediators.) My department is unusual in that we only teach doctoral and master's students, typically individuals seeking a graduate degree to advance their career in education. When I arrived in 2011, the Department had several different program areas; I became a member of the Higher Education program area, based on the substantive content of my research, which primarily focuses on higher education. At the time, the Higher Education program area conferred two degrees, a master's and a doctorate.

In 2015, the College reorganized its doctoral programs into areas separate from the master's degrees; we now refer to these areas as doctoral concentrations. In practice, this separation never occurred for most program areas, including Higher Education, because the faculty for each degree completely overlapped. We held faculty meetings just as before, in which we discussed issues around the master's degree and doctoral concentration in Higher Education; other events, such as orientation, were still jointly held with master's and doctoral students.

Targeted by my new Department Head

My ordeal began at the beginning of the 2017-2018 academic year, with the arrival of a new, very social-justice oriented Department Head, Dr. Penny Pasque. She began by holding one-on-one introductory meetings with all faculty in the department. Expecting a nice chat, I was surprised when she told me that I was described as a "bully" in an anonymous climate study of our department, conducted by the Office for Institutional Equity and Diversity the prior year. Naturally, I asked what the accusation was and who had made it. She refused to identify who made the accusation, and she would only describe one supposed bullying incident, when a representative from the College's Council on Multicultural and Diversity Issues came to our department meeting to discuss a proposed diversity question to be added to our course evaluation. Survey methodology is one my specialties, and during the meeting I asked what the Council had done to establish the reliability and validity of the proposed question (absolutely nothing, as you might suspect). Our discussion was amicable, like any other department meeting. I pointed out that asking questions about survey methodology could hardly be considered bullying, and since the climate study was anonymous, anyone who held a grudge against me could use it to make my life miserable.

I thought that was the end of it until two months later, when Pasque sent me an email summarizing our conversation about my so-called bullying behavior. I realized she was trying to establish a paper trail of problematic behavior on my part, so I asked her if a copy of the climate study was placed in my personnel file. She replied no, which was technically true: when I asked for a copy of my personnel file a year later, I discovered that her summary email (all quoted documents can be found on my website, https://stephenporter.org/badprofs), but not the climate study, had been secretly placed in my file without any opportunity for me to contest it.

In the spring of that academic year, *Inside Higher Ed* broke a story about faculty unrest in the College of Education over the possible hire of a controversial higher education scholar, Dr. Terrell Strayhorn.[2] Strayhorn is a scholar whose research focused on social justice and higher education. He was fired from a center directorship at Ohio State University for misuse of funds, and he resigned from his position as a tenured full professor at Ohio State University, while paying the university $29,000. Part of the controversy was that Dr. Alyssa Rockenbach, a member of our Higher Education program area who chaired the search committee, refused to circulate his resume to the faculty in our department.

I sent an email to the Higher Education faculty referencing the article, saying "This kind of publicity will make sure we rocket to number 1 in the [*U.S. News* graduate program] rankings. Keep up the good work, Alyssa!" This resulted in another meeting with Pasque, where she repeatedly asked me what my intent was in sending the email. Knowing she was trying to entrap me, I countered with a simple question: What was wrong with the email? Not surprisingly, she avoided answering, because she knew I had not violated any University polices or regulations by commenting on this very public, and in terms of impact on our reputation, negative controversy.

Pasque called me into another meeting a few weeks later, which turned out to be quite bizarre. She had spoken with the Graduate School and the Provost's office about me and learned that a tenured faculty member did not need to be a member of any program area if they were still associated with a department. She said that she thought I was unhappy in the Higher Education program area, so I should resign from the program area and continue working as a regular faculty member in the department. I just would not have any doctoral advisees (one of the primary parts of the workload in our department, because we have no undergraduate students to teach or advise), and would not be associated with the program area in any way. I replied that I was perfectly happy in the Higher Education program area and had no desire to resign my position. At this point it was clear she wanted me out of the Higher Education program area completely.

My annual evaluation at the end of the 2017-2018 academic year was fine, except for this odd sentence added to the section discussing my service activities: "It is my expectation that you—and all faculty—maintain collegial relationships as defined by the college [RUL 05.67.204.3.2]." I believe this was her attempt to lay the groundwork that I was somehow not collegial. Note that the addition of the sentence implies uncollegial behavior on my part, but there is no explicit mention of any such behavior.

The beginning of the 2018-2019 academic year was peaceful, until I published my infamous blog post about an academic conference in September.[3] Different sub-areas within the academic discipline of education, such as higher education, have their own professional organizations and conferences. Within higher education, the major organization is the Association for the Study of Higher Education (ASHE), and they host a national research conference every November. As with the rest of academia, the conference shifted during the Great Awokening, from a focus on student success and higher education policy to an emphasis on race and identity politics. Because research on student success and higher education policy tends to be quantitative in nature, this also meant a shift in research methodology used by presenters, from statistical analysis to qualitative research.

A few months before each conference, ASHE produces a program book listing the titles of all the conference presentations. A colleague at another university did a word search for social-justice oriented words as well as words associated with quantitative research. Not surprisingly, he found many mentions of words associated with the leftward shift of the conference, such as *qualitative* (74), *identity* (69), *diversity* (46), *inclusion* (27) and *oppress* (23), and almost no mentions of words like *quantitative* (19), *regression* (13), or *quasi-experimental* (3). I posted his analysis with the title, "ASHE has become a woke joke." Apparently, the post blew up a bit on Twitter, but because I'm not on Twitter, I did not pay any attention to the negative tweets.

The next month I was called into a surprise meeting with Dr. Pasque, Dr. Lee Stiff, the Associate Dean of the College of Education (the number two person in the College after the Dean), the coordinator of the Higher

Education program, Dr. Joy Gaston, and the coordinator from our K-12 policy program area. As the meeting began, I discovered that the subject was a potential spousal hire for our department.

When universities hire faculty, they often must find a position for the spouse of the new hire. These are referred to as "spousal hires." When the spouse is also a professor, universities can struggle to find a position for them. North Carolina State, the University of North Carolina at Chapel Hill, and Duke University have agreements to help one another find positions when hiring one half of an academic couple. In this instance, Chapel Hill was hiring a new faculty member and needed a position for his wife, also an academic.

The potential spousal hire had a strong publication record and was well respected within the field of higher education policy research, but it was clear that the Higher Education faculty did not want to hire her, because she was not seen as focused on social justice. I was a strong advocate for her, not only because of her reputation, but especially because spousal hires are essentially "free" positions: the University covers the cost of their compensation as part of the inter-institutional agreement.

You can imagine my concern when they told me of a wonderful new opportunity: I could resign from the Higher Education program area and create a new doctoral concentration called Higher Education Policy, along with the spousal hire and Dr. Pasque! (At the time, doctoral concentrations required three members.) I protested, saying that we could not just create a new concentration on the spot without consulting with faculty colleagues in our department. Instead, I suggested that she be hired within the Higher Education program area and that she and I could explore the creation of a new doctoral concentration after she arrived. This proposal was immediately rejected.

The tenor of the meeting changed after I refused to resign from the Higher Education program area to join a non-existent concentration. The Associate Dean was very angry and came down hard on me, telling me we were at risk of losing the spousal hire due to my intransigence. It was one of the most stressful meetings of my career, because it felt like a carefully planned ambush. Finally, I blurted out "Give me a fucking break, folks. I was the one who said [the potential spousal hire] should come. And now

I'm the bad guy because I don't want to leave Higher Ed for a non-existent program area?" The meeting finally ended after I repeatedly declined to resign from the Higher Education program area.

A few days later, on October 18th, I was written up by Dr. Pasque for using profanity in the meeting, even though other faculty at the University have used profanity in meetings. At this point I knew I was in her crosshairs and resolved to be quiet in future meetings as much as possible.

Strangely, I received a second letter from Pasque on November 7th. I say strangely, because I had not done anything between the spousal hire meeting and receipt of the letter to provoke her into writing the second letter. Because this occurred only one week before my public chastisement at the ASHE conference (see below), I speculate that either she or Dr. Gaston was contacted in advance by Dr. Lori Patton Davis, the President of ASHE, warning them that she was going to publicly call out one of their faculty members during her presidential address. Thus, Dr. Pasque moved to proactively lay out the groundwork for my removal from the Higher Education program area, so that it would not seem to be in response to the President's speech.

The letter attempted to establish a pattern of problematic behavior on my part. She listed the dates of three conversations she had with me about collegiality, but not their content. The dates of these conversations referred to:

1. The introductory meeting where she told me about the bullying accusation from the Climate Study.

2. My email to Rockenbach about the public controversy over her handling of the search that included Strayhorn as a finalist.

3. The spousal hire meeting where I used profanity (on a single occasion).

She wrote, "Therefore, in order for you to remain in the Higher Education program within ELPHD [acronym for our department], you must refrain from lashing out at faculty members, using negative or disrespectful rhetoric, and trying to intimidate your colleagues. You need to repair the trust between you and your peers, maintain that trust, and foster a stronger climate of collegiality." The first sentence is remarkable: there is no evidence in our meetings to support charges of intimidation or lashing out at faculty. I asked for clarification of these charges and received no response. Note that at this point I had been at NC State for almost a decade, and my "problematic behavior" only cropped up after Pasque became department head.

A week later, on November 15th, a doctoral student texted me from the ASHE conference. She said Dr. Patton Davis was denouncing my "woke joke" blog post during her presidential address to the conference, with a huge picture of me on the screen behind her on the stage. I jokingly texted back, "Does this mean I'm not getting the ASHE lifetime achievement award?" The presidential address is always in a large ballroom, so there were several hundred people in attendance, including faculty and doctoral students from my department.

The week after the conference, Pasque sent me an email saying that graduate students in the department were having "strong reactions" to Dr. Patton Davis' speech and that the department "need[s] to pay attention to" them. She wrote, "I would like to propose we have a community conversation about ASHE (and the field IF warranted) the week after Thanksgiving break, to include faculty and graduate students. I think students would like to hear from you and have some questions for you; they could also hear from Joy [Gaston] as a member of the board; and hear from all the faculty—hoping all could come."

I knew this would turn into a struggle session straight out of Communist China, where I would be at the front of the room and faculty and students would take turns denouncing me and my blog post. I also suspected that Dr. Pasque wanted me in a stressful situation similar to the spousal hire meeting, hoping I would verbally lash out at students in frustration at their criticism. We had a back and forth via email about the so-called community conversation, but Dr. Pasque could not answer questions as to what exactly it would be addressing and what the goal was. Wisely, I declined to take part and instead said that I would be more than happy to meet one-on-one with any student or faculty member (No one took me up on my invitation.) I also suggested that concerned faculty and students could contact Dr. Patton Davis; after all, she made the speech, not me.

At this point I knew I was on thin ice, so I was silent during all program area and department meetings for the rest of the year. I was determined not to give Pasque any pretext for removing me from the Higher Education program area, but that turned out to be a lost cause.

Pasque had received an offer from Ohio State University and was leaving at the end of the 2018-2019 academic year, after spending only two years at NC State. In her last act as Department Head, in July 2019, she removed me from the Higher Education program area. Strangely, she included the removal in my annual evaluation letter instead of a separate personnel action. She wrote that "The Higher Education faculty were not able to make concerted progress on the program and a change is needed. One of a few changes I am making is that you will be removed from the Higher Education Program, but not removed from the Higher Education PAS [doctoral concentration] for the ELPHD PhD." She went on to say that the Master's and PhD programs in higher education would now operate separately, and that because PhD faculty rarely meet, "you will be expected to teach one additional class in the methods program moving from a total of 4 (per approved SME 2015 [Statement of Mutual Expectations, which lists our job duties]) to 5 per academic year."

The normal teaching load for tenured faculty at a major research university like NC State is four courses per year, and I had never heard of anyone being forced to teach a fifth course. Nor had I heard of anyone being involuntarily removed from a degree program. Clearly, Pasque and other faculty wanted me to be as far as possible from the Higher Education program, because of my conservative views and the controversy my "woke joke" blog post had caused within our professional association. But faculty need to be associated with a degree program, so Pasque was forced to let me remain a member of the Higher Education doctoral concentration, while removing me from the master's program.

I believe the addition of a fifth course had one purpose: to get rid of me permanently. Either I would refuse to teach the fifth course and be fired for insubordination, or I would quickly tire of the additional workload and seek a private sector position (she knew I had worked previously with a local research firm).

After carefully studying University regulations, and consulting with an attorney, in August 2019, I decided to file a grievance to contest her action. In retrospect, I think this surprised them; NC State has approximately 2,500 faculty and as far as I can tell, only one or two grievances happen each year. I suspect most administrators at NC State are unaware of the grievance process.

I made the following arguments:

- In Pasque's annual evaluation letter, there was no justification for removing me from the master's program area. Indeed, she stated that the *faculty* had failed to make progress, not me;

- The addition of a fifth course did not make sense in terms of my workload. I was not heavily involved in the master's program, but an additional course would have a huge impact on the time available for my research activities. Simply put, the expansion of my teaching duties made little sense given the small reduction of my time spent on service;

- Changing my teaching load violated University regulations because it was done without my agreement and without the generation of a new statement of faculty responsibilities. It also violated the University teaching workload regulation, which stated that the typical teaching load at NC State was four courses per year. I spoke with several senior colleagues about my situation, and they all agreed that the addition of a fifth course to my workload was unprecedented at NC State.

Going through the grievance process made me aware of how these proceedings are stacked against the accused faculty member, and how universities willingly ignore their own regulations. According to our regulations, the process begins with mandatory mediation between the faculty member and the administrator named in the grievance and must be concluded within 35 days of filing, unless both parties agree to an extension. Furthermore, the extension cannot be more than 90 days from the filing date. I filed my grievance at the end of August, and despite my objections and pointing out that I did not agree to extend the time, the mediation did not occur until the end of November, three months after filing.

The mediation took place with my new department head, Dr. John Lee. He offered to remove the fifth course if I would not contest my removal from the master's program. I refused, of course, and the mediation ended. At this point, the grievance hearing should have been held. It did not occur until the end of May, *a full nine months after filing*. The University delayed the hearing for an entire academic year!

While I waited for the hearing, I was not allowed to attend meetings of the Higher Education master's program area by my new Department Head, John Lee, and the Coordinator of the Higher Education master's program area, Dr. Joy Gaston. I learned from a colleague that all Higher Education doctoral activities were being conducted during these master's meetings, so as a result, I was systematically excluded from all discussions about the Higher Education doctoral program as well as other activities, such as the orientation for new doctoral students, the faculty retreat, where we discuss the future of the master's and doctoral program, and monthly faculty meetings. I was even excluded from the December admissions meeting, and consequently I was not assigned any new doctoral students to advise. I protested to Dr. Lee both in emails and in person, to no avail.

My exclusion at one point became ludicrous. The Higher Education faculty have an annual meeting to discuss doctoral students beginning their second year of studies. We review a writing sample and students' academic performance to see if they should continue with the doctoral program. During the meeting, the faculty panicked when they realized that only a student's advisor has access to their academic transcript, and consequently they had no idea as to whether my second-year advisees had made adequate academic progress. The faculty ended up passing them all without reviewing their performance.

Finally, the grievance hearing was held on May 26, 2020 via Zoom. I was able to call witnesses, and I requested that every Dean in the University participate, so that I could ask about how often they had removed faculty from programs and added a fifth course to their workload. Not surprisingly, they all refused.

During the hearing I presented my arguments. The hearing was structured such that after the grievant presents, the panel considers whether the grievant's evidence, *if* presumed true, would constitute a violation of University policies or regulations. The panel concluded it did not, so the hearing ended before continuing with a rebuttal presentation from Dr. Lee. The panel stated that the master's program removal was within the purview of the Department Head, and that because I was not yet forced to teach the fifth course, I could not establish that I had been adversely affected. The result was disappointing, but not surprising. It was the necessary first step, however, to filing a lawsuit.

Taking legal action and the birth of a new doctoral concentration

The 2020-2021 academic year began the same way, with my continued exclusion from any discussions concerning the Higher Education doctoral program. I continued to complain, and I think it was clear to everyone involved that I was not going to quietly accept my *de facto* exclusion from the Higher Education doctoral program. This became crystal clear in October, when my attorney sent letters of preservation to Drs. Pasque, Lee, Gaston, and Dr. Mary Ann Danowitz, the Dean of the College of Education who had signed off on Pasque's action against me (These letters are formal requests to retain pertinent evidence.) At this point, my obstinacy had become a problem in need of a solution.

Their solution was to create a parallel Higher Education doctoral concentration containing all the Higher Education faculty but me. To see how ridiculous this was, you should understand how doctoral programs in colleges of education are usually structured. Not every college of education has a specialization in higher education, but if they do, there is only one. Our department was unusual in that we had two postsecondary doctoral concentrations: Adult, Workforce, and Continuing Professional Education, and Higher Education. This was so unusual that in her first year as Department Head, Dr. Pasque actually held talks to combine the two concentrations into a single postsecondary concentration. Yet, now there would be a *third* higher education doctoral concentration, called Higher Education, Opportunity, Equity, and Justice. (A better name would have been the Porter Memorial doctoral concentration.) Every member of the

Higher Education doctoral concentration was invited to join but me. All of the other faculty left, and I remained as the sole full-time faculty member of the Higher Education doctoral concentration.

I had retained a local attorney specializing in free-speech issues when I filed my grievance, and he told me I could not file in federal court until the grievance process was finished. Throughout this year he advised me on how to deal with Dr. Lee. When the grievance panel issued its decision in June 2020, I expected to file suit very soon thereafter. But after sending out letters of preservation in October, my attorney became increasingly difficult to reach.

The Black Lives Matter protests over the death of George Floyd occurred that summer, and I began to wonder if he was reluctant to represent a conservative in the current atmosphere. From our conversations it seemed as if almost all of his clients were on the left. After repeated requests, he finally sent me a draft filing in December, 2020, and I thought it was terrible. After consulting with my wife, a former attorney, I decided to fire him and seek new legal counsel.

Luckily, I saw a news item about a professor suing his university over his speech. The report mentioned his attorney, Samantha Harris, a former attorney for the Foundation for Individual Rights and Expression. I contacted her, and she agreed with my assessment of the draft filing and rewrote it from scratch, and we filed a civil rights lawsuit in federal court in September, 2021.[4] She argued that universities were becoming much smarter in targeting outspoken faculty, and instead of outright termination, they subjected them to death by a thousand cuts in an attempt to push them into resigning. We asked for a declaration that NC State had violated my right to free speech, for me to be placed back into the Higher Education Master's program area, and for me to be allowed to join the new Higher Education doctoral concentration.

Unfortunately, I lost when NC State filed a motion to dismiss; the judge argued that the employment actions taken against me were not "materially adverse," and that there was no causal connection between my speech and the employment actions. The 4th Circuit Court of Appeals upheld the lower court's ruling with a split vote and a strong dissent by one member of the three-judge panel. During the hearing, one of the judges made a comment that illustrates the success of the university's strategy of seeking to marginalize me: "What's the issue here? He's still employed, isn't he, and getting a salary?"

In his dissent, Judge Richardson wrote,

> Our job, however, is not to appraise the value of Porter's speech or his personal virtue. It's to take the facts as alleged in the complaint, read them in a light most favorable to Porter, and then decide whether he's plausibly stated a claim for relief. And, drawing all reasonable inferences in Porter's favor, the University threatened his tenure by removing him from his program area because of his protected speech. The University has not yet produced evidence to justify its decision. And no such evidence springs forth from the face of the complaint. So Porter's claims ought to survive, and the district court's contrary decision ought to be reversed. This is not a close call.

> My friends in the majority apparently seek to return to the days of Justice Holmes. But only for certain plaintiffs. In doing so, they have developed a new "bad man" theory of the law: identify the bad man; he loses. But see Oliver Wendell Holmes, The Path of the Law, 10 Harv. L. Rev. 457 (1897). The majority's threadbare analysis willfully abandons both our precedent and the facts in search of its desired result. Even for a Holmesian, that cynicism breaks new ground.[5]

We filed a petition with the Supreme Court, which declined to hear my case in January 2024.[6] Thus ended my legal case after two and a half years.

Aftermath

The past two and a half years have been strangely peaceful, in part because the University succeeded in isolating me in my own doctoral concentration. The university has left me alone, perhaps because the federal government takes a dim view of retaliation for filing a civil rights lawsuit.

However, a recent incident does not bode well for my future. In July 2023, Dr. Gaston was appointed as my new department head. I immediately requested that she be recused from supervising or evaluating me during her tenure as department head, because she was named as one of the parties in my lawsuit. As a result, Dr. Paola Sztajn, Dean of the College of Education, instituted what is known at my university as a conflict of interest management plan, and she assigned an associate dean to evaluate me instead of Gaston.

Dr. Sztajn rescinded the management plan on May 1, 2024, citing the end of my lawsuit as the reason. If an employee does not agree with the Dean's decision regarding conflicts of interest management, University regulations specify they can appeal to the Vice Chancellor for Research and Innovation. I filed that appeal in June 2024, citing the regulations: "Conflict of interest relates to situations in which financial or other personal considerations may compromise, may involve the potential for compromising, *or may have the appearance of compromising an employee's objectivity* in meeting University duties or responsibilities" [emphasis added].[7] I argued that any reasonable person would conclude my suing Gaston in federal court certainly gives the appearance of compromising her objectivity. At the time of this writing, I am waiting on the Vice Chancellor's decision. Whatever his decision, clearly Dean Sztajn strongly desires to have my faculty nemesis in charge of evaluating my job performance.

We will see what the future holds, especially in terms of my annual evaluation and post-tenure review, which takes place every five years. I suspect within the next couple of years the higher education doctoral concentration will be targeted for elimination due to its small number of doctoral students. When Pasque was trying to remove me from higher education, she told me that faculty do not need to belong to a specific master's program or doctoral concentration, if they are a member of a department. So, this might just mean further isolation, or worse, the university could reverse course and claim that I should be terminated due to my lack of association with a master's program or doctoral concentration.

Whatever happens, I will not hesitate to fight back.

Endnotes

[1] Yglesias, Matthew. "The Great Awokening." Vox, April 1, 2019. Available at https://www.vox.com/2019/3/22/18259865/great-awokening-white-liberals-race-polling-trump-2020 (accessed November 9, 2024).

[2] Flaherty, Colleen. "Questions About Job Candidate's Past." *Inside Higher Education.* April 10, 2018. Available at https://www.insidehighered.com/news/2018/04/11/anonymous-faculty-members-nc-state-object-job-candidate-who-was-ousted-ohio-state (accessed November 23, 2024).

[3] Porter, Stephen. "ASHE Has Become a Woke Joke." Last modified September 3, 2018. Available at https://stephenporter.org/ashe-has-become-a-woke-joke (accessed November 9, 2024).

[4] My initial court filing is available at https://stephenporter.org/badprofs/#filing (accessed November 9, 2024).

[5] United States Court of Appeals for the Fourth Circuit, Opinion, July 6, 2023.

[6] Dorrian, Patrick. "Justices Decline to Hear Free-Speech Case Over 'Woke Joke' Blog." January 22, 2024. https://news.bloomberglaw.com/litigation/justices-decline-to-hear-free-speech-case-over-woke-joke-blog (accessed November 9, 2024).

[7] NCSU regulations are available at https://policies.ncsu.edu/regulation/reg-01-25-01 (accessed November 9, 2024).

SkullGate

Elizabeth Weiss

Department of Anthropology

San José State University

This is a modified version of an article that appeared in *Skeptic*, Volume 29, Number 2.

I'm a retired anthropology professor at San José State University (SJSU). My focus is skeletal remains and radiographic images (such as x-rays and CT-scans) to understand both bone biology and past people's lives.

I've investigated diseases, such as leprosy in a Byzantine Carthage collection, and osteoarthritis patterns from Californian Native Americans. I've used x-rays to look at growth fusion lines as age-indicators in remains from autopsy collections, as well as 1.8 million year-old human ancestors, which can be used to inform paleoanthropology and forensic anthropology.[1] And I've tried to reconstruct past people's activities, looking at stress fractures and bone strength in skeletal remains from 18th century European Canadians and Paleoindians.[2] I've also looked at trauma and how it relates to genetic continuity in California Native Americans to help determine that the earliest prehistoric San Francisco Bay Area tribes were replaced by tribes coming in from further inland and further south.[3]

In 2017, as the 30th anniversary of the enactment of the Native American Graves Protection and Repatriation Act (NAGPRA) was approaching, I decided to reach out to now-retired attorney James W. Springer to see if he'd like to co-author a book on the topic of repatriation--the process by which artifacts and skeletal remains are given to Native Americans.[4] The book would take a critical perspective on the law and the ideology behind repatriation. Jim and I had been corresponding for years due to our mutual concern that NAGPRA and similar laws would ruin our ability to accurately understand the past–including the ongoing mystery of how the Americas were first peopled.

Upon getting a book contract, I submitted a request for leave to my chair and my dean. My chair provided an exceedingly supportive statement that also demonstrated that he understood the controversial nature of my position. His statement ended with:

> Finally, since Dr. Weiss holds a controversial position on NAGPRA–focusing upon the ways in which the interpretation and implementation of repatriation and reburial laws may impede intellectual inquiry–her new project is likely to spark lively discussions among various stakeholders. Consequently, her book might potentially boost the department's national reputation as a center that fosters creative and unorthodox viewpoints on important public issues.

My leave was approved. Jim and I published our book, *Repatriation and Erasing the Past*, in September 2020, just in time for the 30th anniversary of the passage of NAGPRA.

Repatriation and Erasing the Past delves into the problem with repatriation laws and the ideology behind it.[5] This ideology stems from post-modern theory, in which there is no such thing as truth and all conclusions are subjective. Repatriation ideology places importance on who is providing the information and whether that individual can claim a victim status; thus, information from Native Americans is considered to have greater validity than information coming from a European American, regardless of its truthfulness.

We also explore NAGPRA's seeming violation of the U.S. Constitution's First Amendment. NAGPRA violates church and state separation by requiring each review committee to have at least two traditional Indian religious leaders; thereby, promoting a specific religion–a traditional Indian religion—as a required component of the law. Further violation of the First Amendment includes NAGPRA's acceptance of creation myths, in the form of oral tradition, as evidence for cultural affiliation (i.e., connection between a present tribe and past peoples) to support repatriation events.

We also looked at how NAGPRA and repatriation ideology encourages censorship: researchers who wish to continue their research will shy away from certain areas of study or fail to publish materials that may lead tribal leaders to stop working with them. Repatriation ideology, accepting that Native American cultures should be held in deference, also promotes discrimination. Anthropologists eager to continue collaboration with tribes will, for instance, heed menstrual taboos that prohibit women who are menstruating from engaging in research and fieldwork. In short, repatriation places ideology, entrenched in creation myths and religious beliefs of cleanliness and status, over science. We called for a return to objective knowledge and an abandonment of anti-scientific values.

When I returned to campus after my leave in Fall 2019 (before the book came out, but after the book had been completed), I was awarded the Warburton Award, which is SJSU's College of Social Sciences highest scholarly award. My title for the Warburton Award talk was "A Collection is Forever" (a play on the title of a famous article called "NAGPRA is Forever.") In my presentation at the award ceremony, I included an extensive slideshow of photos from the Ryan Mound collection (also known as CA-Ala-329), a collection that I curated of prehistoric and precontact Californian Amerindians dating from 2200 years ago to about 220 years ago.

Annu. Rev. Anthropol. 1996. 25:81–103
Copyright © 1996 by Annual Reviews Inc. All rights reserved

A COLLECTION

∧

~~NAGPRA~~ IS FOREVER: Osteology and the Repatriation of Skeletons

Jerome C. Rose,[1] *Thomas J. Green,*[2] *and Victoria D. Green*[3]

[1]Department of Anthropology, University of Arkansas, Fayetteville, Arkansas 727

[2]Arkansas Archeological Survey, University of Arkansas, Fayetteville, Arkansas 72′

[3]Geo-Marine, Inc., 550 East Fifteenth Street, Plano, Texas 75074

KEY WORDS: bioarcheology, Native Americans, federal regulations, reburial, skeletons

ABSTRACT

The 1990 Native American Graves Protection and Repatriation Act requires universities, museums, and federal agencies to inventory their archeological collections to prepare for the repatriation of skeletons to their Native American descendants. The loss of these collections will be a detriment to the study of North

My university, knowing my perspective on repatriation was controversial, was happy to celebrate my scholarly achievements, including my forthcoming book on the subject. Even early on, when I was hired in 2004, I had spoken out against the loss of scientific data through the repatriation of remains. In 2008, I was chosen by then-Provost Gerry Selter to present in the University Scholar Series; my talk was about my scientific research and my work criticizing repatriation and reburial of skeletal remains. I point all this out because shortly after *Repatriation and Erasing the Past* was published, administrators from my chair to the University president started to sing a different tune. Rather than praising my accomplishments and expressing appreciation of the images that exemplified the importance of studying skeletal remains, they started to condemn my scholarship and take retaliatory actions to derail my career.

It is sometimes difficult to spot the moment when things start to unravel. For me, the first sign of trouble ahead was in mid-December 2020, upon receiving a panicked email from my publisher. This was soon followed by a phone call, in which they lamented that they were "in crisis mode" in part because of a letter expressing concern over the publication of *Repatriation and Erasing the Past.*[6] The letter's six original signatories were all anthropologists, some at top universities. When it became an open letter, it attracted nearly 900 signatories, most of whom had listed their academic affiliations. The letter called the book racist and wanted it to be retracted, or at least wanted a halt to providing the book in open access formats to universities and libraries–in other words, they didn't want to give people the opportunity to read it for free. Ironically, after Jim and I responded to the open letter, the repatriation activists advised people not to buy the book, but rather to read through an open access source, such as a library! Through several phone calls with the publisher, Jim and I were able to convince them not to pull the book, but the publishers nevertheless issued an apology, written by University of Florida Press Director Romi Gutierrez:

> I apologize for the pain this publication has caused. It was not our intent to publish a book that uses arguments and terminology associated with scientific racism. I assure you that, months ago, changes to our editorial program had already started to take place, including greater focus to inclusivity and sensitivity, and we will continue and redouble these efforts.

Jim and I stood up for what we had written. We wrote articles defending our work, and fought back in the public press and social media.[7] The campaign to cancel our book failed, and it remains in print.

When this "crisis" was brought to my attention, I was not on social media and, thus had no insight into the campaign against *Repatriation and Erasing the Past*. However, once the publisher informed me of the Twitter campaign against *Repatriation and Erasing the Past*, I reached out to my department chair and my dean. My chair informed me that he had already known about the cancellation attempt. What I didn't know was that both my chair and my dean would become my biggest foes, plotting against me, perhaps from the start of the campaign to cancel me.

Calls for the "depublication" of *Repatriation and Erasing the Past* increased. Upon seeing a number of my colleagues' names on the open letter, I made the decision to post the response Jim and I wrote to my department's anthropology listserv. This led to the end of unmoderated posting on the anthropology department's listserv, after my chair admonished me for my post.

On January 4th, 2021, my chair wrote a letter to all faculty, staff and graduate students in our department "reminding everyone that the opinions expressed. . . don't represent the position of the SJSU anthropology department, and that the principle of academic freedom allows us all to freely pursue our ideas—even if they're controversial or unpopular." His letter concluded with a paragraph in which he states that my book takes a "Victorian-era approach to anthropological inquiry." I replied to his letter and corrected his misunderstanding, making sure that all those who received his letter received mine. I wrote that: "[My chair's] use of the term "Victorian-era" is to misunderstand our perspective though I would like to remind everyone Charles Darwin was from the Victorian-era—and where would we be without him?!"

The result of this exchange was that my chair decided to put together a webinar series, explicitly in reaction to my book and the "harm" it caused: "Emancipatory Theory & Praxis: Confronting Racism in American Society and American Anthropology." His chosen speakers included Agustín Fuentes, who is currently at Princeton University. In his talk, Fuentes's focus was on white supremacy and violence.

In response to this webinar, I asked my chair whether I could put together a similar webinar to focus on academic freedom and diversity of thought. His initial response was that there was no funding and no time to do so. Then, when I suggested we move it to the next semester, he dug up some rules on guest speakers that we never used before and hadn't been used for his own webinar. He had us retroactively vote on whether we approve of his Emancipatory Theory & Praxis webinar and the selected speakers, including Fuentes! After a contentious meeting, guidelines for inviting speakers were hashed out, which were meant to protect academic freedom. But since those guidelines have been in place, I have never been able to get department support to hold a webinar or invite a guest speaker. Ironically, I still held events funded by my chair, which meant that professors wouldn't announce these talks in their classes and the department's support wouldn't be listed on any advertisement. Since I was suing him, he presumably wanted to be seen as acquiescent. But more on that in a minute.

Over the following months, the controversy simmered down, but the environment was to get heated again in the following spring and summer. For one thing, my coauthor Jim and I had decided to submit an abstract to the 2021 Society for American Archaeology (SAA) annual meeting. The SAA was founded in 1934 and states that it is "dedicated to research about and interpretation and protection of the archaeological heritage of the Americas." Our talk, "Has Creationism Crept Back into Archaeology?," advocated for a return to data rather than creation myths to ensure that repatriation can be done as fairly as possible. I compared creation myths of Native Americans to other creation myths while pointing out that the SAA has taken a stand against the teaching and use of biblical interpretations to understand the past. In particular, it has spoken out against intelligent design and other forms of creationist ideology.

Although our topic did not seem particularly controversial to me, there was a movement to prevent the presentation, which was pre-recorded, from being aired.[8] This movement was unsuccessful, and the comments section in the session quickly filled up with name-calling and accusations of racism. I attempted to answer every legitimate question. All talks were supposed to stay on the SAA platform for two months, but after an exchange between the conference organizers and myself, the SAA decided to de-platform me. The outgoing SAA president had supported the inclusion of my presentation as evidence of academic freedom, and stood up for the decision to include it. The incoming president, however, took a very different approach: she apologized for the "harm" Jim and I caused, removing the talk from the platform, and forming a committee to ensure that critics of repatriation ideology would not be allowed on the program again.

On June 3, 2021, my department chair presented a review of the controversy surrounding my research in a panel moderated by my dean at the annual meeting of the Council of Colleges of Art and Sciences, a national professional association for college deans and department chairs. In this presentation, called "What to Do When a Tenured Professor is Branded a Racist," my chair painted me as manipulative, racist, eccentric, and professionally incompetent. He stated that my anti-repatriation position was a reason to withhold resources from me, and to ensure that departmental procedures are always voted on (so I would always be outvoted). He also indicated that my next professional review would state that I was incompetent. He suggested that if I taught my perspective on NAGPRA and repatriation to students or assigned my books in classes, he would consider removing me from the classroom. Throughout the talk he used a pseudonym for me, but it nevertheless was clear that this was a personal attack. He proceeded to describe me as odd, not "warm and fuzzy," and bizarrely suggested that I might lock myself into the curation facility where the university's archaeological collections were held to prevent a repatriation from occurring (although I might disagree with NAGPRA, I've never advocated breaking the law in defiance). Further, he painted my ideas as "scientific racism" and stated that he would have signed the open letter calling for my book to be de-published had he not been serving as department chair.

Perhaps most surreal, my chair painted himself as a victim, claiming that he had no idea of the "skeletons in my closet" (the skeleton being that I'm an anti-repatriation anthropologist). But this was clearly a lie, as seen in the approval for my leave to write the book, his support of my Warburton Award, and the many discussions we held about repatriation over the years. My chair was even on the search committee that hired me, and one of my first papers was on Kennewick Man and how repatriation and reburial of Paleoindians is an affront to scientific inquiry and hinders our ability to reconstruct the past.

It was this talk by my chair that led me to contact the Pacific Legal Foundation. After discussing the issue with the Foundation's lawyers, they suggested that I ask for a complete retraction from both my chair and dean. I did so, but it was to no avail. They would not retract their accusations against me. Since they had deemed me incompetent, it was clear that my job was on the line. Even a tenured professor at San José State University can be fired for incompetence.

Pacific Legal Foundation wrote letters to the university forewarning them that if action were taken against me, such as removing me from the classroom, they would file suit. As Fall 2021 began, I was looking forward to our first in-person classes since March 2020. I returned to SJSU's curation facility that semester, eager to continue ensuring that the skeletal collections would be well-cared for and that research on the remains could be undertaken by myself and others. This facility held many important specimens, including the Ryan Mound collection, a Carthage collection, nonhuman remains from the Ryan Mound, chimpanzee data from Chimpanzoo, and x-rays of the leg bones of the Ryan Mound people.

My duties as curator of the collections were curtailed by COVID-19 and the move to online-only instruction. When returning, I took a few photos of me with the collection–I was genuinely happy to be back at work! I had research hypotheses that I had hoped to test, including some that involved studying the bones directly and others that involved using the x-rays. Yet, shortly after returning to the collection, an activist mob of repatriation supporters ensured that the university would keep me away from all collections for ten months and from any material–human bones, artifacts, animal bones, or x-rays–from the Ryan Mound permanently.

The latest cancellation attempts started up after I published an op-ed in the *San Jose Mercury News* about California's repatriation law called CalNAGPRA, which I described as "NAGPRA on steroids."[9] The passage of CalNAGPRA, further strengthened by the California Native American Cultural Preservation Act, enacted in 2021, set the stage for repatriation events that would hollow out collections in all of the state's universities. CalNAGPRA states that Native American knowledge must be deferred to– that is, if there is disagreement between scientific evidence and Native American oral tradition, it is the Native American oral tradition that must be heeded. Thus, all that is needed for repatriation is for a Native American to say that there is a link between the modern tribe and the past peoples– this would then trump all the DNA and forensic evidence in the world.

There must also be continuous consultation with all tribes in the area, and their requests for handling, access, and repatriation must be followed. When I posted my op-ed on Twitter it quickly garnered over a thousand comments, mostly from angry repatriation activists calling me names like ghoul and grave robber, and puerile insults like "eat shit and die." A common criticism among my critics is the strawman "How would you like it if I dug up your grandma?" In reality, I'd be intrigued to study her remains!

Shortly after the op-ed, I posted a now infamous tweet—I'm holding a skull and it states "So happy to be back with some old friends." This tweet led to another flurry of comments and university reactions. On September 29, 2021, my provost wrote a scathing letter condemning me, stating: "This image has evoked shock and disgust from our Native and Indigenous community on campus and from many people within and outside of SJSU."[10] He went on to criticize the photo by stating: "[I]n what context is it ever ethically appropriate for an academic to handle remains while smiling with ungloved hands while calling these remains 'friends?' I doubt many colleagues in the fields of Forensic Science or Physical Anthropology would find this palatable."

I reached out to the provost and suggested that we discuss the issue and address the public together, but he declined. I then provided him with a letter to send to the same people who had received his letter about the photo.[11] I clarified a variety of misunderstandings; for instance, according to British Museum guidelines, "handling remains with gloves is only necessary if these remains have always been treated with gloved hands and other sterile conditions."[12] Gloves are actually actively discouraged by the National Park Service because it leads to people dropping materials more often. I also stated that SJSU has:

a culture of promoting the anthropology department and the collection; this culture has revolved around interesting images. I have even gotten funding for this and helped promote human diversity by introducing people to the concept of skeletal diversity. There have been promotional posters in which I have a similar pose. This has never been against university, college or departmental protocol. Not long ago, as recently as 2019, this was celebrated (such as when I won the Warburton Award for excellence in scholarly activities in relation to my work on the collection). It instills a love of evolutionary anatomy, a love of anthropology, and a promotion of university resources.

My response led many colleagues to reach out to me, finding similar photos from SJSU and many other institutes, including the Smithsonian, and providing support. However, one supportive colleague faced an onslaught of criticism after he was quoted in the *Mercury News*, which led him to withdraw his support of my freedom of expression. He called to let me know that he was frightened. Others too have expressed quiet support—a former student and lecturer in my department let me know that she didn't think that I was racist at all and felt the need to reach out to me in an email, but she spent all day debating whether to send it from her university account or her private account—she decided on sending it with her private account.

The photo's effect still reverberate. The NAGPRA and CalNAGPRA audit of the California State University stated the audit has been requested in part due to this tweet (which I don't believe since I had heard about the possibility of an audit months before).[13] And, in her presentation on university climate, the new president, Cynthia Teniente-Matson, showed an antiquated photo of a woman sitting at a desk with skeletal remains as an image clearly designed to illustrate old-fashioned and offensive views that purportedly contribute to our poor campus climate. Never mind the decade-long athletics sex scandal that occurred in which senior administrators didn't protect female athletes from a sexual predator coach—and then tried to fire the whistleblower. This resulted in the resignation of the previous president and the athletics director. But, no, the fallout of Skullgate was still clearly in people's minds, and I was the University's chief villain.

These latest twists—the op-ed and Skullgate—led the then-university president to rescind my access to the curation facility. They literally changed the locks. She also stated that no photos were allowed of the Native American collection, or even of the boxes that held the bones.[14] I responded by noting that non-Native American remains and other collections were in the facility and not subject to repatriation law. Thus, I should have immediate access to those collections, such as the Carthage collection. Nevertheless, it took ten months to finally get access to the Carthage collection.

My ongoing discussions with Pacific Legal Foundation led us to the conclusion that letters of warning were not enough. We all agreed there was a serious possibility that my university would summarily fire me. Accordingly, we decided the time had come to be proactive: we initiated legal action against the University for its retaliation against me.

While putting together my case against SJSU, we reached out to senior scholars in physical anthropology and archaeology to seek expert opinion on protocols for handling skeletal remains. Douglas Owsley has worked with many prestigious universities and museums, including the Smithsonian. He is the subject of Jeff Benedict's book *No Bone Unturned: Inside the World of a Top Forensic Scientist and His Work on America's Most Notorious Crimes and Disasters.*[15] Dr. Owsley wrote a supportive *amicus* brief for my lawsuit: "Based on my experience there was nothing improper about Professor Weiss's photograph." He also noted that "it is not standard protocol to use gloves when examining archeological bones in the laboratory."

In her *amicus* brief, Della Cook, who managed the North American skeletal collections held by the Department of Anthropology at Indiana University from 1973 to 2021 and has collected data on skeletal remains around the world, wrote "Photographs of researchers measuring or otherwise doing observations on bones, ancient and modern, are routine in our field, and many anthropologists smile in such photographs." She added that "There are several such photos of me in circulation, and in most of them I am smiling."

As the case against the University moved forward, my chair—abetted by some departmental colleagues and staff—tried to terminate my access to the Carthage collection. One of the most vitriolic attacks came from a colleague who also serves as a tribal liaison: I was a eugenicist and shouldn't get access to any collections. The university also transferred the protocol for access to skeletal collections to the Institute Review Board (i.e., the human subjects committee), a move I fought against. The chair held meetings to try to remove me from my duties as curator, although these duties were written into my job contract; perhaps most tellingly, the department took action to attempt to curtail my ability to take any photos of bones—key to understanding past diseases is sharing and comparing images.

As my department tried to curtail my ability to conduct research, ridiculous moments ensued. One of the cultural anthropology professors in my department asked whether I had written permission from these individuals to take the photos—she of course knew full well that the people had been dead for at least hundreds and sometimes thousands of years! I fought all these restrictions and no policy on non-Native American collection photos was put in place. I'd won a battle, if not the war.

The department also worked with Native Americans and a retired forensic anthropology lecturer—who did not conduct research, never managed collections, and whose previous role at SJSU was to teach a single undergraduate class on forensic anthropology a year—to rewrite protocols that would determine access to collections. The protocol read like a list of all the things that I disagreed with: there was even a menstruation taboo included. Upon seeing this, my lawyers and I cited it as a likely Title IX violation, and that if it wasn't removed, we would file a complaint. The menstruation taboo was removed.[16]

Further complications arose when I requested x-rays and nonhuman animal bones (from refuse piles; not burial goods). These items were quickly seized upon by the Bay Area Native American tribal leaders as now being sacred, and thus out of reach for my research. One of my research areas is bone biology, so these animal bones could be used for my scholarship. Yet, whatever I requested instantly became off-limits and "sacred."

When my lawsuit against SJSU began in May of 2022, Judge Beth Labson misread CalNAGPRA and allowed Native American tribes and the university to abuse the law in order to retaliate against me. Her deference to the tribes included an understanding of "sacred objects" that contravene both NAGPRA and CalNAGPRA: "Specific ceremonial objects which are needed by traditional Native American religious leaders for the practice of traditional Native American religions by their present day adherents." Since there are no ceremonies using x-rays, they could not be needed to practice any religion. In addition, not all artifacts are subject to reburial through NAGPRA and CalNAGPRA; only artifacts that are "funerary objects," "objects of cultural patrimony," or "sacred objects" are included in repatriations. These are also defined in the same way by NAGPRA and CalNAGPRA: for instance, funerary objects are "objects that, as a part of the death rite or ceremony of a culture, are reasonably believed to have been placed with individual human remains either at the time of death or later." Thus, x-rays and animal bones should not be included in repatriation. Judge Labson's decision was clearly flawed, but her initial statement questioning how would she feel if it was her grandmother's skull that I was holding showed her perspective.

On May 10, 2022, the judge dismissed my case, but I was allowed to amend my complaint. The judge stated that the tribes were an "indispensable" party to the case, but that the tribes were considered sovereign and, thus, could not be sued. It's a catch-22 for all who seek to fight cases that include Native American stakeholders. Nevertheless, we filed an amended complaint, excluding the Native American collections, and to everyone's—my council, myself, and the university's council—surprise the judge's previous motion to dismiss my case was overturned. The University lawyer's submission was written in a very angry and unduly personal way; unduly *ad hominem* for a legal brief. Perhaps this played a part in the decision. Unfortunately, I still had no recourse to get access to x-rays, to nonhuman animal bones, or even the ability to enter the curation facility.

Through the Research, Scholarship, and Creative Activity (RSCA) program at SJSU, I proposed conducting research on the Carthage collection and on x-rays from the Ryan Mound. Although the proposal was approved by my provost, he had no intention of following through. Rather, he doubled down by informing me that I would not be able to access the x-rays, that he would not even allow the x-rays to be scanned for me, and I was not to use any previously collected data on the Ryan Mound for research. Stymied by a legal catch-22, I forged ahead with the Carthage collection.

Seeing my research opportunities dwindling, even after approval of my research agenda through the RSCA program, I wanted to ensure that my next academic year was nonetheless productive. Since *Repatriation and Erasing the Past* came out, I've been writing for a number of magazines and websites. I've been involved in *History Reclaimed*, a non-profit organization composed of scholars with "a shared conviction that history requires careful interpretation of complex evidence, and should not be a vehicle for facile propaganda," investigating repatriations and the loss of collections in museums that could lead to the demise of these institutions. Thus, when I saw that Heterodox Academy announced a faculty fellowship through its Center of Academic Pluralism in New York City, I thought it would be a great opportunity to investigate the ideological conformity in museums in New York and DC. My proposal was accepted and, thus, I spent the academic year 2023-2024 on the East Coast.

My leave was approved and normally this would mean half-pay, returning to SJSU to work for an additional year after coming back from leave, and losing half of the year's retirement credit. However, shortly after this approval, I settled my lawsuit with SJSU. As a result, I received full pay during my year in New York, and retired from SJSU in May 2024 with full benefits and emeritus status.

I have had tremendous support throughout my ordeal from a wide range of academics, retired academics, students, professional archaeologists, museum staff, and—perhaps most of all—from people outside the academy and museum worlds. They admired my refusal to compromise my principles for politically-trendy ideologies. They also admired the fact that rather than being a victim, I had gone on the offensive and had taken on SJSU and the might of the California State University system. I was concerned that some of these people might view the settlement of my lawsuit as a disappointment, but with the Native American materials off the negotiating table, any win would have been minor. Just as important, my research program was effectively derailed, and staying at SJSU would have relegated me to teaching without research.

How did we get to a situation in which speaking up against the reburial of human remains is seen as racist, and can derail an anthropologist's career? Anthropology has become an ideological minefield with a focus on victims and tribal (both political and social) identity, rather than an endeavor to give a voice to the past. It doesn't matter who is correct; it matters who is telling the story, and Native American narratives are now considered unimpeachable when it comes to the repatriation of remains.

The next proposed revisions to NAGPRA seem likely to erase the imperfect compromise that was included in the original law—a compromise that tried to ensure that science would still be possible, by allowing for the continued curation of most artifacts and culturally unidentifiable skeletal remains. The revision promises to take a step in the direction of CalNAGPRA—giving deference to Native American traditional knowledge (because "indigenous knowledge is science" as the slogan says) over scientific findings.[17]

The compromise is already falling apart—one can just look at the attack on the University of California, Berkeley's Timothy White for using a teaching collection of skeletal remains.[18] The repatriation of non-Native American materials, including a 16th century Spanish breastplate, from the Phoebe Hearst Museum is yet another example of repatriation law abuse.[19] In the last NAGPRA update, the term "culturally unidentifiable" is slated for deletion; this means all remains will be subject to repatriation. In addition, human remains are now defined to include soil in which human remains were once buried. But even these changes aren't sufficient for the repatriation activists. Some Native American tribes, like the San Carlos Apache Tribe, want a definition of human remains that includes naturally-shed material (like hair and skin cells), casts, replicas, and digital data.[20]

It is now my intent to fight the unconstitutional NAGPRA, to try to bring anthropologists—especially the next generation—back to science, and to fight superstition with science. I describe these efforts in my latest book, *On the Warpath: My Battles with Indians, Pretendians, and Woke Warriors*.[21]

Endnotes

[1] Weiss, Elizabeth, Jeremy DeSilva, and Bernhard Zipfel, "Brief Communication: Radiographic Study of Metatarsal One Basal Epiphyseal Fusion: A Note of Caution on Age Determination." *American Journal of Physical Anthropology* 147, no. 3 (March 2012): 489–92.

[2] On stress fractures in California Amerindians, Weiss, Elizabeth. "Spondylolysis in a Pre-contact San Francisco Bay Population: Behavioural and Anatomical Sex Differences." *International Journal of Osteoarchaeology* 19, no. 3 (May 2009): 375–85; on Quebec prisoners of war, Weiss, Elizabeth. "Humeral Cross-sectional Morphology from 18th Century Quebec Prisoners of War: Limits to Activity Reconstruction." *American Journal of Physical Anthropology* 126, no. 3 (March 2005): 311–17; on Paleoindians, Weiss, Elizabeth. "Kennewick Man's Behavior: A CT-Scan Analysis." *American Journal of Physical Anthropology* 32S (2001): 163–163.

[3] Weiss, Elizabeth. "Biological Distance at the Ryan Mound Site." *American Journal of Physical Anthropology* 165, no. 3 (March 2018): 554–64.

[4] National Park Service. National NAGPRA Program. Available at https://www.nps.gov/orgs/1335/index.htm. Accessed January 5, 2024.

[5] Weiss, Elizabeth and James W. Springer, *Repatriation and Erasing the Past* (Gainesville: University of Florida Press, 2020).

[6] Halcrow, Siân, Amber Aranui, Stephanie Halmhofer, Annalisa Heppner, Kristina Killgrove, and Gwen R. Schug, "Open Letter to University Press of Florida (UPF/UFP) and Authors," Google Docs, December 19, 2020. Available at https://docs.google.com/forms/d/e/1FAIpQLScl44V3125po-vz9oX6wp5I8evKk0ECxTAKhJ2kvSBUpOhn9A/viewform?fbclid=IwAR2 spC0ui1XUfSRv7XjOa1dP6TJZ1gIziub8s218bX3wqmCcLwTgI21qQF0 (accessed November 13, 2024).

[7] Weiss, Elizabeth and James W. Springer, James. "Repatriation and the threat to objective knowledge." *Academic Questions, 34*, no. 2 (2021): 64-73; Springer, James W. and Elizabeth Weiss, "Scholarship Versus Racial Identity in Anthropology." Minding The Campus, January 25, 2021. Available at https://www.mindingthecampus.org/2021/01/25/scholarship-versus-racial-identity-in-anthropology/ (accessed 11/14/2024); Springer, James W. and Elizabeth Weiss. "Responding to Claims of Archaeological Racism." National Association of Scholars, April 28, 2021. Available at https://www.nas.org/blogs/article/responding-to-claims-of-archaeological-racism (accessed November 11, 2024).

[8] Weiss, Elizabeth and James W. Springer. "Why is the Society for American Archaeology Promoting Indigenous Creationism?" Quillette, June 13, 2021. Available at https://quillette.com/2021/06/13/why-is-the-society-for-american-archaeology-promoting-indigenous-creationism/ (accessed November 14, 2024).

[9] Weiss, Elizabeth. "Opinion: California Law on Native Americans' Remains Favors Religion over Science." *Mercury News*, August 31, 2021. Available at https://www.mercurynews.com/2021/08/31/8314049-native-american-remains-uc-ab275-graves/ (accessed November 11, 2024).

[10] Del Casino, Vincent. "The Representational Politics of Science." Office of the Provost, San José State University, September 29, 2021. Available at https://www.sjsu.edu/provost/communications/provost-updates/academic-affairs-messages/the-representational-politics-of-science.php (accessed November 15, 2024).

[11] Weiss, Elizabeth. "Response to the Representational Politics of Science." Office of the Provost, San José State University, September 30, 2021. Available at https://www.sjsu.edu/provost/communications/provost-updates/academic-affairs-messages/response-to-the-representational-politics-of-science.php (accessed November 14, 2024).

[12] Fletcher, Alexandra, Daniel Antoine, and JD Hill, eds. "Regarding the Dead: Human Remains in the British Museum." The British Museum, n.d. Available at https://www.britishmuseum.org/sites/default/files/2019-11/Regarding-the-Dead_02102015.pdf (accessed November 15, 2024).

[13] Parks, Grant. California State Auditor. "Native American Graves Protection and Repatriation Act: The California State University Must Do More to Ensure the Timely Return of Native American Remains and Cultural Items to Tribes," June 29, 2023. Available at https://auditor.ca.gov/pdfs/reports/2022-107.pdf (accessed November 14, 2024).

[14] Papazian, Mary. Office of the President. San José State University's Interim Protocol for Curation Spaces in Alignment with NAGPRA, CalNAGPRA, AB 275 (Interim Presidential Directive, PD-2021-03), October 6, 2021. Available at https://www.sjsu.edu/president/docs/Presidential Directive 2021 03 Interim Protocol for Curatorial Spaces in Alignment with NAGPRA CalNAGPRA AB 275.pdf (accessed November 14, 2024).

[15] Benedict, Jeff. *No Bone Unturned: Inside the World of a Top Forensic Scientist and His Work on America's Most Notorious Crimes and Disasters*. New York: Harper Perennial, 2004.

[16] Schneider, Christian. "San Jose State Lifts Ban on 'Menstruating Personnel' Handling Human Remains." The College Fix, April 14, 2022. Available at https://www.thecollegefix.com/san-jose-state-lifts-ban-on-menstruating-personnel-handling-human-remains/ (accessed November 14, 2024).

[17] United States government Federal Register. "Proposed Rule: Native American Graves Protection and Repatriation Act Systematic Process for Disposition and Repatriation of Native American Human Remains, Funerary Objects, Sacred Objects, and Objects of Cultural Patrimony," October 18, 2022. Available at https://www.federalregister.gov/documents/2022/10/18/2022-22376/native-american-graves-protection-and-repatriation-act-systematic-process-for-disposition-and. (accessed November 14, 2024).

[18] Hudetz, Mary and Graham L. Brewer. "A Top UC Berkeley Professor Taught with Remains that May Include Dozens of Native Americans." *ProPublica*,

March 5, 2023. Available at https://www.propublica.org/article/berkeley-professor-taught-suspected-native-american-remains-repatriation (accessed November 14, 2024).

[19] Weiss, Elizabeth/ "'Decolonization' and 'Repatriation:' A Look behind the Scenes." History Reclaimed, January 14, 2023. Available at https://history reclaimed.co.uk/decolonization-and-repatriation-a-look-behind-the-scenes/ (accessed November 14, 2023).

[20] Grant, Vernelda J. Regulations.gov public comment, January 31, 2023, https://www.regulations.gov/comment/NPS-2022-0004-0183 (accessed November 14, 2024).

[21] Weiss, Elizabeth. *On the Warpath: My Battles with Indians, Pretendians, and Woke Warriors*. Washington DC: Aacademica Press, 2024.

Satire Can Be Dangerous

Frances Widdowson

On May 25, 2020, the Canadian academy went mad. The issue that caused the upheaval did not happen at a Canadian university, or even in Canada. It resulted from the death of a black man while in police custody in the United States. That man was George Floyd.

I had been a professor at Mount Royal University (MRU) in Calgary since 2008, Canada. All of a sudden, "anti-racism" became a constant preoccupation of university leaders. It also led to the development of a public presence for the anonymous "Mount Royal Anti-Racism Coalition" —alleged to be made up of about 70 people, mostly MRU faculty members—and its claim that there was pervasive racism in our institution.[1] The first three Twitter followers of this group were MRU professors Leanne Hollander, Doreen Dornan, and Mark Truffle. Hollander, Truffle, and another MRU professor, Reese Walker, would eventually officially declare their membership in the coalition in November 2020. Dornan and Walker, as well as another faculty member, Giselle Lancaster, would end up filing harassment complaints against me, while I pursued complaints against Hollander, Truffle, and 16 other colleagues (Pseudonyms have been used for all MRU professors.) Hollander also had sent a private email to MRU President Tim Rahilly claiming that I had engaged in harassment and discrimination against Lancaster, other colleagues, and students.[2]

I first became aware of the Mount Royal Anti-Racism Coalition (MRARC) when its Twitter account (@MRUAntiRacism) made a post on June 5, 2020 quoting a statement that I was "associated with or allegedly affiliated with discrimination, white supremacy, or hate speech. . . ."[3] Then on June 24, 2020, it retweeted a student newspaper article. This piece quoted MRARC's concern with the MRU administration's "tepid" response to "anti-Indigenous propaganda circulating on campus" that was "hateful" and engaged in the "target[ing]" of faculty, staff and students. This statement referred to me, as I was the one person at MRU publicly challenging the university's Indigenization initiative (that is, policies that incorporate indigenous symbolism and "ways of knowing" into university campuses and curriculum, and implement targets for indigenous student admissions and faculty hiring ads.)[4] As I was criticizing a key policy associated with MRU's "You Belong Here" campaign, many of those who were benefiting from the resources made available by this initiative believed that I was an existential threat to their livelihood.

At the same time as the reaction to George Floyd's death was unfolding, MRU was in the midst of a COVID lockdown. This led many faculty members to spend more time on social media. While the forces of "woke-ism"—identity politics, purporting to pursue social justice, that has become illiberal—had been gaining momentum since 2014 with MRU's official promotion of Indigenization, they reached a tipping point in June 2020. As a result of the acceleration of anti-racism rhetoric on social media, MRU became unmoored from its academic mission.

This was apparent when President Rahilly and the executive of my union, the Mount Royal Faculty Association (MRFA), both put out political statements about George Floyd's death and the alleged pervasiveness of racism at universities and in Canada more generally. MRU President Tim Rahilly, on June 5, 2020, stated: "I learned long ago to accept people's accounts of incidents of racism as their lived experience."[5] (This worried me because I recently had been unjustly implicated on such a basis.) The MRFA Executive opened its statement with the following claim:

> George Floyd, Tony McDade, and Breonna Taylor in the United States; Regis Korchinski-Paquet and D'Andre Campbell in Canada, are just a few people added in the last month or so to the long list of Black people killed in encounters with police. These murders stem from persistent anti-Black racism, white supremacy, and systemic violence.[6]

Regis Korchinski-Paquet was included in this list despite the fact that she had accidentally fallen to her death when she jumped from a balcony trying to escape the police after she wielded a knife against family members.[7]

In response to these statements, one of my colleagues, MRU philosophy professor Sinclair MacRae, wrote an eight-page letter to Rahilly and the MRFA Executive criticizing them.[8] In this letter, MacRae pointed out that such official pronouncements had the effect of "contributing to an environment in which free and open enquiry and the search for truth at Mount Royal is threatened." This was because the official posts

> seem[ed] to regard these questions [about racism] as settled, and so I am concerned that they will, ironically, promote a culture at our institution that inhibits learning because they will have the effect of foreclosing avenues of thinking and lines of enquiry that are becoming stigmatized as themselves evidence of 'systemic racism.' This would be a terrible failing on our part and an Orwellian state of affairs.

To my surprise, this letter was ignored. Instead of considering MacRae's arguments, 62 faculty members signed an "Open Letter to Mount Royal University" demanding mandatory anti-racism training for all professors. The letter was distributed by an anonymous Twitter account associated with the MRARC, @RacialAdvMRU (MRU Racial Advocacy), which claimed to be a student-led initiative. Mandatory anti-racism training was necessary, according to the letter, because "[r]ecent events on and/or involving our campus have created a chilly climate for BIPOC students, faculty." This "chilly climate" included, once again, a reference to "anti-Indigenous rhetoric" on campus.[9] What this consisted of was never specified.

Because MacRae's compelling letter was ignored, I thought about how I could contribute to the conversation. If no one had acknowledged MacRae's empathetic and persuasive arguments, why would anyone listen to a blunt rational intervention from me? At this point, I recalled listening to Toby Young, the head of the Free Speech Union in the United Kingdom, who mentioned that humour was often an effective way to expose the irrationality of "woke-ism." I also was aware of Andrew Doyle's satirical character, Titania McGrath, and how satisfying his humorous social media commentary had been in fighting back against censoriousness. This led me to compose a satirical reply to the open letter posted by @RacialAdvMRU. In this reply, I said that George Orwell had "come to me in a dream" and told me that "intersectional postmodern theory" was the "right way." This, I claimed, had led me to develop an "Oppression Point System" where faculty could now be evaluated according to whether they were "white/white passing," "cisgendered," or male (those who had a high number of "oppression points," I opined, should obviously resign their positions to make space for "BIPOC voices.") I signed off with the following salutation: "Your faithful and obedient Big Brother lover."

Although many colleagues appreciated my satirical reply, the anonymous member(s) of MRU Racial Advocacy became very angry. The person/people involved declared that they were now blocking me on Twitter for not taking their open letter seriously. Then the group began to take a more hostile stance towards me on social media.

In addition to the developments concerning the open letter, another controversy was unfolding at almost the same time. On June 9, 2020, the distinguished Canadian Broadcasting Corporation journalist, Wendy Mesley, was suspended from hosting her program *The Weekly* for mentioning (but not using) a racial epithet in an anti-racist context in a private editorial meeting. She also had enunciated this epithet when referring to the title of the Quebec Marxist Pierre Vallières' famous book *White Niggers of America*. Although it is hard to believe, it was on this basis that her employer decided to discipline her.

What was most striking was that no one provided a principled defense of Mesley, explaining how her references to this word were justified. This was especially true in the case of the book title, as Vallières had been using the epithet as a rhetorical device to show that it was economic class, not race, that was at the roots of people being demeaned and discriminated against. Appalled by this treatment of Mesley, I defended her on Twitter, saying that she had done nothing wrong. For a number of posts I intentionally avoided mentioning this epithet because I knew it would cause people to become upset. Instead, I posted screenshots of the Vallières book cover and an article from Wikipedia about the epithet. This led a troll (who eventually revealed that he was a student) to ask "if the word is so benign, why do you refuse to say it?"[10]

Although I knew I was being set up—because the troll/student had been previously agitating against my employment at MRU—I realized that it was important to take a stand on this issue. After all, my position was that Wendy Mesley had done nothing wrong. If this were the case, why wouldn't I mention the word in the same way that she had? This led me to post the following tweet: "The word itself does not have some kind of spiritual power. We need to separate a user's intent from recognizing a word that exists. There should be no problem with saying *White Niggers of America*, or asserting that 'the word n____ ethnic slur that is typically directed at black [sic] people.'[11] To this, I again attached the book cover and the Wikipedia entry about the epithet from which the quote was extracted.[12]

This tweet eventually came to the attention of Giselle Lancaster, an Indigenous scholar/activist at MRU. Lancaster had been unhappy with my presence even before she was hired at MRU because of my criticisms of the Indigenization initiative. This led her to repost my offending reply severed from the troll-student's question, which had been previously reposted by MRU Racial Advocacy, with the following statement: "Students are raising critical.awareness [sic] around certain faculty that hide behind academia to spread racist views! No one knows another person's intent. Focus less on intent and more on outcome." She then encouraged the purportedly student-led MRU Racial Advocacy to complain about me and make my position at MRU untenable. In response to this group's claim that "[my post] was violent and makes you wonder how can someone like this teach and grade without racial bias. What will be the last straw? @mountroyal4u," Lancaster asserted the following: "She's been at it for so long that we seriously need to consider your question! What will it take for the university to stop in their complicity? A student or faculty member who's pushed to the edge? @mountroyal4u." Then, in response to an alumnus' question about how she could complain about my conduct, Lancaster suggested the following course of action: "The office of the President. . . go right to the top!"[13]

Lancaster was Indigenous, and an important face of MRU's Indigenization initiative. About 40 faculty members publicly supported her, implying that I was a racist and a hatemonger who was engaged in discrimination for defending Wendy Mesley's reference to a book title. After trying to communicate with my colleagues about how referring to a book title was not racist, people just kept on repeating that this *was* racist, even noting that they were shocked that I would need to have this explained. One professor then encouraged students to ask MRU administration to set up exceptions so that they could avoid taking my classes.

As a result of this pervasive anti-intellectualism, I turned my Twitter account into the home of the satirical character "francXs mcgrath (NOT frances widdowson)" —the "nemesis" of "Prof Frances Widdowson" and "xister-in-law" of Andrew Doyle's character Titania McGrath. Every time Lancaster and her allies would attack me and try to poison my work environment, francXs mcgrath (NOT frances widdowson) would enthusiastically agree with them, repeating the words of my adversaries that I should be fired for my "harassing tweet mockery," "racist gaslighting" and "epistemic terrorism." I also satirized Lancaster's claim that she was "loving and kind" and just trying to "bring people together with humility and grace." It seemed to me that trying to get a colleague fired and mobilizing an anonymous, supposedly student-led initiative against them for referring to a book title was not loving, kind, or indicative of humility and grace.

However, my challenging of Lancaster's unethical behaviour could have no place in a woke university. It resulted in Lancaster and a number of members of the MRARC going to the MRU administration to complain about my behaviour. Soon, Lancaster would file a formal complaint against me with the assistance of MRU and the MRFA. Although the dated and signed complaint was withheld because it was alleged this would negatively impact procedural fairness for the complainant, specific allegations were compiled by MRU-retained investigator Nancy Rice (This is also a pseudonym). These identified the "racist and discriminatory" questions that I had asked about "indigenous science," and social media posts that were critical of Lancaster's attempts to end my career.

Shortly afterwards, Doreen Dornan (the second follower of the Mount Royal Anti-Racism Coalition) would also file a harassment complaint against me. Dornan was in the same department as Lancaster – the Department of Humanities and home of MRU's indigenous studies program. Dornan was also a board member on the MRFA Executive. As a board member, Dornan had been using the position to facilitate a workshop examining the alleged impact of white supremacy on the union. A few days before I received the Notice of Investigation for Dornan's complaint, I had tried to get accountability regarding the honorarium Dornan had received for facilitating this workshop. At the time, I did not know that Dornan had made this allegation, because the complaint had been, once again, withheld on the grounds that "The release of the document of complaint could result in issues around procedural fairness for the complainant."[14]

In the particulars of Dornan's complaint, compiled by the investigator hired by MRU, Jane Halton, it was alleged that I had asked "argumentative" and "combative" questions at two pronouns workshops Dornan had facilitated. I had also proposed a motion (which passed) supporting "critical thinking and open inquiry about feminist philosophies pertaining to sex and gender," which Dornan criticized because the motion did "not speak to the anti-transgender feminist philosophies." Finally, I had posted one tweet satirizing a cartoon Dornan had posted on the internet about "misgendering fatigue" and the mushrooming LGBT+ initialism (I had referred to it as "TGBQ2SLMNOP.")[15]

At the time, I was sure that the allegations from Lancaster and Dornan would not be upheld because they were patently frivolous. In addition, social media had not been grounds for investigations in the past. I knew this because I had been alerting MRU administrators to the fact that faculty members had been trying to ostracize me and denigrate my academic accomplishments on social media for years. The administration had never intervened, although the Personal Harassment Policy obligated them to do so if they believed that harassment had occurred.

It turned out that none of my activities in the workplace were considered to be harassment by the investigators. This was not surprising, as making a motion at a faculty council that passes obviously should not be complained about in the first place. Of particular note was Lancaster's allegation about a question that I had asked that she claimed was "racist and discriminatory." Fortunately, I had recorded the talk and was able to show that Lancaster had engaged in misrepresentation. A transcription of the talk revealed the actual question:

> Thank you very much for your talk. My name's Frances. We are at Mount Royal University currently trying to indigenize the science curriculum. I am just wondering about your thoughts on how this material with respect to astronomy could be incorporated into, for example, astronomy classes or other science classes. I am not quite sure whether this presentation is looking at how indigenous people understood the stars and so on historically, or whether you think that this can actually contribute to existing science courses, especially things like astronomy courses. Because you are a science teacher yourself, you are probably aware that the discovery of the telescope, especially beginning in the times of Galileo, and the astronomy that occurred there, astronomy has advanced tremendously in the last couple of hundred years, and if you didn't have a telescope, if these cultures didn't have a telescope, I am not sure how these stories would be able to contribute to the courses in the actual sciences at Mount Royal. Thank you.[16]

Investigator Rice, however, did not think that Lancaster's misrepresentation had any negative implications for her credibility. Instead, Rice stated that she "found GL [Giselle Lancaster] to be forthright and expressing her honestly held beliefs and genuinely felt emotions."

Although none of my workplace activities were impugned by the investigation, I was shocked to learn that some of my off-duty social media posts on my personal account were deemed to be harassing. This was because social media activities now were being redefined as being part of the workplace. Investigators were not concerned about the fact that MRU had allowed me to be defamed on social media for years without any intervention. Finally, they disregarded the fact that MRU's collective bargaining agreement protected academic freedom and freedom of expression rights, and that we had an Expression and Free Speech Policy stating that "[t]he University will not suppress presentations or debate whether or not the points of view being expressed are thought to be offensive, unwise, immoral, extreme, harmful, incorrect or wrongheaded."[17]

As a result, my tweet satirizing the 'misgendering fatigue' cartoon and the LGBT+ initialism was found to violate three MRU policies and two provincial laws. In the case of Lancaster, it was argued that some of my "tweets mentioning GL" had engaged in "sarcasm, public reprimand and ridicule" and did not constitute interacting with Lancaster in a "mutually respectful manner, respecting the personal dignity of all. . . ." Of particular significance was that I had replied to Lancaster's ridiculing of my claim that she had mobilized students against me. Immediately after going onto my Twitter account and provoking me in this way, Lancaster blocked me, which led me to satirize her blocking me with screenshots documenting how she had, in fact, engaged in such student mobilization.

The supposed legal violations concerning Dornan were never pursued in the courts, but they made it possible for Acting Provost Evans to claim that "the evidence presented constituted Discrimination under Alberta's Human Rights Act and Harassment under Alberta's Occupational Health and Safety Act." This, along with my tweets about Lancaster, resulted in my suspension without pay for two weeks on this basis of this "serious matter," despite the fact that I had no previous incidents of being disciplined. I was instructed to not direct my satire at any member of the MRU community. I also was informed that I would have to take respectful workplace training. My detailed arguments about how the two investigations violated procedural fairness and natural justice protections were ignored. (Natural justice and procedural fairness require that respondents receive complaints and that investigations proceed according to a neutral and clearly specified procedure.)

As a result of these findings of harassment and discrimination on the basis that social media was now considered to be part of the workplace, even though this expectation had not been promulgated, I filed 18 complaints under MRU's Personal Harassment Policy against my colleagues that resulted in MRU pursuing two separate investigations undertaken by Sam Epstein of Field Law (I was not able to file a complaint against Giselle Lancaster for her harassment of me, as she had resigned from MRU immediately after she filed her complaint and accepted a position at the University of Calgary). In the first of these investigations (involving 17 respondents), Epstein and MRU found that six faculty members had harassed me. Investigator Epstein stipulated that these faculty members had committed acts of "ostracism" and the "trivializing of academic achievements."[18]

In the first investigation, concerning 17 of my complaints, Epstein decided arbitrarily to investigate conduct only if it occurred in 2019 or after (unlike the Halton and Rice investigations, that looked at my conduct as far back as 2018, because they did not consider time limitations). As a result, Mark Truffle, who had called me a "pathetic racist" wanting to "associate with white supremacists" in 2018, was not found to have engaged in harassment by Epstein and MRU. Also, academic freedom and freedom of expression protections were extensively considered by Epstein. This led Kaitlin Peacock, who had posted a petition demanding that I be fired on her Facebook page, to be exempted from a harassment finding by Epstein and MRU. According to Epstein, Peacock should not be found to have engaged in harassment because, while calling for a colleague's termination was harassment, this was mitigated by the fact that it was based on a deeply held belief. He also pointed to the fact that it was only one post (i.e. it was analogous to my one tweet that had been linked to Dornan.)

Epstein was also concerned about whether my colleagues had specifically mentioned me, and was sure to place all their social media activity in context. This meant that, if the faculty members that I had complained about were responding to what he considered to be a provocation, this was not seen to be harassment. This can be contrasted with the Rice investigation: Rice did not consider that I was reacting to constant insults from Giselle Lancaster and her attempts to poison my work environment. As Rice put it,

> in determining whether FW's [Frances Widdowson's] conduct
> breached the Policies and the law, GL's [Giselle Lancaster's]

conduct provides only context and is not determinative in my assessment. Although GL may have also behaved in ways that fell below the standards of conduct as outlined in the Policies and the law, I have been tasked with examining only FW's behaviour.

In the first Epstein investigation, one of the six faculty members who was found to have engaged in harassment of me was Reese Walker, a declared member of the MRARC. In spite of Walker's impending departure from MRU (she had been hired by McMaster University), she immediately filed a retaliatory complaint against me after she was notified that MRU was investigating her for harassing me The result was a bizarre seven page document that listed 15 alleged wrongdoings. These concerned infractions such as not capitalizing "I" in indigenous and referring to Equity, Diversity, and Inclusion initiatives as "DIE." Walker's complaint also included 18 pages of attachments that bore no relation to the allegations that she had made. Only one of the attachments, in fact, even mentioned Walker, and this concerned her declared membership in the MRARC, which had been defaming me on social media for a year.

I then entered into a long interaction with the person hired by MRU to investigate the Walker complaint, George Holt (also of Field Law, the same firm as Epstein's). This complaint eventually involved two meetings totaling six and a half hours. In preparing for the meetings, the investigator did not rely only on what Walker had provided as evidence. Instead, he went through my entire Facebook account and Twitter feed. Even though the posts that he compiled were not directed at Walker, he found that I had engaged in harassment and the creation of a toxic workplace. The reason? Because I had "denigrated the viewpoints" of my colleagues. In the case of the satirical reply that I had posted about George Orwell coming to me in a dream, for example, it was found to "[degenerate] into ridicule and [be] demeaning of others" and "sarcastically undermine and mock proponents of a viewpoint." This resulted in the finding that I was guilty of "personal harassment" and had contributed to "tension and toxicity in the workplace."

While interacting with investigator Holt about the Walker complaint, another faculty member began to agitate against me on Twitter for disputing the claim that the indigenous residential schools were genocidal

(I had argued that, while the residential schools had caused a great deal of harm, the education that they provided was beneficial to indigenous students.)[19] This led this faculty member to amplify claims that I was a "residential school denialist" (implying that my views were similar to being a Holocaust denier) and to claim the following:

> I support academic freedom, of course, but universities must absolutely fire racists who deny the real harm of residential schools for indigenous peoples, arguing the RS [residential schools] somehow carried benefits. Kowtowing to them undermines everything a university does for decolonization.[20]

This faculty member also supported the MRU Students' Association's July 14, 2021 press release that denounced me and asserted that I had created a culture of fear by satirizing the comparison being made between the residential schools and the Holocaust. The press release also asserted that students should be given options so that they could avoid taking classes with me because my satire had shown a "tolerance for violent and lethal behaviour" that indicated that I was "misus[ing] academic power." This, the Students' Association argued, was likely to result in me grading students unfairly.

This professor's posts were similar to the posts that qualified as harassment in Epstein's first investigation. Yet Epstein now found, in his second investigation, that my complaint was "frivolous, vexatious, and not made in good faith." Epstein gave two reasons for this: first, he claimed that I should not have included parts of the complaint that could have been pursued when the other 17 complaints were filed. Second, he maintained that I had an unspecified "myriad of avenues of recourse available" to challenge MRU's standard for harassing social media behaviour. According to Epstein in his second investigation, "in making these complaints to the degree that" I had, "with the breadth" that I had, this meant that the complaints were "frivolous and vexatious" and "not in good faith." I continue to find the logic of the second Epstein investigation report to be baffling.

As a result of the findings of the Holt and second Epstein investigations, I was called into a second disciplinary meeting with Acting Provost Evans. At the time, I thought that termination was a possibility, because, as a board member for the Society for Academic Freedom and Scholarship, I was well aware of the unfairness of university investigations and disciplinary processes. Also, the previous discipline meeting with Evans about the Rice and Halton findings showed that she was not interested in discussing anything. It was obvious that the meeting in April was just a box-checking exercise to enable preordained disciplinary action to be administered.

However, unlike professors who enter into these disciplinary processes unaware of these dynamics, I was prepared for the possibility that the mob would come for me. As a result, I had been keeping records, and alerting administration for several years about how my work environment was becoming poisoned. I also had recorded all meetings and events where I had spoken publicly for the past two years; I did not intend to be accosted with trumped-up allegations, as had occurred in the case of another colleague. This colleague had been subjected to a Star Chamber investigation where four feminist scholar-activists colluded and made up false claims about him. In contrast to his case, where he was not even allowed to have access to the investigation report, my colleagues advocating for academic freedom had made me well aware of the procedures required by administrative law—procedures of which my union was either woefully unaware or chose to ignore because I was at ideological odds with the union faction that was controlling it.

Unfortunately, justice was not to prevail. Instead, the second disciplinary meeting turned out to be even more of a kangaroo court than the first. At this meeting, the provost brought up a new allegation that colleagues were now refusing to work with me. I told the provost that my dean had never raised this issue with me, and demanded that she provide evidence for this claim. In response, the provost said that we were going to have to "leave that matter" because we couldn't resolve it here, and went on to try to get me to "accept responsibility" and "show remorse" for my conduct. I replied that I was not able to do this because I couldn't "accept responsibility" for violating rules that I did not know existed, and that showing remorse was impossible because I was just defending myself from a mob that was trying to get me fired.

When I refused to acknowledge any wrongdoing, and instead stated that it was MRU that should show remorse for not promulgating its rules while dragging dozens of faculty members through unfair investigations, the provost asserted that it looked to her as if my employment relationship with MRU had "become unviable." This led my union representative to warn me that the provost's comments likely meant that MRU was planning to fire me. As a result, I ceased hoping for a positive outcome and expected to be terminated after I finished marking my exams. But I was not prepared for what was to happen next.

The day of December 20, 2021 began ordinarily enough. I was attending an indigenous studies hiring talk with one of the candidates. In this talk, I asked a question, as did a number of other people, including the Associate Provost Matt Quayle. After attending this meeting, I prepared to invigilate my last exam for the fall semester, which began at 2:30 p.m. (ironically in B101; room 101 was Winston Smith's torture chamber in *1984*.) After I had finished the invigilation three hours later, I encountered Dr. Quayle again in very different circumstances. This occurred as I was walking back to my office along a deserted corridor after the exam had finished. At this time, Quayle came up behind me and called out "Dr. Widdowson, Dr. Widdowson." He then asked if I could "just step in here for a moment," gesturing to a classroom across the hall. I assumed that, because of my earlier interaction with him about the job candidate, he wanted to discuss the hiring process further.

When I stepped into the classroom and saw two human resources representatives sitting at a table, I realized that I was going to be fired, and immediately demanded union representation (as was required for any disciplinary meeting, per the collective bargaining agreement.) When this was not provided to me, I said that they would have to provide me with notice and I tried to exit the room. This led Quayle to move in front of me to block the door. At this point, I began to panic, as it was after hours and I felt that I had been ambushed, lured, and deceived. I yelled at Quayle that he was forcibly confining me, which led him to step aside, enabling me to brush past him and run back to my office. In a completely agitated state, I tried to send an email to the union, but discovered that my computer had been locked down. This led me to call one of my colleagues asking her to have the union contact me immediately.

Instead of backing off and allowing me to connect with the union, Quayle and several university administrators followed me to my office and placed two security guards at either end of the hall. Feeling terrorized and alone, and fearing that I could be held against my will, I called 911 so that I could exit the building unmolested and liaise with the union about my rights. I went out to the parking lot and locked myself in my car until the police arrived. I discussed the matter with them, and then left to meet the union.[21] Later I learned that while I was fleeing from Quayle and campus security, the Dean of Arts had sent out a communication to about 50 faculty members and Chairs in the liberal arts faculty informing them that I was "no longer employed at Mount Royal University."[22]

It seems obvious in hindsight that the university's draconian actions were attempting to justify portraying me as a threat. This was an escalation of the pattern of many faculty members labeling me as racist, and MRU accepting that I had engaged in harassment and discrimination because I defended myself from the attacks against me. In reviewing how all of the investigations involving me unfolded, it appeared that the standards being applied to me for satirizing "woke-ism" were much higher than those used when I was complaining about a mob actually trying to poison my workplace and end my career.

Some of this differential treatment can be attributed to the fact that no procedures were in place to oversee investigations, which enabled MRU to employ arbitrary standards. Perhaps more important was the conflict of interest: the investigators were being paid by MRU. This problem has been identified by the employment lawyer Howard Levitt, who argues that often there is collusion between investigators and the employer to obtain a result that the employer desires. If the investigator does not provide the desired outcome, he or she will not get contracts for future investigations.

The different standards in the investigations where I was a respondent and a complainant show how the investigations were deployed to purge a professor whose ideas were not consistent with a university's brand. (MRU's motto is Orwellian doublespeak: "You Belong Here.") This was indicated by the fact that the second Epstein investigation and the Holt investigation had results that were almost polar opposites from one another, even though the investigators worked at the same legal firm. In the case of the Holt investigation, posts that were not even about the complainant (Walker) were seen to be "harassing" because they "denigrated" certain "viewpoints." Using Holt's standard in the Epstein investigations would have meant that all, and not six, faulty members would have been found to have engaged in harassment because my viewpoint was constantly denigrated. This also would have negated the frivolous and vexatious finding in the second Epstein investigation because calling me a "residential school denialist" was certainly insulting, thereby resulting in a finding of harassment under the Holt standard.

The unfairness was further exacerbated by the fact that illiberal identity politics has seeped into the legal profession. As a result, those belonging to groups perceived to be oppressed are given leniency in disputes because they are viewed as "punching up" against oppression. Those who are perceived to be members of oppressor groups, on the other hand, are purportedly punching down, and therefore less entitled to legal protections. This is why Lancaster, Dornan, Walker and Peacock's feelings were seen as being so important in the investigations.

Although my satire was what was used as a pretext for my firing, the real issue was my questioning of the politics of Indigenization. This was shown by the fact that my colleagues had poisoned my work environment for years because I had critically analyzed these politics, but MRU decided to not intervene. When Giselle Lancaster became upset because I defended myself after she instigated a mob against me, many people rallied to her defense. My assailants claimed that off-duty social media posts not related to Lancaster's workplace were harassing and discriminatory, and MRU, after being pressured by a union controlled by leaders sympathetic to the mob, decided that this should be a matter for investigation.

The inevitability of my firing was actually revealed in early December 2021, a few weeks before it occurred. This was when Giselle Lancaster was interviewed for a Canada Research Chair position in indigenous studies at MRU. In the interview, Lancaster claimed that she "missed MRU," even though she had previously stated that she had left because MRU had failed to protect her from the harm caused by what she claimed were my racist and discriminatory actions. According to Lancaster, these instances of racism and discrimination involved challenging the validity of indigenous "ways of knowing" while "passing it off as academic freedom." It does not seem to be a coincidence that, soon after I was fired, Lancaster returned to MRU.

In order for Lancaster to feel "safe" at MRU, I would not be able to continue to occupy the same institutional space. MRU, because it had built its "You Belong Here" brand on directing that indigenous "ways of knowing" be "respected" and "valued," could not tolerate the presence of any dissenting faculty member. "Inclusivity," in other words, meant excluding any voice that dared to ask critical questions about the prescribed doctrine concerning Indigenization.

My firing resulted in ten grievances against MRU being taken to arbitration by the MRFA. My union's legal case was then taken over by the Canadian Association of University Teachers because of its broad implications for Canadian higher education, and it was adjudicated over 30 hearing days in January, May, June, October and November 2023. In the arbitration, MRU introduced no new substantiated evidence, and because I had been recording all meetings since September 2019, the false statements of all of MRU's witnesses were effectively refuted. The decision of the arbitrator is still pending, and will be precedent-setting for academic freedom in Canada.

I am demanding to be reinstated because I really enjoyed my role as a professor, in spite of how I was treated, and think that my ability to think critically and pursue the truth made a great contribution to the university. In fact, I continue to have meaningful interactions with several colleagues and even have drinks with some of them at the Faculty Centre on Friday nights. But because MRU erroneously implied that I had engaged in discrimination, and because the former chair of my department falsely stated that I had been fired for my "personal conduct towards faculty and administration, and especially students."[23] I have been unable to secure an interview for even a part-time teaching position. MRU, through its enabling of a mob to deprive me of my academic freedom, has sent a message that critical thinking and honest discussion no longer belong on campus. For the sake of all universities in Canada, one hopes that MRU will not be able to get away with such a flagrant violation of due process rights and academic principles.

Endnotes

[1] Widdowson, Frances. "Anonymity: The Cowardly Enabler of Cancellation." *Minding the Campus*, November 3, 2022. Available at https://www.mindingthecampus.org/2022/11/03/anonymity-the-cowardly-enabler-of-cancellation/ (accessed January 27, 2024).

[2] Widdowson, Frances. "Evidence for 'Satire Can Be Dangerous.'" Blog, n.d. Available at https://wokeacademy.info/evidence-for-satire-can-be-dangerous/ (accessed March 9, 2024).

[3] Mount Royal Anti-Racism Coalition. tweet, June 5, 2020. Available at https://twitter.com/MRUAntiRacism/status/1269030399931379712 (accessed November 15, 2024).

[4] Hagenaars, Stephanie. "MRU Professor Challenges Traditional Indigenous Research, Despite Critics." *Calgary Journal*, February 14, 2018. https://calgaryjournal.ca/2018/02/14/mru-professor-challenges-traditional-indigenous-research-despite-critics/ (accessed January 28, 2024).

[5] Rahilly, Tim. "What Do I Think About Racism?" June 5, 2020. Available at https://wokeacademy.info/rahilly-what-do-i-think-about-racism/ (accessed January 27, 2024).

[6] Mount Royal Faculty Association. "Mount Royal Faculty Association Statement." Available at https://mrfa.net/mount-royal-faculty-association-statement/ (accessed January 27, 2024).

[7] Gillis, Wendy. "What Happened the Night Regis Korchinski-Paquet Died, According to Ontario's Police Watchdog." *Toronto Star*, August 26, 2020. Available at https://www.thestar.com/news/gta/what-happened-the-night-regis-korchinski-paquet-died-according-to-ontario-s-police-watchdog/article_0a1b0360-789f-5e9d-9602-0bfbd6a3cbf2.html (accessed January 27, 2024).

[8] MacRae, Sinclair . Letter to Tim Rahilly and Members of the Mount Royal Faculty Association Executive, June 17, 2020. Available at https://safs.ca/issuescases/university-racism/Letter%20of%20dissent%20to%20PR%20and%20the%20MRFA%20-%20Sinclair%20MacRae.pdf (accessed January 27, 2024).

[9] Widdowson, Frances. "Episode 6: The Satirical Letter that was 'Demeaning of Others.'" Blog, n.d. Available at https://wokeacademy.info/episode-6-the-satirical-letter/ (accessed January 27, 2024).

[10] Widdowson, Frances. "Naming the Title of *White Niggers of America: I will Die on This Hill.*" *SAFS Newsletter*, January 2023. Available at

https://safs.ca/newsletters/ article.php?article=1216 (accessed January 27, 2024).

[11] My preference is to write the word out. The abbreviation has been used at the request of the editor.

[12] Widdowson, Frances. "Episode 5: 'Anti-Racism' and Defending Wendy Mesley." Blog, n.d. Available at https://wokeacademy.info/episode-5-anti-racism-and-defending-wendy-mesley/ (accessed January 27, 2024).

[13] Widdowson, Frances. "Episode 12: Did Gabrielle Lindstrom 'Harass' Frances Widdowson?" Blog, n.d. Available at https://wokeacademy.info/episode-12/ (accessed January 27. 2024).

[14] Widdowson, Frances. "The Woke Academy's Rejection of the Rule of Law" *Minding the Campus*, December 12, 2023. Available at https://www.mindingthecampus.org/2022/12/12/the-woke-academys-rejection-of-the-rule-of-law/ (accessed January 27, 2024).

[15] Widdowson, Frances. "D.A. Dirks Complaint Documents." Blog, n.d. Available at https://wokeacademy.info/d-a-dirks-complaint-documents/ (accessed January 27, 2024).

[16] Widdowson, Frances. "Episode 3: Questioning Indigenous 'Star Knowledge.'" Blog, n.d. Available at https://wokeacademy.info/episode-3-when-defending-science-is-believed-to-be-racist-and-discriminatory/ (accessed January 27, 2024).

[17] Mount Royal University. Expression and Free Speech Policy. October 28, 2019. Available at https://www.mtroyal.ca/Applications/PoliciesAndProcedures/view/1tI6oaPmpb92L07oA63JwQ-ucRKT1plXZ (accessed January 27, 2024).

[18] Widdowson, Frances. "Episode 1: The Renae Watchman Complaint." Blog, n.d. Available at https://wokeacademy.info/episode-1-the-renae-watchman-complaint/ (accessed January 27, 2024) and "Steven Eichler's 'Gang of 17' Investigation." Blog, n.d. Available at https://wokeacademy.info/steven-eichlers-gang-of-17-investigation/ (accessed January 27, 2024).

[19] After the false claim, announced by the Kamloops band on May 27, 2021, that the remains of 215 children had been found in an apple orchard next to a residential school, the charge of "genocide" became much more pronounced. However, no clandestine graves have been found. For a discussion of this, see Champion, C. P. and Tom Flanagan, eds. *Grave Error: How the Media Misled Us (and the Truth about the Residential Schools)*. True North Media, 2023.

[20] Widdowson, Frances. "Steven Eichler's Investigation of Tim Haney." Blog, n.d. Available at https://wokeacademy.info/steven-eichlers-investigation-of-tim-haney/ (accessed January 27, 2024)

[21] "Frances Widdowson Firing Aftermath – Constable Kress' Bodycam Footage." Video, April 15, 2022. Available at https://www.youtube.com/watch?v=1Ip8Cj-Pkgg (accessed January 28, 2024).

22 Widdowson, Frances. "Frances Widdowson's Privacy Complaint Against MRU." Blog, July 1, 2022. Available at https://wokeacademy.info/frances-widdowsons-privacy-complaint-against-mru/ (accessed January 27, 2024).

23 Steward, Gillian. "When Critics Attack Universities for Being Too Woke, What's Really Going On?" *Toronto Star*, February 27, 2023. Available at https://www.thestar.com/opinion/contributors/when-critics-attack-universities-for-being-too-woke-what-s-really-going-on/article_65ca6f13-739a-5f08-8873-182fead9b3b4.html (accessed March 8, 2024).

Religion
and
Politics

US Academia and the Censoring
of an Anti-Zionist Professor*

Fawzia Afzal-Khan

In what follows I will describe my journey through the pitfalls of United States academia from my graduate student days in the 1980s to a tenured full professorship, and how I've experienced repeated attempts at silencing and censorship. I begin with a description of how I was harassed as a grad student at Tufts University because of my advocacy for Palestinian human rights and the right to self-determination. After completing my first year on a tenure-track position several years later, I describe my department chair's attempt at intimidating me after I challenged Susan Sontag during a talk she gave on my campus. I did get tenure, but had to fight for promotion to Associate Professor rank, and in the decades that followed, endured several forms of harassment and discouragement by pro-Zionist colleagues, which I'll outline in some detail. After finally becoming a full professor and being elected director of our Women's and Gender Studies program, I had to endure an unjustified dismissal from my directorship due to a right-wing reporter coming after me on trumped-up charges, for supposedly hiring an instructor who'd tweeted about wishing Trump dead. I traced the backstory to this reporter later, and discovered he was connected to an anti-Muslim extremist group, American Freedom Defense Initiative, whose connections to Zionist think tanks, racist views and Islamophobic activities I had exposed in an article I'd published earlier in *Counterpunch*. My Administration over the decades has continued to view me with suspicion because of my political views since that fateful public encounter with Sontag, so this reporter's exposure of my "biased" hiring of someone calling for Trump's assassination on Facebook provided a convenient excuse to relieve me of a leadership position. It didn't matter that, in fact, I had had nothing to do with hiring said instructor.

Beginnings

When I arrived at Tufts from Pakistan at the end of the 1970s, as a graduate student in English, I was hardly aware of the influence Zionism exercised on college campuses, an extension of its hold in the halls of Congress and United States politics in general. Like many who grew up in what was then called the Third World, my generation had bought into the ideal of the U.S. as a bastion of free speech, equality, and a haven for immigrants of all races, colors and creeds. The history of its genocide of Native Americans and the enslavement of African peoples were often elided in the popular narrative of America as the Land of the Free and the Brave.

Very quickly after my immersion in my graduate studies in 1979, my political education began to be shaped by cataclysmic global events like the Iranian Islamic revolution, the Afghanistan debacle in which US and USSR battled for control of the region that heralded the end of the Cold War, followed by the failure of the Camp David Accords to uphold the UN's charter: the right of return, national independence, and sovereignty in Palestine. and participation of the PLO in all decisions pertaining to its future.

Together with some of my fellow international students from Lebanon and Iran, I realized that most students were ignorant of history beyond the American borders, and unaware of media bias regarding the Third World. We decided to focus on one particularly egregious case of mis and dis-information: Palestine. I became a founding member of the first-ever student-led Committee on Information about Palestine on my campus, and soon learned how risky it was to speak out on behalf of Palestine. Our event posters were routinely torn down: I actually caught someone from Hillel in the act of defacing one such poster. Threatening messages were left on our answering machines. At one point, our committee members wrote a letter to the editor of the Tufts student newspaper, *The Observer,* outlining some of these incidents:

May 8 '81

tufts
Obs

Group claims actions unjust

To the Editor:

We The Commttee on Palestine would like to record a list of harassments that we have undergone since November. **Before** we became an official group, we presented a UN movie entitled **The Palestinians Do Have Rights**. At that time one member received an anonymous hate call. Worse, the majority of our posters announcing the event were torn down. One we became an official group the harassment worsened. The afternoon of our first event false notices were distributed in professors' mailboxes announcing that the event was cancelled, presumably signed by us. Professor John Gibson, for one, read this notice and was later appalled when he realized that he had been used to disseminate false information.

Written on some posters were the words "Marc Iden (the speaker) is a traitor" and "Jew hater." The harassment now spread to include our speakers. Our next guest was Dr. Khalil Nakleh, President of the Arab-American University Graduates, and, once again, anti-democratic people saw fit to tear down the majority of our posters. In addition, our ad did not appear for three consecutive days in The Tufts Daily, despite repeated assurances that it would go in. The following week, when Professor Bob Lange from Brandeis University spoke on the suppres-_on of Palestinian education on the _____ the life expectancy of our posters was reduced to ten or fifteen minutes maximum.

The harassment surrounding our final event was appalling. A few hours before Dr. Husseini

"Every kibbutz is a military target." That statement was in response to the question, "Name me one military target that the PLO tries to hit."

We would like to stress that the purpose of our group is educational. None of us is Palestinian but, having studied the issue carefully, we are convinced of the legitimacy of Palestinian complaints. Further, we saw that there was a complete lack of information on campus on the Palestinian point-of-view and we feel that Americans have the right to hear the Palestinians speak for themselves, especialy considering the extensive American support for Israel. Since the vast majority of Palestinians see the PLO as their sole, legitimate representative—and 103 countries in the world agree with them—we see no reason to continue to deny the right of the PLO to speak unharassed here or anywhere. We will not trample on Palestinian rights by telling them where they should live or who their representatives should be.

There are two sides to every conflict. If the supporters of Israel are so convinced of the justness of their views, why do they feel so threatened by a group that presents the other side? That they do feel this way is clear from the numerous harassments detailed here. If they are indeed correct, what are they so worried about?

The Committee on Palestine
Molly Greene
Mojdeh Pirasieh
Fawzia Afzel
Youssef Khlat
Ralph Eid

The consequences we are seeing today for students and faculty protesting, against what the ICJ has ruled as a likely case of Israeli genocide in Gaza, are much worse.[1] Back then, the reactions to our student efforts at presenting an alternative viewpoint on the question of Palestine were limited to messages meant to intimidate us. It did not result in a loss of future employment, as it has for many student supporters today, or firings and arrests of even tenured professors who are raising voices in support of Palestinian rights.

My own professional trajectory proceeded fairly smoothly after finishing graduate studies at Tufts. I was hired to a tenure-track position in the Department of English at Montclair State University (MSU) a year after I graduated. Aside from a few visiting professor gigs at Harvard, NYU Abu Dhabi, and several universities in my home country of Pakistan over the past several decades, MSU has been my tenure home since 1987. My 38-year career is a study in surviving in academia, at times even thriving, despite the many obstacles small and large that are thrown into the paths of faculty like me who challenge the political narrative around Zionism.

First Act of Resistance as Assistant Professor:

During my second year at MSU, I attended what was then an annual campus event, the Presidential Lecture. That year, our speaker was the famed New York intellectual, Susan Sontag, who was introduced to us by a deferential group of administrators, including the Acting President, and a leading member of our English Department faculty. Sontag spoke on the unit of time known as the decade—what it is, what it signifies, how it came to be a temporal marker, and so on; the usual arcane stuff intellectuals like to ponder. She honed in on a specific decade to provide some concrete examples to buttress her larger argument: the decade that the world witnessed the holocaust of the Jewish peoples by the Nazis.

The Holocaust was horrific. But this same decade also witnessed numerous other horrors, including the creation of the state of Israel on Palestinian lands and the concomitant Nakba (catastrophe) visited on the Palestinian natives of those lands, thousands of whom were forced to flee Israeli forces. Many were massacred, many more witnessed the destruction of their homes, their olive and lemon groves, their villages. When I raised this issue for Sontag to comment on, asking why she had not alluded to this other group of people affected so badly during the decade under scrutiny—she started to tremble on the stage, and ultimately responded with anger at my temerity in asking such a question.

I remember how several junior faculty had approached me nervously as we streamed out of the auditorium. Wasn't I afraid of jeopardizing my tenure and promotion at the institution, they asked? As if on cue, the following day I received a summons to my chair's office, who told me she wished to school me in Zionism, and that in order to allay my ignorance regarding the God-given right of Jewish peoples to the Land of Israel, she recommended I read Maimonides (a medieval Jewish scholar). It was a meeting designed to humiliate and intimidate; I was treated as a child in need of guidance for my ignorance. I realized I would have to proceed with caution if I was going to get through the next few years, and past the tenure and promotion decision. Luckily for me, I had a wonderful defender in the person of a senior member of the department, a popular and well-respected colleague. She wrote a strong op-ed for the campus student newspaper, *The Montclarion*, defending my right to free speech and expressing disdain for the globally renowned author (Sontag) who could not respond to a fair question except by berating me in public. In the weeks that followed, I was amazed to discover daily messages left on my voicemail by university faculty and staff whom I did not know, acknowledging my courage in speaking out on a controversial topic.

Since these were the days before social media, my encounter with Susan Sontag did not go viral, avoiding what today would likely be some sort of cancellation. Several years later I did get tenure—but no promotion (tenure and promotion almost always go hand in hand). For that I had to fight hard, to the point of threatening a lawsuit, but with the help of our union I was promoted to Associate Professor the following year.

Post-tenure Obstacles and Resistance

The politics of fear that I observed among non-tenured faculty especially, and among those aspiring to leadership positions in the department and institution, operated on the unspoken assumption that criticism of Israel was unthinkable. This resulted in a self-imposed censorship on the faculty at my university. Only one other senior tenured faculty member of my department was vocal in support of the Palestinian right to self-determination, and he has been effectively sidelined as an extremist who defends Stalin. He and I were the only ones who would speak out against Israeli apartheid policies consistently. We were especially vocal during moments of crisis such as during the two *intifadas* and the reprisals these invited by the Israeli Defense Forces (more appropriately referred to as Israeli Occupation Forces) against civilians, mostly women and children.

When I tried to organize a day long teach-in with scholars and artists at my university to educate our student body as well as the larger community on the scale of atrocities being committed by Israel in Gaza during Operation Cast Lead (2008-2009), I was taken aside by department members who later went on to hold leadership roles. They tried to discourage me from inviting some of the speakers I had lined up, specifically, the Israel critic academic and activist, Norman Finkelstein, who had been denied tenure at DePaul university for purely *ad hominem* reasons. When I asked why, I was told that "he is not a scholar."

Finkelstein, the son of Holocaust survivors and the author of more than a dozen books, has been repeatedly targeted by pro-Israeli extremists and often silenced in the process. Unfortunately that was the effect my colleagues' persuasive tactics had on me. In the end, I invited Joseph Massad instead, a scholar of Palestinian history at Columbia, who hadn't yet been targeted the way Finkelstein had. The two English department colleagues who tried to dissuade me from inviting Finkelstein (and even Massad) to campus, are respectable scholars who've been kind and gracious in their dealings with me through the decades. I'm sure these colleagues wouldn't recognize or even agree that what they were doing was a form of censorship by invoking the specter of anti-Semitism. Their approach to censoring opinions like mine is far more sophisticated than the more obvious intimidation practiced by some other colleagues.

An example of the latter was the behavior of a self-proclaimed Christian Zionist who was chair of our College's Department of Religion and Philosophy for many years. Let's call him Michael. He had a large Confederate battle flag affixed to his office wall. For displaying a racist, treasonous emblem extolling the virtues of a slaveholding past, this colleague was never sanctioned or told he couldn't fly the flag in full view of students (and faculty) walking past his office, many of whom surely felt intimidated or unsafe by such a display. Yet after the Oct 7th 2023 Hamas attack on southern Israel that immediately resulted in Israel's disproportionate assault on Gaza, the little Palestinian flag I affixed to my office door drew notice and condemnation from several faculty members, including my previous department chair (one of the two colleagues who in 2008 had argued against issuing an invitation to Norman Finkelstein). He told me during a private exchange that he was hurt to see this display of support for Palestinians so soon after Hamas had attacked Israel. I pointed out in a friendly exchange of views, and without endorsing Hamas actions, that there really was no comparison in terms of number of lives lost—27,000 then (now over 64,000, according to The Lancet, 70% being children and women in UN estimates, vs. 1,200 Israelis) (now over 35,000) vs. 1,200—nor had the Hamas attack resulted in damage to civilian infrastructure on the Israeli side anywhere close to what Israeli counterattacks on Gaza's schools, hospitals, homes delivered in retaliation. The sign on his door, announcing his office as a safe space for all students experiencing "anti-Semitism, anti Zionism, Islamophobia" had, on the other hand, by equating anti-Semitism with anti-Zionism, opened up a dangerous space; one that encourages attacks from students on those of us who proffer critiques of Zionism as a racist nationalist ideology, an ideology that is unacceptable to many people of the Jewish faith. Sure enough, a student in one of my classes this past semester brought a charge of anti-Semitism against me, which I managed to effectively debunk because of meticulous record-keeping I have learnt to do precisely to ward off such attacks. Whilst within a week of my putting up the little Palestinian flag in a display of solidarity, it was gone, my former Chair's sign, despite requests like mine to alter its wording, remained on his door. Despite our cordial relationship, I cannot get him to see how the views his office door presents—conflating anti-Zionism with anti-Semitism—poses a threat to freedom of speech in our classes. It's not anti-Semitic to question the Israeli state. The passage of HR 3016, the anti-boycott bill that has been passed by the House of Representatives, if signed into law, would have a similarly chilling effect.

Struggle to Be Given Due Recognition for my Scholarly Output

Between 2005 and 2015 I sought the University's highest award, the rank of Distinguished Scholar. Michael, my Christian Zionist colleague, was a powerful faculty member back then (he's since retired and recently passed away). Michael headed up the committee in charge of selecting our College's nominee for this award. Winning it was important to me, as it would legitimize the kind of scholar-activism my career emphasized, since my work combines a transnational and postcolonial feminist literary and cultural analysis to advance a social justice agenda My work combined literary and cultural critique to advance a social justice agenda. I believe that it was the activist nature of my scholarly work and my open advocacy for justice for Palestine that led Michael and his neoconservative protégés to deny me appointment as distinguished scholar for over a decade. I had to apply ten years in a row before I got it—something that has never happened before or since then. I was named as Distinguished Scholar only after I finally brought a complaint against Michael, insisting he be relieved as chair of the selection committee; no one is supposed to serve continuously on any faculty committee for that length of time.

Here are some of the steps Michael took to prevent me from being appointed as Distinguished Scholar. One year, his committee selected an unqualified nominee rather than me. This proved to be such a ridiculously partisan decision that even the university president, no supporter of mine—denied Michael's pick, with the unprecedented result that *no one* was awarded this honor that year. The faculty member the committee selected had published nothing except a few newsletter entries and an article in a non-peer-reviewed journal; by that point I'd published five books and over fifty articles, many of them in peer-reviewed journals. A colleague on Michael's committee shared this faculty member's application with me. It was just two pages long. I used this pitifully short application to compose a letter to my dean and the university president to let them know that if Michael wasn't removed from his position of power, I would be forced to take up the matter with our union. My letter also established that many recent Distinguished Scholar nominees had far less distinguished publication records than I had.

Sure enough, the next year I got the Distinguished Scholar appointment I should have received a decade earlier. I can only believe that threatening to involve the faculty union had helped. Maybe also my university administrators had come to realize how capricious and prejudicial Michael's leadership had been. Perhaps because my scholarly publications had nothing to do with Israel-Palestine, I was helped with a strong case made on my behalf by my department's representative to the Awards committee—the same colleague who was (and remains) unhappy with my anti-Zionist views.

In the aforementioned episodes with Michael and my former department chair, the latter has been very subtle in this area of curbing my right to free expression through a soft "guidance" approach, at times even by helping me advance certain career goals, whilst the former made blatant attempts to deny me a platform of visibility and scholarly prominence due to my views on a particular issue. The real problem is that these two very different types of censoring actions, one within the bounds of friendly collegiality, the other not—are united under the banner of a shared Zionist ideology that has huge clout in academia and politics. It works to isolate people like me through efforts to curb our speech and actions, thus effectively diminishing our influence and contributions. Despite, for example, pleading for the past two decades for a tenure-track line hire in Arab and Arab-American literature and culture, or another hire in postcolonial studies like myself who could teach courses I've created, such as *Images of Muslim Women*, which currently gets offered only when I am available to teach it—my requests have been effectively sidelined. Hiring another brown South Asianist like me or an Arabist has proved impossible over the past 37 years, and so we remain a white-and male-dominated department, teaching a largely traditional curriculum, despite an increasingly diverse student body.

Post 9/11 Harassment

Michael, the Christian Zionist colleague who prevented me from obtaining the Distinguished Scholar award for a decade, in the aftermath of 9/11 started posting outrageous racist and xenophobic comments about me on a several-thousand strong university-wide faculty and staff listserv.

One such comment, directed at me, was "Go back to the caves you crawled out from." This came as response to an email I sent to the listserv in which I insisted on historicizing the 9/11 tragedy. I'd placed the September 11 attacks in the context of arguments being made by activist writers like Arundhati Roy, who have described the many 9/11s that preceded what happened on US soil, in so many countries of the global south, thanks to unrelenting military and economic interference by the United States's military-industrial imperialist complex. Part of my own historicizing argument was to link unqualified US backing of the Zionist colonial-settler Israeli apartheid nation to the state of general distrust and dislike of the US by many of the world's brown and black peoples. Making such arguments obviously did not go down well with people like Michael. Accordingly, he made vocal attempts to silence me. Many of our colleagues came to see him as the bigot he is, including those who may have had similar reservations about my views.

Becoming the Anti-Zionist "Muslim Woman:" How I was Ousted as Director of Women's Studies

A strange confluence of pressures formed around me in the decades after 9/11. I became the "Muslim Woman," made to represent *both* the exception to the rule of Muslim fundamentalism in western academia, as well as a suspicious "other" for harboring sentiments which, because they were at odds with the US-Zionist machine of Empire, rendered me unpatriotic (hence a traitor) in the eyes of many. Several students, especially in classes where I taught Palestinian writers like Ghassan Kanafani or Arab feminists like Nawal el Saadawi, both of whom sharply criticize Zionism, US imperialism, patriarchy, racial capitalism, and so-called Islamic fundamentalism, called me anti-American, complaining about me in student evaluations. At times some students expressed anger at my views, but in recent years, the number of anti-Zionist Jewish students has grown exponentially on campus. I'd like to think this has been a result of exposure to critiques of Zionist discourse, taught by college faculty like me. In any case, the net result of the confluence of both admiration as well as distrust for what I stood for, for the views I espoused unambiguously in my teaching and my writings, exposing the links between all manner of pieties, combined to result in a number of attempts to silence me.

The first of these was the discovery that my name was on the AMCHA list of professors "inimical to Israel," and hence to be avoided and denounced. Here is the Amcha Initiative's website announcement of their stated objectives:

> As the fall semester begins, many students will consider taking courses offered by Middle East scholars on their respective campuses, in order to better understand the current turmoil raging in the Middle East, especially the Israel-Gaza conflict. AMCHA Initiative has posted a list of 218 professors identifying themselves as Middle East scholars, who recently called for the academic boycott of Israel in a petition signed. *Students who wish to become better educated on the Middle East without subjecting themselves to anti-Israel bias, or possibly even antisemitic rhetoric*, may want to check which faculty members from their university are signatories before registering. (my emphasis)

I'm the only such signatory listed from Montclair State University.[2]

I believe accusations of anti-Semitism, combined with the fact that I am of Muslim Pakistani background, led to the events that got me fired from my position as Director of Women's and Gender Studies several years later. During the 2016-2017 academic year, after a semester teaching abroad at NYU in Abu Dhabi, during which time another person had succeeded me as Director to WGS, I returned to Montclair State. Unfortunately, the woman who had succeeded me as Director of Women and Gender Studies suddenly resigned, and I was requested by colleagues teaching in the program, as well as the Provost, to take up the post once more. I agreed to do so for one year, to ensure that a program I had built up over the past six years would not fall apart. Over the summer I worked to restore some order in the program prior to the start of the academic year, which included finalizing the hiring of two new adjunct instructors. One of these new instructors, who had already been hired by the outgoing Director, had recently tweeted his disgust about President Trump, stating, "Trump is a f—ing joke. This is all a sham. I wish someone would just shoot him outright." I did not know about this tweet and Facebook post. Even if I had, I would have treated it as protected speech that occurred off campus. A few weeks prior to the start of the Fall term, I was asked to meet with the Dean of my college. He informed me that I had been relieved of my position as Director of Women and Gender Studies.

The reason I was given for this ignominious firing from a leadership position that I had been invited —nay begged—to fill, was that a letter had been sent to the President of the University asking how someone calling for the assassination of our country's President, had "slipped through the cracks" in the hiring process. Since I was the Director of the Program to which the instructor had been hired, the accusation was clearly pointed at me, and had its desired effect: the adjunct was fired and I was relieved of my directorship. Here is how I saw what happened, as I outlined in an article published soon thereafter in *Counterpunch:*

> I believe strongly that my "firing" was in response to the Islamophobic rant sent to the President, Provost and Dean of my university by right wing columnist James Merse (who writes for a rag called the *Daily Caller* [co-founded by Tucker Carlson] in NJ [New Jersey])—and on which he also copied me. In this email he threatened the university, claiming he and his "cohort" of right-wing supporters would have marched in protest onto the campus had the admin not fired Allred! He kept asking in that email "how did Allred's hire slip through the cracks" (he had previously stated such things publicly)-and since I was the new Director in charge of the Program at this time, the question was obviously pointed at me. Now all the administrators knew I had had *nothing* to do with hiring this Allred guy—so why remove me then? It doesn't take a genius to figure out that these right-wing nuts like Merse knew of my public writings exposing their outfits and the individuals that head them and that right now in the US, these scary folks are exercising their financial and political clout to pressurize university administrators to fire or otherwise silence voices like mine who are anathema to them.[3]

An article I had published a few years prior, also in *Counterpunch*, traces precisely this money-trail of funders of Islamophobia which, as I argued in the article, is quite clearly linked to pro-Israeli sources and conservative dark money. My research into these links was prompted in the fall of 2012 by huge billboards appearing at my Hudson Valley town's train station, touting nakedly Islamophobic ads. I bring this up as I believe this type of public-facing writing puts folks like me under surveillance by right-wing operatives, and which led in my case to a well-orchestrated attack linking me to the adjunct instructor advocating Trump's assassination. I had claimed in earlier *Counterpunch* article that,

> I was stunned to see an ad on a billboard staring me in the face from across the train tracks stating the following: "19,250 deadly Islamic attacks since 9/11/01. And counting. It's not Islamophobia, it's Islamorealism."

> The ad was paid for by two organizations called "Jihad watch.org" and "Atlasshrugged." Jihad Watch is a program of the David Horowitz Freedom Center, and its Director is a man named Robert Spencer who is the author of twelve books, including two *New York Times* bestsellers, *The Truth About Muhammad* and *The Politically Incorrect Guide to Islam (and the Crusades)*. According to the *Jihadwatch* website:

> Spencer has led seminars on Islam and jihad for the United States Central Command, United States Army Command and General Staff College, the U.S. Army's Asymmetric Warfare Group, the FBI, the Joint Terrorism Task Force, and the U.S. intelligence community. *Stealth Jihad: How Radical Islam is Subverting America without Guns or Bombs* (Regnery), is a supposed "expose" of how jihadist groups are advancing their agenda in the U.S.[4]

Spencer was joined in weaving his web of anti-Muslim (and more specifically, anti-Arab and anti-Palestinian) conspiracy theories—which are still being taught to the US military—by his colleague Pamela Geller, an acolyte of the 20th century writer Ayn Rand, a libertarian conservative and uber-capitalist—hence the name of the blog she sponsored, Atlasshrugs.com. which today has become https://gellerreport.com/ and is spewing forth venomous stories repeating unsubstantiated Israeli *hasbara* claims about Hamas' rapes of Israeli women (which have been proved to be utterly factitious, relying on uncorroborated accounts of two unreliable witnesses belonging to a very suspect and morally compromised militia group called ZAKA).[5]

Jihadwatch and *AtlasShrugged* were also behind another series of ads posted on municipal buses in San Francisco and on municipal buses: "In any war between the civilized man and the savage, support the civilized man. Support Israel, Defeat Jihad."

The equation of "civilized man" with the State of Israel, the "savage" with that of the absent Arab, is lifted verbatim from a 1974 lecture by American author Ayn Rand, which have been echoed by Golda Meir and other past and present leaders of Israel. Muslim brown women like myself, proclaiming solidarity with Palestine, are subject to the same propaganda/hasbara that renders us dangerous "others" who are a threat to the values of western "civilization."

Connecting the Dots, Past to Present

What I've tried to do throughout my academic career, is to connect the dots between phenomena the academy wishes to keep separate and de-linked. Most of all, drawing connections between Zionism, US militarism, racialized capitalism and white liberal feminism, is the kind of display of disobedience to the norms of our profession that must needs be punished by the powers that be.

It was therefore no surprise that the administration responded to the threat by the reporter for the *Daily Caller*, James Merse, that he would "organize and lead significant peaceful-but loud—protests and campaigns" if the aforementioned adjunct wasn't let go, by firing him prior to the beginning of the term, and publicly dismissing me as well from my position as director of WGS. Doing so can be read as a decision to a) appease a university president wary of someone with my political views leading a small but thriving program with a reputation for disobedience; and b) to perform damage control in order to mollify conservative donors potentially triggered by the *Daily Caller* article. Media coverage favorable to me failed to sway my university president.[6]

What I had argued several years prior to my wrongful dismissal—that a confluence of interests in the US political and cultural sphere threatened to fill the polity with hatred, xenophobia, Islamophobia, and racism—presaged this challenging outcome in my professional life: as a brown Muslim woman who had painstakingly exposed the influence of Zionism on American political life, I would not be given a public-facing in the university.[7]

Where I Am /Where We Are Today

We obviously live in a surveillance state, and today we are seeing the consequences of speaking truth to power. Students and faculty across our campuses who dare to condemn Israeli genocide and show empathy with Palestinian civilians being butchered in the thousands, are being doxxed, fired, and otherwise harassed.

With a handful of other faculty, I am active in discussions nationally and on campus, providing analysis and information beyond state-sponsored media narratives. Once more, we are the victims of name-calling, and one of my departmental colleagues was publicly silenced for several months due to complaints against him of "creating a hostile work environment." Since his comments are posted on a public faculty listserv, everyone there is on a coeval footing; my colleague is not in any way in a supervisory role for others on this list. The complaint was therefore nonsensical. I have just published an essay outlining this outrageous turn of events in *Counterpunch*.[8] More recently, I myself was verbally assaulted by the Dean of the College of Humanities and Social Sciences, who accused me at a university event in full view and hearing of colleagues and students, of making assertions and comments on the university listserv he found insulting and egregious which, given I had only been posting articles critical of Israel, indicated to me that he found my comments to be anti-semitic—a claim he in fact made during a later meeting between him, myself and the Provost. When I politely asked if he could identify these remarks, he replied, "I don't want to talk to you." Given his role as my supervisor, such behavior definitely constitutes the creation of a hostile work environment.

His attack followed on the heels of an initial refusal by my department chair to allow me to post notice of a lecture I had organized on our department's social media sites. The lecturer was a well-respected scholar, Andrew Ross, and His talk was titled "Why Palestine Matters." My chairperson eventually consented to my request to post the event on our sites after I pointed out that his refusal was undemocratic and tantamount to censorship of faculty and student rights. However, he made it a point to let me and others know that his initial refusal was occasioned by the fact that the talk was being co-sponsored by SJP (Students for Justice in

Palestine), whom he considers a "terrorist" organization (a totally unsupported accusation), and that in order for the flyer to go out on our sites, I had to remove an image of blood dripping from beneath a woman wearing Palestinian embroidery. To him, the image was upsetting as he saw in it a reference to the antisemitic trope of Jewish blood libel, even though I explained (after apologizing for having hurt his sensibilities) that what was being referenced was the ongoing bloodshed of the Palestinians of Gaza. I paste below both the original flyer and the revised one, to show how my language and art were policed:

Original:

In the streets all over the world and on American college campuses, many more of us than ever before are refusing to be silenced or intimidated. Helped by several colleagues, I am proud to announce the formation of Montclair State's chapter of Faculty for Justice in Palestine. We are slowly seeing our membership grow, although many members have requested anonymity. We hear almost daily about the firing and suspension of untenured faculty who are vocal in their support of Palestine. Meanwhile, pro-Palestinian students are being doxxed, and have had job offers rescinded and on our campus, student and faculty protests have been continuously policed, and participants harassed.

While I have been deliberately sidelined in the decision-making apparatus of university life, I believe that justice will always prevail in the end. I am proud of having remained a disobedient voice, of questioning the norms that compel us to be compliant to authority in and outside of academe. I'd like to end by citing a passage from Steven Salaita's latest essay, in which he pulls no punches regarding the compromises we as scholars working for remuneration and rewards make; at the same time, he exhorts us to do the right thing, to embrace disobedience and class disloyalty, in order to refuse compliance to a genocidal world order:

> Maybe it's time for scholars to disobey our own compunctions—that we're important or even indispensable, that our education gives us special insight, that innovation would die if we suddenly went away. Our main compunction, as with all the professions, is to obey class loyalties. Disobedience should be introspective, then. We have to disrupt the norms and procedures that advantage the compliant. How can this be done? It's hard to say. But that it needs doing is by now beyond doubt.[9]

Steven paid the ultimate price for disobedience—he was fired from his faculty position even before setting foot on the campus that had hired him, for a series of tweets condemning Israeli slaughter in Gaza during Operation Cast Lead in 2008 and 2009. I am lucky I managed to get tenure, and within the constraints and privileges afforded by it, have tried and will continue to try to speak truth to power.

Postscript

The dean of the College of Humanities and Social Sciences has stepped down from his position effective May 2025. I had reported him to the Provost for his inappropriate conduct towards me when he publicly accused me of making anti-Semitic comments on the campus listserv following Oct 7th 2023. This development occurred after I'd sent a letter outlining reasons for possible litigation to the provost, who had held an unsatisfactory meeting between the (former) dean and me in his (the provost's) presence. I was then contacted by the university's Director of Institutional Compliance (who was simultaneously the Title IX coordinator and its Equal Employment Opportunity and Affirmative

Action officer). This university official, my attorney, and I agreed to an informal resolution of the matter pending an apology letter from the former dean. I would be permitted to share this letter with those who had either witnessed or been informed of the dean's humiliating attack on me. The letter would also state clearly that no retaliatory action would be taken against me, or anyone else, for our protected speech under the 1st amendment. The fact of the dean's resignation the fact of the dean's resignation and expressed willingness to issue an official apology can be seen as evidence that it is occasionally possible for beleaguered faculty who push back against unjust treatment to succeed. Those of us working at state universities like me, obviously have more leverage in this regard than those at private institutions, who lack the same 1st amendment speech protections. But one has to be willing to fight back.

Our Faculty for Justice in Palestine chapter has been similarly engaged in resisting harassment and intimidation unleashed on us since September 1st 2024, when our silent protest holding aloft placards of children killed by Israeli forces in Gaza since last October's air and ground incursion was deemed an act of "insubordination" due to our refusal to relocate to a designated "free speech zone" on campus. These zones have no foot traffic, so they aren't effective places for demonstrations. We have succeeded thus far in staving off administrative attempts to shut us down. The Foundation for Individual Rights and Expression (FIRE) wrote a cease-and-desist letter to the university, which points out the unconstitutionality of so-called free speech zones—and made clear that these zones violate the terms of Montclair State University's own stated policies!

I conclude by drawing attention to these recent successes in our resistance against censorship and threats of disciplinary action for exercising our free speech rights, in order to encourage others to stand up and do the right thing, and to use legal means as much as possible in order to fight back against institutional attempts at censorship and silencing.

Endnotes

* A previous version of this essay was published in *Counterpunch* on July 19, 2024. Available at https://www.counterpunch.org/2024/07/19/us-academia-and-the-censoring-of-an-anti-zionist-professor/ (accessed November 8, 2024).

[1] On genocide in Gaza, Al-Kassab, Fatima. "A top U.N. court says Gaza genocide is 'plausible' but does not order cease-fire." NPR, January 26, 2024. Available at https://www.npr.org/2024/01/26/1227078791/icj-israel-genocide-gaza-palestinians-south-africa#:~:text=ICJ%20says%20it's%20'plausible'%20Israel%20committed%20genocide%20in%20Gaza%20The,call%20for%20a%20cease%2Dfire (accessed May 29, 2024).

[2] AMCHA Initiative. n.d. "AMCHA Publishes List of Over 200 Anti-Israel Middle East Studies Professors." Available at https://amchainitiative.org/amcha-publishes-list-of-over-200-anti-israel-middle-east-studies-professors/ (accessed May 30, 2024).

[3] Afzal-Khan, Fawzia. "Of Dramas Big and Small in the USA Today: From ISIS to Islamophobia to the Solar Eclipse." *Counterpunch*, August 28, 2017, available at https://www.counterpunch.org/2017/08/28/of-dramas-big-and-small-in-the-usa-today-from-isis-to-islamophobia-to-the-solar-eclipse/ (accessed April 12, 2024).

[4] Afzal-Khan, Fawzia. "Islamophobia in America." *Counterpunch*, August 24, 2012, available at https://www.counterpunch.org/2012/08/24/islamophobia-in-america/ (accessed May 30, 2024).

[5] See Sayegh, Nadine. "Israel's 'Purple-Washing' and the Dehumanisation of Palestinian Men and Women." *The New Arab*, February 8, 2024. Available at https://www.newarab.com/features/purple-washing-and-abuses-against-palestinians (accessed November 9, 2024).

[6] Quintana, Chris. "A Professor Says She Was Penalized for an Instructor's Tweet." *Chronicle of Higher Education*, August 18, 2017, available at https://www.chronicle.com/article/a-professor-says-she-was-penalized-for-an-instructors-tweet/ (accessed June 3, 2024); Stewart, Andrew. "The Liberal Lockdown in Academia: The Case of Fawzia Afzal-Khan." *Counterpunch*, September 1, 2017, available at https://www.counterpunch.org/2017/09/01/the-liberal-lockdown-in-academia-the-case-of-fawzia-afzal-khan/ (accessed June 4, 2024).

[7] Afzal-Khan 2012.

[8] Afzal-Khan, Fawzia. "The New McCarthyism on US Campuses." *Counterpunch*, December 11, 2023. Available at https://www.counterpunch.org/2023/12/11/the-new-mccarthyism-on-us-campuses/ (accessed May 30, 2024); Lennard, Natasha. "University Professors Are Losing Their Jobs over 'New McCarthyism' on Gaza." *The Intercept*, May 16 2024. Available at https://theintercept.com/2024/05/16/university-college-professors-israel-

palestine-firing/#:~:text=via%20Getty%20Images-,University%20
Professors%20Are%20Losing%20Their%20Jobs%20Over%20%E2%80%9
CNew%20McCarthyism%E2%80%9D%20on,Palestine%20faculty%20me
mbers%20without%20tenure.&text=May%2016%202024%2C%205%3A0
0%20a.m.&text=Many%20scholars%20committed%20to%20Palestinian%
20liberation%20can%20no%20longer%20do%20their%20jobs   (accessed
May 30, 2024).

⁹ Salaita, Steve. "Customs of Obedience in Academe." Blog post, February 12,
2024. Available at https://stevesalaita.com/the-customs-of-obedience-in-
academe/ (accessed May 31, 2024).

The 9/11 Terror Attacks, Racial Profiling, and Its Aftermath

Abdul Jabbar,
City College of San Francisco

In the immediate aftermath of the terror attacks on the United States on September 11, 2001, police personnel of City College of San Francisco accused me of being a terrorism sympathizer and even a potential terrorist. An investigation was initiated when the mother of one of my students called the campus police, accusing me of saying in class that the U.S. deserved those terror attacks because of its foreign policy.

The campus police acted based on hearsay. The San Francisco Police Department wisely reconsidered, and refused to take any action against me. As the following account will reveal, one of the campus officers, who identified himself as an army reservist, made up his mind concerning my guilt without ever asking for my account. He also compelled two of my students to make incriminating statements about the contents of my lecture of September 12, 2001. The students later retracted those statements, stating they had made them under duress.

My lecture of September 12, 2001

On September 12, I had an English literature class to teach. The College administration had requested all faculty members speak to our students about the terror attacks instead of sticking to the syllabus. After condemning terrorism unequivocally and deploring the loss of innocent lives, I invited my students to ask me questions.

They were unanimous in wanting to know the reasons for the barbaric 9/11 terror attacks. Most students did not know about the U.S. foreign policy in the Middle East that might have prompted those attacks. Since the 19 attackers were from Middle Eastern countries whose governments were close U.S. allies (chiefly, Saudi Arabia), it did not seem to make sense to my students that citizens of those countries would attack the United States. I explained to my puzzled students that even though the elite in the governments of Egypt and Saudi Arabia had cordial ties with the U.S., many of their people hated the U.S, government for its military, financial, and diplomatic support of Israel's illegal settlements on occupied Palestinian territories, in violation of U.N. Security Council's resolutions, such as Resolution 242, the frequent massacres of Palestinians, and the illegal campaign of ethnic cleansing of Palestinians from their homeland. None of my students knew that a complete takeover of Palestine has been the Zionist leaders' agenda from its nineteenth-century founder Theodor Herzl to the present Israeli leaders. They had no idea that in view of the U.S. government's and Israel's actions, the notion of a two-state solution that they seemed to support was perceived to be insincere. It was used by the U.S. and Israel just to give Israel more time to complete its occupation of Palestine.

My students wondered why their government had adopted such a foreign policy. I said that one of the reasons could be that the U.S. uses Israel as its military base to control the resource-rich and strategically located region of the Middle East. The U.S. government shows little interest in the dispossession of Palestinians from their own land. With limited time for news, my students relied on mainstream media that was biased in favor of Israel and portrayed Palestinians as the problem, making the victim look like the victimizer.

The U.S. government's perceived hypocrisy made some Middle Eastern people furious. Its declared policy has been that it is opposed to Israel's settlement building on the occupied land. In reality, however, it tolerated Israel's confiscation of Palestinian land to the point that a viable two-state solution seems nearly impossible. Similarly, the U.S. government declares that it supports democracy when in reality, it has been propping up repressive regimes. I mentioned other grievances that had been accumulating over time and exploded in the form of the 9/11 terror attacks. Among them was the 1953 U.S. collusion with the United Kingdom to overthrow Iran's democratically elected government just because Iran wanted a fair share of the revenues from the oil extracted from its soil by British and U.S. oil companies. My article, "U.S., Iran, Israel, and Palestine: the Fateful Quadrangle," offers historical background on this complex topic.[1] The other possible irritants that I mentioned were the U.S. invasion of Iraq in 1991 and the green-lighting of the Israeli invasion of Lebanon in 1982.

I stayed focused on what my students wanted to know. It was easy to see but difficult to accept the possibility that our foreign policy might be a factor in transforming potential friends into foes. I also repeated throughout my lecture that I was unequivocally against terrorism. At the same time, I reiterated my stance that in order to end the scourge of terrorism, we must trace its roots and answer this question: What makes people so mad that they resort to suicide bombings?

I did not think asking such questions was unpatriotic. Nor did I see this view as condoning terrorism. I shared with my students what I knew about U.S. foreign policy and about the politics of the Middle East. I was exercising my right of academic freedom while answering my students' questions honestly. The class appreciated what to many of them was new knowledge about the world and about their own country. A number of students stayed after class to talk to me and ask further questions. Many of them sent me emails to thank me for my lecture.

Fallout from my lecture of 9-12-2001

As I mentioned earlier, one of my students talked about my lecture to his mother, who somehow inferred that I was sympathetic to the 9/11 attackers. In that overheated political climate, one could not speak about "reasons" for the attacks. Doing so was deemed unpatriotic. But analyzing causes of a phenomenon is the job of an educator.

The student's mother called the campus police. The police had instructions that any such complaints should be forwarded to FBI right away. Thus the complaint against me ended up with the FBI. San Francisco Police had wisely refused to act on such a frivolous complaint. I knew nothing about all that happened after my lecture until I heard two phone messages from my Department Chair, alerting me that the police or FBI might take me in for questioning.

My family and I were out all day on September 13, 2001. When my wife and I came home around midnight, I heard the Department Chairman's messages. I wasn't fearful, just very surprised. I'd said nothing that would warrant questioning by police, FBI (or anyone else, for that matter). I am told that when the campus police went to the College administration for their permission to take me in for questioning, they were shocked and assured the police that there must have been some misunderstanding. The Chancellor and Vice-Chancellor knew me well, as I'd worked closely with them for six years as Chair of the Department of Interdisciplinary Studies. The two administrators offered to conduct an internal investigation and if they found it necessary, I could be questioned by the police or the FBI. They knew that the police had no reason to question me.

Racial profiling and its lingering scars

When my white colleagues offered their students the same kind of analysis that I did, none of them were questioned or investigated. The prejudicial treatment that I received from the police made me painfully aware that in spite of my over 30 years of meritorious service with the College, my flawless record as a law-abiding citizen, and my popularity with my students and colleagues, I was still a second-class citizen who was to be treated differently because of my name, ethnicity, and country of origin. I was deeply hurt by this blatant example of racial profiling and the attempt to frame me as a terrorism sympathizer.

I wanted to leave the United States, but not before clearing my name. At the same time, I could not ignore the fact that with the exception of a few police officers, almost every colleague, every student, and every administrator stood by me unequivocally. It was not right to equate the entire country with the actions of a few police officers. So I decided to fight back. I asked my union for legal representation. It was a harrowing time for me and my family. Fortunately, it was a time before the Patriot Act, which decimated civil liberties for all Americans.

I was far from the only faculty member with a Muslim or Arab name who came under intense scrutiny from law-enforcement after 9/11. The

Palestinian American Professor Sami El-Arian had made remarks similar to mine. He was eventually arrested, and deported after 12 years in prison.[2]

Campus police pressure two of my students to make incriminating statements about me

From September 14, 2001, events unfolded with dizzying speed. The student whose mother had called the police had a girlfriend who was also taking my class. To build a strong case against me, she and her boyfriend were taken into the police office and "persuaded" to make an incriminating statement about my lecture about 9/11. When the students showed surprise as to the purpose of that interrogation and hesitated to sign a statement, the police officer threatened the male student with dire consequences if he did not cooperate since, according to the officer, his mother had already told the police everything.

Both of my students were frightened when they came to my office to ask my permission if they could report the police pressure to the press. The female student had the courage to go to the press and also write to the College administration about the police coercion. In the meantime, probably in response to pressure from my male student's mother, City College Police told her that action against me could be taken only if I posed a threat to the safety of her son. The mother then added the "fear factor" to her original complaint against me: She claimed that her son was afraid of me!

City College conducts an investigation

City College held off the FBI by promising to conduct an inquiry into what I had said in my lecture after 9/11. The results of the investigation were then to be submitted to the FBI. The Chair of the English Department was tasked with questioning me. In response to his questions, I expressed my feelings like this:

In the farrago of malicious lies that led to my investigation, the fiction that my student was scared of me added gravely to my hurt, anger, and disappointment. I wondered if my student was really scared of coming to my class. I could not believe that my student considered me a potential terrorist, as his mother had reported to the police. Answering questions about what I had said in class on September 12, 2001, was easy for me, but the allegation that I was a potential terrorist left me bewildered and furious. Was I supposed to say that I was not carrying explosives in my briefcase? I answered the allegations of terrorism with sarcasm. I did not think it warranted a straightforward answer. This is what I wrote to the Department Chair:

I told him I was very sorry that I made even one student feel fearful to be in my class.[3] To assure the student, his mother, the Department Chair, and everyone else that I did not carry weapons or explosives to class, I mentioned in my letter the ways I would make everyone feel safe in my class. I said that I would stop carrying my briefcase to class. If students were still concerned, I would stop wearing my topcoat. If that was not enough, to prove to everyone that I was not carrying any explosives, I would consider teaching naked, even though I'd find that embarrassing. I knew that my classroom nudity might be against the law and that I could be arrested, but I preferred arrest and punishment for a real act than be hounded by imaginary, false charges. I also felt that my sacrifice would at least end the fear and panic that my fully clothed, briefcase-carrying self was causing in tender hearts.

Despite the accuser's retraction of her allegations, the police did not stop pursuing me

In a surprising and welcome turn of events, my student's mother called the police and the English Department Chair to retract her accusations against me after her son explained to her that she had misunderstood my words. To her credit, she apologized, expressed her regret, and requested the police to make sure that no harm was done to me because of her complaint. Since it was her call to the campus police that had initiated the police and departmental investigation, the police should have stopped pursuing me after her retraction. Unfortunately, they continued with their planned action against me, thus extending my harassment for several months.

Some encouraging letters

The English Department chair sent me a letter dated September 19, 2001, informing me that the student's mother had retracted her accusation:

> This morning I talked to. . . the mother of your English 1B student. . . . The mother apologized for her son's misinterpretation of your comments made in class on September 12 concerning the September 11 terrorist attack on America. She said she had asked her son to apologize to you but felt that he might not do so because he was too embarrassed. . . . As you are aware, it was this student and his mother's complaint that the City College of San Francisco Police forwarded to San Francisco Police Department.

The two students wrote letters to City College's chancellor, and sent copies to the campus paper and the English department. Here is an excerpt from the female student's letter, dated November 6, 2001:

> My experience in the days following September 11th taught me not to trust that people in positions of authority are free from racial prejudices that will influence their behavior. I am extremely disappointed in the conduct of the San Francisco City College Police and would like to alert the administration. I experienced extreme pressure to make a statement that would corroborate the feelings of the uniformed officer present. I was placed in a closed room and when I expressed reluctance to cooperate, the officer informed me that I needed to make the statement because "we can't let people get away with saying these kinds of things." Of course what makes living in America so great is that we do in fact have the ability to exercise our right to free speech. The officer also expressed his personal feelings and let me know that he felt strongly about the issue and my responsibility to corroborate the story that was later retracted. I would never have made a statement on my own volition. . . . I am ashamed to see incidences of racial profiling emanating from an educational institution.[4]

Here is what the male student had to say in his letter of November 7, 2001:

> He [the police officer] also let me know that he was in the reserves and that he was personally affected by the incident of September 11 because he might have to serve and that all possible leads should be investigated....another officer entered the room and

asked me if I knew who [Professor Jabbar]. . . . was. My stomach immediately felt like it dropped out. At this point I felt tricked and began seriously feeling like this was a huge mistake. We began telling the officer that we didn't feel right about writing statements concerning Professor Jabbar's lecture. At this point the Officer told me that I had already given a verbal statement and that in itself was enough to open an investigation. After several minutes of extreme pressure we finally wrote our statements. I want to make a few issues very clear: I never felt threatened by Professor Jabbar; if I did I would have taken action without being prompted. I never would have on my own initiative filed any sort of complaint about Professor Jabbar. Although I might not [have] at the time agreed with what Professor Jabbar was saying, I feel he had every right to express his opinion without fear of being harassed. I feel the campus police abused their leadership and authoritative position and coerced me into giving a statement. Furthermore I would like to apologize to Professor Jabbar for having made bad decisions that caused him to be the target of racially motivated attacks....I hope that Dr. Jabbar as well as the school will forgive these serious errors in my judgment. In closing I would also ask that some responsibility be placed on the campus police and their handling of these events. I think it is pretty clear that people in the department had their own motives and used my friend and myself as instruments in pursuing them.[5]

In another positive development, the police officer who had initiated the investigation wrote to me and explained that he himself was a person of color and knew very well how minorities are too often treated with prejudice in this country. He wrote that in the emergency that had gripped the entire country, a day after the terror attacks, he had no choice but to follow the orders of his supervisors to report all terrorism-related complaints to City police and FBI. What was missing in his explanation was an acknowledgement of his error in responding to hearsay and not consulting me before contacting the FBI.

Here is part of what I wrote to my chancellor on November 14, 2001, after my meeting with him on October 31, 2001:

1. Since my meeting with you on October 31, 2001, a new revelation of an extremely serious nature has come about, which makes it

evident that a campus security official has been guilty of a hate crime against me. In their letters dated November 6 and November 7, addressed to you with a copy to me (copies enclosed) two of my students have recorded the details of a City College security official's use of coercion to make them sign statements against me. This particular official not only tried his best to hurt my career by using unlawful means but also terrorized the students by taking them into his office and coercing them into signing statements against their will.

2. As we now know from the English Department Chair's letter that I left with you on October 31 (copy enclosed), two or three days after making her allegation against me, my student's mother retracted it and apologized for her 'son's misinterpretation of my words,' which really was her misinterpretation, not her son's. She withdrew the allegation after the student challenged her absurd misinterpretation of my words. The allegation was withdrawn but not before this hate crime perpetrating Security official, without ever hearing my side, forwarded the complaint to San Francisco Police Department, inviting them and possibly the FBI to go after me and arrest me as a potential terrorist. Another disturbing fact that the student has mentioned to me is that when the Security official was busy coercing the students behind closed doors, he told them. . . that as an army reservist, he could not allow persons like me 'to get away with it.' . . . The problem seems to be not what I had said in class on September 12 because everyone was saying the same thing. The problem was that I have a Muslim name and happen to be of Pakistani origin.

3. The onslaught on academic freedom, on my well-being, and career, combined with blatant racism and unlawful action of the said official, leaves me with no choice but to initiate legal action to have him convicted of a hate crime against me. If the charges against him are proved to be true, I will be seeking his dismissal from service at City College of San Francisco. All of my colleagues who know about this case agree with me that a person

of this official's mentality has no business working in an academic institution.

4. After giving you a brief summary of the case, the action that I would like to request on your part in this letter is as follows:

1. Obtain the bogus file that City College Campus Police are keeping on me. The police sergeant told me on the phone of the existence of this file. It consists of the now null and void statements by the students, obtained from them under coercion by a CCSF Security official. The only other paper in that file is the mother's now retracted allegation. Therefore, there is no justification for a file on me with CCSF Campus Police. I would like you to obtain that file and hand it over to me, please.

2. Order immediate suspension of the Security official involved in this illegal action and start an investigation. If he is found guilty of the charge, remove him from service with City College of San Francisco.

Two of my students and the City College newspaper came to my rescue

On November 26, 2001, *Guardsman*, the City College of San Francisco newspaper, headlined its coverage with these words: "Professor Accuses Police Officer of Racial Profiling."[6] Under my photo, this caption was added: "Professor Abdul Jabbar has been a member of the City College community for over thirty years. In addition to instructing English classes, Jabbar served as the chair of Interdisciplinary Studies for six years. Since September 11, Jabbar has been active in educating people about Middle-Eastern culture." The article cited my words to explain why I thought it was a case of racial profiling:

Somehow my name, place of origin, my religion, played a negative part in the thinking of the officer [who received the complaint] and of the [student's] mother who made the complaint]. . . pointing out that his English Department colleagues discussed the same topics [American foreign policy and Middle Eastern politics] in their classes.

The Guardsman reporter included some crucial details that strengthened my position: "During the investigation, the student and his girlfriend, who is also in Jabbar's class were pulled out of class by the officer in question and asked to issue a written statement about what had been said by Jabbar." The story mentioned that both students later retracted their statements because they had been coerced to make them by college police. In a letter dated November 6, 2001, addressed to the Chancellor and other members of the administration, "she expressed her disappointment in police handling of the situation." This is how the newspaper described the investigating officer's conduct in my female student's words:

> I was placed in a closed room and when I expressed reluctance to cooperate, the officer informed me that I needed to make the statement. This guy is in uniform, telling me it's my responsibility [to make the statement]. He exerted a lot of power.

Once this news became public after *The Guardsman*'s unbiased coverage of the incident, my position became strong. It had taken nearly three months of mental anguish to reach that stage.

My decision not to take legal action, and my reconciliation with police

After the press coverage, the mother's retraction of her charge, and the two students' letters to the College administration, the police were left with no evidence to justify continuation of my harassment. Perhaps I could have obtained a settlement, but I decided not to take legal action, when it would have been the College that had to pay, not the FBI: or the campus police (because it was the campus police that had initiated the case against me). I even stopped asking that the offending police officer be removed from service at the College after receiving his note, in which he detailed his own experience with discrimination.

I did not want to collect damages from a college whose administration had stood by me. How could I ever forget the great favor my college had done for me in 1971, when it created a special job for me to protect me from unemployment. I had taken a one-year leave of absence with the intention of returning to Pakistan after receiving a good job offer there. When that offer did not materialize, I was left without a job for one full year. City College had already hired my replacement while I was on the leave of absence. The College's effort to create a position for me won my life-long loyalty.

The police chief gave me the written apology that I had asked for as a part of resolving my grievance.[7] I needed his apology in writing because it was the proof of my innocence. I could use it if there were to be any future attempts to frame me as a terrorism sympathizer. In that letter of apology, the police chief also stated that in any future incidents similar to mine, the accused faculty member would be asked for his or her account before any further action would be taken.

As a part of the agreement and my union's intercession, I insisted that the police officers who initiated the case against me without giving me a chance to explain the content of my lecture of September 12, 2001, should undergo a cultural sensitivity training with me, which they did. This way I turned this my painful experience into an educational moment. Throughout this crisis, the College administration, my colleagues, and my students stood by me. It was through their help, especially my aforementioned two students and the newspaper coverage of the incident, that I was exonerated.

New curriculum related to Islam and the Middle East as a result of this case against me

After this very unpleasant and nerve-wracking experience, at the request of the College administration I introduced a new course, called Introduction to Islam (later changed to Islam: Identity & Culture). The course is meant to provide information about the core teachings of Islam that condemn terrorism, and offer guidelines for leading a life based on humanitarian ethical values. Such courses started to appear in the curricula of most colleges and universities across the country after 9/11. They are essential for national unity, because they show that the 19 hijackers responsible for the 9/11 terror attacks did not represent American Muslims and over 99% of 1.8 billion Muslims worldwide.

The continuing damage done to me
as a result of a City College police officer's mistake

It is a matter of great satisfaction to me that all allegations against me were withdrawn. However, the damage was done, and to this day I am suffering the consequences of a police officer's mistake in forwarding to the FBI a frivolous complaint that the complainant later retracted. The campus police closed its file on me, but the FBI file on me is still active and has resulted in a lot of harassment over the decades in the form of invasive searches at airports, freezing my Weebly website account for months until my name, conflated with a terrorist namesake, was cleared by a U.S. investigative agency. There was also an attempt to prevent me from teaching a class on the Politics of the Middle East at San Francisco State University, infringement of my academic freedom at City College in the form of censorship of the instructional material that I used in my teaching, and many more punitive measures taken against me.

Over 150 innocent people have been held without charge or trial and subjected to torture at the Guantanamo Bay prison. Some were released after many years of illegal imprisonment when they were found innocent of any wrongdoing. I shudder to think that I had a close brush with that dreaded possibility simply because of a racially motivated complaint by a student's mother, retracted a few days later, and an error by a City College police officer in forwarding the complaint to San Francisco Police and the FBI. One of the most painful aspects of this experience is that this matter could and should have been resolved in a matter of two or three days—the time between the student's mother's complaint with the City College campus police and her quick retraction. Sadly, however, the FBI continued to pursue me long after the need for any investigation had become irrelevant and unnecessary, thus prolonging my tortuous suspense as to what would happen to me.

Harassment by anti-Palestine lobbies and groups

Guardsman's coverage of my case contained my analysis of U.S. policy on the Israel-Palestine conflict, and drew the attention of pro-Israel activists. The Canary Mission maintains a watch list of faculty and students it perceives to be critical of Israel. CM is prone to conflate criticism of Israel with anti-Semitism. It has collected all of my comments from my public lectures, social media postings, and other sources.[8] Professor watch lists like this have resulted in a lot of targeted harassment. They can also be used to deny employment, academic or otherwise. Anti-Palestine activists have successfully prevented well-known scholars like Norman Finkelstein from getting tenure.[9] He was dubbed antisemitic, even though he himself is Jewish and a descendent of Holocaust survivors.

Harassment at airports continued for over ten years after I was cleared of all allegations in 2001

As a part of the settlement with the police, I was to be given my police file, which I was to shred in the presence of my union representative, a college administrator, and the police chief. To my disappointment, this never happened. The police cited legal reasons why such records could not be destroyed. However, they assured me that my file was closed. I thought the matter was settled, but I had not reckoned that the FBI still had a file on me. For more than two decades I have been frequently detained for detailed questioning, sometimes lasting hours, each time I returned to the U.S. from abroad.

Soon after resolving my case with City College Police, I was detained at the airport for three hours of questioning. Each item in my baggage was checked, and I was asked totally irrelevant questions about the printed draft of my then-unpublished book manuscript, titled "Reading and Writing with Multicultural Literature." I guess they were doing their duty in closely scrutinizing each of nearly 500 pages to see if any secret was encoded in my academic prose.

The most bizarre of the searches related to a small bottle of a homeopathic medicine that a doctor in Pakistan had given me for acid reflux. The inspectors kept asking me what the bottle contained. After I explained to them a dozen times what it was, I got frustrated and asked them to keep the bottle and send it to a lab to verify my statement. They ended up letting me keep the bottle. When unpacking my baggage at home, I looked at that bottle carefully for the first time to satisfy my curiosity as to why the inspectors were so interested in it. Unknown to me, the medicine had been prescribed by a doctor at the Osama Clinic (Osama is a very common name in Pakistan.). They must have thought that I was carrying some bomb-making secret in that bottle. My wife had to wait for me for three hours, not knowing what had happened to me. I was not allowed to exit the interrogation area to use a pay phone, so that I could ask a friend to drive to the airport and tell my wife what had happened.

FBI inspectors interrogate me at an Islamic Center

My harassment wasn't limited to airports. On two different occasions, FBI inspectors came to question me at an Islamic Center, where I used to go for Friday congregational prayers. They also wanted to see what went on at the Center. Both inspectors were very polite and friendly. They asked me detailed questions about the content of the courses that I was teaching and requested me to send that information to them if I did not mind doing so. I was happy to oblige and even invited them to come to any of my classes, no prior notice necessary.

Endnotes

[1] Jabbar, Abdul. "U.S., Iran, Israel, and Palestine: The Fateful Quadrangle." *The Journal of America*, May 1, 2015. Available at https://www.journal2016 .ghazali.net/U.S.-_Iran-_Israel-_and_Palestine_--_The_Fateful_Quadrangle _5-27-15.pdf (accessed June 17, 2024).

[2] Gerstein, Josh. "Al-Arian Saga Ends with Deportation." *Politico*, February 6, 2015. Available at https://www.politico.com/blogs/under-the-radar/2015/ 02/al-arian-saga-ends-with-deportation-202233#:~:text=Last%20June% 2C%20prosecutors%20moved%20to,Virginia%20to%20Istanbul%2C%20o fficials%20said (accessed April 27, 2024); see also the United Faculty of Florida. n.d. "On the Termination of a Controversial Professor." Available at http://web.usf.edu/uff/AlArian/ (accessed June 17, 2024).

[3] Abdul Jabbar to Michael Hulbert, Chair, Department of English, City College of San Francisco, September 18, 2001. Available at

https://drive.google.com/file/d/1mwsrvGrGa1tTaxab_FK4dMpcMGHVID8h/view?usp=drive_link (accessed June 17, 2024).

[4] Cara Naiditch to Dr. Philip Day, Chancellor, City College of San Francisco, November 6, 2001. Available at https://drive.google.com/file/d/1N1cpf49SvN12AqC6-O-8HWl931jz7fsD/view?usp=drive_link (accessed June 17, 2024).

[5] Philip B. Rose to Dr. Philip Day, Chancellor, City College of San Francisco, November 7, 2001. Available at https://drive.google.com/file/d/13yiH4FRsGtdVSKAcU0l-dDAht-w6eU1c/view (accessed June 17, 2024).

[6] Jonathan Villar. "Professor Accuses Police Officer of Racial Profiling." *The Guardsman*, November 26, 2001. Available at https://drive.google.com/file/d/1U1QUK7k2NACCZIW_k2JOGYuka-MWqOD0/view (accessed June 17, 2024).

[7] Chief Gerald De Girolamo to Abdul Jabbar, October 25, 2001. Available at https://drive.google.com/file/d/1cDN_00rpiv6H6zLYT365vWGpB7HXly38/view?usp=drive_link (accessed June 17, 2024).

[8] Canary Mission. Abdul Jabbar. Available at https://canarymission.org/professor/Abdul_Jabbar (accessed April 28, 2024).

[9] Klein, David. "Why is Norman Finkelstein Not Allowed to Teach?" *Works & Days*, Special Issue: Academic Freedom in the Post-9/11 University, Vols. 26 & 27, pp 307-322 (2009). Available at http://www.csun.edu/~vcmth00m/finkelstein.html (accessed April 28, 2024).

Stomp on Jesus:
The True Story of What Happened

Deandre Poole,
Florida Atlantic University

I was the first African American male hired to teach full-time in the School of Communication and Multimedia Studies at Florida Atlantic University. This was a major accomplishment in my life, especially because I had earned undergraduate and graduate degrees in the same program. I remember first stepping onto campus at FAU in the fall of 1999. I was nervous and excited about my future. I was the first in my immediate family to attend a university. I earned a bachelor's degree in communication, a master's degree in communication, and served as a graduate teaching associate at FAU. In 2006, after earning my masters, I went on to earn my doctorate in communication and culture from Howard University, where I also served as a teaching associate. In 2011, I was hired as a full-time instructor on an annual contract at FAU. I never imagined that three years later I would be in a situation where my reputation and career would be on the line over an in-class activity that I had conducted many times before.

I prepared for class as normal on Monday, February 25, 2013. Evening classes were my preference, in order to accommodate working students. I enjoyed a healthy enrollment of students each semester and taught a gamut of courses in communication. The course I was teaching that night was Intercultural Communication, an upper-division course that was popular among students in our program. My focus was on helping students develop critical thinking and problem-solving skills. Like most faculty members in my program, I engage my students using hands-on learning class activities paired with open class dialogue. These discussions encourage students to develop cultural communication competency and become skilled communicators in a complex global world. The activity I selected that night had been used it in previous classes without incident. Each time I did the activity, it opened a dialogue about the power of symbols, how people reach different conclusions based on their cultural beliefs, and how the meaning of symbols varies in diverse cultures.

The "Stomp on Jesus" Exercise

I walked into my Intercultural Communication class that day and greeted my students as I normally did while setting up my PowerPoint slides. I began my lesson on verbal and nonverbal codes. This course was regularly taught in our academic program and was an "overload" course. As an instructor, I have a four-course teaching load per semester, but Intercultural Communications did not count against my normal load.

That night class began at 7:10 p.m. I lectured for the first half of the class and took a break at 8:25 p.m. After the break, I began to discuss with students the day's course material. The classroom activity was based on James W. Neuliep's textbook *Intercultural Communication: A Contextual Approach*, 5th Edition. I had used this textbook in a previous offering of Intercultural Communication without incident.

The purpose of the assignment was to start a conversation on the power of symbolism and its role in our culture, and that symbols need to be put into a cultural context. This material was ordinary enough that it was part of the supplemental instructor teaching resources that accompanied the textbook. The activity asked students to take out a sheet of paper and write the letters J-E-S-U-S on the paper. After writing on the paper, place the paper on the floor, and think about it for a moment. Then I asked the students to step on the paper. There were some students who did step on the paper and there were others who did not. I asked a student who did step on the paper why he did so. The student responded, "Sir, it was just a name on a piece of paper." I asked another student who did not step on the paper why she did not, and she responded, "the name has symbolic meaning to me."

At no time were any students told they had to step on the paper. Indeed, a decision to not step on the paper was part of the lesson. Students needed to understand that in society, symbols mean different things to different people. Context and various cultures attach different meanings to words.

There was one student in the class who objected to the activity. After I told students to write the letters J-E-S-U-S on a piece of paper, and place it on the floor, one student yelled out, "Hey brother, hey brother, how dare you disrespect someone's religion?" The irony of this student's question is that I am a devout Christian. I engaged the student and replied, "this is not disrespecting someone's religion… if you don't want to participate, you don't have to." This back-and-forth between the student and myself continued, creating a chaotic learning environment, which in turn lead to an early dismissal of class and a homework assignment instead. As everyone left, the agitated student remained behind, as did a second student. The agitated student approached me as I stood at the front of the classroom next to the computer table. He approached me and yelled as He was pounding his fist into his open hand multiple times, "Don't you ever do that again! Do you hear me?!" As he approached me yelling, I worried that he was about to hit me, and my body reacted defensively. All I could think to do was to pound on the computer table and yell, "Leave right now!" The student turned and walked out of the classroom while the second student looked on in shock at what had just occurred.

After both students left, I called campus security. When a campus security officer arrived, I explained to him the situation and immediately filed a campus incident report before leaving the classroom. Without this incident report documented, there would have been no record of the student's threat towards me. In this report, it clearly stated that the student threatened me with physical harm over his dislike of the course activity. I also emailed my department chair and explained the situation to her, making copies of the incident report and ensured that those copies were delivered to both my department chair and area coordinator. The student who witnessed the incident sent me an email that said, "I am at a loss for words in regarding what happened tonight. I just wanted to make it clear that I do not share the same views as my colleague and have the utmost respect for you as a professor."

The Campus Fallout

A few days later, I heard from the dean of students, who had received the incident report from the security officer. She made it clear to me that she would proceed with her initial investigation into the student's conduct. On March 8, 2013, the student was sent a notice of charges that stated: ". . . after an initial determination by this Office that the student conduct process should proceed, you are being charged with violating FAU student code of conduct, regulation 4.007, specifically: in acts of verbal, written, including electronic communications of physical abuse, threats, intimidation, harassment, coercion, or other conduct which threatens the sale, health, safety, or welfare of any person."

About 10 days later, the media picked up the story. I received an email from a local newspaper reporter asking for a comment. Not only was I shocked, but deeply disturbed by the content of the email I'd received. The reporter said he had received a call from a student in my Intercultural Communications class, who said "he was facing disciplinary action because he complained about an incident in my classroom where students were asked to write Jesus on pieces of paper and throw them on the floor and stomp on them." The following day, March 20, 2013, a local news station ran a story that was picked up by other local news outlets. National media soon followed. In their coverage, they continuously used the word "stomp" (I had never used this language in class.) At no time did they mention that the student had threatened me, nor that he was being disciplined for violating the student code of conduct.

The dean of students sent me an email explaining that the student had been instructed not to attend class until his conduct case had been resolved. I did not want him back in the classroom for safety reasons. My department chair at the time had agreed to teach the course as an independent study for the student. There was no other section of the course offered that semester that the student could have joined.

On March 29, 2013, I was placed on paid administrative leave. During my leave, I was not allowed to teach my classes or to appear on campus. The letter from the associate provost further explained that the University was concerned for my safety, and had decided to address the disruptions across campus. These disruptions had to do with students protesting the

University's decision to accept a large donation from a for-profit prison corporation for the naming rights of the football stadium. Students protested across campus and one incident involved a student protestor being side-swiped by the university president as she drove away from one of the protests. Eventually, the University dropped the deal. All of this was happening at the same time as the "Stomp on Jesus" controversy continued to play out on campus and in the news.

In terms of my being placed on paid administrative leave, I believe this action was in response to a death threat I received. This particular death threat was called into the local Democratic Party office, where I served as an officer. The local Democratic Party turned over the audio of the death threat to the sheriff's department, who then contacted me and alerted me of the threat. The sheriff's department also alerted the local police department in my city, and a police officer visited my home. During that visit, they registered my telephone number so that any 911 calls made would alert them to an imminent threat to my life. Eventually, other colleagues in my department would take over teaching my classes. My dean, who was extremely concerned for my safety that morning even prior to the emailed letter from the associate provost, called to see how I was doing. Most of my colleagues told me they viewed my administrative leave as a punishment, while members of administration were preoccupied with my personal safety, and that of other University personnel. While I had mixed feelings about being placed on administrative leave, in retrospect I believe it was for the best. I was an emotional wreck, and the death threats paired with the racist hate mail only added to my instability. The following are examples of some of the emails I received during that time:

> You have no business being a professor of anything. Your influence upon FAU students is irrational and you should be subject to dismissal of your current position. You cannot influence the true believers. You cannot tell students to stop on jesus's [sic] name without first believing.

> Hey Asshole! Be careful. Someone might decide that you'll look good. Hanging from a tree!!!!

Hear [sic] in Europe we read about the shocking assignment you ask your class to do - being to write the name of Jesus and stomp on it. There are millions of people who love and revere Jesus. Obviously you are not one of them and did not ask the class to write the name of someone who you love to be stomped on. 'For there is one God and one mediator between God and man, the man. Christ Jesus 1 Timothy 2:5'

If you do not ask God for forgiveness, you will stand before him and you will be the one stomped on. You ought to be ashamed of yourself!

One of my tormentors apparently had a lot of time on his or her hands:

You sir are a disgrace to education, a disgrace to this Christian nation, a disgrace to your race, a disgrace to your family, a disgrace to your University and a disgrace to humankind. We have college educated idiots going into mass communications, having taken classes from ignoramuses such as yourself, who think that such vitriolic actions are proper. They are going out, showing Muslims Hindus, Buddhists, Greek Orthodox, Russian Orthodox, Christians monrovians [sic] just how totally egotistical and ignorant are educated. College students are because of teachers such as yourself only use the term teacher because I don't use that kind of language that accurate describes you. You haven't earned the distinct honor of being called the teacher as a high school teacher. I have the privilege of counseling students informally. I know one more liberal arts college I will definitely not be recommending my students go to and that I will be spreading the word around to my educational colleagues. This isn't diversity. This is insanity. This is purposeful. Hate speech. Sadly, you're not alone. I have seen egoistical teachers and many universities so full of themselves that they force exchange students to engage in activities against their respective religions. It is no wonder there is so much hatred of Americans. Our college instructors are turning their minds into jelly. If we as Americans are going to regain respect in the world, we are going to need a new generation of instructors in our colleges; a generation who are not afraid to teach humility, kindness, good communication skills—not the kind of racist activity you have your students engaging. You need to start over in kindergarten. Apparently you were asleep. Or skipping when they taught all the things I needed to know in life I learned in kindergarten.

The Political Fallout

The fallout from the coverage of the incident by the news media reached the highest political offices, both in Florida and in the U.S. Senate. Rick Scott, the Florida governor at the time, sent a letter to the president of the university, requesting a report of the incident and how the University would handle this matter to ensure that the lesson would never be taught again:

> As we enter the week memorializing the events of Christ's passion, this incident gave me great concern over the lessons we are teaching our students. Initial news report said the student was suspended from class because he refused to participate in activity. I am told that these reports are disputed by the university and that FAU has apologized for the activity. Whether the student was reprimanded or whether an apology was given is in many ways and consequent to the larger issue of a professor's poor judgment. The professor's lesson was offensive and even intolerant to Christians and those of all faiths who deserve to be respected as Americans entitled to religious freedom, our public higher education institutions are designed to shape the minds of Florida's future leaders. We should provide educational leadership that is respectful of religious freedom of all people. Florida's parents and students deserve nothing less.[1]

Likewise, on March 22nd, 2013, Senator Marco Rubio (R-FL) wrote a letter to the Chancellor of the State University System of Florida, who was the former president of FAU. In his letter, he expressed concern for the student standing up for his religious beliefs. The letter stated:

> It has also been brought to my attention that a student was offended by the exercise, refused to participate for religious reasons, had the courage to tell the professor that this exercise was inappropriate and informed the professor that he would be reporting this exercise to the superiors. It is my understanding that the student has now been suspended from the class. Chastised by the FAU administration, the student appears to have been singled

out for standing up for his religious beliefs. . . .I remain troubled by his claim that he was suspended. Our public institutions of learning should respect the religious freedom of all people. No student in our state should be punished for respectfully expressing his religious and conscientious objections about a classroom activity and also advocating for transparency and accountability in our post-secondary educational system.[2]

On March 25th, 2013, the president of FAU wrote a response letter to both the Chancellor of the State University System of Florida, and the Chair of the Florida Board of Governors, which oversees all Florida universities. In her letter she stated:

You have requested information about the recent classroom exercise that was taught by a non-tenured instructor in an intercultural communication course here at Florida Atlantic University. . . . Based on the offensive nature of the exercise, we will not use it again and have issued an apology to the community. It was insensitive and unacceptable. We continue to apologize to all the people who are offended and deeply regret the situation that has occurred. The student will not be disciplined in any way for anything related to this exercise, either inside or outside the classroom. We are challenged to balance our responsibility to protect student records and academic freedom with common sense, personal judgment and community expectations. This episode has tested those responsibilities. Please be assured that while a public University is a place for open dialogue in debate, we accept that we have a tremendous responsibility. Consider the repercussions of our decision. Again, we sincerely apologize to the student, members of the community and to anyone affected by this incident.

Conflicting Messages

One of the primary steps that should have been taken at the onset of this controversy was for the University to hold a press conference with the dean or another high-ranking administrator and myself to explain what really happened. I think this would have produced a united front for the public in defense of academic freedom and due process. Instead, in addition to the President's letter to state officials, the University released two different statements. The first public statement was crafted by members of FAU's senior administration, including my immediate supervisor, the Director of the School of Communication. It was released on Wednesday, March 20, 2013:

> Students enrolled in an Intercultural Communication course at Florida Atlantic University recently took part in a classroom exercise from the textbook *Intercultural Communication: A Contextual Approach*, 5th Edition, authored by a non-FAU faculty member. As with any academic lesson, the exercise was meant to encourage students to view issues from many perspectives, in direct relation with the course objectives. Faculty and students at academic institutions pursue knowledge and engage in open discourse. While at times the topics discussed may be sensitive, a university environment is a venue for such dialogue and debate.

Two days later, I received a phone call informing me that a second statement was being released on the evening of Friday, March 22, 2013. This statement threw me under the bus. When the president was questioned by members of the University Faculty Senate's Academic and Due Process Committee, she explained that she wanted to diffuse the situation and took responsibility for the second statement, which read:

> A recent classroom exercise in an Intercultural Communication course at Florida Atlantic University has attracted public attention and has aroused concern on the part of some individuals and groups. . . . Based on the offensive nature of the exercise, we will not use it again and have issued an apology to the community. It was insensitive and unacceptable. We continue to apologize to all the people who were offended and deeply regret this situation has occurred.

> No students were forced to take part in this exercise; The instructor told all the students in the class that they could choose whether or not to participate. No students will be disciplined in any way related to this exercise, either inside or outside the classroom.

> The University holds dear its core values. We sincerely apologize for any offense this caused. Florida Atlantic University respects

all religions and welcomes people of all faiths, backgrounds and beliefs.

The dean of my college, my department chair, and my colleagues were all supportive, but no one from the president's office reached out to me during this period of time. I never talked to the university president directly to share my side of the story. She never ascertained what I might need from the university, nor asked how I was doing. I felt abandoned at my worst moment. I was an instructor on an annual contract without tenure and was understandably worried about losing my job.

Why didn't the president stand up for academic freedom or due process? Why did the student not face the consequences of violating the student code of conduct? Perhaps the president's conduct reflected the fact that she was already embroiled in two other campus controversies. One involved student demonstrators on campus who were protesting against the university for accepting a $6 million dollar gift from the Geo Group, a company that invests in private prisons, for the naming rights to the University football stadium. The second involved a student protester who was side-swiped by the president as she sped away from other students surrounding her car on campus. The student was injured and receive no apology.

By the time the second statement had been released to the media, the damage had already been done. The *New York Times*, Fox News, CBS, and other outlets covered the story.[3] It spread across the country and the world. My name became both local and national news. After the story hit the airways, I received massive amounts of hate mail and death threats, along with some letters of support. At the time I sought counsel from a political consultant on what I could do to ensure my version of events would come out. He told me simply that there was nothing I could do. Once the story got out it spread like wildfire and all I could do was wait for it to run its course.

Missing in this whole ordeal was the fact that I am a deeply devout Christian. Today I am an ordained elder in a Pentecostal denomination. The media coverage caused members of my church at that time to question my actions. One member even asked if I told students to "stomp on Jesus." I told them under no circumstances did I instruct students to stomp on the paper. Another member stated they understood the lesson and did not see what I did wrong. They did not understand what all the fuss was about. My pastor at the time offered prayer and support and encouraged other church leaders and members to pray continuously for me and my safety.

I recall a terrifying moment one evening right after I went to bed. It was just after 10:00 p.m., when I heard a loud banging noise on the front door of my apartment. I immediately jumped out of bed onto the floor and crawled around my apartment wondering what to do. In my mind, I was thinking that at any moment someone could jump through the window or burst through my patio door. I got up off the floor, moved to the front of the apartment and looked through the peep hole, only to see my mother, my sister, and my niece standing on the other side of the door. They had tried to call me, and when I did not answer, they had become concerned and rushed over to my apartment. I was not receiving phone calls as I had turned my phone off, and my family worried that something unimaginable had happened to me.

The Community Rallies behind Me

As I sat at home on administrative leave, I received calls from students, people I knew from the community and university colleagues. I was deeply moved when I learned that my class, where the "infamous activity" had occurred, composed a supportive letter:

> When pursuing higher education, students are encouraged to learn how to think, not what to think. During lectures, open discourse and conversations, especially about controversial issues, aid in the learning process and help prepare students for the harsh realities of life. Dr. Poole is a great professor and a man of high moral values. We, the students were not offended by any classroom activities, including the one pertaining to Jesus, which was not specific [sic] to symbolize "Jesus Christ." We stand with Professor Poole during this rough time and refuse to let him continue to be demonized. The purpose of this petition is to let everyone know how the entire class felt collectively and show our support for our professor, Dr. Deandre Poole.

I was overjoyed. I felt vindicated by the most important court of public opinion. Unfortunately, the press never reported on the students' letter. Nor did the university administration ever mention it. But I was glad, because the students who were there knew the truth about what happened that night in class. This offered peace of mind, knowing that I did my job well, and that they had understood the assignment.

Other students expressed their support. One student emailed me on behalf of her peers and expressed horror at the treatment I was receiving. A few students who were in class on that "stomp on Jesus" night contacted the media to give their side of the story. I was pleased that they supported academic freedom! A student from the previous semester emailed me to disagree with the media's portrayal of my class exercise. This student valued the material learned in my classes, as well as my advice. Finally, a group of students organized a rally for academic freedom in support of me on Tuesday, April 9, 2013, on the free speech lawn on campus. They encouraged faculty to attend. The flier promoting the event read:

> Recently, a 30-year-old academic exercise used to teach the importance of symbolism and communication studies has become the height of national controversy. Dr. DeAndre Poole [sic], a Christian man and well-respected professor, is being wrongfully targeted by some in the community as well as unsupported by. Fair Use Administration for issuing this textbook exercise. The students and faculty FAU will be gathering to show our support for Doctor Poole and academic freedom on Tuesday, April 9th at 12:00 PM on the Free speech lawn on the Boca Raton campus. The administration apologizing for and implicitly condemning the exercise, rather than standing up for academic freedom, confirms their inability to adequately represent the FAU community and the principles that define the university.

To top it off, colleagues and students held a rally on my behalf on campus. This rally was well-attended by people I knew from the local community, who held signs in support of me. Students actively demonstrated support of academic freedom and a campus environment that allowed for the free expression of ideas. This rally was covered by the media.[4] Finally, in June of 2013, my contract renewal arrived right after the university faculty senate completed its report. The report, which was very thorough, concluded like this:

> Dr. Poole should not be penalized for his decision to use the exercise. Until the question of Dr. Poole's reappointment is resolved FAU's commitment to academic freedom remains in doubt. Based upon the known facts, The Academic Freedom and Due Process Committee (AFDPC) strongly views Dr. Poole's reappointment for the 2013-2014 academic year as affirmation for academic freedom.[5]

After four grueling and stressful months, my academic career was saved. Yet the controversy was damaging to my professional reputation and has taken years to repair. I applied for a tenure-track position at another college and was one of the finalists. Later, I received a call from one of the search committee members who told me that there was a disagreement among members of the search committee because one member brought up the "Stomp Jesus" Exercise. I found out that the search was cancelled as a result. In the local community, I was stigmatized as the "stomp on Jesus" professor. When I ran for public office the first time, I was warned that my in-class activity would be used against me, and I dropped out of the race. The second time I ran for public office, it was used against me in a piece of mail by my opponent. Moreover, I did not seek counseling and I believe this would have helped me process the trauma I experienced during the ordeal. The controversy rested on a lie told by a student who was in violation of the student code of conduct. The media ran with the story that he was suspended for refusing to "stomp on Jesus," without all the facts. The University was slow to respond, and slow to defend academic freedom and due process. When all the facts finally came to the fore, I was vindicated.

Endnotes

[1] The Scott letter is available on the *Miami Herald* website, https://miamiherald.typepad.com/files/scott-letter-about-fau-incident.pdf (accessed February 10, 2024).

[2] Academic Freedom and Due Process Committee Report to the FAU Faculty Senate June 20, 2013, Addendum D2. Available at https://www.fau.edu /ufsgov/Files/Final%20Report%207-9-2013.pdf (accessed June 14, 2024).

[3] Fish, Stanley. "Stepping on Jesus." *The New York Times*, April 15, 2013; Williams, Juan. "In Defense of Florida University's 'Jesus Stomping' Exercise." Fox News, March 26, 2013. Available at https://www.foxnews. com/opinion/in-defense-of-florida-universitys-jesus-stomping-exercise (accessed June 15, 2024); CBS News. "FAU Professor In "Jesus Stomping" Incident Defends Himself." April 2, 2013. Available at https://www.cbs news.com/miami/news/fau-professor-in-jesus-stomping-incident-defends-himself/ (accessed June 15, 2024).

[4] Brannan, Cealia. "FAU Protesters Fight for Academic Freedom in Support of Dr. Poole." University Press. Available at   https://www.upressonline. com/2013/04/fau-protesters-fight-for-academic-freedom-in-support-of-dr-poole/ (accessed June 11, 2024).

[5] Academic Freedom and Due Process Committee Report to the FAU Faculty Senate June 20, 2013. Available at https://www.fau.edu/ufsgov/Files/ Final%20Report%207-9-2013.pdf (accessed June 14, 2024).

There Must be a Mistake, I'm Jewish!

Jaime Scholnick

I used to think that the best professors were the ones pursuing their passion outside of academia, and teaching on the side. Academia was certainly a rewarding job. The hours were good and, as an adjunct professor, not a huge demand on my time. This allowed me to pursue my art career, my ultimate passion. I naively thought that my successful art career was exactly what academic institutions were seeking.

Back when I was an undergraduate and then a graduate student, I was especially attentive to my professors who maintained a successful art practice alongside their teaching. They were God-like to me, and ultimately inspired me to teach college. I wanted to join the ranks of esteemed artist/professors, believing that I could become the professor I always wished to have. I remained an adjunct professor by choice, rather than seek full-time employment in academia. My focus was always on my art career first and foremost. But I liked teaching and was good at it. I liked exposing students to different ways of seeing, and instilling in them the power of self-expression. When I was an undergraduate at San Francisco State, my professors were on the front lines of campus demonstrations; the climate was political, exciting, and free expression was encouraged. Their activism made their art that much stronger. It's a far cry from where academia is now.

From 2015-2022, I taught a three-credit undergraduate course called Foundations of Three-Dimensional Design Activity at Cal Poly Pomona (the common name for California State Polytechnic University, Pomona). This class is mandatory for all Art and Design students enrolled at the university; it's also listed as an elective for non-art majors. The class is always full with a large waiting list. I loved the cross-disciplinary nature of this introductory three-dimensional design class. The students were mostly diligent and thoughtful in their work. My own professors had been exhibiting professional artists, so I modeled my teaching style after theirs. I maintained a relaxed, open atmosphere in my classes. Students sat around work tables, six to eight students per table. I allowed them to converse or listen to music on their headphones. I believe strongly in peer critiques of assignments, and these became forums where students expressed themselves as to what they were trying to explore in their individual projects.

I always maintained a vibrant studio practice no matter what my teaching load was, exhibiting my work and receiving large public art grants from Los Angeles County and various foundations. My personal work deals, then and now, with subject matter that is invariably difficult and topical. I invited students to follow me on social media, attend my exhibitions and, because they are living in Los Angeles, with its vibrant art scene, visit galleries and museums.

In the Summer of 2015, before I was hired at Cal Poly Pomona, I created a two-dimensional piece called *Gaza; Mowing the Lawn.* As a Jewish person I have always questioned the Apartheid State of Israel.[1] *Gaza; Mowing the Lawn* was composed of 52 small paintings based on images Gaza residents would send me on my social media feeds. They were both powerful and difficult to look at. By obscuring the subject matter with my obsessive line work art style, I drew the viewer into the paintings. As they looked harder, the scene would unfold. *Gaza; Mowing the Lawn* was exhibited at a prestigious art gallery in Los Angeles and garnered a lot of press and interviews. Articles in myriad journals and newspapers about the exhibition were positive.[2]

Yet both the gallery and I received death threats. In 2015 a pro-Palestinian stance was largely ignored by galleries and the art world. I was warned by a collector/curator that if I persisted in doing this work I would "ruin my career." My reply: "That is one of the most idiotic things I have ever been told." At the time I didn't take the threats seriously.

One of my strengths as a professor of art and design is that I am an exhibiting artist. I show my students examples of work in local museums and galleries, but *only* when it highlights a design principle we are studying. I know what is being shown in the art world and take students to see work in person. Los Angeles is an influential art center, and it is exciting to have access to cutting-edge art. This is my teaching method. But *GAZA Mowing the Lawn* was two-dimensional artwork and thus never shown to the students in my 3-D Design Foundation class. It had no relevance to any 3-D design principal we were studying.

My 3-D design classes at Cal Poly were always popular, and my student evaluations were exemplary. This is why what happened to me was so shocking.

In November, 2021, when I was wrapping up my fall semester, I received an email from Ms. Barbara Renguengo, whose preposterously long title was Associate Director and Senior Title IX Deputy Coordinator of the Office of Equity and Compliance. She was writing to inform me of allegations of anti-Semitism filed against me by a former, now graduated student. The incidents were alleged to have happened in the spring semester of 2020, one year earlier. The student had waited until she had graduated to make these accusations against me. They weren't, as yet, formal charges but I was being summoned for a meeting to discuss the allegations against me. My response was incredulity. "You must have the wrong professor!" I wrote, " [this student] earned an A in my class and we never had any issues. Also, I'm Jewish! (albeit anti-Apartheid)." I was, once again, informed that "No, this was not a mistake." She then threatened me by saying "you had better take this seriously and respond." Thus began a year-long administrative ordeal, which ultimately forced me to quit academia.

During many subsequent meetings with Ms. Renguengo and her supervisor, I was treated like a criminal. "Ms. Renguengo has ALWAYS treated faculty with respect and is unbiased in her dealings" I was told. I did have the presence of mind to request that my union reps attend these meetings, and they were shocked at the manner in which I was being treated. In today's climate—the invasion of Gaza and the campus protests—this would not be so shocking but this was 2021. Historically college campuses have been the hotbeds of dissent, I thought. The crazy part of this entire ordeal was that it was based on my *Gaza Mowing the Lawn* piece, an installation made up of 52 two-dimensional paintings that was NEVER shown to the class. This was a 3-D class, and thus my work would have been irrelevant to any design principle we were studying. I was also aware that I had a student who was very vocal in her statements of support for the Israeli government, and Israeli Prime Minister Netanyahu in particular (Consider for a moment how strong this sentiment must have been for it to have become apparent to her art professor!) I would never have shown her "Gaza Mowing the Lawn."

The student in question made five shocking allegations, all of which I easily refuted:

Accusation #1: The student wanted to make a Star of David for a project. I purportedly came to her table and as she told me about the project I dismissed her, telling her "that isn't very original." I then proceeded to tell her to make "a wall of the object because [building walls is] what you Jews do."

My response: Let's remember, I am Jewish. Saying "you Jews" would negate my own faith. Furthermore, I would never tell a beginning sculpture/3D student that their idea was unoriginal. To be that negative with a student is not in my manner of teaching. It just would not happen. That I would tell her what to make and then insult her would be laughable if it wasn't so vicious an allegation. This was a disgusting lie.

Accusation #2: I took the student aside and whispered in her ear, "Netanyahu is a bigoted asshole." To hear this lie, the suggestion that I am that callous and ugly, and would insult anyone with that language is just beyond belief. I do not speak like this. Period. To knowingly insult the leader of her country is just ludicrous as well. And "whispering in her ear???" I do not get physically close to students, ever. Another outrageous lie.

Accusation #3: During class, in a classroom of 23 other students, the student claimed that I took her to a computer lab to show her gruesome images of Palestinians being blown up by Israelis. My response: This is just sick. I do not know why the student told such a vindictive lie and why it was taken seriously. This is frightening. Why would I do such a thing? I wouldn't abandon the rest of my students during class time, nor would I go to a computer lab for any purpose (I pointed out I didn't even know where such a lab was. I do not even leave the classroom to use the ladies' room. And I have both my personal laptop with me and a desktop in the classroom, so I have no need of a computer lab. These facts expose the student's lie (above and beyond the fact that the lie was so outrageous). Beyond the absurd nature of this claim, let me remind you: this is a 3D Design class. We discuss design elements. If the student had been questioned in depth about these facts, I am sure the lie would have fallen apart . No such questioning took place.

The final two allegations were again dealing with me making derogatory comments about the Holocaust or Israel by way of criticism of her pieces. These allegations were absurd and with any questioning from my department chair, or the Office of Equity and Compliance , would have been easily dispelled. No one examined her allegations at all. The department maintained a hands-off policy regarding her claims, saying that they will "let the very fair and unbiased OEC investigate." The student had initially contacted my department chair at the end of 2020 to discuss these alleged incidents. The chair had asked her to schedule a meeting where all three of us would discuss these allegations. The student never followed up. She graduated, and I was never informed that these allegations had been made.

I was threatened with legal action if I ignored the request to meet and discuss the accusations with Barbara Renguengo. I had no intention of ignoring the summons to meet, but this was during the last two weeks of the semester. I was extremely busy with final projects, finals critiques, and frankly I was in shock.

A meeting took place in 2021 with Renguengo. She was hostile and accusatory. I had asked my union reps to be present, and we all felt as if the presumption of my guilt was predetermined. My two union reps were incredulous and claimed that Renguengo's attitude towards me was biased. The former president of my union called me after I had written the dean of my department to ask that Renguengo be disciplined for her biased handling of my situation. The former union president said "Jaime, don't kid yourself, this student was most likely paid to enroll in your class in the first place by organizations like Canary Mission or the IFCJ [The International Fellowship of Christian and Jews]." I had never heard of these groups but now understood that this was no superficial set of allegations that would just go away. I was told that the student in question hadn't yet decided if she was going to file formal charges against me. She had an indefinite period of time in which to do so but the school was now keeping a file on me, which I was unable to see. There was no statute of limitations on these accusations.

I was furious. I contacted a friend who is a contributing editor at *The Markaz Review*. We talked by phone and I gave her all the records I had been keeping about my case. Her article about my situation for Project Censored inspired media coverage—and also ignited a torrent of blowback.[3] My situation was discussed on the Project Censored podcast, which in turn was mentioned by Michael Moore on his podcast.[4] He praised Project Censored, and especially this segment. It was after this media coverage that the student filed formal charges against me. Charges for blatant unfounded lies.

I was incredibly depressed and scared as I recalled the death threats I'd received after *Gaza Mowing the Lawn*. I did not want to be on campus, as I feared for my life. My classes ended at 10pm. The campus is secluded and walking to my car, I was really by myself. How far would these pro-Netanyahu extremists go? I was concerned for my safety. I was just paranoid and looked at both my students and strangers as potential threats. I was scared that they were lying in wait for me. I was paranoid. Ultimately, it was the reason I resigned my position.

My fears were not taken seriously by the administration. I wanted to teach remotely, but was denied this request. I then asked that my dog accompany me to class. The university granted this request.

I was despondent, and had soured on the school and academia in general. I was also deeply suspicious of Barbara Renguengo and the circumstances that led to the complaint against me. When all this started I recalled the case of Norman Finkelstein. After having been denied tenure at De Paul University for his views on Israel and Palestine after an aggressive lobbying campaign by Alan Dershowitz, he was invited to conduct a series of lectures at Cal State Northridge. Subsequent support for a faculty appointment was overwhelmingly positive, but was met with aggressive lobbying by the far-right Jewish Defense League. Ultimately the Provost denied this appointment.[5]

Finkelstein's experience led me to wonder if outside groups like the Jewish Defense League were involved in the case against me. I asked that my Union (and later on the lawyer provided to me by FIRE, the Foundation for Individual Rights and Expression) to investigate Ms. Renguengo's affiliations with rabidly Zionist groups like Canary Mission or the Jewish Defense League. No connection was found, but I remained suspicious.

I received word that FIRE would secure me legal representation through their Faculty Legal Defense Fund. The accusations were not going away without a fight and I was adamant that these trumped up charges were all lies. I initially wanted to sue EVERYONE involved: the student, Cal Poly Pomona, Ms. Renguengo. My lawyer was pragmatic. He asked me if I really wanted to wallow in this ugly episode for the years it would take to bring a case to trial.

In the end, after the university met with the parties involved and interviewed students—who had mostly graduated—in my class at the time these incidents were reported to have taken place, it was determined there was "insufficient evidence" to hold me accountable. I suppose it was over, and I received "congratulations" from my colleague. Seriously? OVER? The fact that a student could get away with leveling these false charges against me has permanently damaged me.

I quit my adjunct position at CAL Poly Pomona. My attitude towards academia has been permanently altered. Ms. Renguengo is also no longer employed at Cal Poly Pomona.

Many of my peers chastised me for quitting. "If you quit then she won!" they cried. Won? I always followed the edict about choosing my battles, and this one was not worth it. I had an adjunct contract that was decided semester to semester. The pay was ridiculously low, the time slot was late at night, and the drive was far. Moreover, I had just received word that I had been awarded the largest public art commission of my career, worth a million dollars. Ultimately, I was the winner here.

I felt the deck is stacked against professors. The present academic climate gives students an overwhelming sense of entitlement. The ability for them to bring any type of false charge against professors without any repercussions is daunting. I was done with academia.

Postscript: I was recently contacted by my former department chair asking if I was interested in him proposing I receive Emeritus status as an Adjunct Professor from Cal Poly Pomona. "Sure," I replied, "I should get something from this school, even if it's just an honorific title."

Endnotes

[1] This is the determination of Human Rights Watch. Fakih, Lama and Omar Shakir. "Does Israel's Treatment of Palestinians Rise to the Level of Apartheid?" Human Rights Watch, December 5, 2023. Available at https://www.hrw.org/news/2023/12/05/does-israels-treatment-palestinians-rise-level-apartheid (accessed March 17, 2024).

[2] Here's one such review. Miranda, Carolina A. "Her Art Forces a Closer Look." *Los Angeles Times*, July 25, 2015.

[3] Geracoulis, Mischa. "Cal State Poly, Pomona Professor Accused of Anti-Semitism." Project Censored, January 31, 2022. Available at https://www.projectcensored.org/cal-state-poly-pomona-professor-threatened-with-cancellation-on-false-charges-of-anti-semitism/ (accessed March 20, 2024).

[4] Rumble with Michael Moore podcast, episode 229, "The Most Censored Stories of the Year (Featuring the Editors of Project Censored," February 3, 2022. Transcript available at https://rumble.media/transcript-episode-229-the-most-censored-stories-of-the-year/ (accessed March 20, 2024).

[5] Klein, David. 2009. "Why is Norman Finkelstein Not Allowed to Teach?" *Works & Days*, Special Issue: Academic Freedom in the Post-9/11 University, Vols 26 & 27, pp 307-322. Available at https://www.csun.edu/~vcmth00m/finkelstein.html (accessed March 21, 2024).

Postscript:
How to Safeguard Your Academic Career

Stephen Porter,
North Carolina State University

Academics, especially those beginning their careers, seldom understand one key vulnerability: how they view their job. They see their university as a rational institution, an intellectual "safe space." Administrators and colleagues will follow the rules and as long as you are productive, then nothing will happen to you, especially in terms of anything you might say. I have learned, not just from my own experience but from the experiences of other faculty at my university, that the modern American research university is instead a very unsafe space. Colleagues will team up with administrators to target faculty they dislike; administrators will retaliate against faculty who are in any way outspoken, whether by espousing wrong political views, or speaking up about sexual harassment or research misconduct; administrators will ignore university regulations whenever it suits them; absolutely no one will have your back if you end up in their sights.

So here are my lessons learned:

Beware of all meetings with administrators and secretly record them if you reside in a one-party consent state. Administrators rarely give detailed agendas for meetings, making it difficult to prepare for them. The more vague the invitation for a meeting is, the more you should be on your guard. Supposedly friendly meetings can also be used against you, as I learned when meeting with my new department head for the first time.

Any of your weaknesses will be exploited (see e.g., my profanity incident). Behavior that is tolerated in others will be used against you, and the argument that others have engaged in this behavior will not protect you. Poor teaching evaluations, for example, will be ignored until you come under scrutiny. So, you must be bulletproof if want to be vocal on your campus. The only reason I have survived so far is that my teaching evaluations are typically in the 4.8-5.0 range on a five-point scale, I am still publishing my research in peer-reviewed journals, and I do a lot of service activities, such as serving on College and University committees, the editorial boards of three journals, and on conference program committees. (Research, teaching, and service are the three areas in which tenure-stream faculty are evaluated annually and during the post-tenure review process.)

Do not let the university establish a pattern with your "problematic" behavior. A colleague in a research unit who supervised others once told me that Human Resources specifically instructed him that he must establish a pattern of behavior to fire anyone. For example, I should have more forcefully pushed back against the bully pronouncement based on the anonymous report, but I was more concerned with my relationship with my new department head. It is far better to be seen as too aggressive when pushing back against attempts to establish a pattern of problematic behavior on your part. In addition, don't believe that simply filing a response to be placed in your personnel file will help when it comes to termination proceedings. The proceedings will focus on the paperwork generated by the university and ignore your responses. Better to make sure the paperwork never enters your file.

When you are retaliated against, use the university bureaucracy to your advantage: file a grievance. I believe the administrators at NC State were shocked that I fought back with my grievance, because they happen so rarely here. Colleges and departments tend to be siloed within universities, and faculty in larger departments are often unaware of what transpires in other program areas in their department. With my grievance, what was concealed in my department in the College of Education was suddenly thrust into the spotlight of the wider institution. For example, as part of my grievance hearing, I asked the Dean of every single academic college in the university to testify during my grievance hearing. All of them turned me down, of course, but I believe I got the Provost's attention with that gambit.

Know your institution's policies and regulations forwards and backwards. One reason the College of Education administrators never made me teach the fifth course is that I pointed out that increasing my course-load without discussing and meeting with me first was a violation of regulations about the University's Statement of Mutual Expectations. My experience is that administrators tend to make decisions based on what they want, not on what is permissible. They are not familiar with the details of institutional policies and regulations, in part because polices and regulations have become so voluminous during the past few decades, so this knowledge can be a powerful tool for you.

The most powerful tool the university has is delay. The university knows it can simply wait you out, and they are not worried about the cost of litigation. The general counsel of my university has been quoted as saying, "We fight everything." After all, why not? There is no downside for the university. However, most faculty do not have the mental and physical stamina to fight the university for years on end, nor do they have the financial resources for a lawsuit or even just for consultations with an attorney.

If you decide to fight back, don't underestimate the toll it will take. Soon after my ordeal began, I had to see a therapist for the first time in my life. If you do not lose your job, you will constantly worry about being fired and whether you will ever hold a job in academia again. Family and friends may lack sympathy, because they do not understand the strange world of higher education. For most people, someone only gets in trouble in their workplace if they deserve it, so they cannot help but wonder if it is really all your fault. If your situation becomes public, you will learn that many of your professional friends will forget you exist. Professional opportunities will dry up. At worst, protestors will target you and your family. A staff member and fellow conservative at NC State who was falsely accused of being a white supremacist eventually shot himself due to what he endured at work and the physical attacks on his home.[1]

Endnotes

[1] Porter, Stephen. "Another University Conservative Kills Himself." Last modified January 29, 2022. https://stephenporter.org/another-university-conservative-kills-himself (accessed November 9, 2024).

About the contributors

Patti Adler is Emeritus Professor of Sociology at the University of Colorado, Boulder. Her areas of interest are qualitative methods, symbolic interactionism, deviant behavior, socialization, and work and occupations. She was forced to resign her tenured position over the incident described in this book. **Peter Adler** is Emeritus Professor of Sociology and Criminology at the University of Denver. His interests include sociology of sport, drugs and society, and social psychology. Together, the Adlers edited the *Journal of Contemporary Ethnography* from 1986-1994, and were founding editors of the annual *Sociological Studies of Children and Adolescents*. They are the authors of over twenty books and anthologies, and more than one hundred peer-reviewed journal articles. In 2010, they were awarded the George H. Mead Award for Lifetime Achievement by the Society for the Study of Symbolic Interactionism, and in 2006-2007, they were the Co-Presidents of the Midwest Sociological Society. They currently reside in Maui, Hawaii.

Fawzia Afzal-Khan is University Distinguished Professor of English at Montclair State University, and currently Visiting Professor of Gender and Sexuality Studies at Princeton University. She was dismissed as director of Women and Gender Studies (now Gender, Sexuality, and Women's Studies) in 2017 after an intervention by a right-wing reporter. Specializing in feminist theory and cultural, performance, and postcolonial studies, Fawzia is the author of eight books, most recently *Siren Song: Understanding Pakistan Through its Women Singers* (Oxford University Press, 2020) and a traveling memoir, *Traveling Feminista: a Modern Muslim Woman Travels Through the World* (The Little Book Company, 2024). She is Contributing Editor at the *The Friday Times of Pakistan* as well as *The Drama Review* (published quarterly by MIT Press), and a regular contributor to *Counterpunch*. Fawzia's extensive theatrical background includes co-founding Compagnie Faim de Siecle, and touring Europe and North America from 1999-2005; she has written, published and performed in several plays.

Teresa Buchanan is a visiting assistant professor at Berea College, where she teaches courses in Child and Family Studies. Her research focuses on early childhood education, particularly the influence of context on teaching practices. She received over a million dollars in funding to support her scholarship and published widely in the area of teaching and learning. Shortly after being recommended for promotion to the rank of full professor at Louisiana State University, Teresa was fired after an eleven and a half hour hearing. She was fired for sexual harassment, something she had never been accused of.

Robert Frodeman is former Professor of Philosophy at the University of North Texas. He is the author or editor of 16 books, including the *Oxford Handbook of Interdisciplinarity, Sustainable Knowledge: A Theory of Interdisciplinarity,* and *Socrates Tenured: The Institutions of 21st Century Philosophy* (with Adam Briggle). He was driven from his position over specious Title IX allegations in 2019.

Dennis S. Gouws is Professor of English at Springfield College in Western Massachusetts, USA. He has published on maleness and masculinity in British literature, and he serves on the editorial board of *New Male Studies: An International Journal.* Between 2013 and 2019 he was investigated by his college because of ideological objections to his scholarship and activism.

Nathan Honeycutt is a visiting scholar at Rutgers University, where he received his PhD in 2022, and a research fellow at the Foundation for Individual Rights and Expression (FIRE). His research has primarily investigated political diversity and discrimination among university faculty and students. He has published articles on political bias, political polarization, scientific integrity, and censorship in higher education. In 2022, prior to graduating from Rutgers, he was investigated three times by the Rutgers Human Subjects Committee.

Abdul Jabbar taught English and Interdisciplinary Studies for 36 years at City College of San Francisco, retiring in 2004. He chaired the Department of Interdisciplinary Studies for six years. Abdul is the author of three books, *Reading and Writing with Multicultural Literature, Not of an Age, but for All Time: Revolutionary Humanism in Iqbal, Manto, and Faiz*, and the forthcoming *American Cultures: A Struggle for Justice (Evidence from History, Literature, and Film)*. Following 9/11, he was investigated by campus police, and ultimately the FBI, as a terrorism suspect.

Lee Jussim is a Distinguished Professor of Psychology and former chair of three different departments (Psychology, Anthropology, Criminal Justice) at Rutgers University, where he has taught since 1987. He has published over 140 academic articles and chapters and seven books, with two more books in press (*The Free Inquiry Papers,* and *The Poisoning of the American Mind)*, both inspired by the types of events described in the present book. Since 2018, he has been formally investigated several times by his internal review board and informally once by his dean's office, and has emerged unscathed each time.

Patanjali Kambhampati was born in India and emigrated to the United States at age four. He is Professor in the Department of Chemistry at McGill University, where he studies semiconductor quantum dots and ultrafast laser science. Pat has generated $7,000,000 in research funding, published over 100 papers, and has lectured at over 60 institutions. He also holds four U.S. patents. In 2020, he was awarded a Lady Davis Visiting Professorship at the Hebrew University in Jerusalem. Pat has been the target of ideological complaints from students, faculty members, and private citizens, and suffered years of harassment from his dean. Ultimately Pat's provost invoked academic freedom and sided with him.

Jason Kilborn is Professor of Law at the University of Illinois Chicago School of Law, where for 17 years he has taught bankruptcy, commercial and business law, and civil procedure. He is a leading authority on the law and policy of personal and small business insolvency, having written over three dozen pioneering articles and a book comparing developing personal insolvency systems in Europe, Asia, the Middle East and North Africa, and South America. Jason also co-authored a book on international cooperation in cross-border business reorganization and is among the authors and editors of a series on comparative corporate liquidation and restructuring, both published by Oxford University Press. He has advised several national governments on personal insolvency law reform, he chaired the drafting group for the World Bank's landmark 2013 *Report on the Treatment of the Insolvency of Natural Persons*, and he drafted and presented the World Bank Group's 2018 report, *Saving Entrepreneurs, Saving Enterprises: Proposals for the Treatment of MSME Insolvency*. Among the hundreds of thousands of words Professor Kilborn has published, a single (abbreviated) word on an exam sparked a university investigation of purported harassment that led to two semester-long teaching suspensions and years of litigation.

Mark Mercer is Professor of Philosophy at Saint Mary's University, in Halifax, Nova Scotia. He was chair of the philosophy department from 2010 to 2019 and president of the Society for Academic Freedom and Scholarship from 2015 to 2023. Mark's collection, *In Praise of Dangerous Universities and Other Essays*, appeared in 2022. Mark works in philosophy of mind and ethics as well as in philosophy of education. He was once summoned to a disciplinary meeting by his university's president.

William "Liam" O'Mara IV is an instructor at the California State University and formerly with Chapman University, where he has taught courses in Middle East, European, and world history. His discipline is the history of ideas with emphasis on questions of social and personal identity. He has chapters published on religion in Israel/Palestine and on imperialism and racism, and in addition to his heavy teaching load is writing a history of the Levant over the *longue durée*. Liam was investigated after a social media post, but it was quickly resolved.

Deandre J. Poole is a University Instructor and associate member of the graduate faculty in the School of Communication and Multimedia Studies at Florida Atlantic University, where he teaches courses in intercultural theory, political communication, leadership and communication, and communication and civic life. He is the immediate past president of the United Faculty of Florida's FAU Chapter, a position he held for four years. In the Spring of 2013, Deandre was placed on paid administrative leave after a media firestorm over a classroom activity, He was later reinstated after the University Faculty Senate found that his academic freedom and due process rights were violated.

Dave Porter was confirmed by the US Senate as a Permanent Professor and Head of the US Air Force Academy's Department of Behavioral Sciences and Leadership in 1996. After retiring from the Air Force with the rank of colonel, he served as Provost and Academic Vice President of Berea College from 2001 to 2005. Dave continued as Professor of Psychology and General Studies at Berea until his dismissal in 2018. He has authored many scholarly articles, and served as a consultant examiner for the North Central Association of Schools and Colleges, Western Association of Schools and Colleges, and Southern Association of Colleges and Schools. His development and distribution with his Industrial/Organizational Psychology class of a survey designed to collect evidence of respondent's perceptions of hostile environments and judgments about academic freedom led to his dismissal from Berea College.

Stephen Porter is Professor of Higher Education in the College of Education at North Carolina State University, where he has taught since 2011. He has published almost 40 peer-reviewed journal articles and has served on the editorial boards of some of the top journals in education. He has chaired several grant review panels for the Institute of Education Sciences, the main research funding arm of the U.S. Department of Education, and served as a Visiting Scholar at RTI International and Nagoya University in Japan. In 2019, he was retaliated against for speaking out against ideological trends in his field and unsuccessfully sued his university in federal court.

Jaime Scholnick is an award winning contemporary artist living and working in Los Angeles, California. From 2017-2022 she was an adjunct lecturer of 3-D design at Cal Poly Pomona. Her decision to resign from her academic position followed a grueling, year-long investigation from the Office of Equity and Compliance at Cal Poly Pomona. Jaime is a recipient of a California Community Foundation Fellowship in visual arts, as well as several prominent pubic art commissions in the Los Angeles area. She is the first place winner of the 2023 ADACHI Contemporary Ukiyo-e Award (Tokyo, Japan). One of her pieces, *Grief,* from her series *Gaza Mowing the Lawn,* will be reproduced in the traditional Japanese woodcut style. She has exhibited her work throughout Europe, Asia, and the United States.

Buddy Ullman is a former Professor of Biochemistry and Molecular Biology who worked at the Oregon Health & Science University located in Portland, Oregon from 1985 through 2017. He was a research scientist who investigated protozoan parasites that cause devastating and often fatal diseases in humans and employed biochemical, genetic, and molecular biological techniques and strategies in his research. His research was funded by the National Institutes of Health for the entirety of his career, and he published over 200 articles in scholarly journals and books. Buddy also taught medical students for 32 years, for which he was accorded over 50 teaching awards and honors. He was forced to resign his academic position in 2017 after facing multiple accusations instigated by members of OHSU administration and enduring five separate investigations over three years.

Elizabeth Weiss is Professor Emeritus of Anthropology at San José State University, where she curated the largest single site of precontact Native American skeletal remains west of the Mississippi since 2004. She is the author of *Paleopathology in Perspective: Bone Health and Disease through Time* (Rowman and Littlefield, 2014), *Reading the Bones:*

Activity, Biology, and Culture (University of Press Florida, 2017), *Repatriation and Erasing the Past* (University of Florida Press, 2020) with co-author James W. Springer, and *On the Warpath: My Battles with Indians, Pretendians and Woke Warriors* (Academica Press, 2024). Elizabeth's work has been covered by *Science*, *USA Today*, *National Review*, and *the New York Times*. She has published in academic journals in fields ranging from anthropology to medicine. Between 2020 and 2023, she sued her university for their retaliatory actions that barred her from skeletal remains research. From 2023 to 2024, she was a faculty fellow at Heterodox Academy's Center for Academic Pluralism. Currently, Elizabeth sits on the board of directors of the National Association of Scholars.

Frances Widdowson was a professor in the Department of Economics, Justice, and Policy Studies at Mount Royal University from 2008-2021. She is the author of two books, *Disrobing the Aboriginal Industry: The Deception Behind Indigenous Cultural Preservation* (co-authored with Albert Howard) and *Separate but Unequal: How Parallelist Ideology Conceals Indigenous Dependency*. She is a board member for the Society for Academic Freedom and Scholarship and a Senior Fellow with the Frontier Centre for Public Policy. Frances endured five investigations before she was fired on December 20, 2021.

David Wiley was Professor of Health Education at Texas State University in San Marcos, Texas for 30 years. His research interests were adolescent health, with an emphasis on sexuality education and teen pregnancy prevention. He authored or co-authored $4.1 million in grants and contracts and published over 40 peer-reviewed articles in the field. He served as a board member and president of the Texas School Health Association and American School Health Association, and won numerous professional awards. He also served as a school board trustee for an Austin-area school district and was a board member for a large healthcare provider in San Antonio, TX. Fired by Texas State after a Title IX investigation, David spent five years and over $400,000 in unsuccessful litigation with the State of Texas.

Nicholas H. Wolfinger is Professor of Family and Consumer Studies and Adjunct Professor of Sociology at the University of Utah, where he has taught since 1998. He is the author of four other books, most recently *Thanks for Nothing: The Economics of Single Motherhood since 1980* (Oxford University Press, 2024). Nick's work has appeared the *Atlantic*, *National Review*, *Huffington Post*, and various academic journals. Between 2016 and 2021 he was investigated three times by his university.